THE PLAYS AND FILMS OF BAHRAM BEYZAIE

BIPS – Studies in the History and Culture of the Persianate World

Reflecting the British Institute of Persian Studies' role in stimulating and promoting research into all aspects of Persian and Iranian Studies, the BIPS Persian Studies series exists to provide an outlet for the work conducted in this field and welcomes proposals for book length publications in the form of research monographs, conference proceedings or other edited volumes. The series is particularly ready to serve as a vehicle for publishing research undertaken with the support and sponsorship of BIPS and arising out of one of its research programmes. Visit the BIPS website (www.bips.ac.uk/persian-studies-series) for further information about the series and previously published titles.

Series Editor:
Professor Andrew Peacock (University of St Andrews)

Editorial board:
Professor Ali Ansari, (University of St Andrews), Dr Michele Bernardini, and Professor Ahmad Karimi-Hakkak (University of California, Los Angeles), Dr Paul Losensky (Indiana University) and Professor Gabrielle van den Berg (Leiden University)

Published titles
The Practice of Politics in Safavid Iran: Power, Religion, Rhetoric, Colin P. Mitchell

The Ilkhanid Book of Ascension: A Persian-Sunni Prayer Manual, Christiane Gruber

The Ornament of Histories: A History of the Eastern Islamic Lands AD 650–1041 The Original Text of Abū Sa'īd 'Abd al Hayy Gardīzī, Translated and Edited by C. Edmund Bosworth

The Safavid Dynastic Shrine: Architecture, Religion and Power in Early Modern Iran, Kishwar Rizvi

Iran Between Islamic Nationalism and Secularism: The Constitutional Revolution of 1906, Vanessa Martin

Medieval Central Asia and the Persianate World: Iranian Tradition and Islamic Civilisation, Edited by A.C.S. Peacock and D.G. Tor

THE PLAYS AND FILMS OF BAHRAM BEYZAIE

Origins, Forms and Functions

Edited by
Saeed Talajooy

I.B. TAURIS
LONDON • NEW YORK • OXFORD • NEW DELHI • SYDNEY

I.B. TAURIS
Bloomsbury Publishing Plc, 50 Bedford Square, London, WC1B 3DP, UK
Bloomsbury Publishing Inc, 1359 Broadway, 12th Floor, New York, NY 10018, USA
Bloomsbury Publishing Ireland, 29 Earlsfort Terrace, Dublin 2, D02 AY28, Ireland

BLOOMSBURY, I.B. TAURIS and the I.B. Tauris logo are
trademarks of Bloomsbury Publishing Plc

First published in Great Britain 2024
This paperback edition published 2025

Copyright © Saeed Talajooy, 2024

Saeed Talajooy and Contributors have asserted their rights under the Copyright,
Designs and Patents Act, 1988, to be identified as Authors of this work.

For legal purposes the Acknowledgements on p. xii constitute
an extension of this copyright page.

Series design: Toby Way
Cover image: Still from Bahram Beyzaie's *When We Are All Sleeping* (2009),
photograph by Ali Zare

All rights reserved. No part of this publication may be: i) reproduced or transmitted
in any form, electronic or mechanical, including photocopying, recording or by means
of any information storage or retrieval system without prior permission in writing from
the publishers; or ii) used or reproduced in any way for the training, development or
operation of artificial intelligence (AI) technologies, including generative AI technologies.
The rights holders expressly reserve this publication from the text and data mining
exception as per Article 4(3) of the Digital Single Market Directive (EU) 2019/790.

Bloomsbury Publishing Inc does not have any control over, or responsibility for,
any third-party websites referred to or in this book. All internet addresses given
in this book were correct at the time of going to press. The author and publisher
regret any inconvenience caused if addresses have changed or sites have
ceased to exist, but can accept no responsibility for any such changes.

A catalogue record for this book is available from the British Library.

Library of Congress Cataloging-in-Publication Data
Names: Talajooy, Saeed, 1967- editor.
Title: The plays and films of Bahram Beyzaie : origins, forms
and function / edited by Saeed Talajooy.
Description: London; New York: I.B Tauris, 2024. |
Series: I.B. Tauris & BIPS Persian studies series | Includes bibliographical references and index.
Identifiers: LCCN 2023036813 (print) | LCCN 2023036814 (ebook) | ISBN 9780755652693
(hardback) | ISBN 9780755652730 (paperback) | ISBN 9780755652709
(pdf) | ISBN 9780755652716 (epub) | ISBN 9780755652723
Subjects: LCSH: Bayzā'ī, Bahrām–Criticism and interpretation. | Motion
pictures–Iran–History. | Iranian drama–History and criticism.
Classification: LCC PN1998.3.B388 P58 2024 (print) |
LCC PN1998.3.B388 (ebook) | DDC 791.430955–dc23/eng/20230823
LC record available at https://lccn.loc.gov/2023036813
LC ebook record available at https://lccn.loc.gov/2023036814

ISBN: HB: 978-0-7556-5269-3
PB: 978-0-7556-5273-0
ePDF: 978-0-7556-5270-9
eBook: 978-0-7556-5271-6

Typeset by Integra Software Services Pvt. Ltd.

For product safety related questions contact productsafety@bloomsbury.com.

To find out more about our authors and books visit www.bloomsbury.com
and sign up for our newsletters.

CONTENTS

List of Tables and Figures	vii
List of Contributors	ix
Acknowledgements	xii

Chapter 1
BAHRAM BEYZAIE: A CRITICAL INTRODUCTION   1
   Saeed Talajooy

Section A
BEYZAIE'S EARLY PLAYS – GENEALOGIES OF HEROES

Chapter 2
THE GENEALOGY OF ĀRASH, A HERO: FROM *NAQQĀLI* TO BEYZAIE'S RECITATION PLAYS AND FROM ĀRASH THE MYTHICAL HERO TO BEYZAIE'S MARGINALIZED ĀRASH   23
   Saeed Talajooy

Chapter 3
A PAHLEVĀN'S DREAMS OF BELONGING: RECONFIGURATION OF THE IDEALS OF HEROISM IN BAHRAM BEYZAIE'S *SO DIES PAHLEVĀN AKBAR*   57
   Saeed Talajooy

Section B
BEYZAIE'S EARLY FILMS – TEXTS AND CONTEXTS

Chapter 4
THE CHALLENGES OF CENTRE AND MARGIN: BEYZAIE'S COOPERATION WITH THE INSTITUTE FOR THE INTELLECTUAL DEVELOPMENT OF CHILDREN AND YOUNG ADULTS FOR *UNCLE MOUSTACHE, JOURNEY* AND *BĀSHU, THE LITTLE STRANGER*   97
   Amir Hosein Siadat

Chapter 5
THE LANGUAGE OF NATURE AND EARTH: AN ECOCRITICAL READING OF *STRANGER AND THE FOG, BALLAD OF TĀRĀ*, AND *BĀSHU, THE LITTLE STRANGER*   115
   Fatemeh-Mehr Khansalar

Chapter 6
BĀSHU'S OTHER NAMES: A STUDY OF BĀSHU'S IDENTITY IN *BĀSHU, THE LITTLE STRANGER* 135
  Naghmeh Samini

Section C
BEYZAIE THE FILMMAKER – GENRES AND TECHNIQUES

Chapter 7
THE CINEMATIC TRANSLATION OF *TA'ZIYEH* IN BEYZAIE'S *TRAVELLERS* 157
  Farshad Zahedi

Chapter 8
CRIME THRILLER ELEMENTS IN BAHRAM BEYZAIE'S FILMS 179
  Parviz Jahed

Section D
BEYZAIE'S FILMS IN THEIR COMPARATIVE CONTEXTS

Chapter 9
MULTILINGUALITY IN IRANIAN CINEMA: A COMPARATIVE ANALYSIS 197
  Saeed Zeydabadi-Nejad

Chapter 10
LITTLE STRANGERS: REPRESENTATIONS OF DISPLACED YOUTH IN IRANIAN NEW WAVE CINEMA 217
  Nina Khamsy

Index 244

LIST OF TABLES AND FIGURES

Chapter 1

Table 1.1: List of Beyzaie's masterpieces   9

Chapter 2

Figure 2.1: A contemporary pictorial *naqqāl* recounting *Shahnameh* legends   27
Figure 2.2: Parviz Pourhosseini as Jamshid recounting his achievements like a pictorial *naqqāl*   31

Chapter 3

Figure 3.1: Pahlevān Akbar giving water to Mother and overhearing the girl praying for Heidar   74
Figure 3.2: Black-wearing man killing Akbar. Watchman accusing wine-seller of robbery   83

Chapter 5

Figure 5.1: The triangle of mediation   120
Table 5.1: The protagonists' level of self-awareness and relationship with their space   120
Figure 5.2: Plan of Ra'nā's house and natural environment   121
Figure 5.3: Tārā's relationship with the living and the dead worlds and the two men   125
Figure 5.4: Plan of Tārā's house and natural environment   126
Figure 5.5: Plan of Nāei's house and natural environment   128

Chapter 7

Figure 7.1: Mahtāb directly addressing the camera   161
Figure 7.2: The black telephone at the centre of the frame   167
Figure 7.3: Lieutenant Fallāhi presenting the official version of the accident   171
Figure 7.4: Mahtāb and her family enter with the mirror   173

Chapter 9

Table 9.1: Films with languages other than Persian between 2006 and 2017	198
Figure 9.1: *Bāshu, the Little Stranger* (film poster)	201
Figure 9.2: Nāei and Bāshu communicating across languages	202
Figure 9.3: The ending of *Bāshu, the Little Stranger*	206
Figure 9.4: *The Night Bus* (film poster)	207
Figure 9.5: Saddam Hussein's lookalike leader in *The Night Bus*	208
Figure 9.6: Dog tag close-up	210
Figure 9.7: *Che* (film poster)	211
Figure 9.8: Hana pleading with Sirvan	212
Figure 9.9: Kurds scuffling over a gun as it is fired in the air (top right-hand corner)	213

LIST OF CONTRIBUTORS

Parviz Jahed is a film critic, journalist, filmmaker and lecturer in film studies, scriptwriting and film directing. He is the editor-in-chief of *Cine-Eye* (Cinema-Cheshm), a film journal focused on world cinema and independent films published in the UK. Jahed is also the editor of *The Directory of World Cinema: Iran* (Intellect, 2011). His book, *Writing with a Camera* (Nevashtan ba Dourbin), an in-depth interview with Ebrahim Golestan, was published in Iran in 2005. He has guest-edited a special issue of *Film International* journal focused on Iranian independent cinema (Intellect, January 2015). Jahed's research interests include Iranian cinema (especially the new-wave Iranian cinema and Filmfarsi), world cinema, the French new wave, and the history of film style and film theories. He also made a number of documentaries and short films including *Maria: 24 Hour Peace Picket, Ta'ziyeh, Another Narration, The Grass, The Lark, Day-Break, Coffee-Cup Reading, Solayman Minassian: A Man with a Movie Camera* and *Bonjour Monsieur Ghaffary*. Jahed has recently been working on his research project on the origins of the new wave in Iranian cinema at the University of St Andrews.
Email: pj28@st-andrews.ac.uk

Nina Khamsy is a PhD candidate at the Department of Anthropology and Sociology of the Graduate Institute of International and Development Studies in Geneva, Switzerland. Her doctoral research focuses on the relationship between new technologies and Afghan migration in Europe based on a multi-sited and multi-modal ethnography. Her areas of interest and research are diversity in the Persian-speaking world, new media and migration.
Email: ninakhamsy@gmail.com

Fatemeh-Mehr Khansalar holds an MLitt in Middle Eastern Literary and Cultural Studies from the University of St Andrews. She has published two collections of short stories in 2002 and 2018, and several short stories and literary articles in Zendeh-rood, Asr-e Panjshanbeh, and Mehraveh literary journals. Her second short story collection is also to be published soon. After moving to Scotland in 2009, she has run a workshop for Persian miniature painting on a weekly basis. She is currently working on her novel, *Herala*, as well as her research on 'Narrative Identity' in the works and life of Houshang Golshiri.
Email: f.khansalar@gmail.com

Naghmeh Samini is a playwright, scriptwriter and Assistant Professor in Dramatic Arts. More than thirty of Samini's plays have been staged in Iran, France, India, Canada, the United States and other countries. Her screenplays, including *Main*

Line, *Heirān* and *3 Women*, have won awards. The series (Shahrzad-2015) for which she wrote the script was the most popular series in Iran after the revolution. Her play *The King and the Mathematician: A Legend* (2012) was selected by UNESCO as one of the cultural achievements of the year. Samini has been an Assistant Professor in Dramatic Literature at the University of Tehran since 2005. She was also affiliated with the School of Drama, University of Washington, between 2012 and 2017 and is currently a Visiting Professor at Near Eastern Languages and Civilizations (NELC), University of Washington. As a researcher, she has three monographs: *The Book of Love and Magic* (Tehran: Markaz, 2000) on *One Thousand and One Night*; *The Theatre of Myths* (Tehran: Ney, 2008) on reflections of Iranian mythology in Iranian drama; and *Battles and Bodies* (Tehran: Ney, 2019) on the semiotics of human body in post-war Japanese cinema. She has published many articles and delivered lectures on cinema, theatre and cultural studies in Persian and English.
Email: nsamini@uw.edu

Amirhosein Siadat is a curator of the Art and Experience of Cinema, Tehran, Iran. He holds a master's degree in art studies and has been a critic and researcher of theatre and cinema for twelve years. He has published numerous articles on Iranian cinema. He was the director of the cinematheque of the Tehran Museum of Contemporary Arts from 2013 to 2019. He currently works as a curator for the Art and Experience of Cinema.
Email: amir.siadat60@gmail.com

Saeed Talajooy is Senior Lecturer in Persian at the University of St Andrews. Talajooy has taught and published on literature, drama and cinema in Iran and the UK and is currently teaching comparative literature, Persian literature, and Iranian cinema and drama. His research is on the reflections of the changing patterns of Iranian identities in Persian literature and Iranian theatre and cinema. It involves analysing the works of Iranian playwrights and filmmakers to find how they refashion indigenous forms and characters or adapt Iranian and non-Iranian myths, history and literary narratives, to challenge dominant political and cultural discourses. Another aspect of his research involves comparative studies of cultural resistance in Africa and the Middle East. His publications include articles and chapters on Iranian theatre and cinema, a co-edited volume entitled *Resistance in Contemporary Middle Eastern Studies: Literature, Cinema and Music* (Routledge 2012) a two-volume monograph on Bahram Beyzaie.
Email: st83@st-andrews.ac.uk

Farshad Zahedi is Lecturer in Film Studies at the University of Carlos III de Madrid (UC3M). In recent years he has published widely on Iranian cinema. His publications include *40 años del cine iraní: el caso de Dariush Mehryui* (Madrid: Fragua, 2010), 'Who Are You Mr. Kiarostami: Koker Trilogy and European Critics and Scholars', *Quarterly Review of Film and Video*. 2018 35(8), 741–61, and 'Myth

of Bastoor and Children of Iranian Independent Cinema', *Film International.* 2014 12(3), 21–30. He is also an associate member of the Centre for Iranian Studies at SOAS and secretary of the research group TECMERIN (UC3M).
Email: fzahedi@hum.uc3m.es

Saeed Zeydabadi-Nejad has been lecturing at SOAS, University of London, on film and media since 2004; has done consultancy work for BBC World Service; and has lectured at the Institute of Ismaili Studies on a joint degree awarded by University College London. He has authored *The Politics of Iranian Cinema* (2010) based on ethnographic fieldwork. His recent publications include 'Watching the Forbidden: Reception of Banned Films in Iran' in *The State of Post-Cinema* (Hagener et al. 2016). His media appearances include radio and TV programmes on BBC Radio Three and Four as well as BBC World Service.
Email: sz10@soas.ac.uk

ACKNOWLEDGEMENTS

First and foremost, I would like to thank Professor Bahram Beyzaie for his creative and scholarly contributions to Iranian culture and producing the masterpieces that have inspired the writers of this book to probe into various aspects of Iranian life, history, arts, culture and cinema to understand and write about human experience, particularly Iranian's life, from new angles. I would also like to thank Professor Beyzaie for granting me several interviews and responding to my questions whenever I could not find the details of a performance or wanted to discuss a particular comparative perspective. The same goes with Mrs Mojdeh Shamsaie for supporting us in the process and also answering some of the questions herself.

I would also like to thank my contributors for their hard work and patience during the years this book was in preparation. Their valuable analyses have enriched this book with perspectives that cannot be found in a single book. Equally valuable has been the work of those who helped me in the original review process, including Golbarg Rekabtalaei, Nahid Ahmadian, Maryam Ghorbankarimi, Hamid Amjad, Parmis Mozafari and Khatereh Sheibani, as well as Naghmeh Samini and Parviz Jahed who joined me in the peer-review process before contributing their own chapters. I am indebted to all my reviewers for their readiness to share their time and expertise to improve the quality of the chapters. I also benefitted from the support of many friends, relatives and colleagues in the process of finding material and photos, including Hamid Amjad, Jila Esmailian, Mehdi Talajooy, Shaghayegh Talajooy and Ehsan Omidvar.

Last but not least, I should also thank the Institute of Iranian Studies and the School of Modern Languages at the University of St Andrews, The Honeyman Foundation and the British Institute for Persian Studies whose initial financial support made this project possible, and their ongoing academic and peer-review support facilitated the publication of this book.

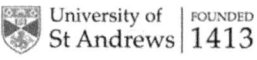   **HONEYMAN FOUNDATION**

BIPS

Chapter 1

BAHRAM BEYZAIE: A CRITICAL INTRODUCTION

Saeed Talajooy

Bahram Beyzaie and the continuity of the past in the present

In 1971, in an interview with John K. Simon, Michel Foucault specified the purpose of his methods of enquiry, the archaeology and genealogy of knowledge, as follows:

> My problem is essentially the definition of the implicit systems in which we find ourselves prisoners: what I would like to grasp is the system of limits and exclusion which we practice without knowing it; I would like to make the cultural unconscious apparent […,] grasp the implicit systems which determine our most familiar behavior without our knowing it […,] find their origin, […] show their formation, the constraint they impose upon us; I am therefore trying to place myself at a distance from them and to show how one could escape.[1]

Thus, Foucault explains his method in terms of examining the origin, the formation, the rise to centrality, the transformation and the contemporary consequences of the ingrained mentalities and practices that distort the hi/story of the present and blind us to what is wrong with the culture in which we grow up. In the same interview, he also explains how when he travels, he sees cultural failures that he does not notice in France and how such experiences encourage him to go back to those failures and try to identify their genealogy and make them more visible.

The ability to see what is wrong with one's culture is essential to progress in any culture and usually occurs due to two reasons. One is because one has suffered marginalization and has, thus, experienced how cultural obsessions and political oppression may distort human potential at personal and national levels. The other is because one has been exposed to intercultural cross-fertilization of perception and thought and knows that inherited cultural practices can be changed for better results. In most cases, of course, both reasons are involved, or one triggers the other. Foucault's projects, however, can also be defined as theoretically charged historical studies, in which his sublimated minority gaze (epistemic privilege) and his defamiliarizing amateur gaze, as a philosopher and psychologist dealing with history, enable him to identify some of the failures of the recycling process involved in history writing. Such theoretically charged amateur reconfigurations, as observed in Foucault's case, are not immune to mistakes in details. However, due to the deviating types of foregrounding they offer, they have the potential to break the chain of habitually recycled materials and perspectives to introduce marginalized or neglected outlooks that may change the disciplinary approaches within a field of study.[2] Of course, all disciplines, including history, are revisionist by nature.[3] The key, however, is to transcend the dominant revisionist trends of a period and create momentum for the rise of new ways of seeing and interpreting. In cultural production, some act as rebel visionaries who introduce new templates and perspectives but never achieve the full potential of the templates or ideas that they have generated. Some, however, as in the cases of scholars such as Karl Marx, Sigmund Freud, Michel Foucault and Edward Said, or creative authors such as William Shakespeare, Henrik Ibsen, Frantz Kafka, or Bertolt Brecht manage to do both.

Bahram Beyzaie is of the latter type. In fact, no one in the history of modern Iranian cultural production fits this ideal of sublimated minority perspective or perceptive amateurism as well as Beyzaie. Perceptive amateurism in his work simply occurs because of the vast range of the subjects that he has worked on and the meta-disciplinary and transgressive nature of dissenting art which can transform any field of human interaction into a subject of aesthetic contemplation to display its problems. The case of epistemic privilege, however, is more subtle because the primary requirement of such a status is that the people who have it have often suffered traumatic marginalization and oppression continuously or at least in a critical period during the early stages of their identity formation. However, what is always more imperative is that such individuals have neither accepted nor reacted in physical violence against such forms of marginalization. They have also transcended the limits of their marginalized background probably because, since they believed in their own centrality to their culture, they obtained unique blends of 'cultural capitals' and skills that made them more central to their culture or because the interactions between their desire for belonging and their quest for recognition triggered a desire to change their culture rather than bend or hate it.[4]

The result has been a body of creative and scholarly works that have led to the rise of modern indigenous-style drama and, to some extent, cinema in Iran. With more than one hundred plays, films and film scripts, his oeuvre is also like a treasure house of techniques hidden in the domains of a culture that has been misrepresented since it was hijacked by Islamic extremists in 1979. This is particularly the case with his plays which have mostly remained untranslated. Being conscious of the contributions that Beyzaie's innovative forms and ideas can make to the visual arts, drama and cinema in a global context, I and the other scholars involved in producing this volume have worked together to highlight some of his qualities in nine chapters on different aspects of his oeuvre and his individual works. Before reading these chapters, however, the reader needs to know more about Beyzaie's life and the cultural contexts in which he has worked to have the background required to engage with his works at a more profound level. In this introduction, therefore, I will first trace Beyzaie's development as an artist and thinker concerned with cultural authenticity and reflect on how he has responded to this concern by reformulating the literary, mythical and artistic resources of his culture for modern theatre and cinema. I will, then, provide examples of how his deconstructive artistic vision evolved to offer new perspectives about different aspects of Iranian culture. In the final section, I will briefly discuss the vision of the volume and the chapters that I have included.

The evolution of an intellectually divergent artist

Beyzaie was born in Tehran in December 1938. His father was a state employee and a poet who led a literary circle, and his mother was a well-read housewife and poet whose erudite native wit and her mother's knowledge of folktales gave Beyzaie a satiric gaze and a treasure of folktales. His family belonged to that category of educated Iranians who were to act as the building blocks of the authoritarian modernization of the Pahlavi era. Beyzaie's parents, however, had converted to Bahaism, a religion from which he distanced himself in his teens when he became enchanted with the myths of all religions and disenchanted with their supernatural pretensions and hostility towards one another. This literary and divergent origin gave Beyzaie a unique cultural capital, but it also exposed him to violence, particularly during the 1950s when Shah's fear of communism and his indebtedness to the clerics who had helped him during the 1953 coup meant that they were given a freer hand and were even helped by the police to harass the Bahais. His family also suffered discrimination. His father was a lawyer, but he had to work as a clerk in the general notary, where even normal promotions were denied to him.[5] Occurring in a context in which he also observed how the state suppressed political dissidents during and after the 1953 coup, these traumatic experiences functioned as a space of revelation for the teenage Beyzaie and demonstrated how the centre in its Shiite or royalist manifestations demonized its assumed others.

Beyzaie's family background was also important to his work at three other levels. The fact that his ancestors were ta'ziyeh directors facilitated his later research on ta'ziyeh. His daily exposure to classical and classical-style modern poetry due to his parents' literary interests and his father's interest in modern law, Arabic and religious debates informed his preoccupation with different registers of Persian. His own fascination with history, cinema, theatre, folk culture and folk heroes in a context in which heated political debates imbued the everyday lives of people in the 1940s and 1950s also expanded this already rich background. His interest in folk heroes and folk culture was also reinforced by the lifelong research of his older cousin, Hossein Parto Beyzaie, on Iranian *Javānmardi* (chivalry) cults. Originating in Mithraic ideas and continuing in the rituals of Iran's traditional sports club, *Zurkhāneh*, the subject intensified Beyzaie's interest in myths and the continuity of ancient heroic archetypes in modern Iran.

Another source of intellectual exchange for Beyzaie was the expansion of return-to-the-roots discourses during the 1950s. These discourses ranged from the retrogressive nativism of some Islamists to the more open culture-conscious pro-Soviet leftists, independent socialists and liberal cosmopolitans whose work on Iran and other Asian cultures aspired to revitalize Iran's cultural life by expanding its intercultural dialogue beyond the West.[6] Such discourses were also political as the post-coup crackdown on constitutionalists and leftists had increased the intelligentsia's sympathy for them, and thus, from the mid-1950s, the intellectual zeitgeist showed signs of tending towards non-Western approaches to reviving the culture in reaction to the state's pro-American policies.[7] This meant that while the state expanded its plans to revitalize the culture by exposing it to Western ways of seeing and doing, some of those who were in charge of fulfilling the process used dissenting liberal or leftist methods to undermine the modernizing discourses of royalist nationalism.

Beyzaie of the late 1950s had liberal socialist tendencies yet distanced himself from fashionable isms of the time as he found most of them equally distorting in the narratives that they used to describe Iran. Thus, he was fully aware that he must find his place in a culture whose potential for growth had been distorted by religious dogma, political tribalism and mimicry of the West.[8] Politically, he remained neutral as he found that most parties displayed the same exclusionist qualities that he observed in the state, the clergy and the people who followed their biddings. Yet he seems to have respected people of Khalil Maleki's type whose reformist vision of liberal socialist constitutionalism offered a path for working with the state without bending to its authoritarian diktats. This suggests that though he found the Iranian left non-democratic and exclusionist, his own views were not completely at odds with people of Maleki's type.[9] Beyzaie denies having any political tendencies at the time but speaks well of Maleki:

> He had a positive future-directed vision of what Iran should be. I met him a few times in the 1960s, and once, he proposed that I launch a non-political film viewing and discussion group to familiarize the youth with cinema, but the plan never materialised.[10]

This post-coup culture, with its web of inherited and imported leftist, liberal, royalist, archaist, religious, mystical, mythical and folklore ideas, which exposed people to several progressive or regressive forces, was for Beyzaie a site of contention and revelation where his ambivalent relationship with his culture evolved. As he probed further into the roots of the exclusionist practices around him, he also noticed that they often contradicted the ideal origins or the founding texts that they glorified. Having suffered religious violence, Beyzaie was more in line with the secular nation-building narratives which were to replace religion with other forms of togetherness. Yet, as reflected in the democratic thrust and the attention to the impacts of marginalization in his early works, his ideal of nationhood was far more democratic and inclusive than the state's royalist nationalism, which tried to create a modern society by mixing Western institutions with a despotic, political system inspired by ancient Iranian empires. For this discourse, as reflected in the slogan '*Khodā, Shāh, Mihan*' (God, King, Homeland), God and the King were placed above 'Homeland,' and people were only imagined as the upholders and performers of the ideology of the slogan. For Beyzaie, people, their education and their rise to responsible citizenship and political awareness were the essence of a modern nation.

As reiterated in one of his recent interviews, Beyzaie was from the beginning concerned with the absence of a history of people and knew that this history could only be extracted from the folk culture.[11] Yet he also knew that for this history to be acknowledged, it must be articulated aesthetically in a language that charms the elite culture. His works, therefore, display as much experimentation with the registers of language as with artistic forms. This experimentation, whether engaging with traditional elite forms, the West-obsessed elite art of the time, or Far Eastern and Euro-American theatre and cinema, is always at the service of reshaping Iranian folk forms to modernize their already gripping carnival motifs for emancipatory purposes.

The language aspect was also essential to him as he saw himself in a literary tradition that represented the best that his culture had given him. His dramatic and filmic oeuvre, therefore, displays a versatile use of linguistic registers that aspire to echo the mythical, historical or modern eras in which the plays or the films are set and the social class or educational levels of the characters. Thus, in such plays as *Ārash* (1959) or *Ardāvirāf's Report* (1999) due to their pre-Islamic settings, he uses pure Persian yet maintains the performability of the dialogue.[12] In his folk plays, including *Snake King* (1966) or *Tārābnāmeh* (2006) he uses a lively language that echoes the qualities of Iranian *taqlid* comedies. In *Parchment of Master Sharzin* (1986), *A New Preface to the Shāhnāmeh* (1986) or *Day of Incident* (1982) he creates a poetic dialogue that echoes the linguistic registers of the secular intellectuals of the medieval era and contrasts it with that of the clerics and the common people of the era. In *The Crow* (1976) or *Maybe Some Other Time* (1987) he displays the contemporary registers of various strata in society. Or in his works on *ayyārs* or other figures of Iranian chivalry cults, including *Ayyār-Nāmeh* (1984) or *So Dies Pahlevān Akbar* (1963), he echoes the speech qualities of such individuals in the twelfth and nineteenth centuries. In all these cases, Beyzaie does not copy the language of the texts that have remained from the relevant eras. Instead, he echoes their main features but adds features or contemporary elements that make the dialogues performable. This attention to language has created positive and negative reactions among critics. From my perspective, although in a handful of scenes in his works, Beyzaie has not been entirely convincing in his use of language, his experimentations with registers of Persian have made major contributions to the development of stage and screen language in Iran and turned the drama into a key genre in Persian literature. I have also noticed that those who have only read or seen one or two of his plays, particularly those set in pre-Islamic or medieval Iran, may find his language difficult. However, those who have gone through his oeuvre and understand his works in terms of their contribution to Iran's aesthetic revolution often find the range of registers that he has adapted for his characters, settings and moods fascinating. Many readers or viewers have also been mesmerized by his witty and versatile pure Persian in such plays as *Death of Yazdgerd* or *Account of Bondar the Premier* (1961/1997) or poetically erudite and powerful medieval Persian in *Kallāt Claimed* (1982), *Day of the Event* or *Parchment of Master Sharzin*.[13]

The range of registers and the literary qualities of Beyzaie's dramatic masterpieces make their translation difficult, particularly because such a historical range of registers does not exist in many languages, or if such registers exist, they are not as understandable as the ones in new Persian which has been around for at least 1,300 years. Furthermore, whereas theatre companies may willingly stage Shakespeare's plays despite their demanding language, they are not willing to do such a thing for a translated play. Therefore, the translator is forced to sacrifice range for performability. It is, thus, important to say that none of the current translations of Beyzaie's works, including my own, reflect the linguistic qualities of the original works in Persian.[14]

This language aspect, however, is also important in that it contains strong subversive elements which reflect what James C. Scott identifies as one of the major spaces of cultural resistance against dominant discourses. Let me unpack this further. In his analysis of popular resistance, Scott distinguishes between three realms of transcripts. The first, the 'public transcript,' is 'the self-portrait of dominant elites as they would have themselves seen'. This 'is designed to be impressive and naturalize' their power to let them 'conceal or euphemize the dirty linen of their rule'. Due to this charade of excellence, however, since they aspire to have 'hegemony in the Gramscian sense of that term', the elite also need to pretend to be ruling on behalf of people and thus their discourse contains gaps which allow the ruled to find representation and rights 'in the prevailing ideology without appearing seditious'. The second is the dissenting discourse which is often 'off stage' where the rebels gather 'outside the intimidating gaze of power' to assert their message of change which causes them harm if expressed in the public space. The final transcript, which, like the first, occurs in the public, reveals itself in encoded cultural forms that undermine the hegemony of the ruling elite not by direct dissent but by challenging the cultural constructs on which their hegemony is built, reinforced and preserved. This latter transcript contains a 'politics of disguise and anonymity that takes place in public view but is designed to have a double meaning or to shield the identity of the actors'. To this domain belong not just 'rumor, gossip, folktale, jokes, songs, rituals, codes, and euphemism'[15] but also the artistic works which bring into formal art the carnival force of folk practices and manipulate their comedy and sentimental morality to trigger action by avoiding catharsis.

Beyzaie's first plays reveal this feature in a style in which all dramatic elements function as codes and join the dialogue to deflate the discourses of the ruling political, religious, economic and even intellectual elites. The process, thus, involves reformulating the Persian language and Iranian folktales, myths, *taqlid* comedies, *naqqāli* storytelling and *kheimeh-shab-bāzi* puppet shows for emancipatory purposes. His first plays engaged with *naqqāli* for three reasons. The first two were the relative ease of writing in a narrative form and his own penchant for myths and ideals of heroism. The third, however, was due to his interest in cinema as a form which, like *naqqāli*, was focused on heroes and used moving from one image to another for narration. During his early teens in the early 1950s, Beyzaie had developed a passion for cinema as an escape from the violence of his ignorant peers and teachers who harassed or penalized him for his parents' religion. This escape space, however, evolved in his mind to become an artistic means to question the exclusionist beliefs and religious discourses that fuelled this violence.[16] Cinema was a major space of entertainment and intercultural cross-fertilization for the youth. In Beyzaie's case, however, as his high school friend, the philosopher Dariush Ashoori states, even when he was 18, his love for cinema was no longer a teenage love of actors and action. He sometimes saw a film several times to analyse its framing, mise en scène, editing techniques and camerawork.[17] In 1959, he joined Farrokh Ghaffary's Cine Club, where he could watch foreign art films and participate in discussions led by Ghaffary and other film experts. Beyzaie, thus, became well versed in how words and images produce divergent meanings in the minds of viewers when placed in loci of aesthetic attention. Cinema was also crucial to him as it was the main space for learning about alternative ways of being and models of behaviour.[18] If until the 1940s theatre was the carrier of the models and role models of modernity or new forms of being, now it was cinema that negotiated those images in people's minds.

Beyzaie, therefore, first experimented with those indigenous forms that were like the magic box of cinema: dramatic recounting with paintings (*naqqāli* & *pardeh-khāni*) and puppet shows (*kheimeh-shab-bāzi*). In one, a narrator used a large painting to move from one scene to another while telling an exciting story. In the other, a puppeteer used a magic box to move and dub his puppets who acted like humans in comic situations, while a narrator engaged with them and the audience in a meta-theatrical dialogue. Both were significant, but, since *naqqāli* was focused on myths and legends, Beyzaie's engagement with the form also commented on Iranian myths which have always been a scene of contention about the origins of Iranian cultural identity.

Beyzaie's concern with cultural identity is also reflected in his focus on writing plays that contributed to the rise of indigenous-style modern Iranian drama and publishing books on Iranian, Japanese, Chinese and Indian dramatic traditions to make Iranian cultural production more cosmopolitan in its intercultural exchanges. This concern also triggered his reflections on the continuity of the negative or positive beliefs and practices of the past. Thus, his works also display how the best aspects of his culture have been maintained by the people of his type – creative thinkers, writers and artists – rather than the exclusionist religious and political elites and their ignorant or opportunistic followers who prosecuted the former. This meant that for him, the main battlefield was that of culture, where the past narratives are used to claim authenticity for dominant discourses. He was, thus, determined, perhaps in defence of himself, to extract the best that his culture can offer and reformulate it for the present to confront those discourses that impede emancipatory change by hiding behind their readings of the past.

In my writing on Beyzaie I usually move from aesthetic, textual and intertextual analysis to cultural and socio-political analysis to display the dialogue of his works with Iranian culture. I also use the evidence of my analysis to argue that Beyzaie is a prime example of a person who has reconfigured his experience of marginalization and his epistemic privilege into a defamiliarizing gaze and a positive, creative impulse for emancipation. He has, thus, in almost every subject that he has touched, introduced new templates and promoted marginalized, life-affirming perspectives that undermine the reductive narratives of the dominant discourses of Iranian identity.[19] Moreover, due to his knowledge of Iranian and non-Iranian dramatic and artistic forms, mythology and history, he has also managed to turn this epistemic privilege into 'epistemic authority'. This has enabled him to articulate his critical questions and perspectives in convincing creative products that are in dialogue with the origins and contemporary conditions of Iranian culture and thus attract attention in the Iranian public space.[20]

Creativity always involves intercultural and intracultural reformulations of old and new ideas, templates, characters, narratives and lived experience.[21] Beyzaie has excelled in both. With more than sixty years of involvement in perceptive cultural production, Beyzaie has also been one of the most prolific playwrights and filmmakers of modern Iran. During this continuous cultural production, with more than 100 plays, screenplays, films and monographs, like all creative artists or scholars, including people like Ibsen, Brecht, Foucault or Said, he may have made mistakes in grasping the reality of a situation or produced mediocre artistic templates, or made occasional mistakes in his visions for theatre, cinema, society, culture or emancipatory art. Nevertheless, his importance has been constantly increasing because even his average works contain valuable experiments with indigenous or global artistic forms and he has always asked the right questions and highlighted alternative ways of seeing, hearing and representing which have high potential for cultural, political and aesthetic regeneration.[22] More importantly, he has created more than thirty masterpieces which have inspired several generations of Iranian artists and writers due to their cultural perspectives and linguistic and artistic qualities. These works have also introduced underrepresented characters and protagonists, such as crushed heroes, suppressed minorities, creative intellectuals, independent or intellectual women, or aspiring homeless children into Iranian cinema and theatre. As noted above and discussed in the chapters of this volume, this process has also involved analysing indigenous dramatic forms and rituals in his research writings and experimenting with them in normal or self-reflexive scenes in his plays and films. In other words, Beyzaie has also been the foremost contributor to the modernization of Iran's indigenous performing traditions. To document this quality for quick referencing, in Table 1.1, I have provided an overview of these masterpieces with attention to the character types and indigenous forms that they have engaged with. Some of these works have been examined in the chapters of this volume. These chapters demonstrate how

1. Bahram Beyzaie: A Critical Introduction

Table 1.1 List of Beyzaie's masterpieces

Female Protagonist [Bold], Male & Female Protagonists [Shaded], Male Protagonist [Normal].

Year	P (Plays), SP (Screenplays), F (Film), RM (Research Monograph)	New Character Types or Ideas	Indigenous Forms[23]
1959	1. *Ārash* (P)	1. Tormented Individual as Saviour	1. Naqqāli
1961	2. *Account of Bondar, the Premier/1997* (P)	2. Creative Intellectual and Opportunistic Tyrant	2. Naqqāli
1962 1963	3. *Puppet Trilogy (The Marionettes, Sunset in a Strange Land, Tale of the Hidden Moon)* (P)	3. Tormented Hero, Demonized Minority, Heroic Black, Self-reliant Woman	3. Kheimeh-Shab-Bāzi, Taqlid, Heroic Folktales
1963	4. *So Dies Pahlevān Akbar* (P)	4. Tormented Individual as Hero, Religious Minority	4. Naqqāli, Ayyāri Tales, Saqqākhāneh and Zurkhāneh
1964	5. *The Eighth Voyage of Sinbad* (P)	5. Misrepresented Hero and Death as a character	5. Taʿziyeh, Naqqāli and Tamāshā
1965	6. *Theatre in Iran* (RM)	6. Iranian Theatrical Forms	6. All Indigenous Forms
1966	7. *The Snake King* (P)	7. Anti-Establishment King, Demonized Minority, Heroic Woman	7. Taqlid, Taʿziyeh, Folktales of Questing Women
1970	8. *Uncle Moustache* (F)	8. Emancipatory Children and Reformed Old Man	8. Carnival forms and Taqlid
1971	9. *Downpour* (F)	9. Creative Intellectual & Wise Hardworking Woman	9. Carnival forms and Taʿziyeh
	10. *Lonely Warrior (Ayyār-e Tanhā)* (SP)	**10. Wise, Heroic Woman & Reformed Vagabond**	**10. Ayyāri Tales**
1972	11. *Journey* (F)	11. Visionary Children in Search of a Home	11. Epic Quests, Seven Labours
	12. *Stranger and the Fog* (F)	12. Independent Woman & Tormented Fertility Hero	12. Taʿziyeh, Fertility Rituals
1975	**13. *Truths about Leila, the Daughter of Edris* (SP)**	**13. Independent Woman Encountering Toxic Masculinity**	**13. Tales of Questing Women**
1976	**14. *The Crow* (F)**	**14. Intellectual Woman**	**14. Tales of Questing Women**
1977	15. *Mourning Wail (Nodbeh)* (P)	15. Victimized Woman against Toxic Masculinity	15. Taʿziyeh, Taqlid
1978	**16. *Ballad of Tārā* (F)**	**16. Perceptive Woman & Ghostly Hero of the Past**	**16. Taʿziyeh, Fertility Rituals**

1979	17. *Death of Yazdgerd* (P & F1981),	17. Creative Women and Suppressed Man Set against the Elites	17. Performance for Survival (Shahrzād), Taʿziyeh, Naqqāli
	18. *Tales of Shroud-Wearing Leader (Qesseh-hā-ye Mir-e Kafanpush)* (P)	18. Victimized Men & Woman Rising against Tyrants	18. Ayyāri Tales
1981	19. *Memories of an Actor of a Supporting Role* (P)	19. Little Men and Women Used by a System	19. Taʿziyeh, Naqqāli, Carnival
	20. *Occupation* (SP)	20. Questing Intellectual Woman	20. Tales of Questing Women
1982	21. *Conquest of Kallāt (Kallāt Reclaimed)* (P)	21. Creative Intellectual Woman Acting as a Saviour	21. Tales of Questing Women, Taqlid;
	22. *Day of the Event* (SP)	22. Marginalized Man & Woman in Quest for Truth	22. Taʿziyeh
1985	23. *Bashu the Little Stranger* (F)	23. Independent Woman, Marginalized Child	23. Fertility Rituals, Taʿziyeh
1986	24. *Parchment of Master Sharzin* (SP) 25. *A New Preface to the Shahnameh* (SP)	24 & 25. Creative Intellectual As Sacrificial Hero, Tormented Femme Fatale, Dogmatic Rulers & Clergy	24 & 25. Taʿziyeh, Tales of Heroic Intellectuals & Mystics
1992	26. *Reed Panel* (SP) 27. *Killing Mad Dogs* (SP/F 2000)	26. Wise Woman as a Saviour 27. Creative Intellectual Woman as a Saviour	26 & 27. Taqlid, Performance for Survival, Questing Woman
1993	28. *Siyāvush Recitation* (P and SP)	28. Intellectual as Sacrificial Hero	28. Taʿziyeh, Naqqāli, Tales of Heroic Intellectuals & mystics.
1996	29. *Destination* (SP)	29. Rebellious Woman against Toxic Masculinity	29. Tales of questing Women
1997	30. *Afrā or the Day is Passing* (P)	30. Intellectual Woman as Sacrificial Hero	30. Tales of Victimized & Heroic Intellectuals & Mystics
2003	31. *The One Thousand and First Night*	31. Creative Women as Saviours, Despotic Rulers & Clergy, Sacrificial Intellectual, Reformed Bigot	31. Performance for Survival and Saving others (Shahrzād)
2006	32. *Book of Merriment (Tarabnāmeh, 1994)* (P)	32. Women and Men in a Comedy of Emancipation	32. Taqlid, Carnival, Naqqāli
2012	33. *Where is Hezār Afsān? (Book of A Thousand Tales?)* (RM)	33. Reclaiming a Marginalized Cultural Tradition	33. One Thousand and One Night, Persian Literature and Much more

Beyzaie has used these forms for emancipatory purposes in contexts that promote cultural belief and practices that celebrate life, art, love, productivity, fertility, creative education and caring togetherness. They also show how Beyzaie displays the authenticity of Iranian life-affirming beliefs and questions the discourses that lead to discord, exclusionism and suppression by celebrating dogmas, the afterlife and blind obedience to imagined representatives of God.

Another important aspect of Beyzaie's oeuvre has been his critique of Iran's political culture without becoming obsessed with politics. In an article on intellectualism, Javad Mojabi argues that, in Iran, due to the absence of free political parties, the roles of the main intellectual types – theoretical philosophers, creative artists and political thinkers – merge so that the former two are trapped in politics and cannot achieve the aesthetic or philosophical depth that their works require.[24] Mojabi's point about the givens of an over-politicized culture is valid, but a neglected aspect of this debate is the role of interpretive communities in the production of meaning because when a cultural product is released, it may be interpreted, rightly or wrongly, in ways that have nothing to do with what the author has intended. Thus, under the conditions specified by Mojabi, people may prioritize political interpretations to the extent that they miss how a cultural product may question the politics of culture or political culture through its form or by challenging the assumptions that shape the exclusionist essence of seemingly rivalling discourses. Though some of Beyzaie's works, such as *Stranger and the Fog* or *Maybe Some Other Time* (1988), have been deemed apolitical and some, such as *Four Boxes* (1967), too political, he has constantly engaged with the politics of culture rather than politics. Thus, his works critique those cultural failings that lead to totalitarian exclusionism, leave Iranians at the mercy of tyrants or invaders, and undermine productive citizenship by breeding apathy towards the rights of lower classes, minority groups, dissenting thinkers, and women or children.

During the 1960s and 1970s, some of the critiques against Beyzaie's works were from such interpretive sources, particularly the Marxist and Islamic leftists, who marked Beyzaie's concerns with form and the machination of marginalization and domination as self-obsessed, decadent, or not political enough. Jalal Al-e Ahmad, for instance, criticized Beyzaie's pre-occupation with language and aphorism. In his review of Beyzaie's *Puppet Trilogy* (written 1962–3, staged 1965), he also misread Beyzaie's critique of inherited beliefs and dominant discourses to argue that Beyzaie is blaming God for human conditions in order to avoid political criticism.[25] Of course, as evident from the debate that occurred between Beyzaie and Saeed Soltanpur (1940–81) during a conference about Beyzaie's staging of *Mirās* (The Heritage) and *Ziyāfat* (The Feast) in autumn 1967, such critiques could have had positive imports for Iranian cultural production if they had remained in the realm of performance and social theory.[26] However, in the decade leading to the 1979 revolution, such critical animosities intensified to the extent that they added a radical leftist form of policing and censorship to official and Islamic forms of censor. At times, leftist groups even disrupted cultural activities or threatened artists.[27] In 1969, for instance, during the staging of *The Snake King* in Mashhad, radical leftists, who had probably been organized by Soltanpur, tried to disrupt the play. They accused Beyzaie, who had long been involved in the campaign for freedom of speech and was one of the founding members of the *Kānun-e Nevisandegān* (Writers' Association, 1968–), of selling himself to the state, threatened to physically attack him and chanted slogans against the play.[28]

The event exemplifies the debilitating attitudes that Beyzaie later criticized in his speech on censorship during the gatherings at the Goethe Institute in 1977. For him, the tyranny of dominant discourses was not limited to the state. It was equally observed in the arbitrary decisions and violent practices of the proponents of exclusionist religious and intellectual discourses or the thugs and clerics who ruled over city districts like independent kingdoms.[29] However, since the late 1980s, with the demise of the zeal for replacing capitalism and the rise of post-political reformist movements, which aspire to reform capitalism by campaigning for the rights of lower classes and marginalized groups, the emancipatory significance of works produced by the people of Beyzaie's type has become more visible.

The vision and the content of this book

When in 2013, I guest-edited a special issue of *Iranian Studies* on Bahram Beyzaie, I was aware of this significance and knew that much could be said about Beyzaie that had remained unsaid even in Persian. Beyzaie has been engaged in studying and reformulating Iranian folklore, mythology, history, drama and cinema as a scholar, creative writer and filmmaker since 1959, and right now (2023), as he has just passed his eighty-fourth birthday, he is still active and has recently published a film script, *Mahi*, which is as interesting in its form and subject as his previous works.[30] This exemplary perseverance is by itself an achievement that must be acknowledged to empower others who follow the example of such inspiring individuals.

The idea of a second edited volume on Beyzaie occurred to me in June 2017, when I invited Beyzaie to Scotland to receive an honorary doctorate from the University of St Andrews for a lifetime of creative and scholarly contribution to cinema, theatre and folk studies. During his visit, I organized a two-day workshop, funded by the British Institute for Persian Studies and the Honeyman Foundation, in which twelve scholars talked about his films. The workshop, which was entitled 'In Conversation with Bahram Beyzaie', also included a screening and discussion of his early cinematic masterpiece, *Ragbār* (*Downpour*), a lecture by Beyzaie on the Cycle of Jamshid and Zahhāk and a dazzling performance of the first act of Beyzaie's *One Thousand and First Night* (2003) in which Mojdeh Shamsaie (1968–) played the role of ten characters. By then I had studied Beyzaie's works in their general contexts for more than thirty years and as a subject of academic enquiry for more than fourteen years. Thus, I was well versed in the range of forms and ideas that he had introduced to the world of drama, literature, theatre and cinema and knew that his works could have as much impact at the international level as they had in the Persian-speaking world. As a result, I started working on this volume.

Most of the chapters in this volume were first presented during the above workshop by their contributors who are all experts in various aspects of Iranian cinema and cultural production. As in the workshop, their focus is Beyzaie's films either as filmic texts analysed for their technical and cultural qualities or as subjects of comparative or socio-political enquiries. The inclusion of more chapters on cinema was because in the absence of more translations, Beyzaie's films are more accessible in the English-speaking world. The primary criterion of inclusion, however, has been the author's ability to engage with aspects of Beyzaie's works which have not been examined in detail in previous publications. Thus, rather than following a particular approach, they represent the variety of ways that Beyzaie's oeuvre can be approached.

To make the volume chronologically representative and more balanced in addressing different aspects of Beyzaie's oeuvre and the origins of his creativity, I have also included the current extended introduction on Beyzaie's rise as a dramatist, scholar and filmmaker and two comprehensive chapters on his early plays. Analysing two of Beyzaie's early plays in their aesthetic, cultural, archetypal and biographical contexts, these two chapters are longer than the other chapters. In the case of Ārash (1959) this was because the cultural and mythical contexts and the forms which the play works with are so dense that my genealogical approach required introducing several different cultural traditions which have remained understudied in the West. In the case of So Dies Pahlevān Akbar (1963), however, this was because, in addition to the complicated set of ideas and forms that the play deals with, the text has not been translated into English and thus required a more detailed scene-by-scene analysis. These three chapters focus on aspects of Iranian culture and Beyzaie's oeuvre which have remained understudied even in Iran. They provide a detailed analysis of Beyzaie's dialogue with the marginalized aspects of Iranian culture; trace and theorize about the cultural narratives, myths and forms that he worked with in his early plays; and offer a solid background for understanding the following chapters.

The book has been structured in a flexible chronological order that reflects the eras in which the works discussed in the chapters have been produced. Nevertheless, the grouping of the chapters also reflects their subjects and methodologies. Chapters 2 and 3 are genealogical and focus on Beyzaie's early plays. Chapters 4, 5 and 6 focus on the texts and contexts of Beyzaie's early films and their dialogue with the dominant political, identity and gender discourses before and after the 1979s revolution. Chapters 7 and 8 focus on Beyzaie's filmmaking techniques and his use of Iranian and global forms, and Chapters 9 and 10 compare Beyzaie's films with other films in their national contexts. As expected, due to its multi-sided significance in Iranian cinema, Bāshu, the Little Stranger (1985) has received more attention than other films and has been discussed in five chapters. These chapters, however, examine different aspects of the film in diverse contexts, and, indeed, only Chapter 6 is entirely focused on the film.

As stated above, the second chapter is on Beyzaie's dialogue with the myth of Ārash, the sacrificial archer who determined Iran's borders with Turān when the Iranian army was under siege in Tabaristan. The chapter has a genealogical approach which demonstrates how the forms, narratives and the ideas that Beyzaie works with have evolved in Iran and what Beyzaie does to them. The chapter first offers a brief overview of the origins, historical transformations, cultural functions and contemporary uses of *naqqāli*, the indigenous form which Beyzaie has reformulated in the play. I, then, do the same with the myth of Ārash by tracing its potential roots in prehistoric, agricultural myths, its political repurposing in Iranian Arsacid myths, its brief recordings in the Avesta and the medieval texts of the ninth to the eleventh century, and its resurfacing in the works of modernist writers in the 1950s. In the final section, I build on these genealogical outlines to analyse Beyzaie's recitation play as a masterpiece that, despite its aura of youthful despair, has remained the most important rereading of the myth in the modern era. I argue that it comments on citizenship, leadership, marginalization and heroism; highlights despair and desire for belonging, recognition and love as keys to sacrificial heroic action; criticizes hero worship in society; and simultaneously displays Beyzaie's psychological battle with the demonizing discourses that had beleaguered his life in the 1950s.

Chapter 3, which is also mine, focuses on Beyzaie's *Pahlevān Akbar Mimirad* (*So Dies Pahlevān Akbar* or *So Dies Akbar the Hero*, 1963). I have placed this early play at the beginning of the volume after my chapter on *Ārash* (1959) to provide another example of how Beyzaie's plays initiated some of the aesthetic and thematic innovations of Iranian cinema and how the elements that he introduced in them became dominant in his later works. I argue that the play introduced a new conception of heroism and initiated a new interest in the Iranian chivalry cult, *Āyin-e Javānmardi*, and its ideal heroes, *Pahlevān* and *Ayyār*, in contrast with the streetwise tough guys who had become central to Iranian cinema from 1958. The chapter explores the ideals of *javānmardi* before engaging with Beyzaie's depiction of a selfless hero as a victim of marginalization. Using scene-by-scene analysis and thick description along with an eclectic use of cultural theory, I go through the play to identify its dialogue with Iranian folktales, epics, drama and cinema and offer a discussion of the double and the fantastic and their significance in Beyzaie's creation of dramatic sublime in the play.

Chapter 4, by Amir Hosein Siadat, examines the dialogue of Beyzaie's *Uncle Moustache* (1970), *Journey* (1972) and *Bāshu, the Little Stranger* (1985) with the priorities of the producer of these films, the state-run Institute for the Intellectual Development of Children and Young Adults, in two very different eras before and after the 1979 revolution. The chapter is different from the rest of the book in its approach. Rather than analysing the internal qualities of the works, it is more concerned with describing Beyzaie's dialogue with the givens of the eras in which the films were made and his relationship with the institute. It does, however, use these contexts to make valid analytical points about the internal worlds and the techniques used in the film. The chapter has links with the introduction and the previous chapters in that it builds on the socio-political contexts established in the first three chapters. It also engages with *Bāshu, the Little Stranger* from an angle that reinforces but is different from the other chapters that analyse the film. The chapter functions as a turning point in the volume as it also reflects the similarities and differences of the dominant discourses in Iran before and after the revolution. Providing an account of how Beyzaie challenged the intellectual, political and cinematic discourses of the two eras, it also introduces an angle that other chapters discuss only in passing.

Chapter 5, by Fatemeh-Mehr Khansalar, offers a light-touch ecofeminist and ecocritical analysis of the relationships of Beyzaie's female protagonists in his village trilogy with their natural and built environments, the people around them and the strangers who appear in their environments. The chapter expands some of the subjects highlighted in the first four chapters in that it deals with three films in which Beyzaie's discourses on nature, fertility, victimization, marginalization, heroism and agricultural myths gradually evolve to focus on heroines who represent the rising agency of Iranian women. Khansalar argues for a gradual progress in the agency and influence of Beyzaie's female protagonists. This progress begins with Ra'nā's failure to control her destiny in *Stanger and the Fog* (1974) continues with Tārā's loss, rise in awareness and new life-affirming determination in *Ballad of Tārā* (1978–80) and is completed with Nāei's powerfully engineered control over her own life and Bāshu's destiny in *Bāshu, the Little Stranger* (1985). She also demonstrates how each of these female characters transcends the patriarchal norms and exclusionist views of her community to relate to the stranger who enters her community and integrate him into her community.

Naghmeh Samini's piece, Chapter 6, is the only chapter primarily focused on *Bāshu, the Little Stranger*. Explicating the idea of naming to analyse Bāshu's position as an outcast, she analyses the film with specific attention to the dialogue of the film with the Islamic state war propaganda in the 1980s and uses the metaphoric aspect of naming Bāshu to see why and how the film subverts the images of the heroic war migrant and the honourable religious host in the state's propaganda. Building on Beyzaie's frequent use of the figure of a stranger, whose arrival changes the givens of an enclosed community, Samini reflects on how Bāshu's visible physical difference initiates new ways of seeing in Nāei and inspires her to transform the norms of her ethnocentric community to be more accepting towards Bāshu. The chapter has clear links with the first four chapters in the way it focuses on the machination of marginalization with Bāshu as an outcast. It also expands the socio-political approach of Chapter 4 by analysing the film from a fresh perspective and focusing on war propaganda in the 1980s.

Chapter 7, by Farshad Zahedi, discusses Beyzaie's filmic style by focusing on his reformulation of *ta'ziyeh* techniques in *Travellers* (1991) as a secular, filmic *ta'ziyeh* performance contemplating the meaning of death. Zahedi analyses several key scenes in the film to argue that Beyzaie combines *ta'ziyeh* and classical cinematic techniques to engage the spectator in a modern ritual. He examines Beyzaie's manipulation of objective and subjective shots and his framing and editing techniques as strategies that give a sense of inevitability and eternal significance to the ritual. He also argues that the ritual aspect of the film celebrates life and has been constructed to confront the dominant ideology of the Islamic Republic in the late 1980s in which death was glorified more than life. The chapter provides a filmic example of my arguments about Beyzaie's reformulation of Iranian indigenous forms in the first three chapters. It, thus, functions like a perceptive extension of the second chapter in which I discuss Beyzaie's reformulation of *naqqāli* in *Ārash*. It also analyses an angle of creativity in Beyzaie's works which is different from his use of global forms, which Jahed analyses in Chapter 8.

Chapter 8, which is by Parviz Jahed, is focused on another aspect of Beyzaie's filmic style. Jahed analyses the use of crime thriller and noir elements in Beyzaie's city films. Focusing on *The Crow* (1977), *Maybe Some Other Time* (1988) and *Killing Mad Dogs* (2001), Jahed analyses some of the filmic techniques and motifs that Beyzaie uses to create suspense, unexpected twists and hallucinatory dark moods, and the way he depicts his protagonists as detectives engaged in an investigation whose results are essential for their understanding of their cultural, individual and historical identities. The chapter is in dialogue with Chapter 7 in that it offers key examples of how Beyzaie reframes global filmic and dramatic forms, in this case crime-thriller motifs, in plots and settings that transform their protagonists into detectives whose quests for truth reveal the distorted and progressive modalities of Iranian identity and turn the films into sites of negotiation between the past, present and future. The chapter displays how Beyzaie's divergent gaze, discussed in the introduction, functions and analyses aspects of Beyzaie's cinema that have remained understudied.

The next piece, Chapter 9, which opens the comparative section of the volume, is by Saeed Zeydabadi-Nejad, who examines the use of languages other than Persian in Iranian cinema. Highlighting the importance of *Bāshu, the Little Stranger* as a trendsetter, it argues that although it maintains the primacy of Persian as a national language, compared to the films that followed its example, it offers a much more egalitarian discourse. The chapter's comparative analysis contrasts *Bāshu* with Kiumars Pourahmad's *The Night Bus* (2007) which contains scenes in Arabic and Ebrahim Hatamikia's *Che* (2014) which has some dialogue in Kurdish. The chapter's ideas link it to the analysis of Beyzaie's divergent gaze and use of language in the introduction. Zeydabadi-Nejad's comparative angle, however, enables him to address some of the points raised in other chapters in a recent national context and reveal the film's importance while critiquing its exaltation of Persian over other Iranian languages.

The final chapter in the volume is by Nina Khamsy who inspects the depiction of dislocated children in Iranian cinema by offering a comparative analysis of Beyzaie's *Bāshu, the Little Stranger*, Majid Majidi's *Baran* (2001) and Rokhsareh Ghaemmaghami's *Sonita* (2016). Khamsy makes a flexible distinction between two types of depicting dislocated children and teenagers: one in which the narratives are allegorical and more representative of the problems of adults and one in which the focus is a realistic depiction of the impacts of dislocation on the lives of the displaced children and the people of the host cultures with whom the newcomers come into contact. Khamsy's subject and discussions of Beyzaie's *Uncle Moustache* (1970), *Journey* (1972) and *Bāshu, the Little Stranger* (1985) link her chapter to the subject of marginalization in Beyzaie's oeuvre, Siadat's focus on Beyzaie's child-centred films in Chapter 4 and Samini's analysis of Bāshu's name and function as an outcast in Chapter 6. Her comparative analysis and focus on strangers, language and children, however, enable her to establish a dialogue with Zeydabadi-Nejad's analysis of *Bāshu*, present significant insights about the depiction of Afghan refugees in Iranian films, and discuss the impacts of Beyzaie's child-centred films on Iranian cinema.

As evidenced in the above summaries, therefore, these ten chapters work together to suggest the richness of the subjects and forms that Bahram Beyzaie has engaged with during the last sixty-three years. Though it remains limited in its scope, the volume also manages to provide a panoramic view of Beyzaie's life, theatre and cinema, identify and analyse the origins of his creativity and some of the forms and ideas that he has introduced to the Iranian public space. It also discusses the functions that some of his plays and films have had in negotiating more inclusive ways of seeing and doing at artistic, socio-political and conceptual levels.

Notes

1 Simon, 'Conversation with Michel Foucault', 192–201 and 198 and 201.
2 For what perceptive amateurs can bring to a field, see Said, 'Professionals and Amateurs', 65–84. Edward Said himself is a good example of what a scholar of one field can bring to another in which she or he is an amateur.
3 For a discussion of revisionism in history, see Rancière, *Names of History*.
4 Cultural capital is the totality of acquired forms of knowledge, manners, ways of speaking, dress codes and experiences that enhance the individual's opportunities for fulfilling his or her potential in life and achieve social mobility. For more on the subject, see Bourdieu, 'Forms Of', 243–8.
5 For the historical context, see Nikusefat, *Sarkub*, 444–72. For Beyzaie's references to such experiences and his father's status and his own understanding of religion, see Beyzaie in Nikazar, *Reesheh-hā*, particularly the first twelve minutes. See also Beyzaie and Jahed, 'Beyzaie: Qalamro'. In my multiple interviews with Beyzaie between 2019 and 2022, he referred to such forms of violence and his nightmares about them on several occasions.
6 Whereas the first discourse led to the rise of Islamic/Shi'i nativism, the cosmopolitan one evolved with people of Beyzaie, Dariush Ashoori, Shorab Sepehri, Ahmad Shamlu or Dariush Shaygan's types who did not limit their sources of inspiration to Western artistic, literary or philosophical traditions and has continued to play a minor yet positive role in Iranian cultural cosmopolitanism.
7 For Iranian nativism, see Boroujerdi, *Iranian Intellectuals*.
8 For the historical background, see Abrahamian, *Iran Between* and Keddie, *Modern Iran*.
9 For Maleki, see Katouzian and Pishdad, *Yādnāmeh*.
10 Beyzaie and Talajooy, 'Email Interview'.
11 Dabashi, *Close-Up*, 84.
12 The pure Persian that Beyzaie uses to create his pre-Islamic settings has little to do with the Middle Persian or the dialects that were spoken in mythical or Sasanian

Iranian. But this stratagem works well as it draws a historical marker that suggests a world in which Arabic words had not yet entered Persian.
13 For discussions of Beyzaie's language, see Beyzaie et al. 'Naghd', 30–2; and Parsaei, 'Hamāseh-Āfarini'.
14 In my translations of Beyzaie's plays in English, I have tried to strike a balance between keeping the plays performable and maintaining the poetic qualities, the word-based repartees, and the historical and class-based range. My translations include *Afra, or the Day Is Passing* and *The One Thousand and First Night* which have been published along my articles on the plays by Bisheh in 2023. Available translations of Beyzaie's plays include 'The Puppets', 'Evening in a Strange Land' and 'The Story of the Hidden Moon', in *Modern Persian Drama: An Anthology* which is edited by Gisèle Kapuscinski, (Lanham, MD, 1987); *Death of Yazdgerd*, by Manuchehr Anvar (Tehran, 1989); 'Four Boxes', by M. R. Ghanoonparvar in *An Anthology of Iranian Drama*, which is edited by M. R. Ghanoonparvar and John Green (Costa Mesa, 1989); 'Aurash' and 'Death of the King', in *Stories from the Rains of Love and Death: Four Plays from Iran* by Soheil Parsa with Peter Farbridge and Brian Quirt (Toronto, 2007); and *Memoirs of the Actor in a Supporting Role* by Ghanoonparvar (Costa Mesa, Mazda, 2010).
15 Scott, *Domination*, 18–19.
16 See Beyzaie in Beyzaie and Jahed, 'Beyzaie: Qalamro'.
17 Ashoori and Hamed. 'Bahram Beyzaie' Podcast 90. See also Beyzaie in Amiri, *Jedāl*, 37, 35–9.
18 For Beyzaie's life, see Nikazar, *Reesheh-hā*; Qukasiyan, *Goftogu*, 7–31; and Abdi, *Gharibeh*, 13–53. For Cine Club, see Jahed, *Az Sinemātek*, 26–30.
19 For collections, studying Beyzaie's dramatic and cinematic oeuvre, see Amjad, *Simia 2*, Qukasiyan, *Majmuʿeh Maqālāt* and Qukasiyan, *Goftogu*.
20 For epistemic privilege and authority, see Janack, 'Standpoint Epistemology'.
21 For Beyzaie's approach to reformulation, see Talajooy, 'Reformulation' and 'Intellectuals'.
22 See also Talajooy, 'Beyzaie's Formation'.
23 *Taqlid* plays are improvisatory comedies, Taʿziyeh plays are Iranian passion plays on Shiʿi and Islamic saints, *Tamāsha* is a term used for sport and juggling spectacle as well as a variety of carnival forms that involve comic processions, *Ayyāri* tales are heroic tales and romances about Robinhood-like folk heroes. For a study of these forms, see Beyzaie, *Namāyesh*; Ghaffary, 'Evolution of Rituals' and Floor, *History of Theater*. For a study of indigenous-style modern plays by other contemporary practitioners, see Talajooy, 'Indigenous Performing'.
24 Mojabi, *Negāh-e Kāshef*, 135.
25 Al-e Ahmad, 'Darbāreh-ye Pahlevān', 1976–7.
26 Beyzaie and Soltanpur, 'Mizgerd-e Teatr'.
27 Sepanlu, 'Chap-hā Dah Sāl', 46.
28 See Dolatabadi, 'Abbas Āqa', 235 and Beyzaie, 'Āzādi Mikhāstand', 133. Soltanpur was not in Mashhad on the day, but he had visited the city three days earlier (Talajooy, 'Interview with Bahram Beyzaie').
29 Zandian, *Bāzkhāni-ye Dah*, 205–13. See also Beyzaie's comments, in Beyzaie & Jahed, 'Beyzaie: Qalamro-e Man', in which he explains how, despite having an official permit, he had to ask for permission from individuals who made decisions about what was allowed in a district when he was making *Downpour*.
30 Beyzaie, *Mahi*.

Bibliography

Abdi, Mohammad. Ed. *Gharibeh-ye Bozorg: Zendegi va Sinemā-ye Bahram Beyzaie*. Tehran: Sales Publication, 2004.
Abrahamian, *Iran between Two Revolutions*. Princeton: Princeton University Press, 1982.
Al-e Ahmad, Jalal, 'Darbāreh-ye *Pahlevān Akbar Mimirad* va *Ghorub dar Diyāri Gharib* va *Qesseh-ye Māh-e Penhān*' (1965). In *Adab va Honar Emruz-e Iran: Majm'ueh Maqālāt Jalal Al-e Ahmad*. Vol. 4. Ed. Mostafa Zamaninia. Tehran: Mitra, 1994. Pp. 1973–9.
Amiri, Nushabeh. *Jedāl bā Jahl*. Tehran: Sāles, 2009.
Amjad, Hamid. Ed. *Simia: Vizheh-ye Bahram Beyzaie va Tāātr*. Vol. 2. No. 2 (Winter 2008).
Ashoori, Dariush and Hamed Sarrafizadeh. 'Bahram Beyzaie beh Revāyat-e Dariush Ashoori'. In *Haqiqat va Mard Dānā Series. Abadiyat va Yek Ruz*. Podcast 90 (January 2019). Online: https://telegram.me/EternityAndADay. (Accessed 5 January 2021).
Beyzaie, Bahram and Saeed Soltanpur. (Autumn 1967). 'Mizgerd-e Teātr: darbāreh-ye *Mirās* va *Ziyāfat*'. *Simia 2*. Ed. Amjad. *Op. cit*. Pp. 165–88.
Beyzaie, Bahram, et al. 'Naghd va Barresi-ye Seh Barkhani'. *Kārnāmeh*. No. 13 (October 1999). Pp. 28–37.
Beyzaie, Bahram. *Namāyesh dar Iran*. Tehran: Roshangarān, 2001.
Beyzaie, Bahram. 'Āzādi Mikhāstand barā-ye Sānsur Digarān: Goftogu bā Bahram Beyzaie keh dar Shab-hā-ye She'r-e Goethe be Jā-ye Hokumat Roshanfekrān rā beh Naqd Gereft'. *Andisheh-ye Puyā*. Vol. 5. No. 39 (December 2016). P. 133.
Beyzaie, Bahram. *Mahi*. San Francisco: Bisheh, 2020.
Beyzaie, Bahram and Parviz Jahed. 'Beyzaie: Qalamro-e Man Farhang Ast'. *Cinema Chashm*. shorturl.at/oIOTW. (Accessed 12 November 2020).
Beyzaie, Bahram and Saeed Talajooy. 'Email Interview with Bahram Beyzaie' (13 February 2015).
Beyzaie, Bahram and Saeed Talajooy. 'Multiple Interviews'. (December 2019–May 2022).
Boroujerdi, Mehrzad. *Iranian Intellectuals and the West: The Tormented Triumph of Nativism*. Syracuse: Syracuse University Press, 1996.
Bourdieu, Pierre. 'The Forms of Capital'. In *Handbook of Theory and Research for the Sociology of Education*. Ed. John Richardson. Westport, CT: Greenwood, 1986. Pp. 241–58.
Dabashi, Hamid. *Close Up: Iranian Cinema, Past, Present, and Future*. London: Verso, 2001.
Dolatabadi, Mahmud. 'Abbās Āqā to Kehili Shabih-e Hedayat Hasti'. In *Digarān-e Abbas Na'lbandiyan*. Ed. Javad Atefeh. Tehran: Melikan, 2015. Pp. 231–6.
Floor, Willem. *History of Theater in Iran*. Odenton, MD: Mage, 2005.
Ghaffari, Farrokh. 'Evolution of Rituals and Theater in Iran'. *Iranian Studies*. Vol. 17. No. 4 (1984). Pp. 361–89.
Jahed, Parviz. *Az Sinemātek-e Paris tā Kānun-e Film-e Tehran*. Tehran: Ney, 2014.
Janack, Marianne. 'Standpoint Epistemology without the "Standpoint"? An Examination of Epistemic Privilege and Epistemic Authority'. *Hypatia*. Vol. 12. No. 2 (1997). Pp. 125–39.
Katouzian, Homa and Amir Pishdad. Eds. *Yādnāmeh Khalil Maleki*. Tehran: Sherkat-e Enteshār, 1991.
Keddie, Nikki R. *Modern Iran: Roots and Results of Revolution*. New Haven & London: Yale University Press, 2003.

Mojabi, Javad. *Negāh-e Kāshef-e Gostākh*. Tehran: Ofoq, 2004.
Nikazar, Ahmad (dir.). *Reesheh-hā* (A Documentary on Bahram Beyzaie). Online at YouTube: https://www.youtube.com/watch?v=xlNdgLRXbEs. (Accessed 15 January 2021).
Nikusefat, Sohrab. *Sarkub va Koshtār-e Degar-Andishān-e Mazhabi dar Iran: Jeld-e Nokhost, az Safaviyeh tā Enqelāb-e Eslāmi*. Luxemburg: Peyām, 2009.
Parsaei, Hasan. 'Hamāseh-Āfarini-ye Zehn va Zabān dar Fat-h-nāmeh-ye Kallāt'. *Sahneh*. Vol. 7. No. 62 & 63 (December 2008 and January 2009). Pp. 72–9.
Qukasiyan, Zaven. *Majmu'eh Maqālāt dar Naqd va Mo'arrefi Āsār-e Bahram Beyzaie*. Tehran: Āgah, 1989.
Qukasiyan, Zaven. *Goftogu bā Bahram Beyzaie*. Tehran: Āgah, 1989.
Rancière, Jacques. *The Names of History: On the Poetics of Knowledge*. Trans. Hassan Melehy. Foreword Hayden White. Minneapolis: Minnesota University Press. 1994.
Said, Edward. 'Professionals and Amateurs'. In *Representation of Intellectuals, The 1993 Reith Lectures*. New York: Vintage Book, 1997. Pp. 65–84.
Scott, James C. *Domination and the Arts of Resistance: Hidden Transcripts*. Boston: Yale University Press, 1990.
Sepanlu, Mohamad Ali. 'Chap-hā Dah Sāl Ru-ye Āb Mineveshtand'. *Tehran Mosavvar*. Vol. 39. No. 23 (8 Tir 1358 [29 June 1979]). Pp. 23–30 and 46.
Simon, John K. 'A Conversation with Michel Foucault'. *Partisan Review*. Vol. 32. No. 32 (Spring 1971). Pp. 192–201.
Talajooy, Saeed. 'Indigenous Performing Traditions in Post-Revolutionary Iranian Theater'. *Iranian Studies*. Vol. 44. No. 4 (Autumn 2011). Pp. 497–519.
Talajooy, Saeed. 'Beyzaie's Formation, Forms and Themes'. *Iranian Studies*. Vol. 46. No. 5 (Autumn 2013). Pp. 689–93.
Talajooy, Saeed. 'Reformulation of Shahnameh Legends in Bahram Beyzaie's Plays'. *Iranian Studies*. Vol. 46. No. 5 (Autumn 2013). Pp. 695–719.
Talajooy, Saeed. 'Intellectuals as Sacrificial Heroes: A Comparative Study of Bahram Beyzaie and Wole Soyinka'. *Comparative Literature Studies*. Vol. 52. No. 2 (2015). Pp. 379–408.
Zandian, Mandana. *Bāzkhāni-ye Dah Shab*. Hamburg: Dariush Homayun Publication, 2014.

Section A

BEYZAIE'S EARLY PLAYS – GENEALOGIES OF HEROES

Chapter 2

THE GENEALOGY OF ĀRASH, A HERO: FROM
NAQQĀLI TO BEYZAIE'S RECITATION PLAYS AND
FROM ĀRASH THE MYTHICAL HERO TO BEYZAIE'S
MARGINALIZED ĀRASH

Saeed Talajooy

Introduction: Dialogue in the cacophony of exclusionist monologues

Beyzaie's early works reflect his determination to adapt his various lines of creativity in forms that use dramatic presence and dialogue for representation. In his case, however, this determination is also significant in the way he turns dramatic presence and dialogue into subjects of experimental enquiry. These early works combine narration and action. They also comment on the impossibility of dialogue in suppressive societies by creating stifled dialogues that reflect and transcend the cacophonic monologues of the dominant discourses of his time and their manifestations in the monologues of the Iranian state and its equally exclusionist Islamist and leftist nemeses. In his puppet trilogy (1962-3), for instance, the puppets aspire to define independent roles for themselves and initiate new forms of dialogue with each other in a process that may enable them to transcend the monological diktats of their puppeteer-narrator who represents an inherited discourse.[1] This concern with dramatic presence and dialogue was recently reiterated when, in response to the question of why he never writes novels, he said:

> Despite its literary values, the novel is a writer's monologue and belongs to the past, but drama is always in the present even when it is about the past. It is always occurring, and its spirit is innately dialogue-based. The country of monologues needs practice in dialogue, and as I said earlier, I have always tried to avoid becoming a writer.[2]

Beyzaie's description of the novel as a writer's monologue can be challenged by referring to those novels in which although the tense is past, the writer's and reader's dialogic imaginations give presence and voice to characters. Nonetheless, the use of present tense and action with bodies on the stage indicates that whereas drama must be in the present and dialogic, novels can be non-dialogic and in the past. Beyzaie's use of dramatic rather than story-writing techniques in his first pieces was in line with this vision which had evolved in him due to his interest in cinema. However, rather than trying to create this dialogue in Western-style plays, which he considered unfit for creating a modern yet authentic Iranian dramatic tradition, he aspired to extract it from indigenous forms while remaining open to Far Eastern and Western forms.[3] His first works, therefore, were different from those of his contemporary writers such as Bahman Forsi's (1934–) absurdist and Akbar Radi's (1939–2007) realist plays which echoed Western approaches to mise en scène, action and dialogue. Though focused on myths, they were also unlike Arsalan Purya's (1930–94) Greek-style plays which used poetry, prose dialogue and chorus recitations for Iranian myths. Instead, he engaged with two Iranian folk forms.[4]

For the first form, in his recitation plays, which engaged with *naqqāli*, he presented heroes who were far from the original heroes of *naqqāli*. In *Azhdāhāk*, he used *naqqāli*'s narration as a dramatic monologue. In *Ārash*, he manipulated *naqqāli*'s use of occasional dialogues or narrative monologues to create a dialogical space. In *Account of Bondar the Premier*, he created alternating monologues that implied a lack of communication but evolved as dialogue for the audience. These recitations were, therefore, like *naqqāli*, in their use of narration, monologues and costumes along with occasional dialogues and acting. For their units of narration, they also used short sections that began with descriptions which created in the mind images that, if performed along with theatrical tableaus, could function like scenes in the paintings of pictorial *naqqāli*.[5] Beyzaie's arrangement of these elements, however, produced dialogical spaces that subverted the ideologies of the legends traditionally used for *naqqāli*, displayed the impossibility of dialogue under tyranny, reflected neglected views about the positions of heroes in society, and voiced the views of the marginalized who suffered the results of such neglects.[6]

For the second form which engaged with *kheymeh-shab-bāzi* (puppet shows), he repurposed the form's meta-theatrical elements to question the accepted norms of heroism and centrality which reinforced inherited exclusionist discourses. In their origins, these elements involved a puppeteer who used a *sutsutak* or *safir* (a squeaking voice distorter) to talk or sing as the puppets and engage in witty discussions about the action with the audience and the *morshed* (director/narrator) who sat outside the show booth and talked to the puppets and audience.[7] Beyzaie's puppet plays, as noted earlier, used this technique to suggest the puppets' raising awareness as they begin to question the exclusionist discourse that depicts divergent people as demons, celebrates the battles of heroes and demons, and produces the monological show of the puppeteer-narrator who is adamant about dictating the puppets' thoughts, words and actions.

In both cases, the process contradicted the dominant voice of Iranian epic or folk forms by deconstructing its authoritarian perspectives and introducing voices that challenged their presumptions. In other words, for both forms, he introduced new ways of voicing unheard perspectives to break their inherited monological mould and create heteroglossia.

In the context of the theatrical activities of the years between 1955 and 1965, Beyzaie's early works marked a new approach which, alongside the articles and monograph that he published on Iranian and Asian dramatic forms, led to the rise of modern indigenous-style Iranian theatre. The momentum had already begun with the activities of *Goruh-e Honar-e Melli* (National Art Group, 1956–78), particularly Abbas Javanmard's adaptations of Sadeq Hedayat's stories *Mohallel* (Divorce Resolver, 1958) and *Mordeh-Khorhā* (Burial and Inheritance Opportunists, 1958) and Ali Nassirian's free adaptations of Hedayat's 'Dāsh Ākol' in *Af'ei-ye Talāei* (Golden Viper, 1957) and a metamorphosis folk tale in *Bolbol-e Sargashteh* (The Wandering Nightingale, 1956). Nassirian's use of a *naqqāl* in his staging of *The Wandering Nightingale* in 1959 and his expertise in Iranian improvisatory forms which enabled him to write and perform *Siyāh* (The Blackface Prankster, 1961) also inspired Beyzaie in the initial stages of his career.[8] However, whereas in Javanmard's and Nassirian's plays the purpose was more to adapt Iranian subjects and forms for Western-style plays, Beyzaie was more concerned with deconstructing the ideologies of Iranian myths, folk tales and forms while using them to create a modern theatrical tradition that was more in line with Iranian culture.[9] His plays, therefore, generated templates whose emancipatory aesthetics sublimated folk forms to subvert the exclusionist constructs and narratives that led to socio-political, ideological and religious tyranny.

To analyse these qualities, in this chapter I examine Beyzaie's divergent creativity in his recitation plays and offer a close reading of his first play, *Ārash*. The chapter has four main sections. The first offers an overview of *naqqāli* as a dramatic form. The second briefly analyses Beyzaie's heightening of the form's dialogical potential in his recitation plays, *Azhdāhāk*, *Ārash* and *Account of Bondār the Premier*. The third section uses a genealogical approach to explore the mythical and political origins and the modern revisionist uses of the myth of Ārash. This section sets the background for a close reading of Beyzaie's *Ārash* in the fourth section in which I analyse the play and argue that it functions as a site of negotiation about marginalization, nationhood, citizenship, leadership, despair, belonging and rebellion as well as the psychology, ideals and realities of heroism. The chapter also includes brief discussions of the play's potential political interpretations and its reception in the past six decades.

Naqqāli: An overview

Naqqāli (recounting) is a generic term used for several forms of dramatic recounting, which date back to ancient troubadours and their later counterparts such as the Parthian *gōsān(s)*.[10] Originating in the prehistoric forms used by bards and shamans to recount the tales of creation, gods, wars and heroes as the loci for conveying the codes of identity, leadership, morality, religion and heroism to the youths, the form which shares its roots with similar forms across the globe continued to play important roles in Iran up to the middle of the twentieth century.

A key piece of evidence for the form's importance in ancient Iran is given in an article by Mary Boyce in which she quotes Athenaeus's retelling of the myth of 'Zariadres and Odatis' based on the account of Chares of Mytilene, the head of Alexander's Royal entourage. The section deserves attention as it reflects the popularity of such legends in Achaemenian Iran and the use of paintings and murals in recounting them:

> Hystaspes and his younger brother Zariadres were said by the people of their land to be born of Aphrodite and Adonis. Hystaspes ruled Media and the lands below it, Zariadres the region above the Caspian Gates up to Tanaïs. Beyond the Tanaïs lived the Marathi, ruled by Omrates, whose daughter Odatis was the most beautiful of all the women in Asia. Odatis dreamt of Zariadres, and loved him; and he too loved Odaits through dreams. He sought her vainly in marriage, for her father did not wish to give her to a stranger. Soon after, Omrates held a marriage-feast attended by his own kinsmen and nobles and bade Odatis give a cup of wine to him whom she wished to marry. Zariadres, forewarned by Odatis, came in full haste across the Tanaïs, accompanied only by his charioteer, and entered the hall in Scythian dress as weeping Odatis slowly filled the cup. She recognized him with joy, and he carried her off. This tale, Charles states, was greatly esteemed by the barbarians of Asia, who painted scenes from it on the walls of temples, palaces, and even private houses, the nobles giving the name of Odatis to their own daughters.[11]

Chares of Mytilene's reference to the form's popularity in the 300 BC, the legend's similarity to Goshtāsp's adventures in the *Shāhnāmeh* and the diversity of the ancient tales recited by *naqqāl(s)* (raconteurs) of the Islamic era indicate that *naqqāli* is one of the oldest and most important forms of performance in Iran.[12] The original form, as signified by the middle-Persian term *khonyāgar* (minstrel) and the later *bakhshi* raconteurs, was more musical. After Islam, however, due to the restrictions on music, the narration aspects were prioritized and evolved in forms that ranged from sedentary *qessehkhāni* (story reading) to dramatic *naqqāli*. Religious forms also began to evolve to confront the praise of ancient heroes with *fazāyelkhāni* (praise recitation of Sunni dignitaries) and *manāqebkhāni* (praise recitation of Shi'i saints). In time, the Shi'i one branched out into *rozehkhāni* (stories of Islamic saints), *sokhanvari* (competing speech delivery about Shi'i saints), *pardehkhāni* (pictorial recitation on Shi'i saints and their deeds), *suratkhāni* (image recitation on Abrahamic religious figures) and *hamlehkhnāi* (dramatic recitations on the bravery and battles of the Prophet of Islam and Imam Ali).[13]

Naqqāl(s) (raconteurs), clad in old-style costumes and at times equipped with weapons, were accompanied by their apprentice, *pishkhān(s)* (prologue reciters), to present the roles of epic heroes to the audience while reciting legends. Though the terms *pardehkhāni* and *pardehdāri* refer to recounting religious stories with painting, some *naqqāl(s)* of secular tales also performed with *pardeh*, a large painting of the key scenes of the legends, which they pointed at with their sticks while narrating with embellished gestures to attract attention. In the heyday of Persian epic poetry and romance in the medieval era, some poets even had their own *naqqāl(s)* whom they chose based on the quality of their voice, charisma and looks.[14] With the rise in the number of coffeehouses in the Safavid era, *naqqāl(s)* who usually performed in public spaces began to appear in coffeehouses. Every coffeehouse had its *naqqāl(s)*, intriguing customers to frequent the place by reciting a few episodes of an epic cycle every evening.

Though *naqqāl(s)* recounted from memory and used improvisation to introduce exciting twists and personal emotions to make the legends more tangible for their audience, some experienced *naqqāl(s)* also produced *tumār(s)* (parchments or written accounts) in which they recorded their own versions of famous legends. A *tumār* that had the stamp of a famous *naqqāl* was highly valued and sometimes other famous *naqqāl(s)* also confirmed its value by stamping it. These *tumār(s)* were considered valuable if they had the stamp of renowned *naqqāl(s)* and functioned like plays that could be used by less experienced *naqqāl(s)*.[15]

In 1929, in line with the nationalist discourses of the era, an official decree banned *naqqāl(s)* from recounting any romances or epics other than the *Shāhnāmeh*.[16] Though this imposition did not end the popularity of the form, it initiated a process of decline that was completed by the 1950s as radio and then television sets gradually replaced *naqqāl(s)* in coffeehouses, and cinemas became the main loci for enjoying heroic accounts. Thus, although *naqqāli* has continued to fascinate those who love Iranian performing arts and its paintings and *tumār(s)* have become major sources for studying Iranian folk culture, *naqqāli* as a popular

Figure 2.1 A contemporary pictorial *naqqāl* recounting *Shahnameh* legends.

art form has disappeared and is nowadays performed by trained actors in art festivals and research events.[17]

From my perspective, pictorial *naqqāli* is a proto-theatrical form which has affinities to cinema in its use of music, costume, voice and moving from one image to another with narration and occasional action, dialogue and impersonation. Until a few decades ago, it was also the primary multimedia transmitter of Iran's cultural memory. Beyzaie's analysis of the form in *Theatre in Iran* also suggests how, like *ta'ziyeh*, it had high potential for communal participation, which is of primary importance in contemporary emancipatory performance:

> In *naqqāli* sessions in which the legend of Shohrab and Rostam is recounted, when the story reaches the point of Sohrab's death, many people cry, and some get out of the place in order not to hear the part about Sohrab's death. Oftentimes people offer money or, in villages, sheep or cows to the *naqqāl* to stop him from 'killing Sohrab'. [...] It is only when these [*Shāhnāmeh*] legends are narrated that crying is not a sign of unmanliness, and everyone is entitled to cry intensely.[18]

The meta-theatrical force of such a performance transcends the usual functions of dramatic presence and self-reflexivity as it turns the form into communion with the *Nā-Kojā-Ābād*, the nowhere land of Iranian secular and religious 'imaginal' where the heroes of the past, the role models of heroism, are ever present for new interpretations.[19] In this context, the audiences' occasional refusal to accept the ending of an inherited narrative displays the form's democratic potential. The sanctioning of crying over a non-religious subject, particularly over *Shāhnāmeh* tragic legends which often criticize exclusionism, also signifies the form's cathartic force and its power to help the audience see the primacy of familial love and human relations over political and religious beliefs. Together, however, these aspects also show how the form's emancipatory aspects may be reinforced to create new role models and new ways of seeing.

Beyzaie's recitation plays

Between 1959 and 1962, Beyzaie produced three *barkhāni* (recitation) pieces: *Azhdāhāk* (published 1961), *Ārash* (published 1977) and *Account of Bondar the Premier* (published 1995). He coined the pure Persian terms *barkhāni* and *barkhān* to replace the terms *naqqāli* and *naqqāl* and experimented with the form to create new dramatic and linguistic idioms for dramatizing Iranian myths.[20] The results are pieces that can be performed in a stylized manner between impersonating the roles and presenting them to an audience. Their performing potential is so that, though conceived as recitations for one, two or several actors narrating or presenting the roles from text or memory, they can also be staged as plays.

In his 2001 republication of these recitation pieces in his *Divān-e Namāyesh 1* (Collected Plays 1), Beyzaie placed *Azhdāhāk: A Recitation Piece for One Person* as his first work because he completed *Azhdāhāk* before completing his revision of *Ārash*, which he had written a couple of years earlier. *Azhdāhāk* is a narrative monologue in eleven sections. Episodic structure is a common form of structuring plots in theatre and cinema, but whereas in the latter two, each segment depicts characters in action or conversing in a setting to propel the plot, in Beyzaie's recitation plays, each segment begins with a description of the situation, the setting and the position of the character as if to evoke the idea of an image in a series of images in a *naqqāli* painting. These descriptions are different from stage direction in that they are embedded in the narration and their linguistic register is the same as the narrative monologues or the dialogues. In theatre studies the term *tableau* is used when one or several characters create a still pose that represents a situation, an emotion or the climax of a memorable event in a play. In other words, it is as if the bodies of actors on the stage produce a painting or a snapshot that suggests an idea or a theme. Naqqāli paintings offer, in a single canvas, several tableau-like images that the *naqqāl* uses as clues for his accounts. Beyzaie's cuts in his narrative monologues function similarly as if suggesting that the reciter or reciters must start each scene with a tableau.

Azhdāhāk's thematic focus is the centre/periphery binary and how the hero of an exclusionist centre, here Yama (Jamshid), may be the arch-demon of the marginalized people suffering under his rule. Using the most demonized figure of Iranian myths, the dragon king Azhdāhāk (Zahhāk) as its narrator/speaker, the piece is like a prose poem in the style of Robert Browning's dramatic monologues in which a fallible narrator reveals his qualities while presenting a case that he assumes will prove he is right. Thus, Azhdāhāk recounts the events that led to his conflict with Yama mostly in first person but with occasional references to himself in the third person or reporting Yama's or other people's words. The piece begins and ends in a setting in which, like Zahhāk, Azhdāhāk is chained to the walls of a cave. However, rather than focusing on Azhdāhāk's viciousness as Iranian mythology does or depicting him as a champion of egalitarianism as some leftist writers did later,[21] Beyzaie depicts him as the victim of a dominant discourse. When his father is innocently killed by Yama and he is heavily lashed for questioning Yama's deeds, he unsuccessfully tries to emigrate and bury the snakes of his hatred and anger but is rejected due to his appearance. He then tries to control them by means of art, his pipe. However, when he sees how Yama destroys everything to create his exclusionist utopia, he breaks his pipe, rebels against him and is defeated, chained and used eternally for Yama's fear-mongering. In Beyzaie's piece, Azhdāhāk is addressing the night and future to suggest how his voice has been suppressed by people who are hypnotically driven by Yama's accounts or his lashes. The revisionist myth, therefore, focuses on how he fell victim to Yama's distribution of ideas, pain and fear as means of control. The *naqqāl*, therefore, is to impersonate a victimized speaker who suggests that Jamshid's tyranny initiated the snakes of Zahhāk's anger and hatred. Thus, in his first piece, Beyzaie used an extended dramatic monologue instead of *naqqāli* narration to present what can be called a silenced case in a form and with names that suggest he wished the audience to imagine the account as a possible original case.[22]

The play has been repeatedly performed in the last ten years, which suggests its timeless value. Prior to these performances I always imagined it performed in twenty-five to thirty-five minutes like a combination of *naqqāli* and a Beckettian dramatic monologue with intense emotions pouring out of the heart and mouth of a wronged character chained to his rage and hatred of himself and those who have wronged him. The idea of a *naqqāl* in chain moving his hands, head and feet to the extent that he can, while recounting his own story, is also fascinating in that it also highlights the idea of how the suppression of writers and speakers may lead to disasters. Nevertheless, it can also be performed with a free-moving actor presenting his monologue with or without pictures and ending it chained in an imagined cave, or with several other actors playing the roles of Azhdāhāk's father, Jamshid and his cronies.

Whereas *Azhdāhāk* is focused on how symbolic and physical violence and suppression generate conflict by planting hate and anger in their victims, *Ārash* is concerned with how they lead to the rise of a sacrificial saviour who guarantees the continuity of his people by a desperate act that is interpreted as divine intervention. I will deal with the themes and structure of *Ārash* in detail, but suffice it to say that, like *Azhdāhāk*, it has a series of short scenes which are to be performed 'by one, two, three or several reciters'.[23] However, unlike *Azhdāhāk*, the narrator can stand out of the action as a raconteur or play a character depending on the director's approach. The play's twenty-three scenes are characterized by detailed descriptions that function like images on the canvas as the characters appear to deliver their soliloquies or occasional dialogues which display Ārash's despair and the impossibility of transcending cultural diktats when tyranny distorts human relationships. These scenes also function like stages in a dream play or the expressionistic tragedy of a wronged individual in a style that stands between *naqqāli* and *ta'ziyeh*, which is also relevant to the play as it is about a sacrificial hero. The key element of the form is the use of intermittent dialogues between long narrations which gradually reveal the impossibility of having meaningful dialogue when people's minds are programmed by inherited assumptions that make them unable to think independently.

Beyzaie's third recitation piece, *Account of Bondār the Premier*, is made of forty-eight monologues organized for two reciters. The play presents a revisionist myth about how the upholders of dominant discourses marginalize unwanted accounts and how the achievements of artists and scientists of an era may be used as means of self-aggrandizement for devious rulers. The play introduces Bondār, Jamshid's adviser, as the author of Jamshid's civilizational triumphs. He dries marshlands to create farmlands and repels the raids of primitive tribes by using mirrors to dazzle them with sunlight. He then engages in decades of research to invent his masterwork, *jām-e jam* (the all-seeing chalice) to help Jamshid find and resolve people's problems. Jamshid, however, uses the chalice to find and kill dissenting people and so-called demons.

Beyzaie's staging of the play in Iran and Germany (Festival of Silk Road Theatre, 1998) suggests how it was conceived as a cross-breed between *naqqāli* and *ta'ziyeh*.[24] His minimal and symbolic use of props for an account of victimization that triggered anti-tyrannical feelings echoed *ta'ziyeh*. Bondār's qualities, indeed, endorsed him as an ideal citizen and an intellectual sacrificial hero who defends his people against Jamshid, the epitome of devious leadership. However, as seen in Figure 2.2, the *naqqāli* motifs were stronger. In his staging, the two *naqqāl*-like characters delivered their rivalling monologues as if in separate spaces, which suggested the gap between their visions of the world. However, their alternating monologues, which always began with 'I said', and their occasional addressing of each other created a dialogical process for the audience that signified the impossibility of dialogue between the two and the precarious relationship between people in power and carriers of knowledge. In Beyzaie's staging, as in *naqqāli* and *ta'ziyeh*, costume was essential, and stage design was minimal with only a few items that allowed the characters to produce momentary tableaus before moving around and delivering their monologues. A comparison between Figures 2.1 and 2.2 also shows how Beyzaie's stage design, costume and mise en scène scene were used to suggest the affinity of the form with *naqqāli*.[25]

The idea that the all-seeing chalice had been made by *farzānegān* (learned elites) rather than Jamshid has been present in Persian literature since the first references to the chalice which associates it with Kaykhosrow rather than Jamshid.[26] The play, however, goes a step further to create a conflict between the learned elites and Jamshid, who epitomizes both the civilizational bid and the failures of Iranian monarchy. It also suggests that the chalice made Jamshid feel like a god, which, in turn, intensified his tyranny and created the chaos that led to his fall. Beyzaie, thus, depicts Jamshid, the supreme king-priest, as one whose downfall occurred due to

Figure 2.2 Parviz Pourhosseini as Jamshid recounting his achievements like a pictorial *naqqāl*.

his obsession with controlling knowledge and creativity as means of power. He also highlights the dilemmas of exceptional people living under tyranny and how knowledge cannot produce positive results under opportunist leaders.

Thus, an overview of the three recitation pieces suggests that even at this early stage, Beyzaie's approach reveals his idea of modernity as a process of voicing the unvoiced while historicizing and subverting the exclusionist assumptions of the narratives and ritual forms that are central to Iranian cultural memory. Despite the antiquity of their subjects, these recitation plays transcend the traditional poetic penchant for the allegorical expression of ideas as characters. Instead, they create a level of suggestiveness that replaces mythic, mystic or metaphysical images of eternal humanity with characters that can be related to history and are symbolic to the extent that they represent similar individuals in the past and present.

Offering an emancipatory discourse on the position of people in the original myths of Iranian kingship, these three pieces keep a degree of mythic presentation but are organized to imply an imagined situation that may be closer to the actual events that were later mythologized. They also subvert the imagined glories of ancient Iran in the royalist nationalism of the Pahlavi era, which aspired to modernize the country with Western technical and institutional models and a political system that emulated the structures of ancient Iranian empires. At another level, they also critique Iran's post-revolutionary system of governance as they comment on the dangers of adopting an outdated conception of governance, namely absolutist religious or secular monarchy, for a modern society. This is particularly the case with *Account of Bondâr The Premier* as Jamshid is depicted as a priest-king. Despite this critical stance against royalist nationalism and absolutist monarchy, however, the plays maintain the patriotic idea of revitalizing new Persian by creating a dramatic prose that is exemplary in its use of wordplays and imagery in pure Persian.[27] This seemingly contradictory stance, however, was justified in that the plays' setting was ancient Iran, and to create the aura of the era, the language was supposed to have qualities that distinguished it from Persian as spoken after Islam.

Beyzaie, thus, combined an elitist language that was used to glorify ancient Iran with a folk form to produce plays that undermined the political discourse for which the Iranian myths were used at the time of annunciation. He specifies that rather than planning to write in pure Persian, he intended to experiment with stage language, but the subject evolved into a language that was close to pure Persian. He also adds that in 1990 when he was revising them for post-revolution publication, he decided that his experiments with language would not be complete without changing a few words of non-Persian origin which were not really necessary.[28] The need for a linguistic register appropriate for the setting remains central to this choice. However, one may also argue that the state's obsession with Islam- and Arab-centred discourses after the revolution reinforced Beyzaie's leaning towards democratic nationalism and subverting oppressive dominant discourses and urged him to intensify his work with pure Persian.

The question that remains here, however, is why a young artist should preoccupy himself with ancient myths. Such subjects are, of course, fascinating for any age, but one may also argue that Beyzaie was more concerned with writing alternative hi/stories of the present in which as Walter Benjamin puts it, history can be brushed 'against the grain' to reveal the voice of the silenced of the present.[29] This desire to change the meaning of the present by rewriting the past is also expressed by many key thinkers of the twentieth centuries, such as Michel Foucault whose *Discipline and Punish: The Birth of the Prison* directly comments on this desire:

> I would like to write the history of this prison, with all the political investments of the body that it gathers together in its closed architecture. Why? Simply because I am interested in the past? No, if one means by that writing a history of the past in terms of the present. Yes, if one means writing a history of the present.[30]

All histories are revisionist in nature as they recount the past according to present assumptions, perspectives and formulas, but in creative works the process also involves other factors. One is the inevitable result of mythical and historical adaptation itself, which necessitates travelling between epistemic paradigms and inserting one's own contemporary visions and imaginations into such narratives. The second is the artist's conscious challenging of the origins of the present practices and the knowledge basis of the power relations that have determined what is socio-politically and aesthetically presentable or capable of being seen, heard and understood in the public or even private domains. In Beyzaie's works, the conscious aspect has been central. In his own words, 'the roots of many of our problems and the meaning and formation of many of our attitudes are in our past. The past must be analysed and acknowledged so that we can know ourselves, snap out of our illusions and change our conditions'.[31]

Since I have already written on Beyzaie's reformulation of the cycle of Jamshid and Zahhāk in *Azhdāhāk* and *Account of Bondar the Premier*,[32] I will here end my general analysis of his recitation plays to focus on the myth of Ārash and how it is reformulated in Beyzaie's *Ārash*. To this end, I will first focus on the evolution of the myth in religious and historical reports and then focus on how Beyzaie's *Ārash* enriches the dialogical potential of *naqqāli*, deflates the idea of heroes as born rather than made, reflects on heroes as victims of a society incapable of taking responsibility for liberating itself, explores the pitfalls and reconstructs the ideals of heroism and subverts the dominant nation-building discourse of the time.

Ārash: *The genealogy of a hero*

The earliest references to the myth of Ārash appear in the Zoroastrian scriptures, in Tishtar Yasht, parts 6, 7, 37 and 38, with the main sections being as follows:

> 37. We sacrifice unto Tistrya [Sirius], the bright and glorious star, swift-flying and swift-moving, who flies towards the sea Vouru-Kasha [The earth-surrounding ocean], as swiftly as the arrow darted through the heavenly space,

which Erekhsha, the swift archer, the Arya amongst the Aryas whose arrow was the swiftest, shot from Mount Khshaotha to Mount Hvanva*nt*.

38. Ahura Mazda gave him assistance, and the Amesha-Spentas and Mithra, the lord of wide pastures, pointed him the way: behind him went the tall Ashi*s* Vanguhi [goddess of piety, fortune and riches] and Pârendi [goddess of resources and treasures] on her light chariot: always till, in his course, he reached Mount Hvanva*nt* on the shining waters.[33]

Other Zoroastrian texts referring to the event are 'Māh-e Farvardin Ruz-e Khordad' which specifies that 'Manuchehr and Ārash, of the swift arrow took back the land from Afrāsiyāb the Turanian' and 'Dadistan-e Minui-ye Kherad' which refers to Manuchehr as the one who recaptured the Iranian territory.[34]

Although Iranian epics and romances include reformulated accounts of the deeds of many ancient heroes, they have remained silent about Ārash. This silence may have been accidental or because epic poets of the post-Islamic era considered the myth too slim to dedicate a poem to it. From my perspective, however, this lack of attention had to do with the absence of an authoritative account caused by the centre/periphery or king/hero binaries of cultural centrality which can already be seen in some of the Zoroastrian texts that highlight the role of the king rather than the heroes who fulfilled the act. This is particularly relevant as the Sassanians were more centralized than the Parthians, and thus, they tended to emphasize the centrality of kings rather than regional rulers or heroes. More important, however, was probably the conflict between Khosrow Parviz and the rebel warrior Bahrām Chubin. As reflected in the *Shāhnāmeh*, which is, in this case, close to historical accounts, Khsorow Parviz tells Bahram, who prides himself in being a descendent of Ārash, that whereas Ārash served his king, Manuchehr, Bahram continues to defy his king.[35] It is, thus, clear that both sides believed that Parthian families, including Bahram's, descended from Ārash, which suggests that the conflict may have led to the omission of the myth from the Sassanian *Khodāynāmags* (Books of Lords), the official chronicles of kings and heroes that the *Shāhnāmeh* is partly based on. This account also corresponds to the fact that although Parthian narratives have influenced the depiction of heroes in the *Shāhnāmeh*, the accounts of Parthian kings are absent in the text.[36] Bahram's achievements are included in the text probably because of Bahram's popularity in Khurasan and the access of the writers of the prose *Shāhnāmeh* and Ferdowsi to the translations of a Pahlavi epic entitled *Bahrām Chubin Nameh* whose accounts they adapted to the *Shāhnāmeh*'s unifying vision and the *Khodāynāmags* pro-Khosrow narrative.[37] Ultimately, however, the text does not dedicate a distinct passage to the sacrificial myth of the Parthians' ancestor, and the inclusion of Bahram's deeds functions more like a highlighter for Khosrow Parviz's greatness as a hero-king who was able to defeat a warrior of Bahram's capacity.

With the fall of the Sasanians, the legends of peripheral rulers and heroes throve and became central in post-Islamic folklore. This may have occurred due to the gap that already existed between the Iranians and their overlords or because folk tales give more centrality to heroes and women. Ārash, however, was unique as he remained neglected even in post-Islamic sources.

Despite this limitation, some sources emphasize the sacrificial aspect of Ārash's task which is central to Beyzaie's play. Biruni's examination of the legend in the context of Tirgān festival on 13th Tir (4 July) is the most elaborate among these:

> Having subdued Erānshahr, Afrāsiyāb besieged Manuchehr in Tabaristan. Manuchehr asked Afrāsiyāb to restore to him a part of Erānshahr that falls within the distance covered by an arrowshot. As mentioned in the Avesta, an angel called Esfandārmaz appeared and ordered Manuchehr to have a bow and arrow made according to instructions she gave to the craftsman. Then they summoned Ārash, a noble and pious man and told him 'You must take this bow and arrow and shoot the arrow'. Ārash stood up, took off his clothes and said: 'Behold, my king and my people, see my body is marked by no wounds or maladies. I am sure that when I shoot this arrow with this bow, I will shatter into pieces and lose my life, but I am determined to sacrifice myself for you.' Then, while still naked, with the might and force that God had given him, he pulled the bowstring right back to his ear and when he released it, he fell apart into pieces. God ordered the wind to bear the arrow away from Mount Ruyan to the furthest frontiers of Khurasan, from Tabaristan and Ferghana, where it landed on a huge walnut three whose size had no equal in the world. Some say the expanse from where the arrow was shot to where it fell was 1,000 Parasangs [about 6,240 kilometres]. Afrāsiyāb and Manuchehr agreed on this land expanse and made a treaty. These events took place over a few days that people later marked as a holiday.[38]

Biruni then goes on to specify the rituals carried out during the holiday. These included general cleaning, breaking old cooking vessels, and then grinding wheat and preparing fruit and food for a feast in commemoration of the hardship that Iranians faced during the siege and Ārash's sacrificial act as a saviour. The ritual, thus, had all the markers of a communal purification rite in honour of a sacrificial hero whose commemoration guarantees survival and prosperity.

Another notable aspect of this account is the status of the non-human figures involved in the action. Tir Yasht refers to plants, waters, Ahura Mazda (the supreme god), Mithra (the herald of light and protector of wide pastures and oaths), and two goddesses associated with prosperity and piety as those who assisted Ārash. Biruni's post-Islamic version, however, has relegated the animist gods to an element and an angle: (1) the good wind, embodying the cloud-bearing good Vayu, and (2) 'Esfandārmaz' the goddess of earth, mother nature, fertility and farmers.[39] Both accounts, however, carry the archetypal motifs of fertility, which suggests that the legend repurposed an agricultural myth to celebrate a later hero. This becomes evident if one notes that Afrāsiyāb's name echoes that of a demon responsible for 'the suppression of waters, draining of rivers, and causing of drought, famine, and desolation,' and that according to another myth, 'the earth was a young virgin' who was 'betrothed' to the demon Parsiag (Farāsiyāt/Afrāsiyāb), prior to her liberation. Thus, Afrāsiyāb was already linked to a myth that 'viewed drought as the result of the rape of the earth by a powerful demon'.⁴⁰ The repurposed myth, however, depicted Ārash as a dying fertility hero who helped Esfandārmaz save herself from the demon and be betrothed to the rightful king, Manuchehr.

Scholars have tried to find a more detailed account of the original myth or its echoes in earlier myths and have identified the Indo-Iranian legend of the Ārashkas family in Rigveda as one that contains certain aspects of the myth of Ārash that has not survived in Iran.⁴¹ This is likely as the Indo-Iranians who settled in Iran and India shared agricultural myths that evolved for new functions when they settled in their new homelands. The same is also evident in the affinity of the name Ārash not only with Ārashkas but also with arch- (leader/curved) and archery-related nouns in Indo-European languages and with Mahabharata's invincible archer Arjuna, who, remarkably for my argument below, is also known as Partha.

In any case, the repurposed myth preserved the mythic motif of the hero as a pure agent of fertility by involving Esfandārmaz, the earth herself, and the cloud-carrying wind in a process that suggests Esfandārmaz achieves her liberation and returns to fertility through Ārash's sacrificial act. Based on a more detailed analysis of the myth's archetypal motifs, however, one can argue that this repurposing may have had a political function which celebrated the contribution of the Parthians (of Parthia) to the defence of Iranian lands against Central Asian invaders before their rise to prominence under Arsaces I (247–217 BC). The Iranian Parthians originated in the lands extending from the north of Kashan to the Caspian Sea and continuing to the north and east to central Asia. Their centres were, therefore, located in the place specified in the legend. As warriors, the Parthians (Arshkāniān/Ashkāniān in Persian) were known for their speed on horseback, which associates them with the wind. Their archery skills and ability to shoot backward while on horseback (the Parthian shot) also associate them with the concept of vibrating or twinkling swift arrow in the descriptions of the star Sirius (Tishtar), the harbinger of rain, in Avesta and in Ārash's epithet, *khshviwi-ishuf* (of twinkling/vibrating arrow),⁴² which later evolved into *shevātir* or *shivā-tir* (of ongoing, unstopping arrow).

Interestingly, Tishtar, the divine figure in whose Yasht Ārash appears as a hero, like Sirius the star that represents it, is associated with rain and rain season, which confirms the link with agricultural archetypes. Similarly, when Tishtar fights against Apush, the demon of drought, he appears as a horse, and when defeated, he is helped by the wind and Ahura Mazda's and people's prayers,⁴³ which, as reflected in the still-in-use Persian expression, 'tir-e niyāyesh' or 'tir-e doʻā' (prayer arrows), may also be compared with arrows against demons.

As stated earlier, unlike other major legends, Ferdowsi's *Shāhnāmeh* does not feature the legend in a distinct passage. However, the references to Ārash as a great archer suggest that Ferdowsi knew its basic points. In one case, for instance, Zarir is described as having a mace like Sām's and arrows like Ārash's; in another Ārash is mentioned as the ancestor of the Parthians, and in another Bahram Chubin claims to be his descendent.⁴⁴ Tabari does not mention the latter but makes a similar link by recounting how Bahram defeated the Turkic Shābeh Shah (Sāveh Shah of the *Shāhnāmeh*) by shooting an arrow that killed Shābeh: 'In Iranian lands, three arrows are renowned, one is Ārashshiātir's arrow in the account of Manuchehr and Farāsiāt [Afrāsiyāb], another is Sukhrā's (Sufrā) arrow against the Turks and another Bahram's arrow.'⁴⁵ In Thaʿālabi, the events occur after Afrāsiyāb has executed Nozar and ruled over Iran for twelve years. Zu, who is elected as king by Iranian warriors, engages in peace negotiations with Afrāsiyāb as the land is ravished by famine and plague. Thaʿālabi emphasizes Zu's inspiration-based wisdom in choosing the wood, the metal and the eagle feather of the arrow, and his role in bringing fertility and health to the land. His Ārash is also an old man who shoots the arrow with divine assistance.⁴⁶ The myth also has versions that further support the idea that it had evolved to celebrate the grafting of Parthian regions and warriors into the idea of Iran. In one of these, reported by Tabari, 'Ārashsiātir' or 'Erash' survives: 'Manuchehr [...] added archery to the activities of warriors and assigned Ārashsiātir to command the archers because of the arrow that he had shot.'⁴⁷ Balʿami confirms the same but specifies 'the prosperous Amol' [near Sari] as the place of the siege, Mount Damavand as where the arrow was shot from, and the banks of Oxus as where it landed.⁴⁸

Similar accounts appear in other epics, romances, poems or histories. Among these, Fakhreddin Asʿad Gorgani, a poet from the heartland of the Parthians, Gorgan, alludes to the legend in a way that highlights both the horse and the archery motifs:

If Ārash is called the Archer because he shot an arrow from Sari to Marv // You shoot from Gourab a hundred arrows at me every hour // It befits you more than Ārash to be called a [warrior] rider as you are a hundred parasang further [west] than Sari.⁴⁹

This relative absence resulted in a situation in which the legend was only referred to in allusions and did not receive any literary treatment until the twentieth century. This was also because, apart from Balʿami's translation of some parts of Tabari's history, no other Persian sources had dealt with the myth at length. With the rise of modern nationalism and Iranian studies in the nineteenth century, scholars occasionally referred to the legend in their writing, but it was with Ehsan Yarshater's two-page account in his *Dāstānhā-ye Irān-e Bāstān* (Stories of Ancient Iran, 1336/1957) that the legend began to evolve as a subject of literary enquiry. The intellectual zeitgeist of the country which was marked by the early vestiges of nativism, as well as leftist and non-royalist nationalism, urged a few creative writers to enhance the legend's prioritization of the role of heroes over the king and produce several epic and anti-epic cultural products.

Beyzaie's Ārash: *The heroic product of marginalization*

Beyzaie's play was one of these products, but it differed from the others in its subversion of the hierarchies of epic form and its depiction of heroes as victims. It distanced itself from Yarshater's folk-tale account, Arsalan Purya's Greek-style poetry and prose play *Ārash-e Tir Andāz* (Ārash the Shooter, 1959) or Siyavash

Kasraei's pseudo-epic poem *Ārash-e Kamāngir* (Ārash the Archer, 1959). Kasraei's poem was momentous in its modernist form, epic beauty, and effort to reconcile leftist views with Iranian myths. However, to avoid antagonizing the left, right, and literary elites and gain more readers, he had created a poem in which the hero's relationship with people was too neat as if people can easily produce heroes who solve their problems. Beyzaie was fascinated by the poem, but the depiction of the hero's relationship with people contradicted his reading of Iranian and non-Iranian legends, including those of Rostam, Gilgamesh or Hercules, in which the hero has moments of serious conflict with his people, and he rarely solves his people's problems. For him heroes were victims, and they were also hard to come by: 'if it were so easy for Iranians to produce heroes, so why are we in this dire state?'[50]

Thus, unlike Kasraei's poem, in Beyzaie's play, it is not the people's unified wrath that emits Ārash as an oyster emits a pearl from its chest.[51] Here, Ārash is reborn as a desperate hero when he is cornered by his people and the enemy. He also does not claim 'to rule the winds' or have a 'fire-bound' 'arrow'.[52] He is filled with contradictory feelings about his place among his people and is not even sure how he is going to shoot the arrow.[53] Though he shares his doubts and innocence with Nader Ebrahimi's Ārash in the short story, *Ārash dar qalamro-e Tardid* (Ārash in the Realm of Qualms, 1959/1963), he is not a modern intellectual who refuses to act as a saviour in a timeless zone. Beyzaie's Ārash is a shepherd, drafted into the army as a groom, who is forced by the tyranny of his overlords, the treachery of the enemy and the hatred of his compatriots to accept the challenge of determining Iran's border by shooting an arrow.

The play begins in section 1 with the narrator delivering an apocalyptic report of a war-stricken wasteland in which 'every man was a storm-afflicted plant whose roots had dried'.[54] Section 2 then offers a tableau of Ārash gazing at the tent of victorious enemies after burying a horse and the narrator's philosophical words on the permeance of Mount Alborz as an observer of the brevity of human life.[55] In section 3, Kashvād, the supreme archer, is summoned by an officer to shoot the arrow that is to determine Iran's border. However, as the narration turns into dialogue, Kashvād refuses to obey and argues that their failure is the fault of their leaders who alienated people, led them to defeat and accepted a challenge that is nothing but a mocking gesture. Ārash is then sent to the enemy as an envoi to ask for a respite until Iranians can find an archer for shooting the arrow. This is followed by sections 4 and 5 in which the narrator talks of the ruined houses and the arid lands before Ārash's meeting with the Turāniān king.

The poetically charged style of expression and the mixture of narration and dialogue, past and present tenses, and war action and philosophical comments on nature and brevity of life immediately remind the reader of *Yādgār-e Zarirān* (The Book of Zarir, extant version, *ca.* 500s) which was probably a tragic recitation or performance piece that commemorated Zarir as a sacrificial hero.[56] The use of narration in a style that describes the sceneries like tableaus is also a new approach to drama which is in dialogue with pictorial *naqqāli*, fiction and cinema.

Sections 3 to 5 offer key elements to the rising action as they unravel Kashvād's intellectual and physical rebellion against the elite and set the challenge that transforms Ārash's life. It is also in section 5 that the Turāniān king sees Ārash's presence as an opportunity to further degrade Iranians. He first tries to make Ārash shoot the arrow by threatening to kill him, but facing his refusal, he threatens to massacre captured Iranian soldiers. Humān, the champion archer of the Iranian army, who has defected to the enemy side, also appears to corroborate that Ārash is not a warrior and to write the message declaring that Ārash must shoot the arrow.

Section 6 which begins with another descriptive narration shows how Ārash becomes the object of his compatriots' ridicule and hate when a dove takes the message that Humān wrote to them. His knowledge of both languages as a shepherd in borderlands leads to further suspicion and the commander's deduction that he has been a spy from the beginning. Thus, although he is illiterate, they insist that he has written the letter. Using a distorted logic reminiscent of the Iranian police's tactic of linking any protests to espionage, the commander also states that Ārash's former support for Kashvād's refusal to shoot the arrow proves that he wanted to do the job himself. The dramatic irony is reinforced when Humān's bow is delivered as a gift from the Turāniān king, and everyone begins mourning Humān and cursing Ārash.

In section 7, Beyzaie builds on Ārash's loneliness to create one of his scenes of collective victimization which, as in his later films and plays, such as *Stranger and the Fog, Journey, Parchment of Master Sharzin*, or *Afrā Or the Day Is Passing*, displays an innocent individual being cursed and stoned by ignorant people who, being obsessed with their assumptions, act as police, judge and executioner without any hesitation. Despite their anger, however, they do not dare to kill Ārash as they are afraid of Turāniāns' retaliation.

Directly after this meeting, the irony of Humān's heroism is reinforced in section 8 in which Ārash encounters a lookout soldier. Here Beyzaie initiates the play's discourse on how the illusions of hero worship deprive people of their agency and their potential to become responsible citizens. The scene also comments on the real intentions of those who make pretentious proclamations about heroes. When Ārash tells him that Humān is alive, the soldier who also spies for Afrāsiyāb turns his words on his head to deliver a hero-worship cliché: 'Yes, Humān is alive. In our hearts he is alive.' Cornered by violent ostracization and unable to convince anyone that he is not a spy, Ārash then makes a suicidal leap: he rises and 'standing on his two feet roars at Alborz: I will shoot the arrow' (34–5).

Beyzaie, thus, uses this encounter to deliver Ārash's statement as a turning point in the rising action. The encounter displays the force of a monologue-like dominant discourse that, being incapable of evolving into a dialogue, crushes any person who opposes its ideological constructs. This display subverts the adoration of born heroes in the monological voice of epic narratives and *naqqāli* routines to initiate a dialogue about who heroes are and initiates the play's exposure of *naqqāli*'s mythical discourse on heroism to a modern psychological gaze. It also creates a three-sided dialogical space that sets Ārash's dialogue with himself and the natural elements against the discourses of the benevolence-born hero Kashvād and the evil-born hero/warrior Humān and his glorifiers who ostracize Ārash and ultimately never learn that Humān has been a traitor. The detailed descriptions and narrations, which are also used for Ārash's monologues, continue to hold the play's ties with *naqqāli*, but simultaneously they problematize it by emphasizing Ārash's internal conflict, doubts and interior dialogues as he, a man who is not a born hero, rises in stature to fulfil a sacrificial feat, which Beyzaie ultimately marks as 'useless' and disruptive for long-term emancipation.

The discussion on Beyzaie's take on born heroes deserves some analysis as upon first enquiry it seems as if divinely favoured born heroes are not essential to *naqqāli*. Though this is correct at a surface level, a detailed study demonstrates that the common people who appear in *naqqāli* accounts are either sidekicks or, as in the case of Samak Ayyār or Hossein-e Kurd, enjoy divine favour in their physical power, intelligence or luck. In other words, though they are born as commoners, they enjoy divine favour in their birth and luck. This is true even in the case of Kaveh, the only lower-class hero of the *Shāhnāmeh* as, despite his courage and the divine favour that prevents Zahhāk form hurting him in their first encounter, he is overshadowed by Fereydun once the latter appears in the horizon. Another point that must be explained is that although nowadays *naqqāli* is considered a form of performance with specific techniques that can be adopted for any subject or character type, prior to Nassirian's and Beyzaie's experiments with the form, *naqqāli* was just *naqqāli*, a performing tradition for specific heroic tales, which, despite its potentials, had remained untouched by modern playwrights.

Ārash's determination to shoot the arrow leads to sections 9 to 12 which relate the beginning of his ascent toward the pick of Alborz as he is mocked by his enemies. From section 13 to the end, Beyzaie's episodic structure, which focuses on Ārash's journey of self-discovery during his ascent, employs dreamlike, archetypal and expressionistic motifs in scenes that besides being reminiscent of *naqqāli* paintings are like scenes in a screenplay with jump-cut transitions. An example of this jump-cut form occurs in sections 11 to 13. As Ārash is climbing up the outskirts of Alborz, repeating to himself in a soliloquy the questions dropped at him by both the enemy and his compatriots, a sentence at the end of section 11 depicts him seeing an entity from afar. Rather than continuing the scene, however, Beyzaie leaves Ārash dazzled on the path and switches to the Turānian camp in section 12, in which the Turānian king is disturbed by the thought that Iranians may have tricked him through Humān, who then makes an oath on his life that Ārash cannot shoot the arrow further than himself. Section 13 then returns to Ārash to reveal the entity to be Kashvād, the benevolent hero who warns Ārash about the consequences of his action in a dialogue that marks the pitfalls of living under tyranny:

> — He [Kashvād] says: The enemy has captured hundreds of miles and you are in your way to free one; this is absurd.
> [...] Tomorrow they will all return to their homes, Ārash, and you remain with your broken conscience. You are just covering for the failure of the

lords! Your arrow becomes the lords' excuse to give the enemy the land with thousands and thousands of serfs included!
—Ārash says: Step aside from my path.
—And the shadow of the hero, strong: You man, think of the serfs!
—Ārash yells: I am one of them.
—Kashvād roars wrathfully: Does this arrow end their bondage?
[...]
No, this arrow does not help them. (38)

The scene ends with a conflict in which Ārash, the desperate rebel, shouts in agony to declare that he is shooting the arrow to die and gets his way by threatening to shoot Kashvād who is reluctant to hurt him. Thus, Beyzaie subverts the diktats of royalist, archaist nationalism, which defined itself in terms of ancient Iranian empires as a model of governance for modern Iran. Instead, it suggests that these empires were erected on people's toil and, thus, collapsed when external pressure strained their military might. The scene also marks the relationship between the kind, intellectual hero and the common rebel, a subject Beyzaie expands later in the play to subvert the idea of waiting for saviours in Iranian culture.

The dreamlike archetypal and expressionistic elements that evolve from section 13 onward can also be explained from two perspectives: the origins of such forms in modern visual arts and Beyzaie's exposure to them. In Euro-American theatre and later cinema, such elements began to appear between the 1890s and the 1920s due to artists' desire to supplant naturalistic drama with forms that enabled them to depict intense human emotions by means of hallucinatory projections in contexts that revealed the failure of social structures. Such forms were in dialogue with contemporary findings of psychology and the Dionysian pole in Nietzsche's theory of tragedy. However, as observed in their romantic prototypes, like Henrik Ibsen's *Brand* (1865) and *Peer Gynt* (1876) or their fully evolved examples like August Strindberg's *The Road to Damascus* (1898) or Eugene O'Neill's *The Emperor Jones* (1920), they also carried the markers of picaresque tales, eerie folk tales and medieval station drama. The difference was that rather than tricksters, demons or nightmarish situations, the form relied on uncanny events and figures that reflect the hallucinations of a tormented individual.

Beyzaie's episodic scenes bear similarities to the dreamlike, expressionistic scenes of such plays. However, these scenes can also, once more, be linked to the cinema not only because of their jump-cut-like transitions but also due to their dreamlike, expressionistic elements because dream plays and German expressionism directly influenced the early years of silent cinema.[57] With the latter point in mind, one can argue that the expressionistic aspects of Beyzaie's episodes may have originated in his own dreams, anxieties and nightmares,[58] but his exposure to such films made him define these images in their current form. Beyzaie had been a film fan since his early teens, and it is likely that when he was revising *Ārash*, he combined *naqqāli* with dreamlike and expressionistic elements that he had observed in such films. Nevertheless, even if Beyzaie was consciously or subconsciously influenced by episodic and expressionistic dream plays and films, his ultimate product is different. In *Ārash*, the main feature of such forms, the hallucinatory adventures of an individual in conflict with his own internal turmoil and his unsympathetic society, and the emphasis on scenery rather than dialogue do not lead to his being crushed. Instead, they are orchestrated in a plot that shows how a despairing person may be empowered by despair while depicting him as a hero and a victim.

Section 14 contains Beyzaie's first engagement with the idea of psychological double or shadow, the side of hesitation, fear, denial and suppressed desires or opportunist tendencies, which pushes the individual to surrender, bend, abandon and refrain from asserting itself or trying to have his dreams fulfilled.[59] This interior dialogue also marks the rise of a powerful Ārash as his despair, hatred of his former self and anger towards the world and himself distance him from the obedient slave in him and pushes him to fulfil the impossible.

> Now, he – Ārash – stands before Ārash. He stares at him, and they both set off. The steps of none of them is longer than the other; and the wind blows equally in their hair.
>
> — Don't come with me Ārash. Stay away; you are contaminating me with yourself.
> — Where can I stay Ārash? You only have me! Where can you escape from me? This morning I saw bad luck flying in the sky to land on someone's head. I knew it was looking for you.
> — I did not deserve this.
> — You deserve worse Ārash! You are being censured for your honesty; and you deserve it! Why didn't you escape to the mountains, surrender your life to a dagger in the chaos, or embrace the victorious enemy? Why did you not bend? [...] Imagine what will happen when your arrow falls before your feet. Every finger would point at you, every donkey renter would mock you. The world would be filled with your moans, sarcastic remarks of old women and widows, slanting smiles of warriors and nomads, and the curses of those who grow old behind spinning wheels.

Here when Ārash asks his shadow about the source of the incredible determination and power that is arising in him, he responds:

> — Think well Ārash. Isn't it despair?
> — Hail this despair, Thousands of hails. If I shoot a useless arrow, one that brings shame to any man, and if the earth and the sky mocks me with laughter, I won't be more dishonoured than I am now. (40)

Beyzaie's poetic, pure Persian makes the dialogue poignant. The same quality is also present in section 15 when the narration specifies the perspective of Mount

Alborz as it bewails the forgone fertility of the land and its people in the absence of love and hope. The reveries remind Ārash of the prosperous meadows, fertile orchards and beautiful maidens of his land, now lost forever to him: 'Remember that the springs became rocks; and the eyes [of the beloved] remained closed, that no foundations remained of the walls and no branches of the orchard. Ārash was climbing Alborz and the earth moaned under his feet' (41). The play, thus, echoes the motifs of fertility in the original myth as in Ārash's mind Alborz urges him to do something, but it also suggests how to become the mythical dying agent of fertility; the hero falls victim to a discourse that deprives him of the possibility of individual love and fertility. The dialogue with the natural elements is also a precursor to Beyzaie's use of natural elements in *Stranger and the Fog*, *Ballad of Tārā* and *Bāshu, the Little Stranger* in which the elements reflect the qualities of the protagonists or guide them in their path to fulfilment or failure.

Ārash's marginalization is then emphasized in section 16 in which a transition takes the play to the camp of Iranian warriors where they decide to slay Ārash after he shoots the arrow as they believe that the Turāniān king would no longer protect him when he achieves his purpose. Once more, therefore, the play highlights how internal conflicts, misunderstandings and illusions drain the forces that can be used against foreign invaders. This juxtaposition reinforces the scenes in which Ārash's loneliness and origin as a shepherd make him capable of communion with nature. Ārash then in section 17, faces the apparition of a divine father figure clad in armour and armed with a double-pronged spear in the style of Bahram, the ancient god of victory, who urges him to shoot the arrow with his heart. The divine, Bahram-like figure, who also seems to work like a father-figure to Arash, roars 'further' each time Ārash specifies a potential landing place for his arrow. Thus, rather than remaining content with Ārash's suggested destinations for the arrow – beyond 'the camps', 'the meadow where our house was' or 'the border' – he wants Ārash to shoot the arrow 'further' than all of them. The repetition of Ārash's expectations and the term 'further' evolves into an incantation that marks the emotional climax of the play as Ārash is emotionally provoked to become like a divinely inspired figure.

Beyzaie, thus, demythologizes the idea of divinely favoured born heroes to mythologize the process that may enable individuals to sublimate their despair and act as heroes. He marks the terrestrial worldliness of the divine and the heroic to suggest the potential of every individual to become a citizen and achieve heroic agency. His de- and re-mythologizing, therefore, remains earth-bound. When Ārash tells this apparition, the subconscious incarnation of his idea of manhood, that he hates his friends as much as his foes, at first, he becomes upset, but when Ārash asks him to teach him 'to love' and give him 'strength', he states: 'No! – If you hate this, this that is now, I have nothing to give you; for you are stronger than I am. It is your heart that will shoot the arrow and not your arms' (43).

At one level, therefore, the play glorifies the power of sublimated hate and despair to change the world. Yet as the emotional climax evolves in sections 18 to 21 to produce the climactic action in section 22, the plot highlights the issues involved in the idea of rebellion. Thus, like other writers who have written on the emotional ambivalence of the swing between love and hate in revolutionary contexts,[60] Beyzaie suggests that rather than hatred of past suffering or a utopian pipedream of future fulfilment, what leads to emancipatory reform is a rejection of the present informed by awareness, love and hope for a better future. The arguments about the two positions are, of course, not limited to literature. For instance, Walter Benjamin argues that 'images of enslaved ancestors rather than that of liberated grandchildren' make the oppressed rebel against the oppressor,[61] or Herbert Marcuse states that the memory of past fulfilments and the utopian desire to recapture that joy triggers reform and liberation.[62] However, it is usually in literary reflections on the psychological ambivalence between love and hate, hope and despair, and faith and doubt, and their reflections in the dichotomy between reform and rebellion that one finds that neither the hatred of the present nor the love and hope for a better future can alone lead to emancipation. An action rooted in hate can only lead to the replacement of one perpetrator of repression with a new one representing a different set of obsessions.

In these final sections, Beyzaie's blend of descriptive narration of scenery and action, Ārash's long soliloquies and intermittent dialogues further optimize the new form the play has created for mythical narrations. Ārash's soul-searching soliloquies in this narrative context prolong the scenes of climbing to make the audience share the feeling of lonely despair in an arduous climb towards an unknown fate. As the battlefield and its people look tinnier and tinnier,

> [h]e hears nothing but the sound of his own steps on the shoulders of the earth, and yet he continues as the seven ovens of his body burn. He has learned from his father that when a tiny scorpion is surrounded by fire, it stings itself and turns into ashes. And he – Ārash – looks at himself as he is burning in the fire of his thoughts.
>
> (44)

Ārash, thus, provides Beyzaie with a space of self-projection in which he reflects his own resolve to love a people that have high potential but waste it due to obsession with superstitious and divisive beliefs, a people who failed to give him the sense of belonging that generates happiness. Ārash, the marginalized, is set to gain recognition and a sense of belonging with a desperate deed that, he hopes, may awaken his people into an awareness of the immorality of the tortures they impose on their assumed others. Thus, like Beyzaie's, Ārash's climbing works like a purgation ritual that sublimates his anger to give him the emotional nobility that enables him to forgive his people. If, in Ārash's case, this rising agency turns a shepherd into a hero who does the job of an army, in Beyzaie's, it generated the creative urge that has enabled him to create the most influential oeuvre of Iranian plays, film scripts and films of the last sixty-three years.

In section 19, in the middle of these moments of ambivalence between hate and love, Kashvād, who is probably as much hated by his compatriot as Ārash, appears again to warn Ārash against another pitfall in individual acts of rebellion.

Aware of the strength that exudes from Ārash, Kashvād appears to warn him against playing the saviour for his people. Beyzaie, thus, refuses to perpetuate the regressive belief in saviours through a counterargument that he delivers through Kashvād. As a veteran warrior, and the grandson of Kaveh, the only working-class hero and the initiator of the cult of heroes in the *Shāhnāmeh*, Kashvād is an apt choice for this function. Earlier in the play, when he is ordered to shoot the arrow to avoid servitude, he says, 'Was servitude not there before this enemy? […] They did not defeat us; we were defeated before we fought [….] The defeat was not the failure of one person. We were all defeated. If I shoot the arrow, the future will curse me' (21–2). Now, once more, he comes to Ārash to warn him against making himself 'the site of people's hopes' and illusions (39) and to debunk his futile act of saving as merely a temporary solace in a world distorted by tyranny:

> — And the man whose words are sharper than warriors' axes, says: *Ārash, this freedom is not eternal. Every truce is breached one day. Where will you be on such a day?* [Ārash stays with his lips closed.] *Ārash, there will be hundreds of standoffs. If you save them now, you will become hope,* […] *the hope that in all hard fords a tough man will appear makes the masses indolent and indifferent. In every hardship, they will look to find a chosen one who stands so that they can remain seated.*
> — Ārash roars: Your words are like a heavy axe going for my roots.
> — The man says: *Your arrow may save them once, but it will keep them enslaved forever.* [Ārash listens apprehensively] *You are not scattering a seed that will sprout everywhere. You yourself will sprout, like a tree that dies in the winter and regrows in the spring.* (45; italics are mine)

As a hero whose father, Kaveh, was a working-class man like Ārash, Beyzaie's Kashvād is the only person who understands the real roots of heroism and Ārash's potential to fulfil the role. The scene, therefore, uses him to debunk the obsession with waiting for or acting as saviours. It also raises the same questions that Bertolt Brecht raised in his notorious *Lehrstück, Die Maßnahme* (The Decision, 1930). As in Brecht's play, which Beyzaie is not likely to have read in 1959, Beyzaie suggests that an ideal world is one in which there is no need for heroes. Yet, when it comes to prioritizing the ideal of raising awareness among the oppressed by not giving them temporary solace, Beyzaie's path diverges from Brecht's calculative communism. Thus, instead of Brecht's expressionism in reverse which debunks the Christian ideals of pity and sacrificial heroism by showing how such individuals fail to recognize collective good, Beyzaie implies that such acts of desperate rebellion, though futile, are inevitable so long as people themselves act as tools of tyranny. Thus, though Ārash reflects Beyzaie's own emotional status and rebellion against the beliefs of an exclusionist society, Kashvād reflects his bid for having rational control over his feelings. Whereas Ārash embodies the clash of Eros and Thanatos in Beyzaie's subconscious, Kashvād represents his conscious ego that questions his sacrificial impulses and transcends the love-hate and life-death pulls of belonging and unbelonging to set his creative path for life. Through using his own experience,

Beyzaie's psychoanalytical probing is not just concerned with him. This is because by reflecting the different sides of his interior dialogue he displays the processes that every person may undergo when exposed to traumatic marginalization, and he uses this reflection to show what is wrong with his society. However, even Kashvād is far from being like Brecht's ruthless insurgents, who argue for increasing people's suffering to hasten the revolution and force the young comrade to kill himself because he fails to contain his revolutionary zeal. Kashvād does not support giving futile solace to people as he wants to see them become responsible citizens rather than continue as hopeful serfs, but he does not desert them either and does understand Ārash's state. While advising Ārash against shooting the arrow, Kashvād talks of a people used to servitude, a people who need awareness rather than heroes, but he ultimately respects Ārash's decision as he knows that it is an inevitable result of living among a people who act as tools of tyranny.

Nonetheless, Beyzaie's focus is not on Kashvād. It is rather on the archetypal tragedy of a cornered individual, who is not and does not want to be a hero but, like some other desperate people, embarks on fulfilling an impossible task to regain a sense of belonging in an ignorant exclusionist society. The expressionistic and surrealistic idiom of the play, which is enhanced in sections 19 to 21 as he reaches the highest part of the mountain away from the madding crowds, works with this archetypal focus to generate the play's magical appeal which has made it one of Beyzaie's most performed plays.[63] The seemingly unending ascent of a wronged, honourable loner gradually finding a mission for his life by leaving behind the censure of ignorant people and receiving inspiration from the natural elements and his internal ideals gives a mythical ambiance to the play. His naked ascent towards the clouds; the murmuring of the dust calling him to itself; the mountain that offers to destroy his enemies and declares that he is approaching the seats of gods; his conversation with Mother Earth, Esfandārmaz, about his lower-class origin and the fire that Mithra planted in his heart; the beating of his heart as he gets closer to 'the celestial path of Anahita', all contribute to this sublimity.

Thus, Ārash, 'a commoner, who was free from' the sins of his people and the burden of knowledge 'in the morning' comes to 'know things about this world' that he wishes 'to have remained unknown' (47). He, 'Ārash, to whom Mithra had given a heart of fire, held up his bow, which was more arched than the sky.' Beyzaie's language turns the climax of action in section 22 into a moment of unity with nature as 'Ārash, the son of earth' pulls the string of his bow with his heart. The 'winds roar', 'the sea makes huge waves', 'the earth shakes', 'the sun stops in its passage', 'the seven skies bend', 'the clouds open up', 'the rivers reverse their course' and 'lightnings' acknowledge his uniqueness. And just when he lets the arrow fly and disappears along the arrow, Alborz declares, with a tongue made of tongues of fire, 'How could I carry him on my shoulders?' Beyzaie's metaphoric imagery compares the arrow with the arrow of time and the never-landing arrow of a resurrecting idea. The arrow never lands. The soldiers chasing its trace just assume that the sharp call of a bird that they see flying from a huge tree with a wounded throat means that the arrow landed there.

The play then closes with Ārash's compatriots celebrating his achievement while waiting for him, and a prologue in section 23 in which the narrator marks the continuity of their waiting: 'now standing at the foot of Alborz, we are facing an enemy from our own bloodline, looking at us with an ugly sneer. And I know a people who still say "Ārash will return"' (47-9).

In dialogue with time: The play's socio-political context

Fulfilling a transgressive vision that subverts social and cultural hierarchies, Beyzaie places a commoner at the centre of the politics of Iranian mythology. The low and the high come together to deconstruct the cult of hero worship while celebrating the silenced individuals who may have contributed to the creation of Iran's cultural continuity. This subversive vision is best reflected in the dialogues between Kashvād and Ārash, but the irony of Humān's fate also comments on heroism and history. The arrow is shot with the bow of Humān, the defecting archer, who is ultimately celebrated as a hero when Iranians find his body. It never occurs to them and perhaps the ensuing generations that he had joined the enemy.

Yet, like all aesthetic reformulations, besides its cultural functions, the play engages with its socio-political context. Being the product of an author's rereading of the codes of his culture, such engagements may be intentional, but they often evolve due to the later interpretations, which originate in the historical exigencies that have produced certain ways of seeing in the authors and their readers or audience. In this context, I argue that Beyzaie's focus on examining the ideals and pitfalls of heroism has two major origins: the rising centrality of tough guys in Iranian cultural products of the 1950s and the roles that mercenary thugs and army officers played in suppressing people's democratic desires during the 1953 coup. This means that, at one level, the play responds to the coup, during which the army headed by General Fazlollah Zahedi (1897-1963), who received the epic title of *Tāj Bakhsh* (Crown giver), fought against the people's will. Incidentally, a few years earlier, Zahedi had been banished to Palestine (1942-5) by the allies for having German sympathies. Yet upon his return to Iran, he changed sympathies and joined the British and the Americans to lead the coup against Mohammad Mosaddegh's constitutionalist government. In the play when Ārash censures Humān for joining the enemy, he states, 'There I was the mule of my clan ... I escaped from tyranny to tyranny, from oppressor to enemy! I chose the side that had victory! How can an idiot like you understand warriors? If I must bend and risk my neck, I will do it where I am fed better' (29).

During the coup, notorious thugs, headed by Shaban Jafari, aka *Shaban Bimokh* (Shaban the Brainless, 1921-2006), a *Zurkhāneh* champion, launched street fights, raided the offices of pro-Mosaddegh newspapers in Tehran. They received money from the royal funds but justified their acts by claiming they were defending the Shah against the forces of chaos.[64] Similar atrocities were committed against the Bahais. While Mosaddegh resisted the clerics' pressures to suppress Bahais by insisting that all Iranians had equal rights, the Shah gave a freer hand to the clergy in the 1950s so that Mohamad Tqi Falsafi's sermons in 1955 provoked anti-Bahai sentiments, and thugs, who always looked for opportunities to destroy places and beat people, were, on this occasion, joined by army officers who wished to ingratiate themselves with the clergy.[65]

Beyzaie's symbolic motifs never sink into political or historical allegories. Yet, as a teenager, he had suffered the violence that defined the years immediately after the coup. Thus, though he never practised Bahaism, he suffered the consequences of such hate speeches and their impacts on the mentalities of his teachers and peers who blindly believed in them and acted as instruments of tyranny.[66] Unlike Humān and those who ostracize Ārash, or General Zahedi, the hate-mongering clergy, or their thugs, Ārash is one of the marginalized whose suffering in the grand scheme of power, which manifests itself in inflicting pain on its 'others', does not seem to concern anyone. Ārash achieves his feat not because he was born a hero or was fed by the court but because his despair forces him to sacrifice his life to prove his worth to the people who corner him. Like all creative artists who have suffered marginalization, he puts his soul in the arrow of his creative work to change the people that fail to see his worth. However, as seen in the analysis above, despite the apparent glorification of Ārash's individual growth, Beyzaie provides a counterargument to suggest that such a feat is useless for emancipation.

Summing up, reception and later influences

This chapter was primarily concerned with four interrelated subjects: (1) the genealogy of *naqqāli*, (2) Beyzaie's engagement with *naqqāli* in his recitation plays, (3) the genealogy of the myth of Ārash, and (4) Beyzaie's reformulation of *naqqāli* and the myth of Ārash in his *Ārash*. From a more general angle, therefore, the chapter was focused on the origins, forms and functions of Beyzaie's *Ārash*, and the cultural codes, practices and beliefs it worked with. The section on the myth of Ārash was central to my chapter as it offered new arguments about the myth and provided an example of how, as in the modern era, myths were repurposed to promote a group or an idea in the past. The sections on Beyzaie's recitation plays and *Ārash* also offered fresh perspectives on Beyzaie's reformulations of Iranian myths, *naqqāli*, cinema and global performance traditions. They also analysed the play from a psychoanalytical angle, embedded it in international and theoretical debates on dram and emancipatory aesthetics, and analysed its potential dialogue with the givens of post-coup Iran. The process revealed a few points that I highlight below before engaging with the reception of the play.

As argued in this chapter, in *Ārash*, Beyzaie applies his divergent gaze to the resurfaced myth of a sacrificial saviour to create a new type of hero. The process creates a narrative play that lacks the participatory elements of indigenous forms but creates a dialogical space that critiques the ideology of hero worship and the emphasis on born heroes in myths and *naqqāli*. The result also creates an intertextual dialogue with *Azhdāhāk* to highlight how wronged individuals may achieve self-awareness and agency, confront the failures of their culture and be called heroes by sublimating their traumas into points of redemption in their narratives of selfhood. Beyzaie, thus, suggests that heroism and assumed or actual villainy originate in a person's experience of traumatic marginalization and that a society may avoid both extremes if people become authors of their own fates and refrain from punishing their assumed others for absurd reasons. He also signifies that where individual agency and emancipatory action and dialogue are costly, rather than acting as citizens and changing the systems that distort their lives, people bend to them, become their tools or just wait for saviours. This latter point also highlights a vision of leadership, particularly in Kashvād, whose presence suggests that good leaders do not bend to pressure, do not follow heroic illusions and do not victimize others for their own interests. They rather sacrifice their own interests for the long-term interests of their people.

Thus, Beyzaie's gaze at his mythical hero and Iran's past is neither glorifying nor post-colonial: rather than celebrating Iran's grandeur before the mythical Turāniān or actual Greek, Arab, Turkic, and Mongolian invasions; lamenting the colonial impacts of these invasions; or writing under the gaze of a Western 'other' to excuse his culture, he rereads the disastrous events of Iran's past in terms of cultural failures that leave people at the mercy of internal tyrants and external invaders. Ārash, thus, depicts heroes as victims, defines heroism as moral integrity in the face of political opportunism and ignorance, and offers a counter-hegemonic discourse that subverts the glorification of ancient Persian empires as models for modern Iran. The play also shows how tyranny turns the unifying function of a king into a force that triggers disunity and identifies tyranny as the cause of Iran's disintegration at different points in history.

These qualities have given Ārash a lasting place among Iranian plays. Beyzaie first prepared the play for publication in the third issue of *Ketāb-e Māh-e Keyhān* (Keyhān's Monthly Book) in 1962, but the journal which was edited by Jalal Al-e Ahmad was suspended. It, thus, remained unpublished until 1977 when it was published by Nilufar Publication. The play was an immediate success, evident in that it has been frequently republished ever since. It was not, however, formally staged until after the revolution when its brevity and inspiring language made it a favourite piece for students' performances. It has also been staged by such leading directors as Qotbeddin Sadeqi (1997) and Mohammad Rahmanian (2013). The play was translated into English by Soheil Parsa who also staged it in Canada, the United States, and the UK.[67]

In June 2010 I worked as an advisor with a group of students from the University of Reading, headed by Rosanna Jahangard, and then included their performance in a symposium I had organized at University College London. There were altogether four actors, and Jahangard used flags and items of clothing to help the audience follow the narration. The performance had the normal problems of an amateur student work, but it was engaging. It was also received well, and the Q and A session suggested that the audience was impressed by the play's poetic power. The four actors, who were of non-Iranian origins, argued that the play had high intercultural potential and reminded them of Shakespeare's works, but the form had elements that made it like Japanese theatre. Later they also performed the play at the University of Reading.

Beyzaie, who had never found the opportunity to stage the play, directed a stylized reading of the play at Standford University in 2103. In this animated reading Mozhdeh Shamsaie and Mohsen Namjou recited the play in a vocal style that sounded like Avesta recitations. Though the reading was innovative and suggestive of another way in which the play can be performed, Beyzaie did not intend it to be representative of the full performing potential of the play.[68]

Along with Beyzaie's other recitation plays, the play has also been influential in the rise of a template in which alternating monologues delivered in a presentational style are used to reflect alternative views about an event or a character. Notable plays in this style include Abbas Na'lbandiyān's *Nāgahān* (Suddenly, 1971), Beyzaie's own *Afra, or the Day Is Passing* (1997) and Amir Reza Kuhestani's *Quartet: A Trip to the North* (2007). While in dialogue with Ryūnosuke Akutagawa's stories 'In A Grove' and 'Rashomon' (1922) and Akira Kurosawa's film *Rashomon* (1950), these plays and others written in this template also echo Beyzaie's engagement with *naqqāli*'s presentational style in his early works.[69] Thus, like his other works, Beyzaie's recitation plays, including *Ārash*, played a central role in initiating new templates for modern indigenous-style Iranian drama and new ways of examining Iranian myths.

Notes

1 For more, see Talajooy, 'Chapter 2' in *Iranian Culture*.
2 Beyzaie, 'Cheh Mahkameh', 122.
3 Beyzaie in Qukasiyan, *Goftogu*, 20-30.
4 For more on his choice of form, see Beyzaie et al., 'Naghd', 30.
5 For an analysis of the form see the next section.
6 For Beyzaie's own comments, see Beyzaie et al., 'Naghd', 28-37.
7 Beyzaie, *Namāyesh*, 104-6, and 84-112, and Floor, *History*, 76, 62-81.
8 Beyzaie in Qukasiyan, *Goftogu*, 21.
9 For studies on this era and the activities of National Art Group, see Javanmard, *Didār*, and Jafari R., *Goruh-e Honar, Vol. 1*. For Nassirian, see also Ghaderi and Ghorbaninejad. 'Ali Nassirian'.
10 Beyzaie, *Namāyesh*, 65-83. Ashurpur, *Namāyesh*, Vol. 4; Ghaffary, 'Evolution', 361-89.
11 Boyce, 'Zariadres', 463. Boyce quotes Athenaeus, *Deipnosophists*, 919-20. See also Boyce, 'Parthian', 10-45.
12 For ancient spectacles, carnivals and ritual forms, see Beyzaie, *Namāyesh*, 27-47, Talajooy, *Mythologizing*, 6-22, and Ashurpur, *Namāyesh-hā-ye*, Vol. 1, 2, 3 and 5.
13 Beyzaie, *Namāyesh*, 65-83, and Floor, *History*, 82-104.
14 Shahriari, *Ketāb-e Namāyesh 1*, 286.
15 Jafari M., 'Tumār'.
16 Kumiko. 'NAQQĀLI'. These included, among others, *Amir Arsālān, Hamzeh-nāmeh*, and *Hossein-e Kurd*.
17 For more on *naqqāli* in general, see Beyzaie, *Namāyesh*, 65-83; Ashurpur, *Namāyesh, Vol 2*. See also Ghaffary, 'Evolution', 361-89, and Floor, *History*, 82-106.

18 Beyzaie, *Namāyesh*, 82.
19 For *Nā-Kojā-Ābād*, which is also central to *ta'ziyeh*, see Corbin, 'Mundus'.
20 Beyzaie et al., 'Naghd', 28–37.
21 For some of these arguments, see Shamlu, *Negarāni-hā*. See also Hosouri, *Sarnevesht-e*.
22 For Beyzaie's views about his dialogue with the myth, see Beyzaie et al., 'Naghd', 28–31.
23 Beyzaie, 'Ārash', 1.
24 *Ta'ziyeh* is Iran's passion play tradition which in its current form has been used to commemorate Shi'i saints since the late Safavid era. See Beyzaie, *Namāyesh*, 113–56, and Chelkowski, *Ta'ziyeh*.
25 For a short film of Beyzaie's performance, see Arte at shorturl.at/kqru4.
26 For an overview of *jām-e jam* as a trope in Persian literature, see A'zamiyān, 'Jām-e Jam'.
27 Pure Persian (Pārsi-e Sareh) is a register of new Persian (700s–the present) which evolved in the 1800s in the poetry and prose of proto-nationalist writers. Originally evolving naturally from the works of those who emulated the language of the *Shahnameh* in the return literary movement, it later turned into a nationalist discourse for eliminating all foreign loanwords from Persian.
28 Beyzaie, *Divān*: Panj. For his views on radial nationalism, see also Amiri, *Jedāl*, 35–9. For his extended comments on his language in the three recitations, see Beyzaie et al., 'Naghd', 30–2.
29 Benjamin, 'Theses', VII, 256–7.
30 Foucault, *Discipline*, 30.
31 Beyzaie in Amiri, *Jedāl*, 25–6.
32 Talajooy, 'Reformulation'.
33 Darmesteter, *Zend-Avesta*, Part 2, 11, 54, 94–5, 103–4 and 270.
34 Tafazzoli and Hanaway, 'ĀRAŠ'.
35 Ferdowsi, 'Khosrow Parviz', Vol. 8, 31–3.
36 The omission of these accounts may have happened earlier when the Sasanians took power.
37 The arguments are mine, but for detailed discussions of Bahram Chubin's life and popularity, I have used Shabazi, 'Bahrām VI Čōbīn', and Pourshariati, *Decline*, 122–9.
38 Biruni, *Āsārolbāqiyeh*, 334–5. Translation is mine.
39 For Esfandārmaz, see Boyce, *History 1*, 206. See also Skjærvø, 'Ahura Mazdā', 404–9.
40 Theodor Bar Kōnay writing specified by E. Benveniste, 'Le témoignage de Théodore bar Kōnay sur le Zoroastrisme', quoted in Yarshater, 'AFRĀSĪĀB'.
41 For the link with the Indo-Iranian myth of Ārksha's family, see Daryaee, 'Ārash', 172–7.
42 For Ārash's epithet, see Darmesteter, *Zend-Avesta*, 95 (footnote 2); Daryaee, 'Ārash', and Kellens, 'Vibrations', 196–8.
43 For Vayu, Tishtar and Apush, see Hinnells, *Shenākht*, 34–8, Panaino, 'TIŠTRYA', and Brunner, 'APŌŠ'.
44 Ferdowsi, 'Razm Arjāsb bā Goshtāsp', Vol. 5.129; 'Ashkāniān', Vol. 6.138; 'Khosrow Parviz', Vol. 8.31–3.
45 Tabari, *Tārikh*, Vol. 2, 726. Tabari's spelling here is Ārashshiātir rather than Ārashsiātir.
46 Tha'ālabi, *Ghorar*, 89–91.
47 Tabari, *Tārikh*, Vol. 1, 291. Translation is mine.
48 Bal'ami, *Tārikhnāmeh*, 253–6.

49 Gorgani, *Vis o Rāmin*, (1054 AD), Fifth Letter, 273. Gourab is near Malayer in Hamedan province.
اگر خوانند آرش را کمانگیر// که از ساری به مرو انداخت یک تیر
تو اندازی به جان من ز گوراب// همی هر ساعتی صد تیر پرتاب
ترا زیبد نه آرش را سواری// که صد فرسنگ بگذشتی ز ساری
50 Beyzaie, 'Cheh Mahkameh', 119.
51 Kasraei, 'Ārash'.
خلق چون بحری بر آشفته/به جوش آمد/ خروشان شد/ به موج افتاد/ برش بگرفت و مردی چون صدف/ از سینه بیرون داد.
52 Kasraei, 'Ārash'.
مرا تیر است آتش پر/ مرا باد است فرمانبر
53 For Beyzaie's views about the play, see Beyzaie in Amiri, *Jedāl*, 25–31.
54 Beyzaie, 'Ārash', *Divān 1*, 19–20.
55 Beyzaie uses *Alborz Kuh* to evoke the mythical mountain of Iranian myths rather than *Kuh-hā-ye Alborz* which refers to a mountain range extending in the southern coasts of the Caspian Sea.
56 See Yarshater, 'Taʿziyeh', 88–90. For a translation of the text, see Bahar, *Pazhuheshi*, 263–74.
57 For expressionistic and dream plays, see Innes, *Avant Garde*, 19–58 and 215–22.
58 For Beyzaie's reference to these anxieties and nightmares, see Qukasiyan, *Goftogu*, 83–5 and 99–100, 251–5, and Beyzaie and Jahed, 'Qalamro'.
59 I have dealt with Beyzaie's use of double and shadow motifs in the next chapter.
60 Examples include Percy Bysshe Shelley's mythic reformulation *Prometheus Unbound* (1820) and Eugene O'Neill's analysis of the lives of downtrodden Afro-Americans in *All God's Chillun Got Wings* (1924).
61 Benjamin, 'Theses', XII, 260.
62 Marcuse, *Eros*, 11–21.
63 The play has been repeatedly republished in Iran and has been performed not only in Iran but also in Canada, United States and Britain in English and Persian; in Columbia and Cuba in Spanish; and in Bosnia in Serbian. See Parsa, 'Ārash-e', and Anonymous, 'Ārash Sād-e'.
64 For more on these thugs, see Sarshar, *Khāterāt-e*, 123–59, particularly 111–12, 123–7, 145–9.
65 Fischer, Iran: 'From Religious', 187, and Davani, *Khāterāt*, 200.
66 See Beyzaie in Nikazar, *Reesheh-hā*.
67 Beyzaie, 'Aurash', 1. See also note 65.
68 A report on the reading is available at https://www.youtube.com/watch?v=BdeuZTflMrg.
69 For an analysis of this template, see Talajooy, 'Afrā'.

Bibliography

Aʿzamiyān, Jamileh. 'Jām-e Jam'. *Markaz-e Dāeratolmaʿāref-e Bozorg-e Eslāmi*. (2020). Online: shorturl.at/lQVX5 (Accessed 12 July 2022).
Anonymous. 'Ārash Sād-e Rahmanian Do Ejrāei Shod'. *Isna*. 4 January 2014. Online: shorturl.at/owyW6. (Accessed 24 January 2021).
Amiri, Nushabeh. *Jedāl ba Jahl*. Tehran: Sāles, 2009.
Ashurpur, Sadeq. *Namāyesh-hā-ye Irāni 4: Naqqāli*. Tehran: Sureh Mehr, 2010.
Athenaeus. *The Deipnosophists*. Trans. C. D. Yonge. London: Henry G. Born, 1854. Vol. 3, Book XIII.

Bahar, Mehrdad. *Pazhuheshi dar Asātir-e Iran*. Tehran: Āgah, 2002.
Bal'ami, Abu Ali. *Tarikhnameh-ye Tabari*. Ed. Mohammad Roshan. Tehran: Sorush, 1999.
Benjamin, Walter. 'Theses on the Philosophy of History'. In *Illuminations*. Ed. and Intro. Hannah Arendt. Trans. Harry Zohn. New York: Schocken, 1969.
Beyzaie, Bahram. *Namāyesh dar Iran*. 1965. Tehran: Roshangaran, 2001.
Beyzaie, Bahram. *Divan-e Namāyesh 1*. Tehran: Roshangaran, 2001.
Beyzaie, Bahram. 'Aurash'. *Stories from the Rains of Love and Death: Four Plays from Iran*. Trans. Soheil Parsa and Brian Quirt with Peter Farbridge. Toronto: Playwrights Canada Press, 2008.
Beyzaie, Bahram, et al. 'Naghd va Barresi-ye Seh Barkhani'. *Kārnāmeh*. Vol. 3. No. 13 (October 1999). Pp. 28–37.
Beyzaie, Bahram and Andisheh Puyā. 'Cheh Mahkameh-hā-ye Roshanfekri keh Nagozarāndam'. *Andisheh Puyā*. Vol. 2. No. 12. (January 2014). Pp. 119–20.
Beyzaie Kashani, H. *Tārikh-e Varzesh-e Bāstani dar Iran, Zurkhāneh*. Tehran: Heidari, 1958.
Biruni, Mohammad Abu Rayhan. *Āsārolbāqiyeh En Alqorun Al-Khālyeh*. Persian. Trans. Ali Akbar Danaseresht. Tehran: Amir Kabir, 1984.
Boyce, Mary. 'Zariadres and Zarēr'. *Bulletin of the School of Oriental and African Studies*. Vol. 17. No. 3 (1955). Pp. 463–77.
Boyce, Mary. 'The Parthian "Gōsān" and Iranian Minstrel Tradition'. *Journal of Royal Asiatic Society*. Vol. 89. No. 1/2 (April 1957). Pp. 10–45.
Brook, Peter. *The Empty Space*. New York: Touchstone, 1996.
Brunner, C. J. 'APŌŠ'. *Encyclopaedia Iranica Online*, © Trustees of Columbia University in the City of New York. Online: http://dx.doi.org/10.1163/2330-4804_EIRO_COM_5535 (Accessed 16 February 2021).
Chelkowski, Peter. Ed. *Ta'ziyeh: Ritual and Drama in Iran*. New York: New York University Press, 1979.
Corbin, Henry. 'Mundus Imaginalis or the Imaginary and the Imaginal'. 1964. In *H.C. Corbin*. Online: https://www.amiscorbin.com/bibliographie/mundus-imaginalis-or-the-imaginary-and-the-imaginal/. (Accessed 30 June 2021).
Darmesteter, James. 'The Zend-Avesta: Part II, the Sirozahs, Yashts and Nyāyis'. In *the Sacred Books of the East Series*. Oxford: Clarendon, 1883.
Daryaee, Touraj. 'Ārash-e Shevātir keh Bud?' *Bokhara*. No. 95 & 96 (September and October 2013). Pp. 167–76.
Davani, Ali. *Khāterāt va Mobārezāt-e Hojat ol-Eslām Falsafi*. Tehran: Markaz-e Asnād-e Enqelāb-e Eslāmi, 2003.
Ferdowsi, Abolqasem. *The Shāhnāmeh*. Vol. 5, 6, and 8. Ed. Djalal Khaleqi Motlaq and Abolfazl Khatibi. California: Mazda, 1987–2009.
Fischer, Michael. *Iran: From Religious Dispute to Revolution*, Cambridge: Harvard University Press, 1980.
Floor, Willem. *History of Theatre in Iran*. Odenton, MD: Mage, 2005.
Foucault, Michell. *Discipline and Punish: The Birth of Prison*. Trans. Alan Sheridan. New York: Vintage, 1995.
Ghaderi Sohi, Behzad and Masoud Ghorbaninejad. 'Ali Nassirian and a Modern Iranian "National" Theatre'. *Asian Theatre Journal*. Vol. 29. No. 2 (Fall 2012). Pp. 495–527.
Ghaffary, Farrokh, 'Evolution of Rituals and Theatre in Iran'. *Iranian Studies*. Vol. 17. No. 4 (1984). Pp. 361–89.
Gorgani, Fakhreddin As'ad. *Vis o Ramin*. Ed. M. J. Mahjub. Tehran: Andisheh, 1959.

Hinnells, John, *Shenākht-e Asātir-e Iran*. Persian trans. J. Amuzgar and A. Tafazzoli. Tehran: Cheshmeh, 1994.
Hosouri, Ali. *Sarnevesht-e Yek Shaman: Az Zahhāk beh Odin*. Tehran: Cheshmeh, 1388.
Innes, Christopher. *Avant Garde Theatre: 1892–992*. New York and London: Routledge, 1993.
Javanmard, Abbas. *Didār bā Khiesh*. Tehran: Farhang-e Nashr-e Now, 2017.
Jafari, Mohammad. 'Tumār-e Naqqāli'. *Markaz-e Dāeratolmaʿāref-e Bozorg-e Eslāmi*. (2020). Online: shorturl.at/hnoRV. (Accessed 10 July 2022).
Jafari, Ruhollah. *Goruh-e Honar-e Melli az Āghāz tā Pāyān (1335–1357)*. Tehran: Afrāz, 2016.
Kasraie, Siyavash. 'Ārash-e Kamāngir'. In *Az Āvā tā Havā-ye Āftāb*. Tehran: Nāder, 2007.
Kellens, John. 'Vibration and Twinkling'. *Journal of Indo-European Studies*. Vol. 5 (1977). Pp. 197–201.
Marcuse, Herbert. *Eros & Civilization*. Boston: The Beacon Press, 1966.
Nikazar, Ahmad (dir.). *Reesheh-hā* (A Documentary on Bahram Beyzaie). Online: https://www.youtube.com/watch?v=xlNdgLRXbEs. (Accessed 15 January 2021).
Nöldeke, Theodor. 'Der Beste der arischen Pfeilschützen im Awesta und im Tabarî', *ZDMG*. No. 5 (1881). Pp. 445–7.
Panaino, Antonio. 'TIŠTRYA'. *Encyclopaedia Iranica Online*, © Trustees of Columbia University in the City of New York. Online: http://dx.doi.org/10.1163/2330-4804_EIRO_COM_1561. (Accessed 16 February 2021).
Parsa, Soheil. 'Ārash-e Beyzaie Qahremān Nist va Hargez Nemikhāhad keh Qahremān Bāshad'. *Tirgan*. Online: shorturl.at/kBGY6 (Accessed 10 November 2021).
Pourshariati, Parvaneh. *Decline and Fall of the Sasanian Empire: The Sasanian-Parthian Confederacy and the Arab Conquest of Iran*. London and New York: I.B. Tauris, 2008.
Qukasiyan, Zaven. *Goftogu bā Bahram Beyzaie*. Tehran: Āgāh, 1992.
Sarshar, Homa. *Khaterat-e Shaban Jafari*. Tehran: Nashr-e Sāles, 2002.
Shahbazi, Alireza Shapur. 'Bahrām VI Čōbīn'. *Encyclopaedia Iranica*. Vol. III. No. 5 (1989). Pp. 514–22. Online: http://www.iranicaonline.org/articles/bahram-06. (Accessed 30 January 2019).
Shahriari, Khosro. *Ketab-e Namayesh 1*. Tehran: Amir Kabir, 1986.
Shamlu, Ahmad. *Negarāni-hā-ye Man*. New Jersey: CIRA, 1990.
Skjærvø, Prods Oktor. 'Ahura Mazdā and Ārmaiti, Heaven and Earth, in the Old Avesta'. *Journal of the American Oriental Society*. Vol. 122. No. 2 (2002). Pp. 399–410.
Tabarai, Mohammad Ibn-e Jarir-e. *Tarikh Al-Rosol va Al-Moluk. Vol. 1*. Persian translation by Abolqasem Payandeh. Tehran: Asatir, 1996.
Tafazzoli, A. and W. L. Hanaway Jr. 'ĀRAŠ'. *Encyclopaedia Iranica Online*, © Trustees of Columbia University in the City of New York. Online: http://dx.doi.org/10.1163/2330-4804_EIRO_COM_5597. (Accessed 12 February 2021).
Talajooy, Saeed. *Mythologizing the Transition: A Comparative Study of Bahram Beyzaee and Wole Soyinka*. PhD thesis. University of Leeds. January 2008.
Talajooy, Saeed. 'Reformulation of Shahnameh Legends in Bahram Beyzaie's Plays'. *Iranian Studies*. Vol. 46. No. 5 (September 2013). Pp. 695–719.
Talajooy, Saeed. *Iranian Culture in Bahram Beyzaie's Cinema and Theatre: Paradigms of Being and Belonging (1959–1979)*. London and New York: I.B. Tauris, 2023.
Talajooy, Saeed. 'Afrā, Or the Day Is Passing: A Cultural Diagnosis'. In Bahram Beyzaie. *Afrā, Or the Day Is Passing*. Translation & Analysis Saeed Talajooy. San Francisco: Bisheh, 2023.

Thaʿlabi, Abu Ishaq. *Tārikh-e Thaʿlabi: Pāreh-ye Nokhost, Iran-e Bastān*. (*Ghorar-e Akhbār*). Persian Translation Mohammad Fazaeli. Tehran: Noqreh, 1989.

Yamamoto, Kumiko. 'NAQQĀLI'. In *Encyclopaedia Iranica Online*. © Trustees of Columbia University in the City of New York (2021). Online: http://dx.doi.org/10.1163/2330-4804_EIRO_COM_363720. (Accessed 23 August 2022).

Yarshater, Ehsan, 'Taʿziyeh and Pre-Islamic Mourning Rites in Iran'. In *Taʿziyeh: Ritual and Drama in Iran*. Ed. Peter Chelkowski. New York: New York University Press, 1979. Pp. 88–94.

Yarshater, Ehsan. 'Iranian National History'. In *The Cambridge History of Iran Vol. 3 (Part 1)*. Ed. Ehsan Yarshater. Cambridge: Cambridge University Press, 1983.

Yarshater, Ehsan. 'AFRĀSĪĀB'. *Encyclopaedia Iranica Online*, © Trustees of Columbia University in the City of New York. Online: http://dx.doi.org/10.1163/2330-4804_EIRO_COM_4841. (Accessed 13 February 2021).

Chapter 3

A PAHLEVĀN'S DREAMS OF BELONGING:
RECONFIGURATION OF THE IDEALS OF HEROISM IN
BAHRAM BEYZAIE'S *SO DIES PAHLEVĀN AKBAR*

Saeed Talajooy

Introduction: The ideal hero in a modern era

Beyzaie's *So Dies Pahlevān Akbar* was the result of his experiments with Iranian epic and folk forms in his recitation and puppet plays (1959–63). As in these plays, his concern was the status of the marginalized and the ideals of heroism. However, rather than commenting on the present by focusing on a timeless folk-tale world as in his puppet plays or on ancient myths as in *Ārash* or *Azhdāhāk*, in *So Dies Pahlevān Akbar*, he depicts the demise of a *pahlevān* in the pre-moment of the present to reflect on the impossibility of such an ideal in the present.

The term *pahlevān* has a cultural import which transcends its translation as a hero. It represents a form of selfless physical and spiritual heroism rarely achieved but always present as an ideal in the Iranian imaginal and its worldly echoes in *javānmardi* cults. It is associated with the term *javānmard* (noun and adjective) which can be used as a compliment for anyone who has chivalrous qualities or acts as a defender of people. A pahlevān differs from a *javānmard* in that though they may undergo similar forms of training, he has a higher status as a champion of Iranian martial arts. Thus, a pahlevān is expected to be *javānmard*, but the opposite is not necessary. He is also different from an *ayyār* in that though in the past some *ayyārs* were also pahlevāns and participated in open battles to defend an ideal, a leader or their people, an *ayyār* is more a Robinhood-like master of disguise and ruse who engages in commando warfare, climbs walls and digs tunnels for extracting imprisoned friends, kidnapping enemy leaders or obtaining information or tokens of glory. As in Rostam's case, who disguises himself as a merchant to save Bijhan from Turān, a pahlevān may also engage in *ayyāri* activities, but he is more known for his power, generosity and ability to defeat opponents in face-to-face combat.[1]

Continuously idealized in Persian literature,[2] *javānmardi* has defined the ideals of hegemonic masculinity in pre-Islamic military culture, medieval and early modern military and folk cultures and the modern folk culture. Though some scholars, whose focus is Iran's medieval culture, argue that *javānmardi* cults evolved during the 800s, it is almost certain that these beliefs and practices had their precedents in the paladin-king bonds of pre-Islamic Iran.³ Central to these precedents was the Mithraic pledge of mutual loyalty, support and sacrifice between an ideal king and his paladins, who also had their own warriors and codes of conduct for free, honourable men.⁴ *Javānmardi* cults also involved military trainings, which signify their origins in the ritual practices associated with the worship of Mithra, the harbinger of light and the divine protector of covenants that keep the world from falling into chaos. In their Islamic forms, while becoming less class-based, *javānmardi* cults maintained their hierarchical relations, forms of training and codes of conduct. They, thus, evolved to produce codes for all men, with ideals that determine the hegemonic forms of masculinity in popular culture. Despite the positive virtues that these codes endeavour to inculcate in boys from a young age along a desire for physical self-improvement, they have two major failures. One is the intense rivalry they create among men, which means that those failing to achieve their ideals may become bitter and end up acting as hooligans and use their skills to serve opportunistic goals or bully the people the weaker people. The second is that while the codes play positive roles in the education of young men, for an uncreative mind who is obsessed with surfaces, they may lead the tendency to berate others as not manly enough. Thus, as in other cultures with similar codes, men who may seem to fail such codes or pass the ultimate test of masculinity in exerting violence when necessary are denigrated as either dishonourable or feminine.⁵

While the original forms of Mithraic rituals in Iran remain disputed, the idea of acting along a group to prepare oneself physically and spiritually for preserving an ideal covenant or a system of value and purifying oneself by selfless dedication to serving people or a cause has continued in different forms with *khānqāh* and *zurkhāneh* as foremost examples. *Khānqāh* (the dwelling place) is where the initiates and practitioners of a Sufi cult 'meet, reside, study, and assemble and pray together as a group in the presence of a Sufi master [...], who is teacher, educator, and leader of the group'.⁶ It is also where the members perform rituals and engage in debates on correct conducts in specific situations and where Sufi wayfarers or warriors from associated cults reside while traveling. *Zurkhāneh* (the house of strength), however, is where traditional martial arts are practised with the outmost attention to codes of honour. Both spaces have played vital roles in shaping the ideals of heroism in Iran, but since the Safavid era *zurkhāneh* has played more roles in defining the status of a person who achieves the position of pahlevān.

The first point to consider when examining *zurkhāneh* culture is that its ranks bear similarities to those of Mithraic hierarchies. These include (1) *nocheh* (novice, a trainee who has just joined *zurkhāneh*), (2) *nokhāsteh* (a newly rising novice of good wrestling ability ready for initiation), (3) *pahlevān* (hero/champion, a young man who has been initiated due to his character and skills in all *zurkhāneh* exercises), (4) *kohneh-savār* (veteran rider, an established pahlevān with unique wrestling skills), (5) *pishkesvat* (a senior pahlevān with an established reputation as a trainer and guide), (6) *sāheb zang* (a senior pahlevān for whom the bells are sounded whenever he arrives at the *Zurkhāneh*), (7) *sāheb zarb* (a senior pahlevān, a *pir* who acts as a consultant in all matters and for whom the bell and the drum are sounded when he enters the *zurkhāneh*). Among these ranks, the four in the middle – *nokhāsteh, pahlevān, kohneh-savār* and *pishkesvat* – are the ones whose strength and fighting skills play major roles in society. This is particularly the case with the pahlevān who must be in his prime, probably between twenty-five and forty, and function as a major wrestler/fighter and a role model for the initiates while fulfilling important feats of physical and military bravery in defence of people or the cult.[7]

Beyzaie's engagement with the subject

Beyzaie's engagement with the ideals of heroism commenced due to his consciousness of the social roles that *javānmardi* cults had played in Iranian history and the wrong take that Iranian cinema had begun to take by depicting streetwise tough guys as heroes. This was important as such forces can be used to oppress the weak and the marginalized or defend them against exclusionist centres of power. The roles played by Iranian Mithraic, *ayyāri* and *javānmardi* cults in the rise of several dynasties, including the Parthians, Abbasids, Safarids, Sarbedars and Safavids, indicate how this level of group dedication and training and the members' aspiration for rising in ranks generate socio-political, military, economic and cultural power. The same can be observed in how the adoption of Mithraic beliefs, ranks and rituals by Roman civil and military officials played major influences on the formation of chivalry and later freemason cults that had tremendous influence on political and cultural change in Europe.[8] Like any form of power, however, the power generated by such cults can serve people or tyrannical systems. They can also be liberating to a group of people but suppressive to others, particularly if they fail to transcend their cultic origins when they achieve higher forms of power. Their obsession with obeying a master also perpetuates the worst forms of patriarchy in which women's roles in society are underrated, and the decisions of one man are valued above the wisdom of the group and the lives of the people most affected by his decisions.[9]

Beyzaie places his hero, an intellectually gifted and physically strong victim of marginalization, at the nexus of mutually exclusive systems of value in a corrupt society. He then analyses his psychological status through multi-layered dialogues and soliloquies and a sublime use of the double and concludes that fulfilling the ideals of heroism in Iran leads to nothing but death. Beyzaie states that from an early age he was fascinated with finding who heroes were and why and how they became heroes, and that by the time he was twenty he had learned a lot about *javānmardi* and *zurkhāneh* traditions and speech forms due to his cousin's research on the subject.[10]

However, as specified in my chapter on *Ārash*, his first creative engagement with the ideals of heroism was triggered by Kasraei's *Ārash the Archer* as he knew that, unlike what happens in the poem, a hero's relationship with his people was often wrought by conflicts.[11] He, thus, wrote *Ārash*, in which, like all Beyzaie's early heroes, the protagonist is a victim and although his essential goodness and despair turn him into a semi-divine hero, his achievement is useless as it only perpetuates people's obsession with saviours. His puppet plays were also similar in that, though using folk tales instead of myths, they focused on how the puppets aspire to achieve agency when the hero, himself a victim of social pressures, discovers that the demon is an oppressed man whose status is the result of the demonizing narratives of dominant discourses.

With *Pahlevān Akbar*, however, Beyzaie brought this vision to the modern cults of *zurkhāneh* wrestlers by mixing the idealized accounts of Iranian wrestler, mystic and poet Puriyā-ye Vali (1255–1322) with a name reminiscent, but not reflective of the last wrestling champion of the nineteenth century, Pahlevān Akbar Khorasāni (1850–1904).[12] He also subverted the classical idea of born heroes by showing that though some people may be born with unique mental or physical qualities, they become heroes only when they sublimate their anger after suffering ostracization or being placed in tight corners that transform their identity.

The writing circumstances of the play may also offer a key to its discourse on heroism. Having been transferred to the office of theatre from the notary office, where he was employed as a clerk, Beyzaie was asked by his colleague, Ali Nassirian (1935–), who had read his puppet plays, to write a one-act play on Puriyā-ye Vali, which Nassirian promised to perform for the national television. The result, however, was a full-length tragedy that had affinities with Hedayat's *Dāsh Ākol* (1932), Nassirian's *Af'ei-ye Talāei* (*Golden Viper*, 1957) and Puriyā-ye Vali's tale but was more in line with his own puppet plays. It was as if Pahlevān of the puppet plays had been placed in a realistic setting that replaced the timeless vicious circles of magical folk tales with a pre-moment of the present and uncanny motifs that allegorized the history of the present.

Another play with a similar subject that Beyzaie may have seen at the time was Bahman Forsi's *Chub-e Zir-e Baghal* (*Crutches*, 1963). However, whereas Beyzaie was more concerned with the processes that produce and crush a hero and determine the triangular relationship of the hero with the state and the people, Forsi focused on questioning the romantic glorification of ancient Iran and a people's need for heroes. This focus is evident in Forsi's central symbol, a chain with one side stretched to the sky in a ruined *zurkhāneh*. Forsi's semi-absurdist vision shows how when people need a hero, they pull the chain to evoke him but concludes that with the arrival of a paralysed Rostam-like hero who walks with crutches, things may change. Forsi, thus, depicts a society in which people resort to glorifying their spectacular past or heroes because they are unable to face the disastrous present. Beyzaie reflects on hero worship and the failures of the present, but he also reformulates mythic motifs of heroism to restructure them for generating new meanings and new forms of looking at the self and the other.

As Hedayat's story and Nasiriān's and Forsi's plays suggest, Beyzaie was not the first or the only author to explore the subject from a modern perspective. However, while his tragic vision was as psychologically penetrating as Hedayat's *Dāsh Ākol* and his criticism of hero worship was as strong as Forsi's, his play also commented on the pitfalls of heroism in a despotic, exclusionist society. This was a corrective discourse as many tough guys who claimed to embody *javānmardi* ideals in the twentieth century participated in suppressing the street fights of the 1953 coup and from 1958 mainstream Iranian cinema became obsessed with depicting such tough guys as protagonists. Known as *dāsh*, *luti* and *kolāh makhmali* (fedora hat guys) or negatively as *lāt* (thug) or *jāhel* (hooligan), these tough guys had found their way into plays, novels and films since the 1910s with such early examples as Ahmad Mahmoudi's *Ustā Nowruz Pineh Duz* (Master Nowruz, the Cobbler, 1919) where they are depicted as thugs. A turning point, however, occurred with Hossein Madani's comic novel *Esmāl dar New York* (Esmāeil in New York, 1953–4) which allowed the type to evolve into a protagonist and enter Iranian cinema in 1958. At first, as in Majid Mohseni's melodramatic film *Lāt-e Javānmard* (*Chivalrous Lout*, 1958) or Farrokh Ghaffary's bitterly realistic *Jonub-e Shahr* (*South of the City*, 1958), such depictions had potential for modernizing and educating a type that immense presence in the public space. Once the type was adopted by cinema, however, it degenerated in films that were obsessed with cheap entertainment to produce two major types: (1) the fedora hat tough guy who reflected the qualities of pahlevāns and (2) the honourable happy-go-lucky clever type who reflected the features of Robinhood-like *ayyārs*.[13] In time with the publication of works such as Beyzaie's pahlevān-centred plays (1960–3) and Sadeq Chubak's *Tangsir* (Tight Corner 1963), three new types found their ways to cinema. These included (1) pahlevāns and *ayyārs* themselves, (2) marginalized city tough guys facing who rebelled and were crushed by unscrupulous lower- or upper-class rivals, (3) and rebellious village types fighting against corrupt elites.[14] All the new types were influenced by Beyzaie's plays in that rather than saving the day and getting the girl, their protagonists came to tragic ends. In other words, the success of Beyzaie's play opened Iranian cinema to cases of unfulfilled love and tragic ends.

What was also new in Beyzaie was that the ideal types were no longer there, or if they were, they were very different from the tough guys of mainstream cinema or the opportunistic thugs who went against the will of people during the coup. For him, such a hero would side with the people rather than the suppressive elites and thus would have no chance of survival. This approach was also corrective in that it reconfigured an ideal mirror that displayed the failures of contemporary tough guys to them in a language that was poetic but understandable to them as it was rooted in the registers that had been enriched by *javānmardi* cults.

So Dies Pahlevān Akbar: *The hero of the imaginal, the imaginary and the real*

So Dies Pahlevān Akbar or *Pahlevān Akbar Dies* has an enigmatic title which suggests Beyzaie's fascination with the ever-recurring time in theatre and a *ta'ziyeh*-like tragic vision depicting the suffering and death of a protector of the poor and the marginalized. The play concerns a pahlevān's death but instead of using 'death of' or only the protagonist's name as in classical tragedies, Beyzaie uses the concept in its verb form and in a tense that highlights constant as well as current occurrence. Thus, marking Pahlevān Akbar as a hero of the poor rather than the lords, the play conjures his passion for loneliness and dying like a recurrent phenomenon. Indeed, the sentence 'Pahlevān Akbar Mimirad' has three senses in Persian: (1) Pahlevān Akbar dies, (2) Pahlevān Akbar is dying and (3) Pahlevān Akbar will die. The timeless presence suggested by the title is important as it implies a *ta'ziyeh* – or *naqqāli*-like evocation of the imaginal, the nowhere land of collective memory where the heroes of the past await to be reimagined as role models. The play also, however, goes on to present what had never been seen on the Iranian stage, the internal turmoil and fears of a hero, and expand the sense of the title by showing how such a hero always dies, is dying now and will die in the future.

The first extant reformulations of the imaginal after Islam occur in the *Shāhnāmeh* narratives which refer to the myths of Kaykhosrow vanishing into an unseen realm or the ever-existing, invisible utopias, Jamshid's *Vara* (*Varjamkard*) and Siyāvush's *Gang Dezh*, which are inhabited by the pure paladins who are to accompany the savior.[15] Its first mystic elaboration, however, occurs in Shahabuddin Sohravardi's (1154–91) idea of *Nā-Kojā-Ābād* (Nowhere-Land). The idea, which has influenced the Shi'i beliefs in the occulting Twelfth Imam and the ever-presence of Karbala martyrs and other religious figures in an unseen world,[16] occurs in *Aql-e Sorkh* (Crimsoned Archangel/Red Reason) and *Sedā-ye Āvāz-e Par-e Jebreil* (Rustlings of Gabriel's Wings). In these parables, a stranger from the unknown, 'the imaginal' appears to guide the narrator on a journey of self-discovery.[17] The concept of *Nā-Kojā-Ābād* was first introduced into Euro-American scholarship on Iran by Henry Corbin in his 1964's writings on Sohravardi, whom he celebrated as the 'reviver of the theosophy of ancient Persia in Islamic Iran'. Corbin combined the terms 'Image' and 'Original' to discuss *Ālam-e Mesāli* (Mundus Imaginalis/the world of ideas) as an order of reality – also referred to as *Eqlim-e Hashtom* (the eighth climate) or *Nā-Kojā-Ābād* – which transcends the mundane but is not imaginary. In his analysis of *Aql-e Sorkh*, Corbin refers to a person meeting a 'stranger', 'the world's first born', from 'the land of nowhere' who speaks of going on a journey to the world beyond Mount Qāf. The journey always ends where it starts but leads to a sublimated consciousness due to which the individual becomes a 'stranger' to his former self. This journey 'is a matter of entering, passing into the interior and, in passing into the interior, of finding oneself, paradoxically, outside, or, in the language of our authors, "on the convex surface" of the Ninth Sphere – in other words, "beyond the mountain of Qaf"'. Corbin then extracts a definition for a realm of 'spiritual reality' in Iranian conceptualization of the world 'that envelops, surrounds, [and] contains the reality called material'.[18] He specifies that the 'function of the mundus imaginalis and the Imaginal Forms', is reflected in 'their median and mediating situation between the intellectual and sensible worlds', where it 'immaterialises the Sensible Forms, and "imaginalises" the Intellectual Forms to which it gives shape and dimension'.[19]

Whether interpreted metaphorically or literally and religiously, Iranian tales and performing traditions project the idea of this ever-present realm in which the ideal heroes await to be reinterpreted or resurrected. In this light, Beyzaie's play is the locus in which the formation and fate of a single pahlevān and the embodied ideal of sacrificial *pahlevāni* merge to reflect how he becomes a hero due to his determination to transcend his marginalization and how he is doomed to suffer and die due to the elite's tyranny and people's apathy or opportunism.

The hero in his cultural context

The play begins with an image of dilapidation, a traditional arched alley with a collapsed arched roof and abandoned houses and shops, a stone lion facing the audience and a religiously decorated *saqqākhāneh* (a shrine with a water dispensary). Then, an old woman's despair is juxtaposed with Pahlevān's graceful care. Passing the shrine, Pahlevān notices Mother praying and throws her a coin. His dialogue with the Wine-seller about having wine and playing the *tār* (long-necked, waisted lute) evokes the idea of fighting and feasting (*razm o bazm*) in epics or its comic renditions in the attitudes of such figures as Pahlevān Kachal (bald hero) in puppet plays.[20] Before Pahlevān enters the shop, however, the play foreshadows disaster: 'Mother collapses on her knees. Pahlevān who turns to look at her sees Black Wearing Man crossing the end of the alley. Wine-seller, who hears the laughter of two people [watchmen] looks outside worried.'[21] Beyzaie's stage directions continue to introduce these sinister sounds and images as Pahlevān tries to relax with a glass of wine and music before his wrestling match the next day. With Wine-seller as a confidant, the dialogue specifies that Pahlevān grew up among nomads and learned to play the *tar* from a shepherd. Beyzaie uses such references and Pahlevān's soliloquies about being lost in childhood and his loss of love and ostracization by the nomadic tribe to link Pahlevān to the periphery rather than the centre. This is not unique as in Iran's myths and folk tales, the periphery rather than the centre, the son rather than the father and the youngest rather than the oldest son are often the most honourable.[22] This also allows Beyzaie to associate Pahlevān with the image of the lost, marginalized child in a quest for a home and the lonely stranger in an unsympathetic milieu which later became central in his works.[23]

The two watchmen then appear to fulfil the governor's order and extort money from Wine-seller, but seeing Pahlevān, they disappear, upset that his return may disturb their plans. It is, thus, implied that the alley's ruined state is due to the state's corruption and the watchmen are the state's instruments of tyranny, two of the many heads of a hoarding dragon. This is reinforced by the fertility motifs that associate Pahlevān with the shrine's water and fire/light (candles) and the way he reacts to Mother's plea to the god as if he embodies divine intervention. Rather than suggesting arrogance, his reaction signifies his urgent sense of providing hope in a cruel world as his identity has evolved in terms of suffering to make others happy. Mother's prayer at the shrine, which carries the motifs associated with Mithra (the fire and light of prayer candles and the lion) and Anahita (the water), creates a Mithraic ambiance, in which Pahlevān, as a Mithraic upholder of the pledge for protecting the weak and a guarantor of fertility, feels he must respond to Mother's prayers. In pre-Islamic Iran, Mithra, the god invoked in chivalric cults, was the protector of oath, covenant, harvest, pastures and cattle, and Anahita, who was invoked to grant victory, was the goddess of rivers and fertility.[24] Wine-seller's indication that the shrine was a 'fire temple in the past' (187) asserts this point while also echoing Beyzaie's analysis of a similar form of repurposing in his discussion of Sultan Ali temple in Ardahāl.

> One reason I believe this shrine is a Mithraic temple is the existence of yet another shrine very close to it which nobody speaks about. Whatever its name, from what I have seen, it is a female shrine, which is significant as in many cases the temples of Mithra and Anahita were built in the proximity of each other.[25]

The juxtaposition of these motifs with the watchmen's attitude mythologizes the clash between the forces of corruption and prosperity and removes the layers of Islamic symbolism to indicate the agricultural origins of Iranian heroic ideals. The music and wine motifs also highlight that Pahlevān's compassion is beyond religious morality which is often marred by hypocrisy or the trading approach in which good deeds are done to obtain a place in paradise.

Pahlevān then leaves the shop with his *tār* while making a meta-theatrical reference to going to see a puppet show. These words echo his earlier references to his nomadic upbringing and remind the audience that Iranian puppet shows originated among nomads and gypsies.[26] The *tār* and wine are also central motifs in the puppet plays on Pahlevān Kachal's misadventures with hypocritical elites.[27] This relaxed mood, however, is again counterpointed with another sinister tableau in which he sees 'Black Wearing Man standing still on the edge of darkness with an unsheathed machete' (189). This Kafkaesque presence may be interpreted existentially as an expressionistic embodiment of death in Pahlevān's mind, mythically as Ahriman, the epitome of evil, or socio-politically as an assassin or threat of death for a marginalized or dissenting figure living under religious, cultural or political suppression.[28]

Pahlevān's conversation with Mother propels the plot to its rising action. He gives her water while uttering the phrase, 'water brings light', which finds a transcendental meaning in this context. The ensuing dialogue reworks the legend of the old mother and Puriyā-ye Vali. Mother lost a son in a journey thirty years ago, and now his second son, Pahlevān Heidar is to wrestle with the renowned Pahlevān Akbar to fulfil a condition set by his future bride's foster-father, the ruler Khan Beik. Referring to himself in the third person, Pahlevān calms her by promising that 'Akbar' will not kill her son. He then challenges himself in a soliloquy to accept defeat to make her happy and reveals his past and inner conflicts to the audience. Pahlevān's reference to himself in the third person when talking to others and in the second person when talking to himself is interesting. Here, his use of the third person is to avoid terrifying Mother, but on other occasions, it signifies his modesty in refusing to use 'I' when it may sound like bragging. At its existential level, however, it implies a separation between his vision of his innermost self as a lost, lonely boy called Akbar, and the indomitable Pahlevān that others see. His soliloquy also signifies that he thinks he may be Mother's older son because as a child he was lost when travelling with a caravan, and he knows that he may be killed by the phantom-like assassin, who may have been employed by the Khan. Beyzaie, thus, highlights the inner conflicts of a type whose mask of bravado makes people neglect his psychological needs and exposes him to risks posed by both the elites and the enemies of his people. This hero is as much a victim as a scapegoat.

When Mother asks him to warn Pahlevān Akbar against the phantom, he insists that Pahlevān Akbar is not afraid of such things.

> **Pahlevān:** It has been a while now. Someone follows him like a shadow – maybe a man – maybe he has been paid a thousand, two thousand, five thousand gold coins! Do you see that stone lion Mother?
> **Mother:** Yes, Sir.
> **Pahlevān:** How many of these have you seen in the town?
> **Mother:** Many, Sir.
> **Pahlevān:** You may not know Mother, but under each of them a *Pahlevun* is lying dead![29] It's not worth it; this world is not worth any of the things it gives you.
> **Mother:** That man, the one who wants to kill –. Sir, how do you know? Are you a friend of *Pahlevun*?
> **Pahlevān:** No, Mother; *Pahlevun* is my enemy.
> **Mother:** Tell him not to come out of his home!
> **Pahlevān:** [Angry] *Pahlevun* Akbar is not afraid of such things! [Controlling himself] Anyhow; which home?
> **Mother:** What do you mean, Sir? Doesn't he have a home? A house, family, wife, mother – ?
> **Pahlevān:** Let it be, Mother! Tomorrow your son will be honoured!
> **Mother:** How do you know, Sir?
> **Pahlevān:** You prayed for him. There's no one to pray for *Pahlevun* Akbar.
> (191–2)

Pahlevān Akbar, therefore, is characterized by complex familial, socio-political, psychological and existential relations. Viewing his 'Pahlevun' identity as his enemy, he is determined to lose to end the absurd game of public honour in a conflict that may bring happiness to another person. His identification with Mother's lost son also highlights childhood trauma as the root of his quest for belonging through recognition and its inevitable outcome, sacrificial heroism. As in his puppet trilogy, therefore, Beyzaie gives depth to the type and implies that his inner conflict for subduing his urge for glory is more important than his heroic acts. He, thus, reformulates the genre of heroic tales by reframing the folk tale of Puriyā-ye Vali and adding socio-political and psychological details that offer modern perspectives about life in a violent surveillance society. In this regard, the play's title and the juxtaposition of Pahlevān's carefree appearance and his sense of duty to confront the evil inside and around him create a sense of doom, which presages a tragic end for the hero and the community in which he lives.

The poetic uncanny, the double and the sublime

While contemplating his decision, Pahlevān is greeted by the two watchmen. He then asks Wine-seller to give him a mirror, which triggers an uncanny scene. Surprised by what he sees in the mirror, he asks Wine-seller to give him a real mirror:

> **Wine-seller:** Why, what do you see in this mirror, *Pahlevun*?
> **Pahlevān:** Something which is not me! I see a man in black, whose face is covered, a man with a machete, a sharp machete, in his hand. Why does the mirror show this … ?
> **Wine-seller:** Because he is there.[Pahlevān quickly turns; but Black Wearing Man has disappeared.]
> **Pahlevān:** Where?
> **Wine-seller:** What?
> **Pahlevān:** You said he is there.
> **Wine-seller:** I saw nothing; but when the mirror shows something, it must be there.
> **Pahlevān:** [To himself.] Then he is there.
> **Wine-seller:** [Curious.] Who is there, *Pahlevun*?
> **Pahlevān:** [Jokingly] An old drinking pal.
> **Wine-seller:** Why doesn't he join us?
> **Pahlevān:** [Growling.] He's waiting!
> **Wine-seller:** Waiting for what?
> **Pahlevān:** [Turning his head] I don't know; I don't!
> **Wine-seller:** Are you sure you saw something, *Pahlevun*?
> **Pahlevān:** [Distracted.] What?
> **Wine-seller:** Maybe, you imagined him.
> **Pahlevān:** Maybe, maybe –
> **Wine-seller:** Why maybe? Have you seen it a lot?
> **Pahlevān:** [He sets off determined.] I should find him – [He stops.] which way? (195)

The disturbing appearing and disappearing of the phantom-like entity suggest that, at one level, he is Pahlevān's double, his self-resenting Mr Hyde, whose presence implies Pahlevān's frustration with his identity. He has suppressed his desire for belonging with hard work directed towards gaining recognition to prove his worth.

However, living in an unsympathetic society with corrupt officials, dogmatic clerics and people who swing between opportunism and passivity, he has remained an outsider who maintains his sanity by helping the poor. His unfulfilled dreams of belonging, therefore, have been twisted by a nightmarish process of 'condensation, displacement and secondary revision' to produce a murderous double.[30] In this context, Sigmund Freud's idea of '*unheimlich*' (the uncanny) is enlightening:

> The theme of the 'double' has been very thoroughly treated by Otto Rank (1914). He has gone into the connections which the 'double' has with reflections in mirrors, with shadows, with guardian spirits, with the belief in the soul and with the fear of death; but he also lets in a flood of light on the surprising evolution of the idea. For the 'double' was originally an insurance against the destruction of the ego, an 'energetic denial of the power of death', as Rank says; and probably the 'immortal' soul was the first 'double' of the body. This invention of doubling as preservation against extinction has its counterpart in the language of dreams, which is fond of representing castration by a doubling or multiplication of a genital symbol. The same desire led the ancient Egyptians to develop the art of making images of the dead in lasting materials. Such ideas […] have sprung from the soil of unbounded self-love, from the primary narcissism which dominates the mind of the child and of primitive man. But when this stage has been surmounted, the 'double' reverses its aspect. From having been an assurance of immortality, it becomes the uncanny harbinger of death […] A special agency is slowly formed there [from and in the ego], which is able to stand against the rest of the ego, which has the function of observing and of exercising a censorship within the mind, and which we become aware of as our 'conscience'.[31]

Freud then links the transformation of the idea of 'the double' to 'the pathological case of delusions of being constantly watched', in which 'this mental agency becomes isolated, dissociated from the ego and discernible to the physician's eye'. The 'double' then becomes a deadly force that stops the ego from wanting more and having its wishes fulfilled. It functions in the exact opposite way of its early primitive function and becomes 'a thing of terror, just as, after the collapse of their religion the gods turned into demons'.[32] Thus, at one level, Pahlevān's shadow or double embodies his suppressed inferiority complex which, emanating from his feeling of being unwanted, has materialized as a hostile spectre that undermines his happiness. At another level, however, whereas his id or life force drives him to survive, conquer and procreate, the god-turned-demon of his superego undermines his desire for life by triggering his death wish which appears as an executioner that is to relieve him of his guilt complex.

In aesthetics, the origin of the discussions about terror goes back to the distinctions that creative authors and philosophers make between the beautiful and the astounding and their later association under a single system in Edmund Burke's writings on the sublime, which were later expanded by Immanuel Kant. For Burke, awed astonishment is central to any expression of admiration and perception of beauty, and thus 'terror is in all cases whatsoever, either more openly or latently the ruling principle of the sublime'.³³ Though somewhat restricting in its definition, Burke's definition reflects the concurrent popularity of gothic novels in which terror was the dominant mode of the sublime. Nevertheless, it is undeniable that awe and terror are among the main components of the sublime, particularly because, as Kant explains, the moment of the sublime occurs when the mind rejoices in its safety while being exposed to the overwhelming power of nature or the unknown or when it comprehends the specifics of what was feared or seemed inexplicable, unpresentable or beyond human control.³⁴

Beyzaie has stated that Black Wearing Man is 'the hidden self, the unknown side to whom we have no access and most probably we never understand'.³⁵ This confirms his awareness of how self-resentment and death wish transform everything into a threat. Later, in *Maybe Some Other Time*, in which his priority was to make a film that no one could ban, he took this from expressionist nightmares to realistic explanations. Here, however, the play is concerned with the double as the force that censures the hero's desire for self-aggrandizement for being a tough wrestling scarecrow used by the puppeteers of power to ruin other people's happiness.

The use of the double, however, also allows Beyzaie to introduce a political level as Black Wearing Man may simply be an assassin hired by the state to annul Pahlevān's threat to their plans. Beyzaie's hero, like many talented individuals who join a system to control its tyranny, has accepted the title of the city's champion to play a role in curbing the ruler's power over people. Now, however, realizing that the system is beyond reform, he feels he must exit the game of power that requires him to compete as the city's champion. Pahlevān has, thus, reached a state of maturity in which his double is no longer propelling him forward for recognition but requires him to control his desires and subvert his identity as the subservient champion of the city. This is, of course, partly because he has no one to fight for, yet his shadow is also a thing of terror as it calls for self-sacrifice and death as the path to controlling the self. At first, he feels that he can resolve the issue by losing or leaving, but his meeting with his spiritual master reminds him that *javānmardi* codes require him not to escape from a match or dishonour his rival by intentionally losing. This makes his dilemma impossible to manage, but it also suggests how *javānmardi* codes may crush an individual in a tyrannical system.

Beyzaie's use of soliloquies and asides allows him to reflect Pahlevān's interior monologue which highlights his memories of loss and subsequent fear of intimacy and abandonment while reflecting the frightening tangibility of human existential angst. The audience, thus, alternates between existential and political terror and the bitter intellectual satisfaction of realizing that the threatening figure may be a hallucination born from the hero's psychological ambivalence.

Another way to approach this aspect of the play is through Tzvetan Todorov's idea of 'the fantastic'. Todorov defines this concept as the 'hesitation [...] experienced by a person who knows only the laws of nature', when 'confronting an apparently supernatural event'.³⁶ Then while expounding the characteristics of the fantastic, he adds:

The fantastic requires the fulfilment of three conditions. First, the text must oblige the reader to consider the world of the characters as a world of living persons and to hesitate between a natural or supernatural explanation of the events described. Second, this hesitation may also be experienced by a character; thus the reader's role is [...] entrusted to a character, and at the same time the hesitation is represented, it becomes one of the themes of the work – in the case of naive reading, the actual reader identifies himself with the character. Third, the reader must adopt a certain attitude with regard to the text: he will reject allegorical as well as 'poetic' interpretations.[37]

Todorov distinguishes 'the fantastic' from 'the uncanny' and 'the marvellous' by specifying that the latter two eventually provide the reader/audience with a resolution. The uncanny ultimately grounds itself in the natural law and 'the marvellous' in the supernatural.

Beyzaie's dramatic use of the double, as in other cases around the globe, has its origin in folk tales. In Iranian popular lore, there are numerous tales and directives about how to treat, talk to or capture one's *hamzād* (the double), who is sometimes referred to as a jinni, and how to avoid making it angry. In Sufi traditions, depression and loneliness trigger the appearance of the double, a part of the self, which is at first frightening but is then accepted as a confidant. There is, however, always the danger of becoming obsessed with the double, which leads one to behave in a disoriented way as one considers conversing with one's double more important than communicating with others.[38] Prior to Beyzaie, the foremost examples of using the double in modern Persian literature were in Sadeq Hedayat's oeuvre. This is evident in *Arusak-e Posht-e Pardeh* (The Doll behind the Curtain, 1933), *Shabhā-ye Varāmin* (Varāmin's Nights, 1933) and even *Dāsh Ākol* (Tough Guy Ākol, 1932) where Kākā Rostam acts like a double that kills Dāsh Ākol with Dāsh's own machete. In these stories, the action is external and suggests a nightmarish process of displacement and replacement in heroes whose mental states prevent them from functioning coherently in the real world. In his *Seh Qatreh Khun* (Three Drops of Blood, 1932) and *Buf-e Kur* (The Blind Owl, 1936), however, the parallel narrative worlds seem to be projections of the activities of the narrator's doubles acting on his behalf to fulfil his nightmares or dreams. Beyzaie's use of the double is like the first type, but by focusing on Pahlevān's spiritual anguish, he also creates a bridge between external heroism – those who fight the enemies – and the internal ones – those who confront their own desires.

The physical, the spiritual and the political

One of the anomalies of Iranian medieval literature is the shift from the centrality of external heroism in the epics of the tenth and eleventh centuries to spiritual heroism in the later mystic literature in which the real hero is the one who controls his desire for grandeur. As some scholars argue, this sounds as if a worldly system of heroism was replaced by an otherworldly one.[39] An oversimplified interpretation of this shift may conclude that the defeats that Iranians suffered during Turkic and Mongol invasions of the eleventh to fifteenth century led to the suppression of external heroism in poetry, if not in Iranian socio-political life. However, one must remember that Iranian epics feature heroes who combine physical bravado with spiritual profundities, such as Fereydun, Iraj, Siyāvush, Key Khosrow and Zarir, and self-searching or intellectual ones such as Zāl, Pirān, Gudarz and even Rostam. Furthermore, the tenets of post-Islamic *javānmardi* cults which influenced the reformulation of the Sistān Cycle in the ninth century, included ethical directives for both the intellectual elites and the warriors.[40]

The rise in the glorification of spiritual heroism, therefore, was partly due to the prevalence of despair in society and partly as a proactive method to curb the new rulers' desire to display their bravado which meant killing more Iranians or waging more wars. It was also partly because the resources of Iranian epics had been exhausted and 'anxiety of influence' urged leading poets to look for new subjects and modes of speech.[41] The composition of epic-like tales and romances, therefore, became the task of folk writers who also wrote on religious figures such as Imam Ali (600–61), antinomian mystics such as Mansur-e Hallaj (858–922) or Bāyazid Bastāmi (804–78) and folk heroes such as Abu Moslem, Amir Hamzeh and Puriyā-ye Vali, whose physical bravery and practical morality linked them to *ayyārs* and *javānmards*. Folk mystics, on the other hand, wrote codes of conduct (Fotovvat-Nāmeh) for the youth and craftsmen whose power and skills they could use to fulfil their aims or resist their political or religious rivals.[42] Thus, from the earliest Islamic tales such as the ones on Abu Moslem (718–55), physical and spiritual heroism became more linked with Sufism and evolved with mystics and folk writers creating a discourse that became more spiritual from the eleventh century. Beyzaie made extensive use of secular *ayyāri* tales in his later screenplays, but here he focused on the psychology of hesitation and ethical ambivalence and pitfalls of physical heroism. Thus, Pahlevān's soul-searching journey also summarizes the history of Iranian heroism.

This spiritual aspect evolves after Pahlevān's dialogue with Mother. No longer worried about winning, he now returns to the wine shop to bury himself in ruminations about who he is and whether he is Mother's lost son. Beyzaie yokes the motifs of soul-searching identity crisis and altruism to those of marginalization to suggest that, as in Pahlevān's case, only those who have suffered marginalization are capable of sacrificial altruism. Yet he also highlights the woes of religious minorities in Iran. As in pre-modern Iran, Wine-seller is from a religious minority, a Zoroastrian; but though his people have lived near the shrine for centuries, the state treats him like an unwelcome stranger. Their excuse is that his business is religiously forbidden, but the governor's real plan is to confiscate and demolish the whole district to build an arsenal. In Beyzaie's world, such juxtapositions between *zāher va bāten* (the apparent and the real) are central to his depiction of the hypocrisy of the clergy who use the elites' or people's greed or ignorance to ostracize minorities or the elites' use of religion to confiscate people's properties. At its political level, this reflects the state's approach to rapid modernization in the 1950s and 1960s, when the vestiges of the past were being demolished to fulfil the state's Westernization and militarization plans both before and after the breach of the ties between the state and extremist ulama in 1963. This is the era in which the state used oil revenues to assume the role of the Gendarme of the Middle East while appeasing the clergy by limiting the employment of religious minorities in high positions. Thus, in line with its non-democratic ideology, which insisted on modernizing Iran with West-inspired institutions while adhering to a political vision inspired by ancient empires, it used anti-modern policies to fulfil its modernization plans.

Such politically suggestive references to the state of the marginalized or the marginalization of those who do not bend to the state are frequent in Beyzaie's plays, but except for *Four Boxes* (1967), they never take over the play. Thus, having made these political suggestions, Beyzaie takes the action back to its normal multi-layered course with Pahlevān's soliloquies and his dialogue with Wine-seller providing the poetically rendered backstory of his life.

The poetics of love, longing and belonging: Long Day's Journey into Night

In the scene after his encounter with Mother, Pahlevān's drunken reverie reaches a poetic point where he talks of a caravan of which only the bells' sound is heard. The phrase carries a subtle plurisignation. While connoting how the passage of time ushers in loss and death, it denotes the moment Akbar, a boy of about nine, fell behind the caravan of belonging and found himself lost and unwanted in a violent world. Beyzaie intensifies this moment with a Shakespearean comic relief that combines dramatic irony with a choral commentary on the apathy of the world to human misery: a blind character appears to talk passionately about the match and wish that Pahlevān will beat up the upstart. The use of this character is in line with Beyzaie's inclusion of disabled characters in his works. While displaying another aspect of his attention to the disenfranchised, this disabled character, particularly if a child, may see or do things that others fail to see or do.[43] The blind man's presence may, thus, suggest that the rest of the town are blind. At its opposite end, however, it may imply that people depend on hearsay rather than evidence about matters and those who support Pahlevān are unaware of his misery and unable to help him.[44] Yet, like all disabled people in Beyzaie's oeuvre, he supports the hero so keenly that Pahlevān begins to ruminate again about the absurdity of his life and the consequences of losing to Heidar. He asks Wine-seller for his best wine and sits next to the stone lion, thinking of going to see his spiritual guide and reminiscing about his nomadic life and his beloved.

Beyzaie's depiction of a tormented soul lost in reveries reflecting his desire for belonging in soliloquies and asides is stylistically reminiscent of Eugene O'Neill's autobiographical play *Long Day's Journey into Night* (1941, pub. 1956). Beyzaie had seen the play at the time, but he specifies that the performance he saw was too stilted to be inspirational and that it was much later that he saw a good performance of the play.[45] He may, of course, have liked O'Neill's treatment of some dramatic elements without liking the play, but it is more likely that because he and O'Neill were both inspired by Shakespeare's handling of objects as triggers for reveries, their depictions of the thoughts and feelings of their Hamlet-like characters became similar.

The world, characters and cultural codes that Beyzaie explores in his play are too Iranian to have anything to do with O'Neill's, but a comparative overview of these similarities may help my reader further clarify Beyzaie's use of such elements. In O'Neill's play, several objects and a small backroom function as triggers for the multi-layered dialogues and drunken or drug-induced reveries of the Tyrones. Their soliloquies reveal their inner conflicts, past or present illusions, self-defeating attempts for displaying their love for each other, and failure to feel belonged and happy. Similarly, Beyzaie's objects, be it a mirror or a *Tār*, remind Pahlevān of his failures and fears, and the shrine becomes a space for revealing dreams and worries as characters pray for divine intervention. Pahlevān's drunken soliloquies create the setting for reflecting the failures of an exclusionist culture, and the concentration of action in a few hours before a tragic end creates a momentum that comments on the fluidity of time in the mind and the multi-layered nature of human identity. In Beyzaie's play, however, while the desire for belonging and love is essential to the plot, the focus is not to show how addiction and familial or occupational failure produce vicious circles of hope and despair. It is rather to question a culture's obsession with heroes by depicting its impact on the best people of a society in which modern citizenship has been delayed due to elites' opportunism and people's ignorance.

The reveries of this scene are about love and belonging. The audience learns that after he was lost, Akbar was found by nomads, but he was never accepted. Thus, when he fell in love a few years later, the insinuations of the clan's leader's son about his being an unwanted child of impure blood led to his rejection by the girl and a conflict with the slanderer for which he was branded, ostracized and kicked out of the tribe (196–204). This motif is also augmented by an innovative theatrical effect. As if conjured by Pahlevān's thoughts about his beloved, a girl who is like the double of the nomad girl shows up at the shrine to pray for Heidar's victory.

> **Pahlevān:** In the nomad tents, it is now near the sunset: on the village crier's hill the sun is leaving, and the moon is arriving —
>
> [A girl enters the alley, looking just like the one Pahlevān is describing.]
>
> With a red skirt, yellow vest, her face like the day, her hair like the night in a long braid —
>
> [The girl stops in front of the shrine.]
>
> She turns on the lantern, opens her lips, and what does she say?
>
> **Girl:** […] I love Heidar! You know that; what can I say? You wanted it to happen; who am I to decide? — [Scared.] If they find out I've secretly come here! [Passionately holding to the bars of the shrine.] Stealthy under the eyes of so many ogling watchmen! — At every shrine I granted a candle for

your heavenly attention! Everywhere the flame quivered, the candle melted; and the smoke got into my eyes. [Suddenly.] By this alight fire, do not put out the light of our heart! If his back is soiled on the ground, if he's defeated, he'll never — [Crying.] He's fighting for me; don't let him lose his good reputation for me. Don't, don't ...
[Pahlevān, who has quietly departed and reached the end of the alley, turns left. A moment later Black Wearing Man crosses the alley following him. Girl is crying]
— Tell me what else I should do! How can I soften your heart? If he is defeated, it is not just a defeat; it is two! Tell me; you have the answer, the cure, only you know it, only you can help ...
[Wine-seller comes out of his shop with a jug of wine; notices that Akbar has gone, and a girl is crying at the shrine.]
Wine-seller: Cry, good girl; cry. There's no one to cry for Pahlevun Akbar. (203–5)

The appearance of girl at the shrine depicts one of the features of Iranian society where, in the absence of institutional venues for self-improvement or proper communication channels for lovers, prayer at shrines of saints plays a role in people's lives. Girl's emphasis on 'ogling watchmen' also highlights the strains of life in surveillance societies in which the clash of the self with disciplinary and exploiting forces that demand compromise distort the psychological process of individuation which generates authentic integrity rather than hypocritical bending to norms. Equally striking, however, is the poetry of Pahlevān's vision which contrasts the imagined and the real to highlight the clash of hope and despair as well as love and sacrificial honour in his mind. The imagery of water (Anahita), fire/light and lion (Mithra) also support the motifs that link Pahlevān to agricultural myths, and the red wine presages his Christ-like bleeding to death and proposes him as the sacrificial hero who must die to guarantee the fertility that may be evoked by the love and marriage of the youths (Figure 3.1).

The simultaneity of Pahlevān's vision of his beloved and the girl's arrival enriches a realistic scene with the dreamlike effect of a flashback to imply that he also loves Khan's foster daughter because she reminds him of his first beloved. However, these unfulfilled loves, once more, also allude to the mythical association of pahlevāns with heroes of fertility and sacrificial gods in agricultural myths.[46] At an archetypal level, therefore, the girl, who is trapped in Khan's house, is a deity of fertility, or perhaps Iran, in the grasp of a dragon-like usurper who hoards the resources of the land for selfish purposes rather than use them to facilitate prosperity. The match also signifies that this hoarder forces the two heroes of fertility, Akbar and Heidar, to fight each other rather than the usurping state. The energy that can be spent for prosperity is, thus, channelled to break one pahlevān and turn the other into a tool of tyranny.

Both occasions, however, also reflect on how the hierarchies of belonging and power function in different settings to ostracize unwanted practices and reinforce

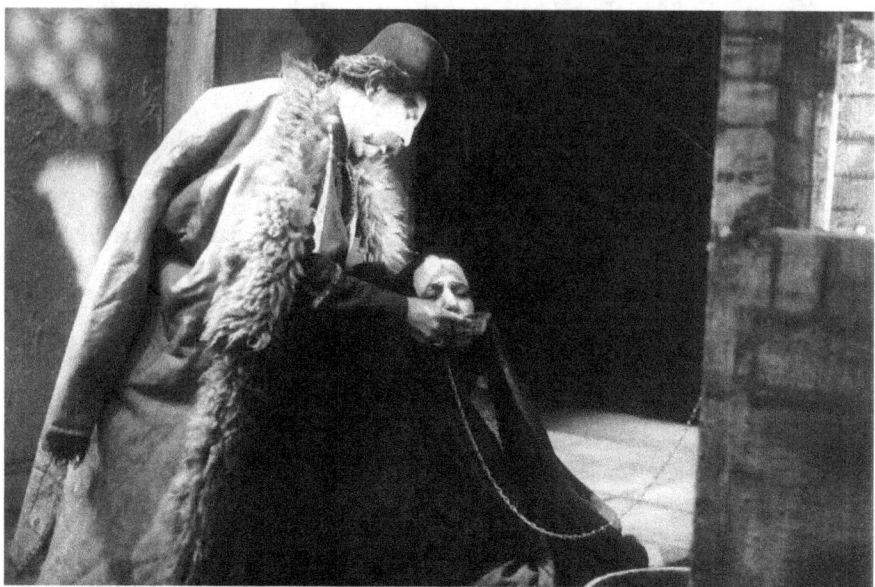

Figure 3.1 Pahlevān Akbar giving water to Mother and overhearing the girl praying for Heidar.[47]

the sadomasochistic chain of obeying the higher ranks and demanding obedience from the lower ranks. Thus, the relationship of strict fathers or mothers with their espouse and children or a tribal leader with his people, and people with people or even children with each other echo the same forms of religious, political, ethnic or aesthetic marginalization observed at national and international levels.

Dramatic recreation of ayyārs' vanishing discourse

The encounter reinforces Pahlevān's desire to lose, a subject which continues in Act 2 with Pahlevān Akbar's wrestling and spiritual master, Pahlevān Asad advising Heidar not to wrestle with Akbar. Mythologizing a strength that originates in hard work and despair, as Beyzaie had already done in *Ārash*, the dialogue reveals that Akbar's strength is beyond anything Heidar can imagine. Asad also reminds Heidar of a major pahlevāni code: it is not appropriate to challenge another pahlevān just to win a girl's hand. Having listed Akbar's global triumphs, Asad states: 'Not only here, but also in India, Iraq and Caucasia every suffering, yet honourable man names his son after him – why? Because his chivalry knows no limits; he's the protector of the oppressed! He has lots of friends but more enemies – tribal leaders, rulers, bailiffs, mullahs, military commanders!' (207). Thus, Beyzaie places Akbar in the same position as dissenting intellectuals, antinomian mystics and protective *ayyārs*. Yet he also uses motifs that echo the legend of Rostam and Esfandiyār in which two great heroes face each other because Esfandiyār's father has promised him he may assume kingship once Rostam is subdued and brought to the court. Esfandiyār aspires to be the king because he thinks he can create a better world, but the fates of those with such beliefs often differ from what they assume. This is because when heroes join a system to change it, as Esfandiyār does, the inherited violence of power relations turns them into tools of tyranny or embodiments of the system after it has slightly changed as if adapting for continuity.[48] Beyzaie, thus, mythologizes the conflict by reframing one of the most tragic clashes of Iranian mythology, in which two heroes face each other because one of them assumes that by becoming the hero of a system he can make it better.

> **Master:** I prefer to die rather than hear that you've become Khan Beig's mercenary.
> **Heidar:** Never.
> **Master:** He has a thousand hands, and every day a new one comes out of his sleeves. Watch that you don't become one of these hands. (209)

Beyzaie makes a distinction between two kinds of public figures. The first fights for his good name or a code of honour and confronts the centres of power to support people even if he is not appreciated. The second fights to gain advantages for himself or join the system with the dream of improving it but is ultimately used by the system as a tool of oppression. Heidar's insistence that Akbar was probably a slave also reveals that he has absorbed Khan Beig's master-slave discourse and is on the verge of becoming a tool of tyranny.

Master: I met him by accident; the year I was returning from your town. He had cleared the mountain passage of all murderous highwaymen.
Heidar: I saw a brand on his arm.
Master: His arms are full of hatred, his heart full of compassion! It's strange; he never said where he was coming from and didn't know where he was going! I brought him here; send him to the wrestling pitch!
Heidar: In the pitch, is it his hatful arms that fight or his compassionate heart?
Master: This against that – that against this. He's always fought; sometimes in the wrestling pitch, mostly outside. He has taken with one hand and given with the other; you may ask what has he taken? He has taken back what belongs to the poor from those who have had the power to take it! What's he given? *Whatever he has taken! He has strange habits and attitudes; he did not accept the state salary for his championship.*
Heidar: I have heard it.
Master: And – at nights he sleeps in the dove house.
Heidar: Yea? – but the armband of championship does not hide the brand on his arm.
Master: These are not your words. You are the son of Pahlevun Avaz!
Heidar: Why not? Don't you see that there is only one night to Heidar's tomorrow?
Master: All right – so are your bad words to push away your fear?
Heidar: Now, you're being unkind.
Master: Of course, you're not afraid of your opponent; but you're afraid that the whole thing may be a mistake; yes, of what comes afterwards! For whom are you going to sharpen and brandish your machete; for those on the top or the ones in the pits? Is it possible to be Khan Beig's son-in-law and not serve him? (209–10)

The emphasis on the combination of hatred and love in Pahlevān Akbar's constitution, his marginality and his hatred of identifying himself with the ruling elite offers a genealogy of heroism and suggests that it must be a dissenting, constructive force that offers social check and balance against absolute power instead of becoming its tool.

Beyzaie's social context here alludes to the debates about the obligations of those with unique talents in society. In *Ārash* Beyzaie's political motifs is focused on how the military elite may betray the country's long-term interests for temporary advantages or self-serving allegiances, as in the 1953 coup which closed Iran's path to constitutional democracy and ushered in the second Pahlavi's autocracy, which, in turn, led to the rise of its more suppressive Islamist double. The coup itself and the rise of a state aligned with the West, however, gave rise to new debates about the roles of intellectuals or people with unique qualities in preserving the country's cultural integrity. These ranged from reactionary nativist to cosmopolitan discourses that aspired to reformulate Iranian culture while remaining open to both East and West. While nativists moved towards Islamism from 1962 onwards, the cosmopolitan return-to-the-roots movements continued to have positive impacts on culture with the activities of artists, poets and philosophers such as Beyzaie, Sohrab Sepehri, Ahmad Shamlou or Darisuh Shaygan. Among these discourses, Jalal Al-e Ahmad's ideas on *gharbzadegi* (Westoxication), gave a new momentum to the nativist discourses about the responsibilities of the educated elites in facing unbridled Westernization.[49] Thus, the debates that had started in the first Pahlavi era about whether intellectuals should support or confront a state that was effective but unconstitutional began to polarize further to include anyone who supported the state or sided with its equally distorting leftist and Islamic nemeses. The range of those expected to take sides was expansive from leading tough guys, army officers and sportsmen to chief civil servants, academics and creative artists and intellectuals. The issue was not working in a state-related job; it was how the job was done and whose interests the person fulfilled. What is important, however, is that despite the dominance of religion in the resistant discourses of 1963 onward, Beyzaie's hero is also hated by the *sheiks* (the clergy). In other words, the alternative that Beyzaie is offering is different from the one promoted by Al-e Ahmad and the other nativists of the era.

Towards the end of the above dialogue, Pahlevān Akbar enters and is forced by Heidar's rudeness to engage in a hostile conversation punctuated with the yelling of the watchmen who order people to stay inside and sleep. This yelling, which adds to the intensity of the dispute between the two, suggests how two unique individuals, perhaps brothers, who can serve their people are facing each other due to the machination of the state. The conversation begins with Akbar's kind words but escalates with Heidar's innuendos about Akbar's absences and the rumours that he is too old and has been exercising to regain the strength of his youth. The scene echoes the encounter between Rostam and Esfandiyār in a language that distances itself from the tough guy speech of the 1960s by using the naturally poetic and rhythmic repartees of *ayyārs*.[50] Heidar censures Akbar for his unknown origins and for having unruly habits:

Pahlevān: [Jumping to a standing position, enraged.] Who are you to brag before me?
Heidar: [Holding Pahlevān's hand in a standing arm wrestle.] These are people's words. Did you not like them?
Master: Enough!
Heidar: Some of the state guards, who had chased him one night, saw him go to a disreputable district, heard him sing in the house of a prostitute, spotted him dancing in the main square and warming himself with the fire of a leper, heard him insult Governor Khan on the market junction! They say Pahlevun can no longer do anything. He's too old. His hands shake [Pahlevān bends Heidar's hand down, causing Heidar to shout in pain –] They say he is turning into an unruly drunken vagabond!
[Laughter of watchmen from outside. Pahlevān Akbar goes to the door, furiously –]
Pahlevān: Shut up, blind bats! Bandits! Looters of sleep! Bragging hooligans. (213)

While Pahlevān's shouting at the watchmen clarifies that his encounters with them have made them spread such rumours, Heidar's repetition of those rumours suggests that he has become the state's mouthpiece. Yet realizing that he is indeed weaker than Pahlevān, before he leaves, he states that he would never confront Pahlevān if 'things could be changed' (214). When Pahlevān's anger makes Master ask whether he also loves Khan's stepdaughter, Pahlevān responds in the third person: 'Akbar can no longer be attached to anything', not because he wants to preserve his strength as Master did, or just because he dislikes Khan Beik and his cohorts, but because nothing can fill the twenty years that has been lost to him after he left the nomads. Beyzaie's emphasis on Pahlevān's fear of intimacy and its roots in his fear of abandonment is not to detract from his positive role in society. It is rather to highlight the complex set of relations that make people behave in particular ways and show how his uniqueness is because he has turned his suffering into a source of blessing. Thus, instead of just glorifying Akbar, which he does, Beyzaie creates a modern character entangled in a web of relations that have determined his identity while depriving him of the generosity of those he has been protecting.

Pahlevān then announces that he has come to bid Master farewell as he will be leaving for India. He adds that Heidar's rudeness has enraged him, so he may hurt him in the match. Master advises him to wrestle with compassion as he has done in the last twelve years. Yet seeing his refusal, he suspects that he has promised Khan's stepdaughter to lose. Thus, he refers to Puriyā-ye Vali and how he lost to an Indian wrestler to keep his promise to the wrestler's mother. The double-layered dialogue then shows how Master, assured that Pahlevān had not promised anything to the girl, refers to a hero's oath as the proof of his honour, which ironically makes Pahlevān more determined to leave. Here, as usual in Beyzaie's world, Pahlevān exposes the folk tale to critical inspection by contending that Puriyā-ye Vali may have really lost rather than pretending to lose and that if he pretended to lose in a way that the referees noticed it, it was worth nothing as it boosted his rather than the Indian wrestler's reputation. Then, he reiterates his desire to leave. Beyzaie's dialogue here is enriched with his knowledge of *zurkhāneh* traditions. Master then insists that being a protector of the poor, the country's most honourable wrestler and the best performer of the 360 wrestling techniques that have reached them from Puriyā-ye Vali, Pahlevān is the only one deserving to receive Puriyā-ye Vali's *kherqeh* (cloak) which is now with Master. Then, noticing that Pahlevān has no interest in this highest token of honour, he delivers a monologue about the honour of a hero being like his afterlife and warns that Pahlevān's departure will destroy his reputation and will be his death in life. While echoing the legend of Rostam and Esfandiyār again, the monologue specifies the tenets of the cult of *nām o nang* (honour and dishonour) for which Rostam and Puriyā-ye Vali function as role models. Even though Rostam knows that killing Esfandiyār means losing the chance of a blessed afterlife, he encounters Esfandiyār because Esfandiyār wants to shackle him. For Pahlevān, however, honour in life or being blessed in the afterlife have lost their senses.[51] His idea of honour is a modern one which is characterized by an awareness of the absurdity of the world and having no interest in playing its games of religion, honour or dishonour. Yet the dialogue is also crucial in that it ends with a reference to Black Wearing Man as if Master can see him:

> **Master:** [...] Animosity does not have a recognizable face; just like that Black Wearing Man, you turn, and you suddenly find him at your door –
> [Pahlevān turns but does not see anything.]
> **Pahlevān:** Which Black Wearing Man?
> **Master:** The one who was there!
> **Pahlevān:** Was?
> **Master:** I am not sure.
> **Pahlevān:** How come?
> **Master:** Maybe it was just something that passed my mind.
> **Pahlevān:** Which way?
> **Master:** God knows.
> **Pahlevān:** [Setting off.] I should find him! (221–2)

The desire to find the double is thus repeated at the end of act two, preparing the audience for Pahlevān's distracted dialogue with Wine-seller and soliloquies about leaving the town, intentionally losing or even suicide: 'No, even if you die you have broken your promise as you will still be the champion of this land not him. [Looking at the sky.] The Seven Brothers (Big Dipper) are silent, the North Star is up; it should be cold in the tents now' (224–5).

In his analysis of the clash between the Eros and the death drive, Freud refers to a melancholic nostalgia for returning to an inanimate state in which the absurd business of life has no place.[52] This nostalgia is reflected in Pahlevān's love for inanimate entities. Yet his fascination with stars can also be read at two other levels: (1) his upbringing among nomads for whom natural landscape and stars act as maps and (2) the mythic link between heroes and constellations as Hercules (pahlevān or *zānu-zadeh* [kneeling] in Persian) or Perseus (*borandeh-ye sar-e diev* [Cutter of Demon's Head] in Persian). The reference to the Seven Brothers also connotes the folk tale of Seven Brothers in which a sister finds her seven brothers after years of separation.[53] Pahlevān's desire to be found is, thus, set along his desire for non-being which explains his self-effacing, sacrificial impulses. The latter is reinforced when Wine-seller refers to a man who had brought a gift for Pahlevān because when the man's horse had died, Pahlevān turned the heavy wheel of his oil-extracting machine for a week so he could buy another horse. The reference clarifies why Pahlevān was happy in the first scene and refutes the claims that his absence was because he was spending his time with prostitutes. It also highlights again that his power is due to his willingness to engage in hard work and suffer to help others.

The hero of the marginalized and the hero of the king

Here Beyzaie's juxtaposition of allusions to estrangement, death and oppression escalates to refer to the condition of the marginalized in Iran and highlight that those who have not suffered marginalization are unable to understand the problem.

> **Wine-seller:** I somehow understand your situation.
> **Pahlevān:** It is now twelve years that I am in this city, but I'm still a stranger.
> **Wine-seller:** I understand this perfectly well. We have been here for a thousand years. They say we have been here since this land was here. We were the owners of this place. But now, we are treated not only as strangers, but as impure. They are closing all the shops in the Zoroastrian district. People avoid this district. If you did not frequent this wineshop, they would already have sealed the shop. If this ancient fire temple were not here, they would have demolished the shop –
> [The sound of fast-paced music.]
> **Pahlevān:** We are strangers! (227)

Then, Wine-seller's references to the year in which his district was attacked, his family was all killed, and his neighbours were tortured, slayed or forced to leave, sends Pahlevān to a frenzy, a ritual dance of despair, because, despite all his power, he has failed to change anything:

> **Pahlevān:** There was torture – here. [Dancing.] Buying and selling human beings. In red castles, shackles, chains, balls and blocks! Dungeons and gallows! [Drunken and mad] Here – there was torture! Whips lashing on bodies! Pulling people's nails! Tearing their chests! Cutting their hands! Breaking their legs! [Helpless.] This broken leg was lost on the roads! [Kicking the ground.] There was torture here! Injustice and cries of –
> [A thunder. Pahlevān regains control.] (227–8)

The monologue challenges the aesthetics of politics in the Iran of the 1960s by expanding the range of the critical views heard and seen in Iranian public space. At a more allegorical level, it also refers to the 1953 coup and its violent aftermaths. It even mentions 'qal'eh-hā-ye sorkh' (red castles) which alludes to the notorious *Zendān-e Qezel Qaleh* (Red Castle Prison). The context, however, criticizes not only the state's use of torture to get confessions from dissidents, but also the atrocities committed by the clergy and their thuggish cohorts against minorities. The language used to describe the events echoes Ferdowsi's lines about Rostam routing the enemies of Iran on the battlefield.[54] The difference, however, is that the people who committed these atrocities on Wine-seller were not slaying the country's enemies but their own helpless people. Pahlevān's ritual dance of despair is followed by another reference to Rostam and Esfandiyār in which Pahlevān states that Simurgh – the epitome of wisdom, who saves Zāl when he is left in the wilderness as a child, and his son, Rostam when he encounters Esfandiyār – is now dead and that he himself cannot even choose to die.

Then, after a moment of sleeping, he jumps up in a rage, lifts the heavy stone seat and throws it at the shrine, censures its silence and expresses his doubts about whether the ideas embodied in the shrine and the stone lion are still alive. Beyzaie emphasizes the absurdity of talking about the metaphysical notions of honour and heroism in the Iranian imaginal when society is reeking of corruption and injustice. He then highlights this corruption in another comic relief. With an exhausted Pahlevān falling into a torpor, the two watchmen appear to talk about sharing the booty of a burglar, rivalries in their job, Pahlevān's alertness, their desire to be sleeping and having sex in their beds, and the demolition of the Zoroastrian district. Thus, rather than protecting the city from burglars, the watchmen are after getting their shares of stolen goods, fulfilling their boss's distorted demands and undermining those who resist their tyranny.

As in Iranian puppet tradition and his own trilogy, Beyzaie then uses the sound of thunder to mark the beginning of a climactic scene in which Pahlevān wakes up to encounter Black Wearing Man. His monologue, here, draws a line between two types of public figures and marks Black Wearing Man as the type that serves tyranny. With Pahlevān's challenging gaze, however, Black Wearing Man disappears. Pahlevān wakes Wine-seller to tell him that he is leaving and that he should give his championship armband to Heidar.

> **Wine-seller:** What about the people whom you have always helped, who are you entrusting them to? Who's going to protect their rights?
> **Pahlevān:** [Setting off, embarrassed.] No hero has lived until the end of the world; never! [Confused but still roaring.] They themselves – themselves should do something! [Turning towards Wine-seller.] Themselves. (240)

Thus, once more, Beyzaie refers to apathy as a pitfall of citizenship as those who allow others to control their lives or wait for saviours to liberate them will get nothing but leaders who treat them like beasts of burden. Pahlevān's despair, thus, signifies that it is people's campaign for their rights and partaking in decision-making which transforms the masses into the public, subjects into citizens and subalterns into resistant voices. Similarly, it is the elites' refusal to become obsessed with power and money that allows for an open public space that facilitates debate, growth and emancipation.

With Wine-seller having gone to deliver the armband to Heidar, Black Wearing Man appears and takes Pahlevān's machete from near the shrine. Yet before the encounter between the two, Beyzaie inserts another comic relief in which the watchmen warn Pahlevān that burglars and bandits have sent someone to kill him. In Shakespearean tragedies such scenes are used just before or after a tragic scene to intensify the range of emotions that the audience undergo or juxtapose a moment of suffering or anagnorisis with a comic episode to suggest the continuity of life despite a tragic event. The comic characters in such scenes are often not aware of the tragic event that has just happened, so they mock about it. Thus, as Alfred Hitchcock did later, Shakespeare used death as a ploy to show how people often do not care if a tragic event does not directly concern them, or if they see such events too often or benefit from them due to their jobs as gravediggers or undertakers. Beyzaie, however, uses this ploy to also criticize the state as caring for nothing but money and power. Thus, the watchmen warn Pahlevān not because they like him but because they want to ingratiate themselves to get some money.

This comic relief is followed by a monologue in which Pahlevān reviews his life, a dialogue with the blind man marking him as a saviour who cannot save himself and the arrival of Black Wearing Man who stabs a resigned Pahlevān from behind (247–50). Marking the play's emotional climax, the monologue reflects the process through which traumatized people try to control their fates by achieving recognition. It also implies Pahlevān's similarity with Beyzaie in that he has extracted strength from within trauma but has found himself championing values that, in the absence of social awareness, have led to his despair and isolation. Like all marginalized people, who achieve recognition, Pahlevān has ambivalent emotions towards his people. He craves to belong to them but resents their failures. This resentment may also make him resent himself as, despite his powers, he may feel unable to cure their failures. Yet the play also shows how, even when successful, the path of recognition which defines such heroic figures may ultimately seem absurd to them in the absence of love. For Pahlevān, therefore, the despair and death that are embodied in Black Wearing Man seem to be the only way out.

Beyzaie, however, does not mystify Pahlevān's intentions. Commenting on the formation and transformation of human identity, the monologue specifies how the complex knots of images, sounds, pains and desires in the memory formulate our identity and how our ultimate desire is always to have fulfilment in production and love. In a balanced society where injustice is less brazen, and people have opportunities to act as co-authors of their lives, he could have been a good father and due to his strength, an efficient craftsman, farmer or a defender of his people. Pahlevān fulfilled his first feats so that the glory of his name may reach his nomadic beloved and the people who rejected him due to their ignorance and their devious leaders (250). Yet, like Hamlet, who is trapped in hesitation, for Pahlevān the 'time' has been 'out of joint' and he is embittered about being 'born to set it right'. Thus, instead of using his power to build a family and contribute to the prosperity of his society, he has spent his life in a war to protect those who are not conscious enough to stand up for themselves.

Black Wearing Man, thus, remains an enigmatic figure. He can be a bandit, a secret agent or Pahlevān's shadow, but what is essential is that he can do his job only because Akbar, who has already rejected his identity as a pahlevān, refuses to defend himself. Thus, more than anything, he is a projection of Akbar's self-hatred and despair in a futile battle in which only heroes are supposed to achieve deeds. The suicidal Pahlevān tells the man to do what he must do, which he does by placing Pahlevān's machete between his shoulders and pressing the blade. Heidar then comes to protest Pahlevān's generosity, but facing a dying Pahlevān and unable to do anything leaves at Pahlevān's insistence. Soon, however, the two watchmen return like 'the twa corbies' of the Scottish ballad and after robbing the dead Pahlevān, plant some evidence in the pocket of the arriving Wine-seller to accuse him of murdering Pahlevān. The play, thus, ends bitterly, leaving the audience with questions about what Pahlevān should have done and a dialogue that reflects Beyzaie's bitterness about cultural philistinism:

> **Wine-seller:** [Trying to grab Pahlevān's cloak.] This has a significant –
> **Watchman 2:** Shut up! [Wine-seller tries futilely to get it back, but they cover his mouth.] [To Watchman 1.] Keep it, we can sell it in the second-hand market. (254–5)

The same hopeless wrath is also reflected in Mother's words after hearing that Pahlevān, the stranger who promised to help her, has left. This despair and the accompanying desire for the return of heroes is also reflected in her feeling that Pahlevān is present like a ghost near the shrine and the roaring of the stone lion when everyone has left the stage. The lion, which, as other stone lions, marks a pahlevān's grave, roars the unseen pain of those who act heroically in response to suffering but are burdened with misery due to people's expectations. Like Gholamreza Takhti (1930–68), the most honourable wrestling champion of modern Iran, whose suspicious death or suicide proved the impossibility of having such heroes in a modern society, Beyzaie's Pahlevān depicts the bleeding heart of a cornered lion trapped by a dying ideal. This bleeding heart, however, is also Beyzaie's as he observed how thugs, clerics and officers who implemented the 1953 coup ripped its benefits in the 1950s. It also reflects the pressures that define the lives of the marginalized people of his or Takhti's type.[55]

 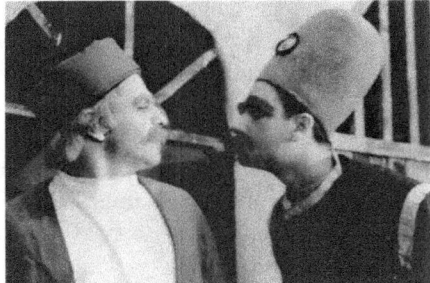

Figure 3.2 Black-wearing man killing Akbar. Watchman accusing wine-seller of robbery.[56]

A unique tragic hero and a poetic language

Writing about Sophocles's *Antigone* in an age of heroic plays in which the conflict between love and honour defined tragedy, Hegel argued that tragedy, at its best, was the result of a hero finding himself torn between mutually exclusive yet equally legitimate systems of value. Pahlevān Akbar's quandary involves his entrapment between mutually exclusive systems of value in a situation in which choosing one will trap him in a whirlpool of consequences.[57] Beyzaie's play has heroic motifs, but in his vision, honour rarely clashes with love. With love already lost and reformulated as honour in the form of protecting the weak, contradictory notions of honour are set in conflict, and sacrificial love becomes the ultimate form of honour. In this vision, the hope of renewal is minimal, and Pahlevān's choice is inevitably destructive. The dice are already cast, and the vicious forces of the watchmen and their leaders are already closing in on him and the voiceless people he is protecting. This is where a Beyzaiean level of meaning evolves. The audience is challenged to identify with Pahlevān but urged to make a different choice in a process that may raise awareness about why a healthy society is one in which people have achieved self-awareness and there is no need for heroes.

Besides its tragic insight, the play's poetic power has continued to attract attention. Al-e Ahmad, who liked the play in general, criticized this poetic quality as 'aphorisms that soften the steel of speech by turning it into three or four cornered, or diamond or six-sided star-shaped bars decoratively inlaid.'[58] Al-e Ahmad's sarcasm and his reference to 'six-sided star-shaped bars' suggest that Beyzaie imprisoned the language in ways that served the Pahlavi's agenda and their support for Israel. What he missed or refused to admit, however, was that Beyzaie used such a language because he respected his form. He used a register fitting for his characters but augmented his poetry to elevate his audience rather than bend to the norms of copying tough guy's speech in Iranian films. Al-e Ahmad also referred to the activities of the office of theatre as state propaganda but failed to see how his ideal of committed literature was as obsessed with propaganda as the state-funded plays that Beyzaie and his colleagues avoided.

Writing at the same time, Azar Rahnama argued that the play was the most gripping play she had ever seen in Iran and argued that its poetic language allowed Beyzaie to create a play that was entirely Iranian but as captivating as the greatest plays in the world: 'The play evokes the spirit of the real pahlevāns of Iran with their authentic expressions, words and proverbs to bring the audience face to face with a system of values, the nucleus of which is honest and steadfast honour and a free spirit, so that they can test the level of their accord with these values.' She then went on to talk about the value of reviving the positive aspects of one's culture in a world overridden with superficial modernity.[59]

Beyzaie's poetic language which reformed a dying register for the stage offered two types of speech with realistic nuances. The first used the metaphorical, rhyming and rhythmic phrases of the *javānmardi* cults. The second was the poetry of Pahlevān's existential ruminations and recollections about love, belonging and costs of real honour. Though recreated with a modernist gaze, even the second type was realistic as some leading pahlevāns, including Puriyā-ye Vali, were also poets. Thus, expressions like the following fascinated many later writers and played a role in changing the nature of dialogue writing in Iranian cinema and theatre.[60]

پهلوان: چراغ دلت روشن باشه مادر، اشکت خشک.

Pahlevān: Your heart's light be alight, Mother, your tears dry. (187)

حیدر: [...] پهلوون پیش پیری سپر انداخته.

Heidar: [...] Pahlevān has dropped his shield in face of old age. (213)

حیدر: ریشه وقتی می لرزه که تیشه‌ی تیز دیده باشه.

Heidar: A root shakes when it sees a sharp hatchet. (214)

پیر: [...] همون عشقی که میوندار بود و نبودِ کون و مکانست. عشق به هر چی که هست، به زن، زندگی، صفای دنیا و وفای آخرت. چه خوش اون مردی که بند فتوت به میون بند مروت بست. می شنوی؟

پهلوان: به گوش دل!

Master: The same love that is the guiding champion [the coach at the centre] of the being and unbeing of the universe and existence. Love of whatever is, wife, life, sincerity in this world and loyalty to the other world. Great is the man who put the belt of chivalry onto the belt of humanity. Do you hear me?

Pahlevān: With my heart's ears. (214–15)

And examples such as the following soliloquy gave a new meaning to poetic dialogue:

پهلوان: های – دختر امشب چه کار می‌کنی؟ زلفات رو می‌بافی یا پریشون می‌کنی؟ فدای سبز چشمهات، سیاه چادرت رو روشن بذار، بذار چشمهای اکبر سیر ببینندت. تو ستاره های ایل ما تو ماه تمومی.

-تو از ایل ما نیستی!

-فدای لب شیرینت که بارش تلخ بود! تو نوچه‌ی این میدونی، من پیش خال تو ابدالم.

-از کدوم خونی؟

-چیزی نمی‌دونم!

[...] به قاطر بستنت، قاطر چموش بود. از **تنگِ نفیر** تا **غار کفتار** روی خس و خاک کشیدت. تو بودی و خاک سرخ، خاک سرخ بود و آسمون کبود! خورشید کوره بود، ماه نعلی برای داغ! از تنگ کبود تا غار مار نگاه رو می‌پیچید. [...] تو خط افق برای کوچ کرنا میزدن، دلت اونجا بود ولی خودت دور می شدی. تو خط افق برای کوچ ولوله بود، اما تو از افق جدا مونده بودی. [...] باز هم تو از قافله جدا مونده بودی.

Pahlevān: Ay – what are you doing tonight, girl? Are you braiding your hair or let them flow on your face and shoulders? I'll give my life for the green of your eyes, let the light of your black tent remain on. Let Akbar's eyes quench their thirst with your beauty. Among the stars of our tribe, you are the full moon.

— You're not of our tribe!

— Akbar's life is nothing for the sweetness of your lips whose fruit was bitter!

— You're the fresh soul of this arena, and I am the pure soul losing to your beauty spot.

— Of what blood are you?
— I don't know!
[...] They tied you to a wild mule, which dragged you on thorns and rocks from the **Valley of Cries** to the **Cave of Hyena**, it was you and the red clay, the red clay, and the cobalt sky! The sun was an oven, and the moon a horseshoe for branding you! Your gaze wandered from **Azure Valley** to the **Cave of Snake**. [...] On the line of horizon, the karnay signalled the time of migration. Your heart was there, but you were getting afar. On the line of horizon, the commotion of migration, but you had been estranged from the horizon. [...] Once more you had remained behind the caravan. (246–7)

Beyzaie's poetic imagery even uses the animal and natural imagery of the names of locations in a nomadic line – from Kermanshah (*Ghār-e Mār/Cave of Snake*) and Lorestan (*Tang-e Kabud/Azure Valley/ Tight Corner of Bruises*) to Isfahan (*Ghār-e Kaftār/Cave of Hyena*) – to echo Pahlevān's sense of loss, pain, frustration and loneliness. Akbar, a teenager in the wilderness, had to hide like a snake to escape punishment after he was tortured, branded and kicked out of the tribe, and like a hyena he had to shadow the tribe in the hope of being reaccepted.

These two types echoed Beyzaie's origin in a family of poets and his knowledge of modern poetry and *javānmardi* discourses. Their emotional intensity, however, reflected his sense of loss every time he was treated as 'not one of us' although he knew his centrality to the best aspects of his culture. It also echoed his experience of love every time love was embittered due to the gap between love and fulfilment in a society ruled by exclusionist discourses.

R. Etemadi, who admired the authenticity of the first type of speech, considered the second type more like 'a modernist poem which, though good in itself' did not match the rest of the dialogue.[61] Etemadi is not entirely wrong, but in my opinion, Pahlevān's poetic soliloquies are like modernized versions of the types of poetic sentiments that one observes in Puriyā-ye Vali's writings. Moreover, despite its modernity which reflects Beyzaie's success in adapting it for the stage, this poetic form is characterized by metaphors whose crude beauty reflects those of folk poetry. Thus, rather than contradicting each other, the play's two types of poetry reinforce each other and, as Ehsan Yarshater argues, give a kind of 'emotional and nostalgic intensity' to the dialogue that elevates the play 'to the level of tense and highly effective drama.'[62]

Reception and conclusion

The play's qualities attracted the attention of those who read it before and after its publication in 1965, but it was its performance that made a major influence on Iranian theatre and cinema. During the months the National Arts Group was preparing for the 1965 Theatre of Nations' Festival in Paris, Ali Nassirian urged Abbas Javanmard to work on *So Dies Pahlevān Akbar*, but the troupe's final decision was to take two of Beyzaie's puppet plays to Paris. Immediately after they returned, however, Javanmard staged the play to great acclaim in *25*

Shahrivar Theatre during the Festival of Iranian National Theatre in October and later for the public from December 1965 to February 1966.[63] As in former cases, Javanmard had his own priorities. Beyzaie had exposed the conditions of Pahlevān's rise and fall as a seemingly indomitable hero to reveal his life as a lonely victim, but Javanmard's directorial gaze and acting as Pahlevān celebrated him as an epic hero who made a sacrificial choice. In any case, as evident in the number of television and cinematic works that copied it and the ensuing recurrence of dying heroes and pahlevān figures in Iranian cinema, the performance was a success.

The success of the play also led to a side history. Mohammad Reza Shah who had heard about the play while watching another during the festival asked Mehrdad Pahlbod (1917–2018), the minister of culture and art, to make arrangements so he could see the play. The authorities involved were hesitant and wanted to change some parts, but Javanmard insisted that as the recommendation had been made based on seeing the play as it was, the King probably preferred to see it with no changes. This led to a performance in which two scenes referred to torture. The first is when Pahlevān reminisces about being tortured after beating the son of the nomadic khan while the *Shāhnāmeh* is being recited. This, of course, alludes to the glorification of the *Shāhnāmeh* in the Pahlavi era while those who spoke truth to power were tortured.[64] The second is when Pahlevān and Wine-seller discuss the violence imposed on the marginalized, and Pahlevān performs a ritual dance of despair and a Brechtian song of injustice.[65]

The King's decision to ignore these allusions and the other dissenting sentiments embedded in the play, however, suggests that he had either already begun to allow a degree of socio-political criticism or was unable or reluctant to see himself in the negative role of the tyrants of the play. In other words, his literalist desire to see himself and his father as the ones who saved Iran from such rulers – the Turkic Khans of the *Qajar* era (1796–1925) – made him unable or unwilling to see that this could also apply to him and the activities of the clerical establishment during the 1950s. The latter is likely because, according to Beyzaie, during the performance the King saw, when referring to the location of tortures, Javanmard unexpectedly changed 'here' to 'there' which increased the likelihood of such an interpretation.[66] However, such reports also prove that, as Beyzaie states, the worst outcome of imposing surveillance on artistic activities is that it breeds self-censorship and the extreme censorship of philistine officials. In both cases fear triggers a tendency to go beyond what may be expected of them.[67]

Javanmard's performance unwittingly decreased the play's potential to produce an alternative cultural narrative and a new kind of audience. Yet some of his advertising tactics worked well. For instance, apart from writing on the necessity of having a national drama in the press,[68] the group also invited Shaban Jafari (1921–2006) and his cohorts to watch the play.[69] Shaban was a leading thug of the 1940s and 1950s, who organized the pro-shah street fights and raids of the 1953 coup and was later employed to organize the state shows that featured *zurkhāneh* sports. This was a new form of dialogue which aspired to influence those claiming to be pahlevāns of the present with values extracted from the *javānmardi* codes that they failed to uphold.

The text itself continued to play a significant role in the Iranian conceptualization of heroism. Its poetically charged dramatic language urged others to pay more attention to the linguistic register for characterization in literature and drama. Beyzaie's scholarly knowledge of *javānmardi* also challenged contemporary conceptions of tough guys as heroes in cinema. As specified above, its impact can be seen in the use of dying heroes or pahlevāns in cinema or the way pahlevāns are depicted in plays and films after 1963. But its more direct impact can be seen in such TV series as Sirus Afhami's *Pahlevānān* (*Pahlevāns*, aka *Pahlevān Nāyeb*, 1970) and Hasan Fathi's *Pahlevānān Nemimirand* (*Pahlevāns Do Not Die*, 1997) and films such as Ali Hatami's *Toqi* (*Wood Pigeon*, 1970), *Bābā Shamal* (1971) and *Qalandar* (1972).

Beyzaie's preoccupation with pahlevāns and *ayyārs* continued in several significant plays and screenplays and was given a filmic fulfilment in *Ballad of Tārā*. Yet, determined to avoid repeating himself, he switched to other subjects in which while the ideals of masculinity remained a subject of enquiry, the focus expanded to include other types of men including intellectuals and artists and more importantly women, children and old people.

Notes

1. Afshari, *Āyin-e Javānmardi*, 15–28. For Rostam's *ayyāri* acts, see Ferdowsi, *Shahnameh*, Vol. 3, 306–97.
2. Ridgeon, *Javanmardi*, 1–27.
3. For more, see Zakeri, *Sasanid Soldiers*.
4. My analysis is based on my reading of King-Paladin relations in the *Shahnameh* and in Arrajāni's retelling of the Mithraic, Parthian romance *Samak-e Ayyār*.
5. For more, see Balslev, *Iranian Masculinities*, 1–53. For masculinity, see Horlacher, *Configuring*, 1–94.
6. Böwering, and Melvin-Koushki. 'ḴĀNAQĀH'.
7. Afshari, *Āyin*, 47–9; and Beyzaei Kashani, *Tārikh*, 40–2. In the past, women, children and non-Muslims were not allowed into *zurkhāneh*, but this prohibition decreased from the 1950s when Shaban Jafari hosted the Shah's foreign guests for special performances. See Chehabi, 'ZUR-ḴĀNA'.
8. For more on Mithraism in Europe, see Vermaseren, *Mithras* and Beck, 'MITHRAISM'.
9. For failures and achievements of Iranian *ayyāri* traditions in medieval and premodern Iran, see Hakemi, *Āyin – Fotovvat* which also includes Saeed Nafisi and Abdol Hussein Zarrinkoub's articles on the subject and on Yaqub Laith of Saffar, an *ayyār*, who established the Saffarid dynasty (861–1003).
10. For his cousin's research, see Beyzaei Kashani, *Tārikh-e Varzesh-e Bāstāni-ye Iran (Zurkhāneh)*.
11. Beyzaie, 'Cheh Mahkameh', 119. Amiri, *Jedāl*, 25–31.
12. Though Abolqasem Janati 'Ataei's *Shrimardi az Khorasan* (A Lion Man from Khorasan, 1963) may have urged Beyzaie to write on *pahlevān*(s) from a totally different perspective, nothing in the play echoes any aspect of Akbar Khorasani's life, except that he also, once when he was in his twenties, fell asleep, and his caravan left

him behind. This is important as Khorasani was a violent and, according to some sources, opportunistic wrestler. Beyzaie is concerned with an ideal rather than an individual, and his character is most probably from the Western parts of Iran. See Beyzaei Kashani, *Tārikh*, 58, 136–8, 148–52, 175, and Ensāfpur, *Tārikh va Frahang*, 166–8.

13. See Esmail Kushan's *Kolāh Makhmali* (1962) for type 1 and Siamak Yasemi's *Ganj Qarun* (1965) for type 2.
14. See Ali Hatami's *Bābā Shamal* (1971), Masoud Kimiaei's *Dāsh Ākol* (1971) or Aman Manteqi's *Pahlevān Mofrad* (1971) for type 1; Kimiaei's *Qeysar* (1969) or *Reza Motori* (1970) for type 2; and Aramis Aqamalian's *Golāqā* (1967), Amir Naderi's *Tangsir* (1972) or Nasser Taghvai's *Sadeq Kordeh* (1972) for type 3.
15. See *Vendidad*, 2, 16–21; *Bundaheshn*, Part 18, 139–14; and Corbin, *Spiritual*, 23–4, 278. While celebrating Siyāvush and Kaykhsorow's spirituality, Ferdowsi's inclusion of Zāl's comment on Kaykhsorow's vanishing, 'the wise would laugh at the business of someone going to god alive', signifies the worldliness of a different type of intellectuality that the *Shahnameh* equally celebrates:
خردمند از این کار خندان شود // که زنده کسی پیش یزدان شود.
16. See also the myth of the *Jazirat Al-Khazrā* (The Ever-green Island), Majlesi, *Bahār*, Vol. 52, 159.
17. *Nā-Koja-Ābād* is the unseen world of eternal heroes and saints between the earthly (گیتی) and the divine (مینو) worlds. Embedded in this cosmology is also the *Shi'i* idea of *shahidān-e shāhed* 'the living, observant martyrs', who reside in a paradisaic limbo as eternal testifiers of the truth of their belief and observant of all human activities.
18. Corbin, 'Mundus Imaginalis', part 1.
19. Corbin, *Spiritual Body*, ix. For an extended discussion, see Talajooy, Chapter 1, *Bahram Beyzaie's*.
20. See Talajooy, 'Chapter 2' of *Iranian Culture*.
21. Beyzaie, 'Pahlevān', 184.
22. Examples include Zāl and his father Sām, Rostam as the hero and Keykāvus as the king, Kaveh and Fereydun as the oppressed periphery under Zahhāk, and Fereydun's youngest son Iraj who is better than Salm and Tur.
23. See *Downpour*, *Journey*, or *Bashu, the Little Stranger*; and Beyzaie in Qukasiyan, *Goftogu*, 163–4.
24. For details, see Darmesteter, 'Aban Yasht' and 'Mehr Yasht'; and Beck, 'MITHRAISM'.
25. See Beyzaie and Amjad, 'From the Land', 721–36.
26. See Beyzaie's discussion of the origins of 'Shadow Plays' in *Jana 1*, 12′–15′.
27. See Talajooy, 'Reformulation', 696–7.
28. However interpreted, this enigmatic figure also appears in Beyzaie's later works including *The Eight Journey of Sinbad*, *Downpour*, and *Stranger and the Fog*.
29. Pahlevān is pronounced Pahlevun in Tehrani accent.
30. Freud, *Interpretation*, 147–58, 159–86 and 295–362.
31. Freud, 'Uncanny', 235.
32. Ibid., 236–37.
33. Burke, *Philosophical Enquiry*, 54.
34. Kant, *Critique*, 103–40.
35. Beyzaie, 'Har Kas'. 20.
36. Todorov, *Fantastic*, 25.
37. Ibid., 33.

38 See also Rezaeian Attar, *Roju'-e Hamzad*.
39 Sadeghi, 'Hero'.
40 For more see Hakemi, *Āyin* which also includes Saeed Nafisi and Abdol Hussein Zarrinkoub's chapters on the subject and on Yaqub Laith of Saffar, an *Ayyār*, who established the Saffarid dynasty (861–1003).
41 For the anxiety of influence as an Oedipal condition that generates innovation in poetry, see Bloom, *Anxiety*.
42 For the links between Sufism and chivalry traditions, see Milani, 'Cultural'; and Ridgeon, *Jawanmardi*, 1–24.
43 See the lame boys in *Downpour* and *Stranger and the Fog*, or the deaf boy in *The Crow*.
44 See also Mahmoudi and Dadkhah, 'Nākhodāgāh-e Matn', 30.
45 Beyzaie and Talajooy, 'Multiple Interviews'.
46 For more see Beyzaie's analysis of the subject in *Hezār Afsān*, 75–376.
47 Abbas Javanamrd's staging of Pahlevān Akbar. The second photo is from Amjad's collection and the first is from Iran Theatre: https://theater.ir/fa/movie/105.
48 For an English rendition of the legend, see Ferdowsi, *Shahnameh*, (Davis), 371–422.
49 For more, see Boroujerdi, *Iranian Intellectuals*.
50 For samples, see Bighami's *Firuznāmeh* and Tarsusi's *Samak-e Ayyār*. As in Samak-e Ayyār's case, who knows several languages and is adaptable to statecraft, an *ayyār* may have unique intellectual and military qualities.
51 For more, see Gholamrezaei, 'Nām o Nang', 39–62.
52 Freud, 'Ego and the Id', 380.
53 This is a variation of ATU410 (Sleeping Beauty) in which the seven dwarfs are the heroine's lost brothers.
54 On the day of battle the glorious warrior*with sword, dagger, mace and lasso // cut, tore, broke and tied*the heads, chests, legs, and hands of enemy warriors:

به روز نبرد آن یل ارجمند // به شمشیر و خنجر به گرز و کمند
برید و درید و شکست و ببست// یلان را سر و سینه و پا و دست.

55 See Beyzaie's interview with Saber, about Takhti, 'Shir', 122–4. For Takhti, see Chehabi, 'TAḴTĪ'.
56 The first photo is from Amjad's collection and the second is from Iran Theatre: https://theater.ir/fa/movie/105.
57 Hegel, *Hegel on Tragedy*, 132.
58 Al-e Ahmad, Kārnāmeh" and 'Darbāreh', 1961–4 and 1975–7.
59 Rahnama, 'Pahlevān', 30.
60 This influence can be seen in a variety of works, but the best examples occur in the tough guy films whose scripts were written by Ahmad Shamlou and the poetic films written and directed by Ali Hatami.
61 Etemadi, 'Pahlevān', (11900), 12 and (11901), 12.
62 Yarshater, 'Modern', 59–60.
63 Javanmard, *Didār*, 183.
64 Beyzaie, *Pahlevān*, 246.
65 Javanmard, *Ghobār-e*, 145–6. See also his *Didār*, 304–08, 407–16.
66 Beyzaie and Talajooy, 'Multiple Interviews'.
67 Beyzaie, 'Pas az', 363–81.
68 Javanmard, 'Honar-e Emruz', 12.
69 Nassirian, 'Mokhalef', 44.

Bibliography

Al-e Ahmad, Jalal. 'Kārnāmeh-ye Taātr-e Hokumati-ye Sanglaj' and 'Darbāreh-ye Pahlevān Akbar Mimirad va Ghorub dar Diyāri Gharib va Qesseh-ye Māh-e Penhān' (1966). In *Adab va Honar Emruz-e Iran: Majmuʻeh Maqālāt-e Jalal Al-e Ahmad.* Vol. 4. Ed. Mostafa Zamaninia. Tehran: Mitra, 1994. Pp. 1959–64 and 1973–9.
Balslev, Sivan. *Iranian Masculinities: Gender and Sexuality in Late Qajar and Early Pahlavi Iran.* Cambridge: Cambridge University Press, 2019.
Beyzaie, Bahram. 'Pahlevān Akbar Mimirad' (1964). In *Divān-e Namāyesh 1.* Tehran: Roshangaran, 2002. Pp. 257–370.
Beyzaie, Bahram. 'Har Kas dar Iran yek Film-e Khub Sākhteh Bāshad, Mo'allem Man Ast'. *Film.* Vol. 8. No. 93. (Mordād 1369/August 1990). Pp. 20–1.
Beyzaie, Bahram. 'Pas az Sad Sal'. *Iran Nāmeh.* Vol. 14. No. 3 (Summer 1996). Pp. 363–81.
Beyzaie, Bahram. *Jana and Baladoor Workshop with Bahram Beyzaie Part 1.* Online at *YouTube*: https://www.youtube.com/watch?v=T3X7ggmWSLI&t=793s (Accessed 08 December 2021).
Beyzaie, Bahram and Hamid Amjad. 'From the Land of the Pure, in Search of the Lost Origin: An Interview with Bahram Beyzaie on Siyavush-Khani (Siyavush Recitation) and Its Mythological and Literary Roots'. *Iranian Studies: Special Issue on Bahram Beyzaie's Cinema and Theatre.* Ed. Saeed Talajooy. Vol. 46. No. 5 (Autumn 2013). Pp. 737–52.
Beyzaie, Bahram and Hoda Saber. 'Shir-e Del Khun'. *Cheshm-andāz-e Iran: Vizheh-nāmeh Jahān Pahlevān Takhti (Jā-ye Khāli, Jā-ye Sabz)* (Winter 1388/2010). Pp. 122–4.
Beyzaie, Bahram and Andisheh Puyā. 'Cheh Mahkameh-hā-ye Roshanfekri keh Nagozarāndam'.*Andisheh Puyā.* Vol. 2. No. 12. (January 2014). Pp. 119–20.
Beyzaie, Bahram and Saeed Talajooy. 'Multiple Interviews'. December 2019–May 2022.
Beyzaei Kashani, Hossein Parto, *Tārikh-e Varzesh-e Bāstani dar Iran, Zurkhāneh.* Tehran: Heidari, 1958.
Bloom, Harold. *The Anxiety of Influence.* 2nd edn. Oxford: Oxford University Press, 1997.
Boroujerdi, Mehrzad. *Iranian Intellectuals and the West: The Tormented Triumph of Nativism.* Syracuse: Syracuse University Press, 1996.
Böwering, Gerhard and Matthew Melvin-Koushki. 'ḴĀNAQĀH'. *Encyclopaedia Iranica Online.* © Trustees of Columbia University in the City of New York. Online: http://dx.doi.org/10.1163/2330-4804_EIRO_COM_10715. (Accessed 2 May 2022).
Burke, Edmund. *A Philosophical Enquiry into the Origin of Our Ideas of the Sublime and the Beautiful* (1757). Ed. Adam Philips. Oxford: Oxford University Press, 2008.
Chehabi, Houchang E. 'ZUR-ḴĀNA'. In *Encyclopaedia Iranica Online,* © Trustees of Columbia University in the City of New York. Online: http://dx.doi.org/10.1163/2330-4804_EIRO_COM_273. (Accessed 25 February 2021).
Corbin, Henry. 'Mundus Imaginalis or the Imaginary and the Imaginal'. 1964. In *H.C. Corbin.* Online: https://www.amiscorbin.com/bibliographie/mundus-imaginalis-or-the-imaginary-and-the-imaginal/. (Accessed 30 June 2021).
Darmesteter, James. '"Aban Yasht" and "Mehr Yasht"'. *Sacred Texts.* Online: <http://www.sacred-texts.com/zor/sbe23/index.htm>. (Accessed 5 February 2011).
Ensāfpur, Gholāmrezā, *Tārikh va Farhang-e Zurkhāneh.* Tehran: Farhang o Honar, 1975.
Etemadi, R. 'Pahlevān Akbar Mimirad'. *Etelāāt.* Nos. 11900, 11901, 11902 (17, 18, 19 Bahman 1344) (6, 7, and 8 February 1966). P. 12.

Ferdowsi, Abolqasem. *The Shahnameh*. Vol. 3. Ed. Jalal Khaleghi Motlagh. New York: Bonyād-e Miras-e Iran, 2002.
Ferdowsi, Abolqasem-. *Shahnameh: The Persian Book of Kings*. Trans. Dick Davis. New York: Penguin, 2007.
Freud, Sigmund. 'The Uncanny'. In *The Standard Edition of the Complete Psychological Works of Sigmund Freud*. Vol. XVII. Ed. and Trans. James Strachey. London: Hogarth, 1953.
Freud, Sigmund. 'The Ego and the Id'. In *On Metapsychology: The Theory of Psychoanalysis*. Middlesex: Penguin, 1987. Pp. 339–408.
Freud, Sigmund. *The Interpretation of Dreams*. Trans. James Strachey. New York: Basic Books, 2010.
Gholamrezaei, Mohamad. 'Nām o Nang az Didgāh-e Pahlevānān-e Shāhnāmeh'. *Majaleh-ye Pazhuheshi-e Dāneshgāh-e Esfahan: Olum-e Ensāni*. Vol. 8. No. 1–2 (Summer 1997). Pp. 39–62.
Hakemi, Esmail. *Āyin Fotovvat va Javānmardi*. Tehran: Asātir, 2003.
Hegel, Fredrich. *Hegel on Tragedy*. Ed. Anne and Henry Paolucci. New York: Harper & Row, 1975.
Horlacher, Stefan. Ed. *Configuring Masculinity in Theory and Literary Practice*. Leiden: Brill, 2015.
Javanmard, Abbas. 'Honar-e Emruz'. *Etelā'āt*. Year. Vol. 40. No. 11888, 11889, 11890, (2, 4, 5 Bahman 1344/22, 24, 25 January 1966). P. 12.
Javanmard, Abbas. *Ghobār-e Maniyat-e Pedar Khāndeh: Naqdi bar Pazhuhesh-e Taātri-ye Mostafa Oskoui*. Tehran: Afkār, 2003.
Javanmard, Abbas. *Didār bā Khiesh*. Tehran: Farhang-e Nashr-e Now, 2017.
Kant, Immanuel. *Critique of Judgment*. Trans. Werner s. Pluhar. Indianapolis/Cambridge: Hackett Publishing Company, 1987.
Mahmoudi Bakhtiari, Behruz and Maryam Dadkhah Tehrani. 'Nākhodāgāh-e Matn va Ideology dar Seh Nemāyehnāmeh-ye *Ghorub dar Diāri Gharib*, *Qesseh-ye Māh-e Penhān* va *Pahlevān Akbar Mimirad*'. *Taātr*. Vol. 23. No. 85 (Summer 2021). Pp. 14–34.
Majlesi, Mohamad Baqer. *Behar al-Anwar*. Bookshia. Online: shorturl.at/ruKLR (Accessed 12 November 2021).
Milani, Milad. 'The Cultural Repository of Persian Sufism: Medieval Chivalry and Mysticism in Iran'. In *Intercultural Transmission in the Medieval Mediterranean*. Ed. Stephanie L Hathaway and W. K. David. London & New York: Continuum, 2012. Pp. 63–83.
Nassirian, Ali. 'Mokhālef Budam bā Estabdād-e Roshanfekri'. *Andisheh Puyā*. Vol. 8. No. 61 (September and October 2019). Pp. 43–4.
Qukasiyan, Zaven. *Goftogu bā Bahram Beyzaie*. Tehran: Āgāh, 1992.
Rahnama, Azar. 'Pahlevān Akbar Mimirad'. *Negin*, Year 1. No. 7 (Azar 1344/December 1965–January 1966). Pp. 29–31.
Rezaeian Attar, Masoud. *Roju'-e Hamzād*. Tehran: Adabestan, 1998.
Ridgeon, Lloyd. *Jawanmardi: A Sufi Code of Honour*. Edinburgh: EUP, 2011.
Sadeghi, Ali. 'Hero and heroism in the Shahnameh and the Masnavi Critique'. *Critical Middle Eastern Studies*. Vol. 13. No. 2. (Summer 2004). Pp. 195–208.
Talajooy, Saeed. 'Indigenous Performing Traditions in Post-Revolutionary Iranian Theatre'. *Iranian Studies*. Vol. 44. No. 4 (July 2011). Pp. 497–519.
Talajooy, Saeed. 'Reformulation of Shahnameh Legends in Bahram Beyzaie's Plays'. *Iranian Studies*. Vol. 46. No. 5 (September 2013). Pp. 695–719.

Talajooy, Saeed. *Iranian Culture in Bahram Beyzaie's Cinema and Theatre: Paradigms of Being and Belonging (1959-1979)*. London: I.B. Tauris, 2023.
Talajooy, Saeed. *Bahram Beyzaie's Cinematic and Dramatic Worlds: In Dialogue with Time (1979-2022)*. London: I.B. Tauris, 2024.
Todorov, Tzvetan. *The Fantastic: A Structural Approach to a Literary Genre*. Trans. Richard Howard. Cleveland: Case Western Reserve University Press, 1973.
Vermaseren, Martin. *Mithras. The Secret God*. London: Chatto & Windus, London, 1963.
Yarshater, Ehsan. 'The Modern Literary Idiom'. In *Critical Perspectives on Modern Persian Literature*. Ed. Thomas M. Ricks. Washington, DC: Three Continents Press. 1984. Pp. 42–62.
Zakeri, Mohsen. *Sasanid Soldiers in Early Muslim Society: The Origins of Ayyaran and Futuwwa*. Wiesbaden: Harrassowitz Verlag, 1995.

Section B

BEYZAIE'S EARLY FILMS – TEXTS AND CONTEXTS

Chapter 4

THE CHALLENGES OF CENTRE AND MARGIN:
BEYZAIE'S COOPERATION WITH THE INSTITUTE FOR
THE INTELLECTUAL DEVELOPMENT OF CHILDREN
AND YOUNG ADULTS FOR *UNCLE MOUSTACHE,
JOURNEY* AND *BĀSHU, THE LITTLE STRANGER*

Amir Hosein Siadat

Introduction

When *Uncle Moustache* was released in 1970, the sheer energy and the comic force of the film took many critics by surprise. This was primarily because most of the filmic products of *Kānun-e Parvaresh-e Fekri-ye Kudakān va Nojavānān* (The Institute for the Intellectual Development of Children and Young Adults from this point 'the Institute') had been noted to be sombre and reflective of the hard conditions of life for many children. Beyzaie's film, however, reflected the hard conditions of children but was more concerned with their energy and how this energy can be used for progress. It also reflected this change in the attitudes of an old person, which, in turn, signified that any change in society can only take place if the older generation is also open to new ideas. This discourse offered a new perspective on change and the relationship between different generations that Beyzaie reintroduced from other perspectives in his later child-centred films.[1] To understand the significance of this discourse, however, one must properly understand the structure of the dominant discourses within which its variations evolved. My first step, therefore, is to examine the Institute's origins, services, significance and transformations before and after the revolution.

The Institute was founded in January 1966 in response to the need to provide contents and facilities for the intellectual development, leisure and recreation of young Iranians. Prior to the launch of the Institute, children's literature had grown significantly over a decade, and many publishers had become much more active in this field. The first step towards dedicating more facilities to the education and entertainment of children and young adults was taken by founding a library for these age groups in Farah (Lāleh) park.

The library was in fact at the core of the idea of forming an institute for the intellectual development of children and young adults. A key figure for the initiative was Leili Amir-Arjomand, a close friend of Iran's queen, Farah Pahlavi. Amir-Arjomand, who had a master's degree in Library and Information Science from Rutgers University, was inspired to create a children's library in Iran when taking a course on children's literature. In 1965, she joined Homa Zahedi, Ardeshir Zahedi's sister who later became the MP for Hamedan to found and manage the new library. The library which began its work in January 1966 also published the Institute's first book, *The Little Mermaid*, by Hans Christian Andersen translated and illustrated as *Dokhtarak-e Daryā* (The Little Sea Girl) by Queen Farah Pahlavi herself. The publication department of the Institute was launched using the profit from the sale of this book.[2]

Another key figure in shaping the policies of the Institute before the revolution was Firuz Shirvanlu who was invited to join the Institute to boost its cultural productions. Shirvanlu, who had studied Sociology of Art at the University of Leeds, started to work as a book designer and editor in Franklin Publishing house upon his return to Iran in 1965.[3] It was during this period that he was arrested in relation to an unsuccessful attempt to assassinate Mohammad-Reza Pahlavi on 10 April 1965. After his acquittal and release in November 1966, he founded Negāreh advertising company, which was also involved in producing books,[4] and, having completed a few projects for the Institute, was invited, most probably by Homa Zahedi, to join the Institute as the main decision-maker for the Institute's production policies.

Samad Behrangi's *The Little Black Fish* (1968), the first product of the Institute's collaboration with Shirvanlu's company, went on to win important awards at the Bologna and Bratislava Biennale in 1969. *The Little Black Fish* is about a small fish who risks his life to see the sea, embarking on a long journey during which he meets several interesting characters and finally acts as a role model through a sacrificial act of resistance against a violent and tyrannical pelican. In the years ending in Iranian revolution this story was interpreted as a manifesto against the government and many considered the black fish as a symbol of the young revolutionary and intellectual generation. The symbolic expression of the story seemed so inspiring to various authors and poets. The book which had been illustrated by Farshid Mesghali was a political allegory whose literary qualities and eloquently written tale 'made the name of the Institute global and set an example for political art'. The story became 'a prototype for the types of children's books that […] mothers read to their children', but this type was precisely the type that later made these children to go to 'the streets to fight for freedom a decade later'.[5]

Behrangi's book has long served as the unofficial, allegorical statement of the leftist guerrilla group, *Sāzemān Cherikhā-ye Fadāei Khalq* (Organization of Iranian People's Sacrificial Guerrilla).[6] Moreover, many of the artists and teachers who joined the Institute wanted to be like Samad Behrangi,[7] whose drowning during swimming in August 1967 was interpreted as a political assassination committed by SAVAK (Iran's security and information office during the Pahlavi era, 1958–79). His own background as a leftist and the publication of Behrangi's story initiated the leftist tendency of the Institute. This tendency was further reinforced when Shirvanlu realized that the number of well-known authors who wrote for children was too few to carry out his large-scale project and, thus, he contacted several leading authors and encouraged them to produce children's stories for the Institute. Since most of these authors had leftist tendencies and little experience in producing children's literature, the intellectual atmosphere of the Institute became one in which artists and authors used the Institute to express their political views in semi-allegorical works that were presumably for children. As Fereydun Moezi Moghadam puts it, this was an important development as 'Shirvanlu played a pivotal role in attracting to Kanun a large number of leading, young modernist intellectual figures in literature and visual arts, who had critical views of the regime's autocratic mode of governance'.[8] The same approach was established in the workshops and training classes in all the branches which were gradually established in different provinces. Shirvanlu was the initiator, leader and supporter of this initiative which established a new approach to political art between 1968 and 1979.

SAVAK's reports and the confidential documents are very interesting in this respect:

> The Institute [...], which is headed by the esteemed Empress of Iran, is run by the people, some of whom are not qualified to serve in this institute since they had previously been arrested and detained on charges of treason. Mrs. Amir-Arjomand, the Institute's director, does not have enough information about the internal situation of this institute. Furthermore, during the recruiting process, they do not examine the volunteer's dossier seriously enough.[9]

The quotation clearly indicates that the people who identified with the state and its security policies considered many of the artists working for the Institute as a sort of unwanted 'other'. This is significant as the imposition of Otherness alienates the person labelled as 'the Other' from the centre of society and places them at the margins of society:

> The ideological view always polarizes culture and non-culture. Representatives of the dominant voice in the political discourse define 'themselves' as the norms and 'others' as abnormal voices and causes of chaotic attitudes. Nevertheless, if the point of view changes, we see that in their works these 'abnormal people' define themselves as the originators of order and calmness, and the representative of the 'norms' as initiators of chaos, aggression and threat.[10]

The statistical studies of the Institute's pre-revolutionary works demonstrate that more than 12 per cent of all books and products had clearly dissenting socio-political themes. Issues such as inquisition and censorship, discrimination and exploitation, and, above all, political resistance and conflict are seen in many of these works.[11] The aforementioned contrast demonstrates that every culture considers 'self' space to be familiar, conventional and human while depicting its 'other' as dangerously unconventional in its narratives, myths, cinema, literature, etc. In fact, the existence of a culture and its normative system of meaning and value is not possible without the existence of its 'other'.[12] This view suggests that the Pahlavi's dominant political discourse did not intend to eliminate these 'others'. It rather wanted them to remain in the 'margin' and have no access to the resources of the 'centre' so that their voices could not reach the wider public and their activities could be put under full surveillance. Some scholars argue that via the strategy of creating a safe territory of freedom of expression and providing the possibility of producing uncensored cultural products, the Institute's directors were pursuing different goals. On the one hand, they could satisfy the intellectuals by providing them with a democratic space which was also useful in proving to more democratic countries that Iran was a free country. On the other hand, they could monitor artists who were potentially against Pahlavi dynasty and control their actions and interactions.[13]

In 1968, Shirvanlu invited the Moscow Circus to Tehran with the intention of using the investment to earn enough money for the Institute to provide a part of the budget necessary for the inauguration of the cinema department of the Institute. The Institute gained a considerable amount from the investment and used it to launch its cinema department in 1970. The policies of the cinema department were not different from the other departments of the Institute.[14]

The cinema tradition that evolved in the Institute was completely at odds with the mainstream cinema of the time. While the views promoted in Iranian commercial cinema were mostly superficial, backward and conservative, the Institute functioned as a safe space to speak the unspoken and retrieve and those reflect aspects of the culture that were ignored by mainstream cinema. The Institute used to produce works that tended to challenge the dominant discourses of the time and engage in aesthetic and thematic experimentation.[15] The pejorative terms used to describe the popular films of mainstream cinema were Filmfarsi. Introduced by Houshang Kavoosi in the early 1960s, the term *Filmfarsi* was used for films characterized by superficial stories about damsels in distress saved by heroic tough guys, shallow characterization, impossible accidents, sudden story twists, and erotic dance episodes in nightclubs and street and bar fights in scenes unrelated to the main narrative. In Filmfarsi, poverty is celebrated, and class conflicts are resolved by love. These films were generally influenced by Hollywood films and were in dialogues with Egyptian and Bollywood cinema.[16] The critical writings of a number of film experts, including Kavoosi, on mainstream films initiated an alternative discourse which later gave birth to what is now known as Iranian New Wave.

Some of the famous filmmakers who contributed to this alternative discourse, including Bahram Beyzaie, Nasser Taghvai, Masoud Kimiaei and Amir Naderi, took the opportunity to work with the Institute in the years before the revolution.[17] Such directors were considered 'subsidiary' and 'marginal' by mainstream cinema and could not work with the market-oriented producers who controlled Iranian cinema, but they had significant artistic visions. As a result, the films that were made in the Institute during the years leading up to the revolution were categorically inconsistent with Filmfarsi and relatively inconsistent with the dominant socio-political discourses of the time. This aesthetic and thematic superiority and the chasteness of the films which had to do with their intended addressees were instrumental in the influence that the films produced by the Institute had on post-revolutionary television.[18] Since the Institute did not need to compete with the private sector or function in accordance with the economic cycle of production and distribution, it opened its doors to creative, leftist artists and intellectuals who established a progressive artistic committee, which was, nevertheless, required to work with the state. This was an exceptional opportunity for the so-called committed filmmakers because they could make films that handled unwanted subjects and were indirectly critical of the state with the government budget.

The Institute, therefore, was instrumental in forming one of the main margins of Iranian cinema by providing opportunities for directors who were not interested in making commercial and superficial films and did not have any place in mainstream cinema. The Institute made it possible for a generation of artists to challenge the readymade formats of mainstream cinema and eliminate the disruptive regulations that guaranteed the continuity of the dominant cinematic, socio-political and artistic discourses. However, new rules and constraints gradually emerged within the Institute itself that can easily be identified today. In the years prior to the revolution, the Institute's artists often considered themselves 'committed' artists, but as stated before, this commitment was not to the intellectual and emotional needs of children but to the delivery of idealistic and political messages and the intellectual demands of socio-political opposition. It seems that the Institute films were made with the remnants of the artists' bitter childhood memories and were more like a review of their childhood from an adult perspective. As Saeed Talajooy puts it, though reflective of life in the lower classes and occasionally still valid, these childhood memories were closer to how children experienced life two decades earlier rather than in the 1970s.[19] They were dominated by sadness, repression, bitter, unspoken emotions and were often always devoid of fun, games and joy.[20] In fact, the target audience of these film were adults, who were to be enlightened about the conditions of life in Iran. The needs of children were supposed to be in the 'centre', but they were brushed away to the 'margins'. By allegorizing them, committed filmmakers approached political taboos with impunity. The allegory is the common denominator of most famous films made in the Institute, namely Amir Naderi's *Sāzdahani* (Harmonica, 1974), Nasser Taghvai's *Rahāei* (Salvation, 1972), Morteza Momayez's *Siā Parandeh* (Black Bird, 1974), Mohammad Reza Aslani's *Badbade* (The Quail, 1971). For instance, Amir Naderi's film tells the story of a boy who uses his harmonica to exploit the neighbourhood children who like to play the instrument. Over the years, this story has always been referred to as an allegory of colonialism and exploitation. The film *Salvation* also creates an allegory for captivity and the desire for freedom out of the story of a fish kept in a small fish tank. As a result, today the Institute is mainly remembered for some dark works which were not really made for children and their atmospheres were not in harmony with the hope and energy observed in children's colourful world.

By the time he embarked on making films, Bahram Beyzaie had been active as a playwright and theatre scholar and director for a decade. The intellectual atmosphere of the Iranian theatre was also completely politicized during the years Beyzaie wrote and staged his first plays. There, too, everyone demanded a commitment to political ideals and saw art as a means for fulfilling an end, which in their case was ideological and political resistance against the state. A roundtable discussion that was held in 1968 on Beyzaie's two plays, *Mirās* (The Heritage) and *Ziāfat* (The Feast), reflects the characteristics of the discourse on committed art and the attitudes and judgements of the intellectuals associated with this discourse. It also clearly shows the inconsistency between this discourse and Beyzaie's views on artistic activities. The word choices and concepts used in the discussions during the roundtable explicitly suggest that the proponents of this discourse were obsessed with and prioritized political propaganda over aesthetic engagement with life, society, politics and arts as well as the artist's individual perspectives. In this dialogue, Saeed Soltanpour, a leading leftist intellectual and theatre practitioner, clearly tries to impose a list of dos and don'ts on Beyzaie and insists on giving priority to his own Marxist idea of how 'truth' is to be reflected and analysed over the reality of historical experiences. This roundtable also shows that Beyzaie fitted into neither the framework of the main voices in the dominant political discourse nor the common leftist discourse of the intellectuals of the time.[21] Despite this divergent attitude or perhaps because of it, the Institute approached Beyzaie in 1969 and initiated cooperation that resulted in two short films, *Amu Sibiliu* (Uncle Moustache) and *Safar* (Journey). Later after the revolution, once more Beyzaie cooperated with the Institute to make *Bāshu, Gharibeh-ye Kuchak* (Bāshu, the Little Stranger). In addition to their numerous technical innovations, these three films are also very thought-provoking because they challenge the governmental and intellectual discourses of their times, and together, they illustrate a clear 'path' that has the markers of the author's individual world in all its motifs and characters.

Uncle Moustache

Bahram Beyzaie, like many other artists, came to the Institute due to Shirvanlu's invitation and was able to make his first film due to Shirvanlu's support.[22] The noticeable difference between *Uncle Moustache* and the majority of the stories and films made for the Institute is that Beyzaie's film is, indeed, dedicated to children. It is a joyful and humorous film for and about children. A middle-aged man with a big moustache has moved from a bustling area of the city to the suburb in order to live a relaxed life in a quiet neighbourhood. In other words, he has come from the 'centre' to the 'margin'. He looks very 'serious' and is constantly engaged in studying and contemplating, but he is unaware that he has actually entered the territory of children. Today, when we put *Uncle Moustache* in a 'long shot' and look at it in the context of the Institute, it seems that Beyzaie had made fun of the extreme and untimely seriousness of the intellectuals of the time and the bleak atmospheres of the products of the Institute. He had stood with the children to remind everyone of the vitality of childhood.

Through the lens of Beyzaie's camera, the spectators see the man standing in the 'foreground', with his back turned to the window, not paying attention to the children playing outside in the 'background'. In this mise en scène, the window frame resembles a cinema screen, a cinema centred on children. From this perspective, relying on cinematic theories derived from Jacques Lacan's views on the mirror and the imaginary realm,[23] one can argue that the 'image' seen through the window is an imaginary and dreamy frame of a lost childhood that the man would rather ignore. He belongs entirely to the symbolic order and is, in a sense, an embodiment of patriarchal authority, while the 'boys' behind the window are more in the imaginary realm. The psychoanalytic perspective tempts the viewer to find the footprint of the transition from the imaginary realm to the symbolic order in this form of space segmentation and interpret the window in terms of the mirror stage. On one side of this window (the mirror) the pleasure principle 'prevails', while on the other side we see the strictness and symbolic order and the 'law of the father'. Thus, the contrast between the children's happy worlds and the violent and patriarchal image of the man has Oedipal echoes. In this context, the moustache is also a characteristic of the leftist intellectuals; therefore, it might not be wrong to regard it as a sarcastic comment as well. Although the film leaves us free to explore these hidden layers and expand the range of its implications, it never falls into the trap of becoming a political metaphor in the conventional intellectual way. It rather constructs and makes a pleasant suggestion to children, which refers to playing as their only serious concern.

The film's driving force is the contrast between the children's playful and boundless world and the man's serious and bounded mind. While the children are running and playing in an open area, the man is often sitting in his small, cramped flat. Children are creative. By drawing temporary lines with chalk and planting unused sticks into the ground, they turn a barren field into a football field. On the contrary, the Moustached man is a stubborn person obsessed with frames and boundaries. Due to the walls, doors, and windows of his house, the composition of his shots is mostly formed by obvious and bold horizontal and vertical lines. Unlike him, children do not fit into any frame. They are constantly breaking down borders: whether these 'borders' are the windows of the man's house, or the curtain or the bed which they want to hide behind or under (as seen in the hospital sequence). They do not easily adapt to lines and limits. No matter how hard they try, eventually their hands or feet would protrude from the corners of the bed and curtains. In the shots related to the man, there are noticeable visual signs indicating limitation and demarcation, which can be interpreted as the boundaries and restraints of adults. From this point of view, the film stands against patriarchal order and takes the side of children wholeheartedly, which, in turn, can be interpreted as Beyzaie's statement against the unwritten rules of the Institute's cultural products and moving in the opposite direction where instead of the adults, children are the winners.

If interpreted at an archetypal level, the film is also the inverse of a quest or the journey of initiation archetype. As Joseph Campbell explains 'atonement with the father' represents a major turning point in the plot of such quests or journeys of self-discovery. It is in this moment of atonement that the hero faces the true purpose of his quest as everything the hero has endured thus far has led to this moment of reckoning with the person or entity that holds the power that rules his life. As a result of his encounter with the symbolic 'father', the hero becomes fully aware of his or her power, purpose or skill during the apotheosis or climax, and this newfound knowledge is the key to the hero's ultimate success.[24] Instead of following the usual instructive anecdotes about puberty, in which the boy goes through a hierarchical set of challenges and his tumultuous past to learn to obey the law of adulthood and the rules of society, it is the father who embraces his forgotten childish excitement.

Unlike most Iranian children's films which tend to converse with their young audience in an advising tone, here, in *Uncle Moustache*, children are not expected to adapt to dos and don'ts of adults. Instead, it is the man who, under the influence of children, alters his strict, patriarchal manner and becomes a different person. It is he who finally shaves his moustache, joins the children, and accompanies them in playing football. The glass that breaks after the man shoots the ball indicates the shattering of his fence of isolation and arrogance, and the echoes of glass being smashed resemble the sound of opening a bottle of champagne to celebrate his rebirth.[25]

Journey

In contrast with *Uncle Moustache*, *Journey* is strange, dark and bitter. It stands miles away from the freshness and warmth of *Uncle Moustache*, and a few steps closer to the general character of the films made in the Institute. This stark difference makes one wonder what happened to Beyzaie in the two years between these two films. The soundtrack diverges from the joyful and lively music of *Uncle Moustache* (by Esfandiyar Monfaredzadeh) to offer a plaintive Turkmen music. While by shaving his moustache, the grumpy, frustrated man of *Uncle Moustache*, symbolically became a child, in *Journey* by shaving a child's hair, they make him look like a bald old man. *Journey* is the story of children who do not experience childhood. To experience childhood, there must be a neighbourhood and a home. The path of the children in *Journey* diverges from the children of *Uncle Moustache* right there. *Journey*'s boys do not belong to anything, but they do not experience freedom either. They are forsaken, rejected and lost. This time, the patriarchal order does not bend to the will of the children and asserts its disruptive presence at every corner. The boys, therefore, desperately look for a refuge which welcomes them. They need reassuring 'limits' and 'boundaries' and a 'roof' that gives them a sense of belonging. They stand in front of the camera of an itinerant photographer to take their photo, and then they run away giggling without paying or even getting their picture. They want to settle down, even within the framework of a photo; the photo that they will never have. It is enough for them to be recorded and inhabit such a 'frame', even for a short moment.

When one of the boys, who has been pushing the other one to join him for the journey, arrives at his destination, the house that he hopes will be his home, he faces a burly man, a cheerless moustached grumpy man standing in front of the house's entrance between the boy and a woman in the background in such a way that his figure splits the shot into two sections. The presence of Parvaneh Masoumi whose appearance in Beyzaie's *Ragbār* (Downpour, 1972) had established her as a great actress gives a remarkable significance to the woman's small role and her eye contact with the boy. Though they exchange no words, a hidden connection evolves between the two. This highly interpretable moment associates the woman with home, roots, nature, and happiness. Analysing the separation of the boy and the woman in this perspective allows for expanding the meaning and the universe of the film as much as possible.[26] The affinity of the woman and the boy is reflected in Beyzaie's mise en scène more than anything else. Both are isolated, ignored, and 'marginalized' in a space dominated by a man. By tracing this masculinity in *Journey*'s dystopian setting, Beyzaie explicitly responds to the dominant and pervasive intellectual tendencies of the time. The construction workers (proletariat), the central characters of the ideology of many of those who dominated the Institute, do not notice the two boys, but the moustached paedophile, who, as Talajooy states, looks like the tough guys of mainstream Iranian cinema, follows them as 'preys' for his pervert desires.[27]

The character type *jāhel* (tough guy) was the central character of most films of the Filmfarsi genre of the era. Typical individuals of the type wore a black velvet suit, a fedora hat, and a white shirt with a few open upper buttons, black shoes and a moustache. They usually had a long silk handkerchief and spoke with a particular accent that reflected the speech patterns of the lower classes. Many of those who belonged to this group of people were proud of their illiteracy and boasted of being tramps.[28] It is not also surprising that they found such a prominent role in Filmfarsi, as, depending on the situation, this character can be considered the embodiment of either a negative form of resistance against modernity or a superficially hybrid and imitative understanding of modernity. In Filmfarsi, in many cases, they represented a heroic type who was portrayed as a strong, honourable and popular man who protected the weak against injustice and was praised for his strength. Nevertheless, the roles they played in the socio-political conflicts of the time were also significant. For example, their interventions in the street fights of the 1953 coup changed the political equation in favour of the proponents of the coup that led to the fall of Mohammad Mosaddegh's government and the return of the Shah to Iran.[29] Beyzaie's depiction of the figure deconstructs him by portraying him in a light that reveals his disgusting habits much more effectively than any other films in Iranian cinema.

When the lumpen thug dives into the poster of a Filmfarsi in a completely exaggerated and comic way, it seems as if the filmmaker is offering a new lens to the audience so they can see that these underclass lumpen thugs are, indeed, very repulsive. This is not a film in which lumpen thugs have epic and heroic presences. It is not a film in which a poor and displaced boy accidentally finds his father in a happy ending. This drastic perspective is significant as, at the time, most Filmfarsi films were designed to suggest that there is a lost blood relation between the affluent minority who dominate the possibilities of modernization and the poor, marginalized urban majority. In other words, in Filmfarsi, the idea of togetherness is often suggested by depicting a situation in which the old and the new and the poor and the rich are related through blood relations. For instance, in *Ganj-e Qārun* (Qārun's Treasure, 1965) the poor, marginalized hero, who adheres to traditional values, may be the lost or runaway child of a wealthy man, who owns new industries but is lonely and unhappy. The two finally come together after problems or initial misunderstandings, and the hidden blood relation is finally revealed. As a result, an optimistic reconciliation occurs, and the happy family builds a bright future. In *Journey*, however, the optimistic illusion of the connection between the marginalized and the modern city, the poor and the rich, or the traditional and modern spaces collapses. This, however, is done not with anger and despair or a desire to destroy the city but with an expression of regret at the lack of dialogue and understanding.[30] *Journey* refrains from giving comfort or fulfilling a feeling of catharsis. It rather disrupts the audience's sleep by showing how the forgotten ones are sleeping in the ghettos and the ruins of old buildings. This nightmarish image of the city is shocking, especially at a time when the state discourse which was intoxicated by oil revenues constantly talked of Iran's grand future.[31]

Journey is truly a film of atmosphere and background. By over-stylizing, relying on installation art, compacting the time, ignoring the objective logic of events, and emphasis on the crowded and cramped spaces, it induces a claustrophobic feeling and portrays a nightmarish Tehran through the eyes of the two boys. Due to this point of view and mise en scène, the film gradually loses its initial neorealist tone and creates an expressionistic mood which goes beyond the social realist cinema of the alternative cinema of the time and its European counterparts to raise existential concerns and fundamental questions about human identity.

Many of Beyzaie's later films contain motifs and ideas that have their origins in *Journey*. Displaced and homeless boys of *Journey* are present in *Stranger and the Fog* and *Bāshu the Little Stranger* with a different appearance. *The Crow* is also about a city lost in the turmoil of a transitional period. *Maybe Some Other Time* is about identity, and its protagonist is a woman who is looking for her real parents. *Journey*'s workers appear in the Sangastani sequence of *Killing Mad Dogs* with the same appearance, and in *When We Are All Sleeping* the machination of commercial mainstream cinema becomes the subject of analysis. This shows that, despite its obvious commonalities with the generally bitter films of the Institute, *Journey* is distinguished by Beyzaie's lifelong preoccupations which make the film much more significant in its cultural concerns. Like other films made in the Institute, the film can be said to be focused on delivering a 'message', but Beyzaie's message is not a simplistic advising message. It is rather a constructive multi-layered discourse about life in Iran. The narrative takes the audience through a journey that does not lead to a safe destination. The path, which seems linear at first, returns to the starting point at the end to form a complete cycle. In other words, although here the seeker is not necessarily the finder, there is no other way but to start searching again. This is Beyzaie's bitter but realistic suggestion. As a result, despite its circular narrative and its emphasis on rotating elements such as tires and wheels,

Journey takes a different path from the common passivity that is observed in the circular hopelessness of the theatre of the absurd. The emphasis, both visually and thematically, is on action, endeavour, human will, and movement, which seems to be in vain but suggests the strength of character. This is an invitation to standing up and trying again, an attitude which echoes Beyzaie's life since its very beginning.

Bāshu, the Little Stranger

Although after the 1979 revolution most institutes affiliated with the Pahlavi state were closed or completely restructured, the Institute continued its activities rather smoothly. Behruz Gharibpour states that it was the phrase, 'Children and Young Adults', in the name of the Institute that saved it.[32] Some other scholars, however, argue that the presence of people like Alireza Zarrin, a manager who believed in the revolution but had an open-minded interested in children, saved the Institute. As Aslani puts it:

> Unlike the newcomers who rose to power quickly after the revolution and tried to deny the Institute's achievements, Zarrin made a great contribution to the continuation of the activities of this institution. His support for the people who worked with the Institute was a risk and required a level of courage that no one expected. While the activities and the functions and atmospheres of many institutions had been disrupted by the influx of opportunists, people like Abbas Kiarostami, Amir Naderi, Ahmad Reza Ahmadi and Nureddin Zarrin Kelk were able to breathe, work and redefine their styles and ideas [in the relatively open atmosphere of the Institute], and this would not have been possible without Zarrin's patient wisdom. He intelligently realized the value of the Institute's managerial structure and functions.[33]

Beyzaie, who had been teaching theatre at the University of Tehran since 1970 and had acted as the Head of the Department of Performing Arts since 1974 was expelled from the university during the Cultural Revolution and was banned from working in theatre. Thus, the Institute was probably the only place he could work with. Four years after his last film, *Marg-e Yazdgerd* (Death of Yazdgerd, 1981), was refused permission and a year after he edited Amir Naderi's *Davandeh* (The Runner, 1984), the Institute supported his plan to make *Bāshu, the Little Stranger*. The film is about a child who flees from his war-torn hometown in southern Iran during an air raid that kills all his family members and takes refuge in a calm green region in northern Iran. Such a subject had never been handled in the films of those who were associated with the new dominant discourse. It had been simply neglected or avoided due to the official focus on the heroism of the warriors fighting at the front. Iranian war films, which evolved to create the new genre 'sacred defence cinema', often made religious epics out of war-related subjects,[34] but *Bāshu* highlighted the voice of the 'marginalized' and the challenges of a stranger and 'other' in a community that is obsessed with its inherited 'self'.

The plot of *Bāshu, the Little Stranger* is designed in a way that suggests the boys in the neighbourhood of *Uncle Moustache* face a boy who is like *Journey*'s dislocated boys. The village boys in *Bāshu* have a community that with the appearance of a stranger functions like a unified bullying gang. They unite against the stranger to assert their collective identity. They tease and ridicule Bāshu in a way that is like their typical attitudes towards the Moustached man in *Uncle Moustache*. They even unite to beat *Bāshu*. At one level, this attitude echoes some of the conflicts observed during the early 1980s due to the immigration of people from war-torn regions to the main Iranian cities. Limited resources in a war-torn country and accommodation problems meant that host communities, those who lived in safer cities (centre), occasionally displayed hostile attitudes towards those who had come from war-torn cities (margins). They saw war immigrants as uninvited guests who, with their untimely arrival, had further disrupted their local resources and culture. Since ethnocentric or racist perceptions are also always passed down to children, schools were also one of the places in which local children (the self) rallied and teamed up to tease or beat children from war-torn cities (the other).

The discourse that constantly talked about unity and tended to hide the cracks of society by presenting the image of a unified people turned a blind eye to the facts that are highlighted in *Bāshu*. While *Bāshu*'s depiction of villagers distanced itself from most artistic films of the 1980s, its interpretation of war subverted the perception of the war reflected in the mainstream state-sponsored films of that era. The otherness of Bāshu and his sense of alienation is clearly reflected in two scenes via Beyzaie's mise en scène. The first is when the villagers come to Nāei's house to see Bāshu. The film depicts the atmosphere of this gathering through Bāshu's eyes and makes the audience experience homelessness as he does. The second is the bazaar scene, in which the documentary-like shots and their juxtaposition with the film's narrative elements enhance and convey the sense of Bāshu's isolation from his environment.

Reflecting on this social phenomenon and the war in general, Beyzaie's film is an invitation to peace and unity at one level and avoidance of wars at another. This was important as at the time Iranian mainstream cinema had mobilized all its resources to glorify and sanctify the war. In *Bāshu*, the war is nothing but destruction: traumatized and maimed individuals and ruined schools, hospitals, houses and farms. Thus, the making of the film may urge a researcher to state that the Institute was still a safe place for those in the 'margins' of Iranian cinema who wanted to reflect on aspects of life that were ignored by the formal discourse. What happened after the completion of the film, however, demonstrated that this was no longer the case. Like Beyzaie's two previous films *Cherikeh-ye Tārā* (Ballad of Tārā, 1978–80) and *Death of Yazdgerd*, *Bāshu* was banned as it was deemed to be critical of the war. The proponents of the dominant discourse could never approve of Bāshu's escape as they expected him to stand and fight the enemy. What was accepted by the dominant discourse can be seen in Kambuzia Partovi's *Bāzi-ye Bozorgān* (Adult's Game, 1990) in which children take up arms and fight.

Nevertheless, unlike *Ballad of Tārā* and *Death of Yazdgerd*, *Bāshu* was finally released three years and a few months later in 1989 and was received so well in Iran and outside Iran that even today it is ranked as one of the greatest films ever made in Iran. Discussing the process that led to the final release of the film is beyond the scope of this chapter, but what is important is that when the war ended the so-called anti-war discourse of the film was considered less of an issue.

Two other important aspects of the film were related to the way it avoided sentimental conclusions and the way it depicted women. Beyzaie's narrative of reconciliation refrains from ideological and sentimental resolutions. After the northern white boys shake hands with the southern brown boy, one expects that the stranger to be accepted as a member of the community and all conflicts get resolved. This, however, is far from reality as Beyzaie knows it. Thus, the local boys become less violent, but they do not really become friendly towards the stranger and continue to use any opportunity to tease and upset him with various excuses. This separation is also reflected in the film's mise en scènes in which, except for one or two scenes in which Bāshu is surrounded by children, his frames are separate from the children's.

One important example of their mischievous attitude is the way they inform Bāshu of the return of Nāei's husband. They probably believe that Nāei's husband, like the man in *Journey*, may stand in the doorway and prevent the homeless boy from entering the house.

These mischievousness attitudes are, in fact, often intended to flaunt their safe position to Bāshu to remind him that as a stranger who is not like them, his position has become more precarious with the arrival of the man of the house. From this point of view, the last scene is psychologically very complicated. As soon as Bāshu hears from the children that Nāei's man has returned home in response to the letter (which was about Bāshu), he picks up a stick from the ground and goes home. It is clear that he can guess who the man who is arguing with Nāei is. However, he goes forward with anger and asks threateningly: 'Who is this man?'

The scene suggests that Bāshu's behaviour combines real emotions with roleplaying to remind the man of his positive role as the defender of Nāei and the house to win his trust. Therefore, this ending, despite its positive signs, is not one of those 'happy endings' that take the character to a safe and secure end. This ending raises questions: Will Bāshu and Nāei's husband truly and deeply become 'father and son' in an imagined sequel? Will the children and Bāshu get along and sit comfortably together in the same classroom?

In *Bāshu*, the house that becomes Bāshu's home belongs to a woman who seems to represent the heart and spirit of the earth, a loving, agile, powerful and lively woman who can even communicate with birds and land animals. Beyzaie's Nāei is the heir to the ancient goddesses and is associated with water, fertility, love and sensuality. Unlike the woman in *Journey*, she speaks loud and clear, and her voice is louder than the man's voice. The significance of Nāei's powerful presence becomes more evident if one remembers that after the revolution, Iranian mainstream cinema pushed women to the 'margins' even more than before. Under the influence of the dominant patriarchal gaze, women were presented as docile and obedient figures and were tolerated on the screen only when they were depicted in their houses and specifically the kitchen, as a mother or a spouse.[35] During such a period when the 'otherness' of women as active individuals was more visible than when *Journey* was made, Nāei, as an assertive, yet compassionate and supportive woman, presented a type of womanhood that went directly against the dominant discourse and its view of women.

In the middle of the film, where Nāei and Bāshu are on the verge of becoming 'mother and son', the viewers see a sequence that is like the sequence of the villagers' initial gathering in Nāei's house. This time the villagers have gathered in Nāei's house again because Bāshu seems to have disappeared. Now it is Nāei who has become a stranger (other) due to her disharmony with the 'tribe'. This time the spectator is made to identify with Nāei's feeling of restless loss and homelessness by being placed in a position to see the world through her eyes. It seems that the film has connected Bāshu and Nāei with this parallel mise en scène (and some other similar situations, such as finding medicine and seeking help, feeding children or sowing seeds in the field). Despite this parallel, however, Nāei's role in the film is different from Bāshu's as she is ultimately the initiator of unity, and thus, in the end, Nāei, her husband, their children and Bāshu become a family and run towards the field to drive the wild boars away.[36]

Conclusion

Uncle Moustache and *Journey* paved the way for the support that the Institute offered to Beyzaie for making *Bāshu, the Little Stranger*. In other words, *Bāshu* was not the result of an accidental cooperation, but the outcome of a process which had begun with Beyzaie's ability to produce two of the early masterpieces of Iranian children's cinema. This becomes more evident if one considers the restrictive stance that the state had taken against Beyzaie after the revolution. Thus, when it comes to *Bāshu*, one should not neglect the impact of the Institute's heritage on the decisions that its management made in the first few years after the revolution. In Beyzaie's case, this experience was ruined by the ban that was imposed on the film after its completion. Though less complicated in their production and release Naderi's *The Runner* (1984) and Kiarostami's *Khāneh-ye Dust Kojāst?* (Where Is the Friend's House, 1986) were also similar in that both directors were able to make their films primarily because they had worked with the Institute for almost a decade before the revolution.

Bāshu was Beyzaie's last collaboration with the Institute. Although he later wrote screenplays such as *Film dar Film* (Film within a Film) or *The Landscape* in which children's conditions and fates are a subject of enquiry, he never returned to the Institute. The ban that was imposed on *Bāshu* was a clear marker of the narrow-mindedness that was becoming more prevalent in the Institute and eventually led to the dismissal of Alireza Zarrin and the departure of Abbas Kiarostami from the Institute in the early 2000s. From then on, the Institute was no longer the locus where leading artists could present their alternative vision and progressive cinema. The philistinism that had transformed many cultural institutes after the revolution and had slowly changed the Institute accelerated, and soon the Institute became an ineffectual and conservative institute.[37] Although it remained in the 'margins', it had now completely bent to the requirements of the 'centre' and was no longer a haven for marginalized perspectives.

Before the revolution, the Institute was considered a rival to such major film producers as the National Iranian Radio and Television and the Ministry of Art and Culture. In the first decade of the revolution, despite the limitation that was imposed on its activities, its vision was sometimes in conflict with the policies of the Ministry of Culture and Islamic Guidance. From the 1990s, however, it gradually lost its independence and eventually went under the complete supervision of the Ministry of Education.[38] However, the milestones of the Institute's cinematic productions in the 1970s and 1980s, particularly Beyzaie's *Uncle Moustache, Journey*, and *Bāshu, the Little Stranger*, illustrate how the inclusion of alternative visions can lead to the production of great cultural products. They also demonstrate how, when it comes to cultural production, proper management, providing the required infrastructure as well as opportunities to experiment with new forms and themes, and long-term planning can lead to lasting results. This is the fact that has been neglected in the last two decades when Iranian cinema has become more reliant on accidental masterpieces produced by individuals rather than believing in organizational planning, supporting, planting and harvesting.

Notes

1. For an analysis of the film, see below. For a detailed analysis, see Talajooy, *Iranian Culture*, 71–90.
2. Bakhtiari, *Iran: RPM*, 12–18.
3. For more on Shirvanlu, see EIr, 'SHIRVANLU, FIRUZ'. The name is also spelled Firouz Shirvanlou.
4. Bakhtiari, *Iran: RPM*, 12.
5. Aslani, 'Yek Olgou-ye', 21.
6. *Fedāei-ye Khalq* signifies those who are ready to sacrifice their lives for people.
7. Gharibpour, 'Padideh-ei Tekrār', 77.
8. Moezi Moghadam, 'KĀNUN-E PARVAREŠ-E'.
9. Anonymous, *Zanān-e Darbār*, 163.
10. Sojoudi, 'Ertebātāt Bein-e', 147.
11. Kadivar, 'Tahlil-e Mohtavā', 75.
12. Sojoudi, 'Ertebātāt Bein-e', 145.
13. Baghban Maher and Shams, 'Jazireh-ye Āzadi', 143.
14. Bakhtiari, *Iran: RPM*, 23.
15. Mehrabi, *Tārikh-e Sinemā-ye*, 352.
16. Moazzezinia, *Filmfārsi Chist?*.
17. Sadr, *Tārikh-e Siasi-ye*, 226.
18. Forouzesh, 'Royā-ye Kudakān-e', 44.
19. Siadat, 'Interview with Talajooy'.
20. Forouzesh, 'Roya-ye Kudakān-e', 47.

21 Beyzaie and Soltanpour, 'Mizgerd-e Tāātr', 165.
22 Qukasiyan, *Goftogu*, 33.
23 Hayward, *Cinema Studies*, 286–306.
24 Campbell, *Hero with*, 116–37.
25 For studies of the film from other angles, see Talajooy, 'Uncle Moustache' 234–6 & *Iranian Culture*, 71–90.
26 Beyzaie further explored this hidden capacity in his next film for the Institute, *Bashu, the Little Stranger*.
27 Talajooy, 'The Journey', 236–8; and Talajooy, *Iranian Culture*, 133–54.
28 Akbari, *Lumpenism*, 54.
29 For more, see Sarshar, *Khāterāt-e Shʿābān-e*, 112.
30 Amjad, 'Az Tārikh', 108.
31 Ejlali, *Degarguni-ye Ejtemāei*, 73–6.
32 Gharibpour, 'Padideh-ei Tekrār', 79.
33 Aslani, 'Yek Olgu-ye', 24.
34 Devictor, *Revâyat-e Jang*, 250–65.
35 Ghorbankarimi, *Colourful Presence*, 45–8.
36 For more on Nāei's character, see Talajooy, 'Jābejāei-ye Marzhā', 48–51.
37 Aslani, 'Yek Olgou-ye'.
38 Gharibpour, 'Padideh-ei Tekrār', 81.

Bibliography

Akbari, Ali Akbar. *Lumpenism*. Tehran: Sepehr, 1974.
Amjad, Hamid. 'Az Tārikh Va Ostoureh Khalasi Nadārim'. *Tajrobeh*. Vol. 1. No. 7 (Winter 2012). Pp. 107–12.
Anonymous. *Zanān-e Darbār be Revāyat-e Asnād-e Sāvāk, Farah Pahlavi*. Tehran: Markaz-e Barrasi-e Asnād-e Tārikhi-ye Vezarāt-e Ettelāāt (Center for the Study of Historical Documents of the Ministry of Intelligence) 2015.
Aslani, Mohammad Reza. 'Yek Olgou-ye Modiriyat-e Farhangi'. *Āngāh*. Vol. 1. No. 2 (Spring 2018). Pp. 20–4.
Baghban Maher, Sajjad and Mohammad Shams. 'Jazireh-ye Āzadi Dar Oqyānus-e Ekhtenāq'. *Āngāh*. Vol. 1. No. 2 (Spring 2018). Pp. 142–5.
Bakhtiari, Ali. *Iran: RPM. Collection of Kānun's Vinyl Record Productions*. Vol. 2. London: Magic of Persia, 2014.
Beyzaie, Bahram and Saeed Soltanpour. 'Mizgerd-e Tāātr: Darbāreh-ye Mirās va Ziyāfat'. *Simia 2: Vizheh-ye Bahram Beyzaie va Tāātr*. Ed. Hamid Amjad. Vol. 2. No. 2 (Winter 2008). Pp. 165–87.
Campbell, Joseph. *The Hero with Thousand Faces*. Princeton: Princeton University Press, 2004.
Devictor, Agnes. *Revāyat-e Jang dar Del-e Jang. Jāigāh Majmuʿeh Mostanad hā-ye shahid Seyyed Morteza Avini*. Tehran, Vāhe, Institut français de recherches en Iran (IFRI), 2020.
Ejlali, Parviz. *Degarguni-ye Ejtemāei va Filmhā-ye Sinemā-ye Irān*. Tehran: Āgah, 2017.
EIr. 'SHIRVANLU, FIRUZ'. In *Encyclopaedia Iranica Online*, © Trustees of Columbia University in the City of New York. Online: http://dx.doi.org/10.1163/2330-4804_EIRO_COM_969. (Accessed 16 February 2022).

Forouzesh, Ebrahim. 'Royā-ye Kudakān-e Dirouz va Emruz'. *Āngāh*. Vol. 1. No. 2 (Spring 2018). Pp. 38–51.

Gharibpour, Behrouz. 'Padideh-ei Tekrār Nashodani' (Interview by Zeinab Lak). *Āngāh*. Vol. 1. No. 2 (Spring 2018). Pp. 74–81.

Ghorbankarimi, Maryam. *A Colourful Presence: The Evolution of Women's Representation in Iranian Cinema*. Cambridge: Cambridge Scholar Publishing, 2015.

Hayward, Suzan. *Cinema Studies: The Key Concepts*. London and New York: Routledge, 2003.

Kadivar, Mansour. 'Tahlil-e Mohtavā-ye Ketābhā-ye Qesseh-ye Kānun-e Parvaresh-e Fekri-ye Kudakān va Nojavānān dar Do Marhaleh-ye Pish va Pas az Enqelāb'. *Pazhuhesh-nāmeh-ye Adabiyāt-e Kudakān va Nojavānān*. Vol. 2. No. 5 (Summer 1996). Pp. 74–6.

Mehrabi, Masoud. *Tarikh-e Sinemā-ye Iran az Āghāz tā 1357*. Tehran: Film, 1985.

Moazzezinia, Hossein. *Filmfārsi Chist?*. Tehran: Saghi, 2002.

Moezi Moghadam, Fereydoun. 'KĀNUN-E PARVAREŠ-E FEKRI-E KUDAKĀN VA NOWJAVĀNĀN' (2012). *Encyclopaedia Iranica Online*. Online: http://dx.doi.org/10.1163/2330-4804_EIRO_COM_10725 (Accessed 30 July 2022).

Naficy, Hamid. *A Social History of Iranian Cinema: Volume 2: The Industrializing Years, 1941–1978*. Durham: Duke University Press, 2011.

Qukasiyan, Zaven. *Goftogu bā Bahram Beyzaie*. Tehran: Āgah, 1993.

Sadr, Hamidreza. *Tārikh-e Siāsi-ye Sinemā-ye Iran*. Tehran: Ney, 2003.

Sarshar, Homa. *Khāterāt-e Shaʿbān-e Jafari* (Memoirs of Shaban Jafari), Tehran: Sales, 2003.

Sojoudi, Farzan. 'Ertebātāt Bein-e Farhangi: Tarjomeh va Naghsh-e ān dar Farāyandhā-ye Jazb va Tard'. In *Neshānehshenāsi: Nazariyeh va Amal*. Collection of Essays by Farzan Sojoudi. Tehran: Elm, 2010. Pp. 143–67.

Talajooy, Saeed. '"Uncle Moustache: Amu Sibiloo" and "The Journey: Safar"'. In *Directory of World Cinema: Iran*. Ed. Parviz Jahed. Bristol: Intellect, 2012. Pp.234–8.

Talajooy, Saeed. 'Jābejāei-ye Marzhā-ye Taʿlloq: Qomiyat, Zabān va Hovyat Melli dar Bāshu, Gharibeh-ye Kuchak'. *Film-e Emruz* (Today's Film). No. 8 (January 2022). Pp. 48–51.

Talajooy, Saeed. *Iranian Culture in Bahram Beyzaie's Cinema and Theatre: Paradigms of Being and Belonging (1959–1979)*. London: I.B. Tauris, 2023.

Chapter 5

THE LANGUAGE OF NATURE AND EARTH: AN ECOCRITICAL READING OF *STRANGER AND THE FOG*, *BALLAD OF TĀRĀ*, AND *BĀSHU, THE LITTLE STRANGER*

Fatemeh-Mehr Khansalar

Introduction

Bahram Beyzaie's village trilogy – *Stranger and the Fog* (1974), *Ballad of Tārā* (1978–80) and *Bāshu, the Little Stranger* (1985) – can be viewed as a coherent narrative that illustrates the relationship between human beings and nature by making nature progressively more visible and tangible as female characters find their agency and power in the course of the trilogy. While gradually distancing his female characters from the gendered metaphorical association with a submissive nature, Beyzaie shows the strength of both women and nature and simultaneously suggests that nature has a life of its own and that both women and men are parts of nature and dependent on nature for survival. The protagonists of the first two films are in love, respectively, with a traveller who has escaped from beyond the fog and with a Historical Man who has returned from the world of the dead. As discussed in this chapter, while in these two cases, the relationships are more symbolic and reflective of the psychological or archetypal states of the protagonists than real, in *Bāshu, the Little Stranger*, the protagonist achieves a multi-layered presence that though representative of archetypal qualities has relationships which are tangible and worldly. This transformative treatment of relationships is also applied to nature. I argue that each of these films displays triangles of relationships between the main characters (male and female) and the spaces around them (home/nature). In each case, the female character has a dynamic relationship with the components of her natural and built environment until the male character, a stranger, appears and introduces the unfamiliar world (space) to the familiar world. From that point on, the female protagonist – as mediator of the process of accepting the stranger into the community – tries to make the unfamiliar familiar. I will show how this mediation depends on the agency of the female protagonist in her community. To analyse these triangles, I examine the natural geography of the location, the floorplans of the protagonists' homes and the positions of their bodies in important scenes in these contexts. I also show how women and their environment are given actual and symbolic voices in their encounters with suppressive patriarchal beliefs. My approach to this trilogy is informed by ecocriticism and ecofeminism. However, before briefly explaining what ecocriticism and ecofeminism have in common, I will offer an overview of the trilogy's plot to contextualize my debates.

Beyzaie's village trilogy: Overview of the plots

The trilogy illustrates the lives of three female farmers whose similarities suggest that they are to represent a single woman in the course of her transformation from a silenced woman who is trying to find her voice and her place in her environment to an independent woman who knows what she wants and manifests powerful and constructive relationships with her natural and built environment and society.

The first part of the trilogy concerns Ra'nā, the young widow of the hero of the village, Āshub. She and her child live with her father in a humble house when Āyat, an injured stranger, arrives in the village by boat. The villagers treat him and, when he wants to become a member of the community, they state that he must marry one of the village girls if he wants to become one of them. Āyat falls in love with Ra'nā, and she accepts him, but Āshub's brothers will not tolerate the marriage. Despite the obstacles, Ra'nā marries Āyat, but one night when all villagers are chasing a wolf in the forest, Āyat encounters Āshub, who has been hiding in the foggy forest, stealing money and food from people. They fight and Āyat kills Āshub. Āshub's corpse is carried by the river into the sea and is found near the village. Āyat confesses the details of the encounter to Ra'nā as she is mourning for Āshub. Āyat reveals Āshub's true nature to Ra'nā. Meanwhile, the mysterious strangers who live beyond the fog emerge to take Āyat with them. When he refuses to leave with them, they attack the village, and a gory war occurs between the villagers and the strangers. Finally, Āyat (who is injured again) decides to venture beyond the fog to find what lies behind it. At the end of the film, Ra'nā tears her white dress and begins to mourn once more in her black dress.

The second film is about Tārā, a charming young widow with two little children. Rahman, her husband, was a fisherman who drowned in the sea. Āshub, Tārā's brother-in-law, is in love with her and has settled in Tārā's village with his sisters, hoping to marry her. However, Tārā refuses him because she believes that Āshub was responsible for Rahman's death. Tārā lives in the home of her late father. She distributes the unwanted belongings of her father (Grandfather) among villagers, but no one wants the sword, which Tārā soon finds has a connection to a deceased Historical Man. Her current love interest, Qelich, desires a real relationship with her, but Tārā finds herself increasingly in love with the dead Historical Man who has returned to the village to reclaim his lost identity and his sword. In the course of the story of the Historical Man, Tārā discovers the history (specifically, the bloody war that occurred in the neighbouring forest) of her village. In the course of their meetings, Tārā decides to be with the Historical Man, but he can be resurrected only if she sacrifices her children. Since Tārā cannot accept that, she asks him to take her with him to the world of the dead. Eventually, the Historical Man returns to the sea without Tārā, leaving his sword for her. Relieved, she agrees to marry Qelich.

The final film in the trilogy concerns Nāei's struggle against her village and her husband after she adopts Bāshu, an orphaned refugee of the Iran-Iraq war. Nāei is a young mother, beautiful and strong, raising two children while working in the fields in the absence of her husband who has left the village in search of work. The plot is focused on Nāei's adoption of Bāshu and how she sympathizes and supports him helps him to settle in the new space and convinces her husband to accept him as a member of their family.

An overview of ecofeminism and ecocriticism

The main matter upon which both ecofeminism and ecocriticism agree is the existence of a patriarchal world view and the domination of men over women and human beings over nature. According to Val Plumwood, ever since human beings have imagined themselves as separate from the rest of nature, a 'discontinuity problem' has occurred which has, in time, been reinforced in different directions resulting in and a false dichotomy between human beings and nature.[1] In other words, human beings prefer to see themselves as standing above the rest of nature at the top of an imagined evolutionary hierarchy. However, human beings are part of nature and cannot be against or separated from it. Equally, the direct result of the imagined separation of human beings and nature is the creation of human-nature and culture-nature dichotomies. Furthermore, when women are, according to their traditional roles, identified with the 'natural and physical', and men are identified with the 'human and mental', one may conclude that, as Victoria Davion has summarized it, nature, physicality and womanhood become inferior to human, mentality and manhood. Consequently, the domination of 'human' and 'mental' and the subordination of their respective 'others' is justified.[2] From this perspective, ecofeminism and the environmental movement present become similar as they both challenge patriarchy. Therefore, ecofeminism seeks to examine and deconstruct the ways human beings exploit nature and the ways gender-based oppression damages and controls women. It also explores the ways nature and women can be empowered so that their agency can be recognized in human discourses. Likewise, when a text is read through an ecocritical perspective, the relations between the text, the writer (artist) and the world are changed since 'the notion of the world expands to include the entire ecosphere'.[3] In this expanded world, humans and nonhumans are seen as equal creatures, with human beings viewed as being continuous with the rest of the world. Accordingly, this approach suspects and attempts to undermine the presumed dichotomies between nature and culture, physical and mental, or sentimental and rational, because, as Plumwood argues, all these relations are rooted in the 'logic of domination'. With this logic, the privileged side of the dichotomy has the right of domination over the other side.[4] In any form of domination (man over woman or humanity over nature), one side of the relationship automatically loses its significance, agency and voice. Therefore, for women to achieve equality with men and for nature to achieve equality with human beings the first step is to embark on a process of communication to reclaim the lost agency and voice of the losing party. If human beings descend from their superior place and see themselves as a part of nature, nature can be seen and heard by them. As Michel Foucault states, social power operates through a regime of privileged speakers such as men, intellectuals and those whose words are taken seriously, while the words of women, children and nature are considered meaningless.[5]

Women and their environments in Beyzaie's village trilogy

In Beyzaie's trilogy, however, one encounters strong women who find new ways to speak up. This becomes particularly visible in *Bāshu, the Little Stranger*, in which Nāei has her own autonomy and voice in her relationships with people, animals and the natural landscape. Nāei is not only attuned to the environment around her but also stands against society and her husband whenever she feels that she is right. Though more outspoken and capable than others, Nāei is not the first woman with such qualities. She is, indeed, the final product of a process of cognitive maturation and initiation which begins with Ra'nā, in *Stranger and the Fog* and Tārā, in *Ballad of Tārā*, who are already challenging their patriarchal communities and voicing their own independent desires and thoughts. Nevertheless, in their relations with the world around them – as I will illustrate later – the first two women are still more metaphorical than real. In the third film, however, Nāei has a tangible relationship with her community, her environment, her husband and with the little stranger whom she saves.

The most efficient way to discuss the transformation of these female protagonists in the context of ecofeminism is to explore their relationship with their locations, societies and male counterparts. I will, therefore, use a location-based (deixis) perspective to identify and locate 'all entities' present in the films in their 'space, time, and social context'.[6] Through deixis, one can highlight the relation of each space with a story and specific action of a character; therefore, every space will be defined in relation to time, characters, relationships and other spaces.[7] In Beyzaie's trilogy, for each female character and her situation, space plays an important role not only as a setting but also as the source of stories which interact with her life. These spaces include a natural environment and a set of man-made buildings.

In the familiar space of the film, the female character confidently lives and creates a dynamic relationship with the components until the male character, a stranger, appears and introduces the unfamiliar world (space) to the current familiar world. From now on, the female protagonist – as a mediator of the acceptance process – tries to make the unfamiliar, familiar. In *Stranger and the Fog*, after the female protagonist forms a bond with a heroic stranger, other strangers attack her village from beyond the fog. In *Ballad of Tārā*, the wandering spirit of an ancient Historical Man walks into the village and confides in Tārā about his terrible fate. In *Bāshu, the Little Stranger*, an orphan boy who has escaped from the war zone enters the village as a homeless refugee. As a result, the relationship between the characters (the woman and the stranger) and the space must alter in a process in which the stranger is either rejected or accepted inside the familiar space. In all these films, the disharmony created by the stranger directly affects the female protagonist's life, either because of the romantic relationship incurred (such as Ra'nā and Āyat or Tārā and the Historical Man) or the mother-son feelings that are gradually created between Nāei and Bāshu. The role of the mediator in balancing the environment is played by the female protagonist who is well-equipped for the challenge and can deal with the instability and disharmony in the village. As indicated before, although the female protagonists are more powerful than the other women in the village, each of them stands on a different level of strength in terms of her self-awareness, independence and relationship with nature. Therefore, the territories of these three women depend on their power, which varies from Ra'nā to Nāei. Regarding this level of power and awareness, the action zone of each woman starts from her home and expands to her farm, neighbourhood and finally the wider nature around her.

To illustrate the action zone of Ra'nā, Tārā and Nāei, it is necessary to compare the actions of these women in relation to their spaces. Their actions are directly related to their environments which are divided into two parts: their homes and nature. These two parts are always related to each other since the three homes are in three villages with access to the sea/river, a forest and a farm. In addition, each village is limited by these natural borders (the sea, forest and mountains) which separate it from other territories. Beyzaie also creates specific atmospheres for these villages by using fog, clouds, wind, thunder and forest sounds. I see each village with its components and its surroundings as a biome, as the biome also contains ecosystems located inside natural borders. A biome remains dynamic and balanced while its ecosystems and members (village, villagers and the environment) are in equilibrium and are working together properly. In other words, each village and their environments have an 'organic human society', in the sense that Aldo Leopold, the father of wildlife ecology, uses the expression when he states that a naturally sustainable society is one in which every member (human and nonhuman) has a reciprocal relationship with the other members.[8] This means that in order to maintain its balance, an 'organic human' community can only accept strangers if they abide by its rules and traditions. Here, the female character, who is as conversant with nature as with her community, becomes a mediator and creates a relationship triangle with the two other counterparts (the male character and the place), which supports the stranger during the process of his acceptance into the community (Figure 5.1). In each film, the balance of this relationship triangle depends on the level of the female protagonist's self-awareness and the reality of her relationship with her space.

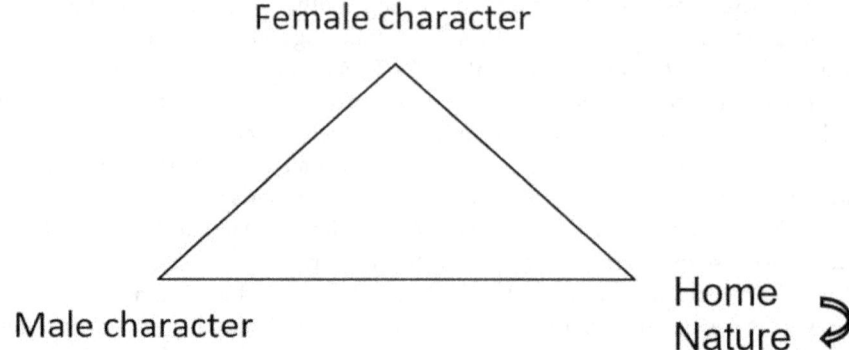

Figure 5.1 The triangle of mediation.

Table 5.1 The protagonists' level of self-awareness and relationship with space

Female Protagonist	Environment		Connecting Tools	Location of Connection
	Familiar	Unfamiliar		
Raʿnā	Nature	Beyond the fog	Boat and sickle	Raʿnā's home
Tārā	Farm House Village	The unseen world	Sword	Forest and seashore
Nāei		Land and language	Language of nature	Nāei's yard and farm

As listed in Table 5.1, the environment around each woman includes familiar and unfamiliar worlds. Nature, farm, house and village are the familiar spaces, while the world beyond the fog (in *Stranger and the Fog*), the world of the dead (in *Ballad of Tārā*) and foreign lands and languages (in *Bāshu, the Little Stranger*) are the unfamiliar spaces. This confrontation of familiar and unfamiliar spaces locates the woman's house at the centre of the village and her action zone will expand from her house to wider nature based on the level of her agency. The more independent and aware of her powers and significance the woman is, the wider action zone she gains. Her agency also depends on both her status in her society and the reality of the interaction between the unfamiliar world and the real environment around her. This can better be observed below as I analyse the way the borders of the protagonists' homes and their action zones expand from their houses to their villages, farms and natural environments to balance the interruption made by the new incomers.

Inside the supernatural borders; the covered body and silenced environment in Stranger and the Fog

The female protagonist's home, like any other home, is a place made by human sensitivity and creativity. As humanistic geographers claim, 'humans make alterations around them to create their own personal places by the emotions, memories, and habits of individuals'.[9] In each part of this trilogy, Beyzaie depicts the link between the protagonist's sensitivity and the place she lives in by creating specific features and floor plans for her home which make them compatible with her body. Therefore, the feminine identity and action zone are reflected in her location and in its relationship to the nature around the house.

As reflected in Figure 5.2, Ra'nā's home is surrounded by a forest and the sea. It is a humble and almost empty house with a dark atmosphere and no signs or sounds of joy. It has an almost empty large, square living room with two doors open to the forest and three windows overlooking the forest and the sea. The only gate of her house also opens towards the forest. Ra'nā comfortably lives with her father and her baby in this home and runs her life very well from her familiar space. Her home is the hub of the village, not only because she is their hero's widow but also because of the affection the villagers hold for her and the role she and her father have as healers. However, as her home is a vital passing point in the village, she can get no privacy. Doors and walls can prevent the intrusion of neither her late husband's family members nor the sounds of nature. Her brothers-in-law

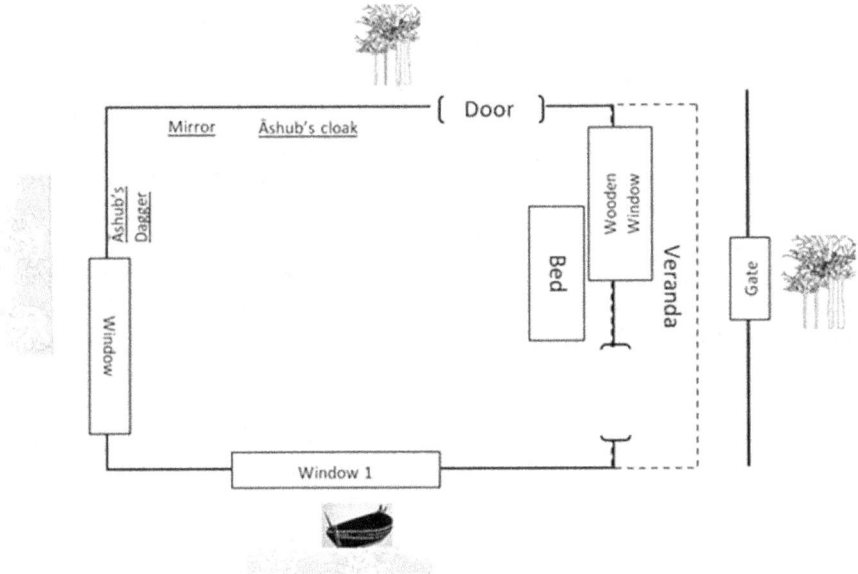

Figure 5.2 Plan of Ra'nā's house and natural environment.

and sister-in-law can freely enter and exit her home, and the sounds of nature are always heard when she is indoors. The main window of the house works as both Ra'nā's watching point and a place for her to be watched by others. As reflected in her home, she is a humble woman with no sign of joy or excitement on her face. She still wears her mourning dress, covers her face and rarely speaks.

When Āyat comes to the village and expresses his love for Ra'nā, and she accepts him, Ra'nā's father cheerfully runs around the village, shouting that she has smiled again. From this point onward, her home becomes cheerful, but simultaneously the level of turbulence rises in her home and village. This is because from the moment her home becomes the location of her connection with Āyat, and her main window becomes her viewing point for Āyat's boat, which is the means of their connection (Table 5.1), her brothers-in-law violate her space to interrogate and impose their opinion on her. They accuse her of breaching her ties with their brother and tell her that she should be ashamed of being in love with Āyat because she is still their late brother's wife. Ra'nā sits on the ground in silence, as if she is sitting in front of a judge in a court. The scene mirrors an earlier hearing that the audience witnessed when Āyat had to sit on the ground at the village square to be interrogated before hearing the chief's verdict. Here again, Ra'nā's older brother-in-law interrogates her to know why she has accepted Āyat after the death of Āshub, her husband. He asks: 'Why? What are you lacking in your life?'[10] He assures her that he will always serve Ra'nā and her child because she holds Āshub's memories in her home. Ra'nā replies that she has no intention of sacrificing herself to a fate like Āshub's (death) by choosing loneliness.

During their long conversation, her brothers-in-law strive to convince Ra'nā that they are protecting her, but she refuses their protection because she views herself as the master of her own life. The moment that Ra'nā breaks her silence is the turning point of the film and her life. She refuses the protection offered by her brothers-in-law because this protection means nothing but surveillance and suppression. Ra'nā can no longer accept suppression because she is aware that she must be free and become herself to be able to love Āyat. Now, the darkness of the house starts to disappear. Her sister-in-law pulls her own dress down to show them how she became uselessly old because of their wrong sense of honour. She then shows them Ra'nā's bare shoulder to remind them that she is made of flesh and blood and that her beautiful skin means that she is still alive, her body is young, and she should be able to love and have a new life. Her sister-in-law then concludes the verdict by saying, 'Ra'nā, do not listen to anybody. Do what you want.'[11] When the two men leave the house by the main door, Ra'nā goes through the back door and exposes her body and hair to the rain as if washing herself. Now, the house is no longer dark because all windows and doors are wide open. Likewise, Ra'nā no longer covers her face and hair. She now wears a white dress and a colourful loose scarf. She smiles and expresses herself more openly during the feast that the village holds in the main square the day after this scene.

Thus, in the first film in Beyzaie's trilogy, a newcomer interrupts the balance of a village because he falls in love with Ra'nā, the wife of their late hero. This is a serious issue because Ra'nā's house and her body are sacred to the villagers.

The holiness associated with her can be interpreted as a manifestation of the oppression imposed by social conventions on Ra'nā and her environment and how these conventions function to make them obedient and silent. However, Ra'nā asserts her right to have a love life because she is strong enough to stand against her brothers-in-law and against these suppressive conventions. Therefore, she not only changes Āyat's status from a foreigner to a member of the village community, but she also alters the reality of her own surrounding geography. By loving Āyat, she expands her space from her gloomy house to her farm, opens herself further to nature with the rain as a point of cleansing and contact and begins to frequent the forest and the fields where she works and ultimately fights against the invading strangers who have come to ruin her newly gained happiness. In addition, she regains control over her body. She wears open dresses and works cheerfully on her farm with Āyat. Nonetheless, the relationship triangle of her, her environment and Āyat cannot follow a dynamic pattern because of the strangers who arrive from beyond the fog to display a marked dominance over the villagers. They violently control everything and attempt to remove Āyat and Ra'nā from the triangle as an unnamed almighty person awaits Āyat. Āyat cannot escape since this person controls everything, including mountains, rivers, woods and the afternoon's nap.[12] The fear and insecurity that engulf Ra'nā's environment transform nature into a pure wilderness. From this moment, the space around Ra'nā experiences a great deal of turmoil: the villagers must kill a wolf that attacks the village, Āyat accidentally encounters Āshub in the foggy forest and kills him, the sea returns Āshub's corpse to the village, and finally a bloody fight occurs between the invading strangers and the villagers. Ra'nā's house becomes gloomy once more, and she mourns again after realizing that Āyat has killed Āshub. Finally, due to the stranger's invasion of her home, the fields and even the forest are damaged. This time, the unknown entities who appear from beyond the fog disrupt the balance of the village and its surroundings. The intruders are ultimately defeated, but the battle changes Āyat's conception of his identity as a man who should serve the land. Thus, injured and grieving for the loss of life that his presence has caused in the village, he decides to leave to find out what is beyond the fog.[13]

With the balance of relationships disrupted, Ra'nā, who has had enough power to stand for herself and change both her geography and Āyat's status, cannot interact fully with her environment because her relationship with Āyat and her environment follows a metaphorical pattern under the imposing pressure of the strangers' presence. There is something supernatural beyond the fog, which powerfully limits the reality of her life and destroys her environment. She is not strong enough to stand against the metaphorical and unknown invading strangers; therefore, she loses Āyat and retreats, wears mourning dress again and becomes silent, as before. However, this time, her silence is not because of mourning for her husband. It is rather because of a powerful, unknown and supernatural entity which has condemned her to silence. In his analysis of the film, Talajooy argues that Ra'nā and Āyat's failure to maintain their natural sense of love and life suggests that overwhelmed by a patriarchal religion, the community and ultimately Āyat, are consumed with a belief in the unknown and the afterlife, and this belief distorts

Ra'nā and Āyat's relationship with nature and their own natural lives.[14] A similar conclusion can be made if one considers Christopher Manes's arguments about the silence of nature, in which he states that such a silence signifies that a voluble subject will shift to a mute object when animistic presence becomes a symbolic one.[15] In this case, Ra'nā's silence is rooted in the oppression incurred by the symbolic presence of creatures from beyond the fog, who can control her private life by force. In *Stranger and the Fog*, the elements of nature – such as the sea, the fog and the forest – are mighty and have power over the villagers, but the villagers know how to deal with them through their traditional feasts and prayers. However, there is still an unknown world beyond the fog which sees itself as the owner of nature and wishes to manipulate the villagers. The strangers from beyond the fog attack the village and disrupt the balanced relationship that Ra'nā has established. As a result, Ra'nā's relationship with Āyat, her power over her own body, and her farming occupation are disrupted by a supernatural existence. Fighting with the invading strangers exhausts her body and ruins her house, her field and her natural environment. As Tahera Aftab states, 'true freedom in mind and soul occurs only when women's access to nature is no longer hindered'.[16] In Ra'nā's case, her freedom is blocked by the invading strangers as her environment – the field, sea and forest – are obstructed or damaged, and she cannot do anything but mourn after Āyat's departure.

Geography of the impossible; desire, Tārā's body and her chamber in Ballad of Tārā

Unlike the gloomy atmosphere of the first film of the trilogy, the second film is bright and cheerful. The story is developed during the harvest season when the villagers work together and enjoy the harvest feasts and commemorate Imam Hossein, the greatest martyr in Shi'i Islam. Tārā's familiar space is real, bright and abundant. Her house is close to the village with access to both the forest and the sea. Like Ra'nā, Tārā and her house are at the centre of attention in the village. She is a charming young widow who has two small kids and the villagers' love and support. When she is returning from her summer residence in the nearby mountains, every man and woman welcomes her. When one of the villagers finally tells her that her father has passed away,[17] she is momentarily upset but the news does not affect her vitality, as if for her, the old man is still present. All men in the village love her, from the teenage boy who ambushes her in the field to see and touch her to Āshub, her brother-in-law, who is a hunter from a southern region but lives in Tārā's northern village with the hope of marrying her now that his brother has passed. Tārā is joyful and full of energy. She lives in her own house, which is fully depicted from the first moment she enters it. The mirror, lamp, cradle and fireplace of the house are framed in a way that the viewer recognizes that despite her father's death, with Tārā's return, her home is ready to return to life again.

Having returned home, Tārā distributes all her father's belongings among villagers, except for an old sword which no one wants. The sword then becomes a mysterious token that links Tārā to the unfamiliar world of the Historical Man. This injured Historical Man who returns from the world of the dead to reclaim his sword is the one who interrupts the harmony of Tārā's world. He changes the triangular relationship between Tārā, her space and Qelich, whose passionate and healthy love for Tārā which is also reciprocated by Tārā plays a significant role in the film. Whereas Ra'nā must deal with one man, Āyat, who is trapped between a natural and a supernatural world, Tārā must decide between one man from the real world of nature and one man from the unreal world of the dead. As a result, Tārā stands at the apex of a pyramid made by her relationships with Qelich and the familiar world of the village, and the Historical Man and the unfamiliar world of history and the dead (Figure 5.3).

Whereas the reality of Ra'nā's village had direct links with the supernatural, Tārā's follows the rules of reality until the arrival of the Historical Man disrupts her mind. Vague signs of the Historical Man's presence are seen by others. For instance, everyone seems to see his horse. Tārā's neighbour, who has earlier returned the sword because he had a nightmare when he had it in his house, sees drops of blood at the doorsteps of Tārā's house and at night hears strange cries and noises from Tārā's yard. However, the villagers do not engage with the imbalanced triangular relationship that unfolds in Tārā's mind as they never see the Historical Man.

As seen in plan B, the yard of Tārā's house has a well, whose windlass has broken in Tārā's absence. Although her house has a veranda, two doors and several rooms, Tārā's living space is practically her chamber with a window that is always out of the spectator's sight. Her chamber with its narrow door is always full of light, either natural or from the fireplace and the oil lamp. This chamber is a place specific to

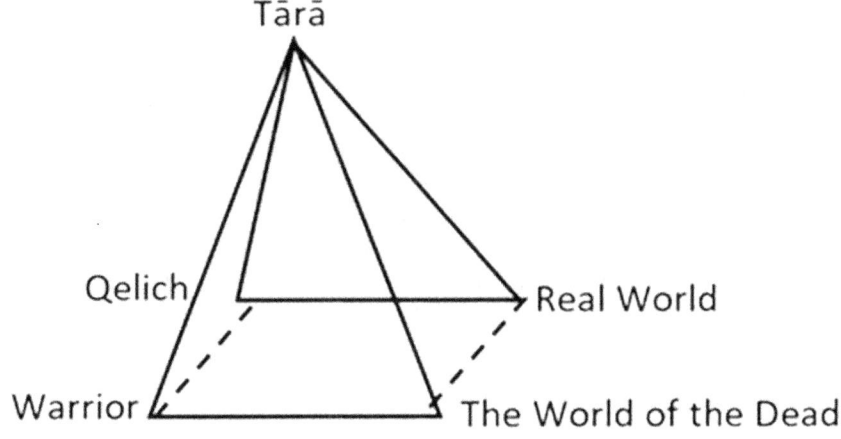

Figure 5.3 Tārā's relationship with the living and the dead worlds and the two men.

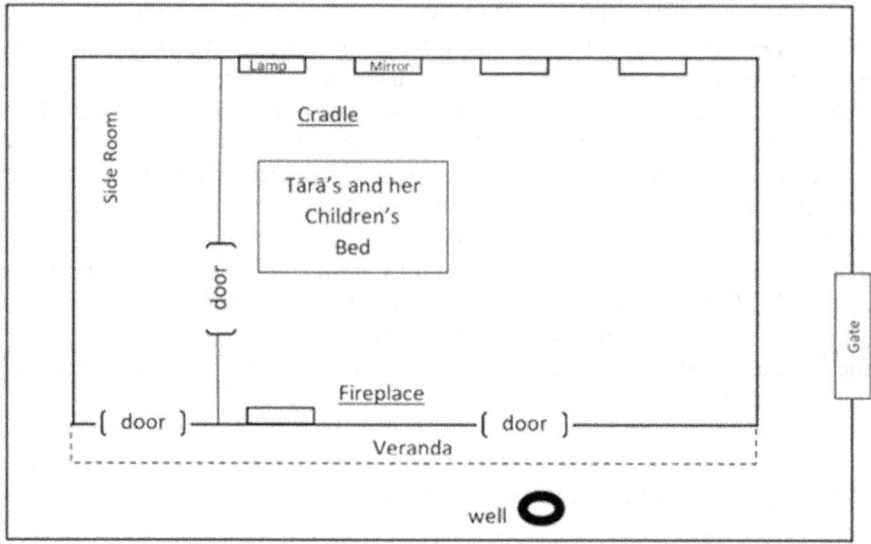

Figure 5.4 Plan of Tārā's house and natural environment.

Tārā and her children. Thus, neither Qelich nor the Historical Man can enter her house. Even when Qelich enters the yard and fixes the broken well-windlass, he goes away in silence without a glimpse at her chamber. The Historical Man can only walk around her yard. Tārā's chamber is like her mind; it is bright and clear during the day, but when Tārā hears the Historical Man's cry at night, it turns into a place of reveries. She sits in the corner of her chamber and prays to defeat the evil spirit. This double feature of her room and its limited floor plan with only one entrance conjure the alternative images of a tomb or a womb. Consequently, passing through this door can be interpreted as her death or birth, which in her case means either directly to the Historical Man and the world of the dead or to Qelich and the world of the living. Tārā's chamber reflects her relationship with the two men and their competing spatial and romantic realities.

Unlike Ra'nā, who could change Āyat's status by sleeping with him and accepting his love, Tārā cannot bring the Historical Man back to life by making love. Tārā's love makes the wandering Historical Man more miserable because being from two different types of worlds, interaction between them is not possible. As the Historical Man says, he can only be revived if Tārā's children die, and Tārā can only join him if she dies. Therefore, any change in the geography of the two places and their relationship is impossible. The border of Tārā's space and the Historical Man's is pictured in two places; firstly, in the forest where Tārā takes her clothes off to seduce him to return and stay, and secondly, on the seacoast where Tārā fights the waves to bring the Historical Man back.[18] Thus, although the Historical Man's horse and sword link the two worlds, crossing the border is impossible. Her nude body, seductively presented in the wet red dress, cannot help the Historical Man to return to life because he belongs to a passive and silenced world. Although she is independent, self-aware and powerful, the passivity of the Historical Man's body and world will break the triangle and Tārā cannot expand her personal space into that of the Historical Man.

At the end of the film, when Tārā's fight against the waves ends in her defeat, she realizes that her relationship with the Historical Man is blocked. Thus, she returns to her familiar world, embodied in her lover, Qelich and her natural and human world, the village. Her request to Qelich to set their marriage date can be interpreted as her desire to return to the harmony of her familiar space again. However, she still has the sword in her hands and knows the story of the Historical Man and his tribe. This knowledge has changed Tārā's understanding of her environment. After hearing the Historical Man's life story, Tārā sees the blood of trees when their trunks are cut by villagers. Tārā is still as cheerful and powerful as she was before meeting the Historical Man, but now, instead of staying in her tomb-like chamber, she comes out through the narrow door of that womb-like place to encounter the real space with her expanded awareness about the history of her environment. In other words, she achieves a higher level of contact with her natural environment. From now on, every single tree in the forest, the sands of the sea, or the stones of the ruined castle relate to something bigger and wider than the familiar world she knew before. As Talajooy states, the process has given a new sense to nature as being not only the great source of life and joy that it has always been to Tārā but also the totality of all the entities that have ever lived, died and returned to nature.[19] Tārā has reached this understanding due to her confrontation with the Historical Man and his miserable life and death. She now can keep the sword as a reminder of his impossible territory when she is living in her new, rebalanced, familiar environment. In the course of the film, Tārā's knowledge about her surroundings and life has been elevated, and she can now accept Qelich as her husband.

Acceptance and unconditional love in Bāshu, the Little Stranger

The third film in Beyzaie's village trilogy introduces Nāei, a remarkably independent woman who rises further to transcend the impositions of her patriarchal society in a world of real relations. Although she is illiterate, she runs her farm and takes care of her children on her own. Her husband, who is away in search of work, returns only in the penultimate scene of the film, but, because of his letters, his power is still felt in Nāei's everyday life. Nāei's life has no privacy, and all the villagers know about her life because the old apothecary, her neighbour, reads and writes her letters for her. Consequently, the surveillance of her husband resonates with the patriarchal community of the village that supports her husband's ideas. However, she is strong enough to withstand all of them and do what she feels is right. In her initial appearance in the film, her determination and power are reflected in a close-up of her face as she is covering her face with a white scarf before dealing with Bāshu's sudden appearance. She is honest towards both people and creatures around her. Her house is open to all villagers, but she is able to push them away when they try to impose their opinions on her. In the same manner, her home and farm are open to animals, but she strongly pushes animals away when they cross their boundaries. She can help humans and non-humans but can also protect her borders against them if they try to impose themselves on her or the balance of her natural environment.

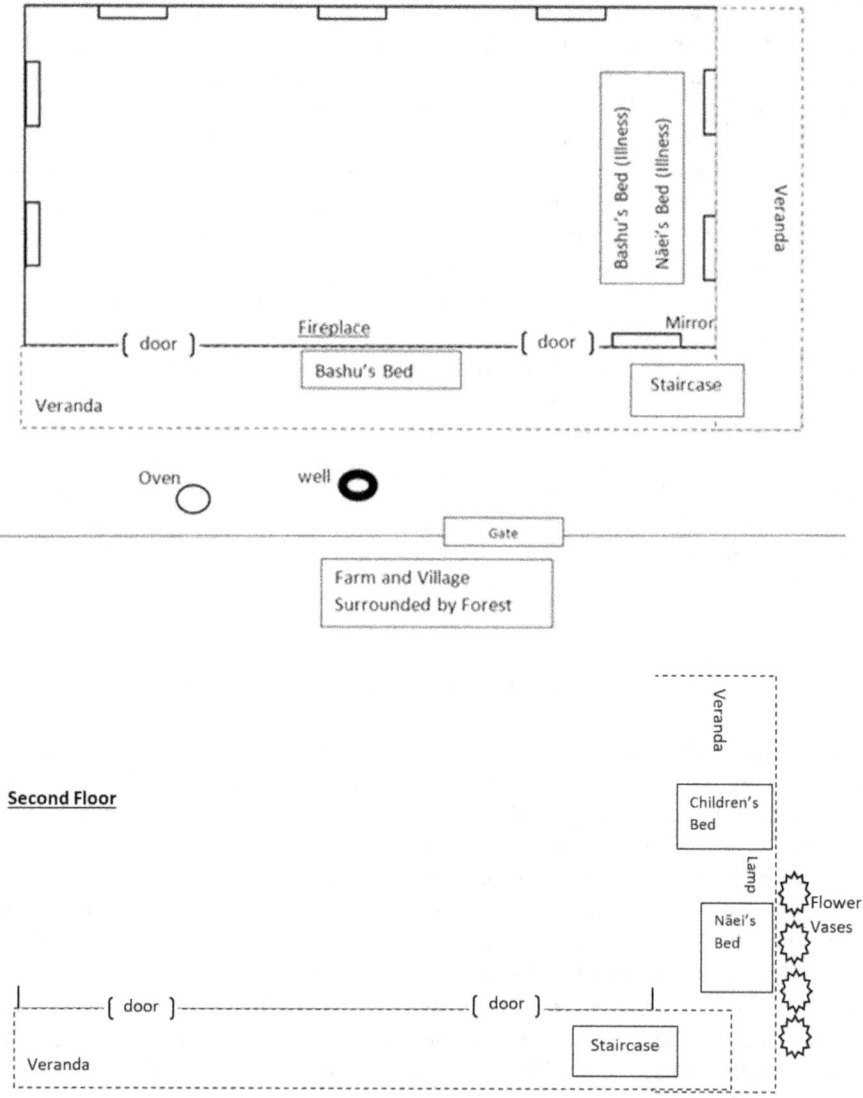

Figure 5.5 Plan of Nāei's house and natural environment.

As depicted in Plan C, the floor plan of Nāei's house is open. Both the first and the second floors have verandas where Nāei, her children and Bāshu sleep. The house has a gate open to the village path and a small bridge leading to her farm. The village and its farms are surrounded by the forest and the mountains where workers are building a tunnel to connect the village to the other side of the mountain. The tunnel is a symbol for the villagers and the audience that the village is going to connect with the outside world, which may bring disruption to the land. Apart from a few war or tunnel-related explosions at the beginning of the film, the rest of the film unfolds in a context characterized by mostly tranquil farms, rivers and forest, where Nāei and her children live and work.

In contrast to Ra'nā's village, Nāei's space is abundant, but, unlike Tārā, who has the support of her fiancé and villagers, Nāei must work hard to run her life single-handedly and draw her own boundaries and stick to them firmly with no flexibility towards imposing villagers or animals. She, thus, stands strong against villagers when they try to impose their opinions on her. When Nāei is feeding her chickens, she talks to the birds flying over her house and invites them to come for food, but she also replies to the eagle's cry and strikes the ground with her foot to keep it away from her birds. When she accepts Bāshu, he also learns to guard Nāei's territory by watching her rice paddy and drumming to scare wild boars away at night.

Nāei is still young and a mother of two children, but, unlike Tārā who is single and thus uses her charming appearance and character to attract men, she shows no desire or signs of seductive charm. Her body is strong, healthy and ready to embrace her children. She is open to both humans and nonhumans and maintains a peaceful relationship with all of them. When Bāshu arrives in the village, the triangle of the relationship is shaped between Nāei, Bāshu and the environment. However, unlike the two strangers in the previous films, Bāshu knows nothing about the space he has entered. Bāshu is an orphan Arab boy from a war-torn region in southern Iran, a boy, who has had to escape the war zone after the deaths of his parents and siblings in an air raid. His escape on the back of a truck has led him to appear by accident in a small village to the south of the Caspian Sea in Gilan province. Therefore, Nāei's familiar space seems unfamiliar and scary to Bāshu, and at the same time, the very existence of Bāshu is unfamiliar to Nāei and her community. Bāshu is different from Nāei in the colour of his complexion and his language; therefore, no communication can be generated between Bāshu and Nāei, nor Bāshu and the villagers. Since Bāshu has accidentally sheltered at Nāei's farm, she personally intervenes in making the unfamiliarity of Bāshu familiar to her community and environment. In the process that leads to Bāshu's acceptance, the first step is for Nāei to know Bāshu in order to help him overcome his traumatic experience of facing death, bereavement and rejection and feel safe at her home. She also has to support him in his encounters with villagers and must argue with her husband about adopting the little stranger.

Nāei's main issue in this first stage is the language difference which makes communication impossible. Bāshu speaks Arabic and Nāei speaks Gilaki, the language spoken on the southwest coast of the Caspian Sea. The lack of communication between Nāei and Bāshu adds a nuance to the triangle of Nāei-Bāshu-environment because both Nāei and Bāshu have to follow their instinct in order to understand each other. The ability to rely on instinct has its roots in a close relationship with nature. Nāei can understand Bāshu because she can read natural signs and can listen to and communicate with nature. Bāshu observes Nāei when she replies to a hunting bird by imitating its call. As the story unfolds, the audiences understand that Bāshu has also developed his own ways to communicate with nature by playing a flute to make the crops grow faster and drumming to help Nāei recover from a fever. When discussing shamanism, Mircea Eliade states: 'learning the language of animals, especially of birds, is equivalent to knowing the secrets of nature and hence to being able to prophesy [...] learning their language, imitating their voice, is equivalent to communicate with the beyond and the heavens'.[20] Nāei's cries to the hunting bird flying over her house confirm that the chickens in the garden belong to her. She makes noise to scare wild boars on her farm. She even replies to the neighbour's horse for fun when she is on her way to the local market with her children and Bāshu.

Like all the animals around her, Nāei has a territory, and her intention is to keep it safe. Therefore, when Bāshu enters her territory (at her farm), she pushes her children behind her, picks up a stick and comes forward to see Bāshu who has been trying to hide from her. Nāei asks Bāshu if he is a human being or a demon, but when he escapes and hides behind bushes, she puts out a piece of bread for him and leaves the place, as though Bāshu is an injured wild creature who needs food. Like the injured Āyat in *Stranger and the Fog*, Bāshu is tired, hungry and alone. Ra'nā's stranger has arrived on a boat injured from an unspecified conflict or war in an unknown land beyond the fogs where he ultimately returns at the end of the film. Nāei's little stranger, however, is a tired boy from a very real Iran-Iraq war zone. Tārā's Historical Man is washed away by the sea of the underworld, but Nāei rescues this little stranger from drowning in the pond and lets him rest in her arms. The world frequented by Nāei is more real and more tangible than the other two in all its relations even in the protagonist's relationship with nature. It is clear from the beginning, therefore, that it is Nāei's duty to rescue her stranger from being rejected by the conservative community that has no desire to accept the newcomer who is different from them. In the scene where Nāei rescues Bāshu from drowning in the pond, the dynamic relationship between Nāei, Bāshu and their space is perfectly depicted. By rescuing Bāshu, Nāei changes Bāshu's status from a little stranger to her son. The way she throws and pulls the fishing net and the sound she makes can be interpreted as delivering a child then she embraces the vulnerable soaked little Bāshu, in front of villagers, as though he is born that very moment.[21] Nāei's body has expanded (figuratively and physically) to coddle another child, and she offers her unconditional love to an orphan child from another land.

In addition, by accepting Bāshu, Nāei incorporates Bāshu's space into her own space. In other words, at that very time and location, she expands her space from her house and farm to Bāshu's homeland, which has been altered by war. Later, in the letter-writing scene, when Nāei dictates the letter to Bāshu, the hedge of her house is expanded to the battlefield from where Bāshu has come, illustrating how Nāei's space expands from the north to the southwest of Iran. As a strong and independent woman who knows the reality of nature and her community, Nāei decides to adopt Bāshu. She instructs Bāshu to write to her husband that she will share her 'own bread' with Bāshu since 'he, like other children, is the son of the sun and the earth'.[22] As such, in the last film of the trilogy, the relationship of Nāei, Bāshu and the environment reaches its most dynamic, tangible and realistic moment because, via a concrete interaction with the world, Nāei is aware of her feelings and purpose in life and asserts them.

Nāei knows how to deal with her familiar space and understands Bāshu's world based on her instincts. In the second half of the film, when the villagers and Nāei understand that they can communicate with Bāshu through Persian, Iran's national language, the language barrier disappears because Persian connects all of them together. Although this approach to the national language perfectly works here, there is a risk of interpreting Nāei's body as a national land and minimizing her function to one of passive maternal action. But, as discussed before, Nāei is an independent woman who has the agency of doing whatever she likes. She consciously decides to adopt Bāshu as her own son and accepts all the responsibilities that this decision entails. She offers her unconditional love to Bāshu and her children, but at the same time she stands against any control that others want to impose on her life. This characteristic prevents the audience from perceiving Nāei's existence as a national land in its traditional sense, as a female territory to be attacked by enemies or protected by heroes. Thus, as Talajooy states, 'even at a symbolic level, Nāei's character represents land, nature or women that have their own priorities and are open and supportive of others but have achieved a level of agency that has made them stronger than the suppressive, patriarchal or anthropocentric discourses that surround them'.[23] This is also reflected by the features of her home floor plan, which is open to nature, the villagers and guests but has marked and strongly protected boundaries. She is now fully capable of repelling any external force which may try to control her home.

Conclusion

Looking at the village trilogy from an environmental perspective leads us to conclude that Ra'nā, Tārā and especially Nāei are not related to nature merely as goddess-like figures whose roles encompass fertility, love and nurture. Instead, the primary reason that they are aligned with nature is agriculture. Being a farmer means that one can communicate with nature and is related to a specific piece of land. Farmers should know the language of nature to synchronize their lives with seasons and soil. The lives of these female farmers are also related to nature and their specific lots; therefore, they respect nature and try to keep it in balance. But the way that they keep their environment in balance is completely related to their agency and their personal real or surreal environment. The agency of all these women comes from two resources: firstly, they are capable of independently managing their lives, and secondly, they are loved by the other members of their societies. Therefore, due to having a combination of qualities, they have already achieved the specific status due to which they have agency and are, thus, heard and seen. However, this voice and agency have been granted inside the patriarchal frame, thus mitigating their agency within the expectation that women should be obedient. In the course of the trilogy, each woman, depending on her level of self-awareness, fights against the oppression imposed by the social hierarchy of power and tries to do what she wants. The success of this, however, depends on the reality of the situation. In the triangle of relationships with the male character and the space, each woman plays the role of a mediator to change the status of the stranger and her own geography. Ra'nā's triangle of relationships with her stranger cannot be wholly manifested because of the overpowering supernatural entities which control nature and Āyat. Tārā's triangle with the Historical Man could not be manifested because the very nature of the Historical Man's world is beyond Tārā's reach. Among the three women, Nāei is the most successful in achieving her goal because while the other two are also powerful and independent, the challenges they face are overwhelming and they are limited by the givens of their environment. Nāei's goal, however, is within the givens of the rational and tangible world of her relationships, environment and home over which she has visible influence, and since she has already achieved a high level of agency, she manages to fulfil her supportive role.

Notes

1. Warren, 'Ecological Feminism', 13.
2. Ibid., 11.
3. Glotfelty, 'Literary Studies', 123.
4. Warren, 'Ecological Feminism', 26.
5. Manes, 'Nature and Silence', 16.
6. Howarth, 'Some Principles', 80.
7. Ibid., 80.
8. Clark, *Cambridge Introduction*, 94.
9. Lenson and Seager, *Companion to Feminist*, 8.
10. *Stranger*, 36'.03".
11. *Stranger*, 38'.05".
12. *Stranger*, 74'.30"–74'.40".
13. For a detailed analysis of the battle scene, see also Talajooy, Iranian Culture, 185–9.
14. Ibid., 155–92.

15 Manes, 'Nature and Silence', 17.
16 Aftab, 'Text and Practice', 155.
17 The man is referred to as Grandfather, so he can be Tārā's grandfather or father depending on whether the term reflects Tārā's or her children's perspective.
18 *Ballad*, 85'.46"–90'.03".
19 Talajooy, Interview.
20 Eliade, *Shamanism*, 98.
21 See also Talajooy, Jābejāei-ye Marzhā, 51.
22 *Bashu*, 101'.37".
23 Talajooy and Khansalar, 'Interview'.

Bibliography

Aftab, Tahera. 'Text and Practice: Women and Nature in Islam'. In *Sacred Custodians of the Earth: Women, Spirituality and the Environment*. Ed. Alaine Low and Soraya Tremayne. Oxford: Berghahn Books, 2001. Pp. 141–58.

Buell, Lawrence. 'Representing the Environment'. In *The Environmental Imagination, Thoreau, Nature, Writing and the Formation of American Culture*. London: Belknap Press of Harvard University Press, 1995. Pp. 83–114.

Clark, Timothy. *The Cambridge Introduction to Literature and the Environment*. Cambridge: Cambridge University Press, 2011.

Eliade, Mircea. *Shamanism, Archaic Techniques of Ecstasy*. Trans. Willard R. Trask. London: Penguin Books, 1989.

Glotfelty, Cheryll. 'Literary Studies in an Age of Environmental Crisis'. In *Ecocriticism: the Essential Reader*. Ed. Ken Hiltner. Abingdon: Routledge, 2015. Pp. 120–30.

Howarth, William. 'Some Principles of Ecocriticism'. In *The Ecocriticism Reader: Landmarks in Literary Ecology*. Ed. Cheryll Glotfelty and Harold Fromm. Athene and London: University of Georgia Press, 1995. Pp. 69–91.

Lenson, Lise and Joni Seager. Ed. *A Companion to Feminist Geography*. Oxford: Blackwell, 2005.

Manes, Christopher. 'Nature and Silence'. In *The Ecocriticism Reader*. Ed. Cheryll Glotfelty and Harold Fromm. Athene and London: University of Georgia Press, 1995. Pp. 15–29.

Nash, Catherine. 'Remapping the Body/Land: New Cartographies of Identity, Gender, and Landscape in Ireland'. In *Writing Women ad Space, Colonial and Postcolonial Geographies*. Ed. Alison Blunt and Gillian Rose. London: The Guilford Press, 1994. Pp. 227–50.

Talajooy, Saeed and Fatemeh Khansalar. 'Interview on Beyzaie's Village Trilogy'. 15 February 2023a.

Talajooy, Saeed. *Iranian Culture in Bahram Beyzaie's Cinema and Theatre: Paradigms of Being and Belonging (1959–1979)*. London and New York: I.B. Tauris, 2023b.

Talajooy, Saeed. 'Jābejāei-ye Marzhā-ye Ta'lloq: Qomiyat, Zabān va Hovyat Melli dar Bāshu, Gharibeh-ye Kuchak'. In *Film-e Emruz*. Vol. 1. No. 8 (January 2022). Pp. 48–51.

Warren, Karen and Barbara Wells-Howe. *Ecological Feminism*. London: Routledge, 1994. Pp. 8–28.

Films:

Stranger and the Fog. Directed by Bahram Beyzaie. Cinema Theatre Rex Company, 1974. http://www.sourehcinema.com/Title/Title.aspx?id=138109160953.

Ballad of Tārā. Directed by Bahram Beyzaie, Iranian Organisation of Cinema and Filmsāz Studio, 1978. http://www.sourehcinema.com/Title/Title.aspx?id=138205060100

Bāshu, the Little Stranger. Directed by Bahram Beyzaie, The Institute of Intellectual Development of Children and Young Adults. IDCYA, 1990. http://www.sourehcinema.com/Title/Title.aspx?id=138109201333.

Chapter 6

BĀSHU'S OTHER NAMES: A STUDY OF BĀSHU'S IDENTITY IN *BĀSHU, THE LITTLE STRANGER*

Naghmeh Samini

Introduction

The war between Iran and Iraq started on September 22 in 1980, less than twenty months after the victory of the Islamic Revolution in Iran. The war lasted for eight years during which the residential areas of many Iranian cities were targeted by airstrikes and rockets, and many civilians lost their lives, homes and communities. Among the consequences of the war the fate of war refugees and the problems of their housing had become one of the most crucial issues during the conflict between Iraq and Iran. According to Iran's central statistics bureau in 1981 alone about 350,000 refugees from Khuzestan province fled to other parts of the country.[1]

In view of the urgent importance of the refugee problem, an organization entitled *Bonyād-e Omur-e Mohājerin-e Jang-e Tahmili* (Foundation for the Affairs of the Immigrants of the Imposed War) was founded. The stated mission of the organization, which was renamed *Bonyād-e Jangzadegān* (War Victims Foundation) in 1981, was to 'plan and organize aid and relief efforts for providing refugees with material and moral support'.[2]

Mustafa Mirsalim who was appointed as the director of the organization expressed his opinion about the importance of the refugee problem in the following words:

[W]e realized that we have one million and a hundred thousand war refugees. The scale of the operation was very large. Housing more than a million people and providing them with basic livelihood was not simple. The refugees' experiences also caused mental and emotional traumas that had to be treated properly.[3]

As the war continued, the number of refugees increased. The refugees were fleeing Iran's war-torn southern regions and migrating to safer cities in the country's northern regions. The more a city was situated towards the north, the safer it would be as a haven for those fleeing the war zone. One can only imagine the challenges arising from such a largescale migration of refugees, particularly because many of them had fled to cities whose inhabitants were of a different ethnicity, culture or talked in a completely different dialect or even language. The issue was aggravated by the fact that the country was engaged in an atrocious war and the government had meagre resources to dedicate to refugee relief efforts.

Ayatollah Khomeini had explicitly stated: 'The war is a blessing', and this short sentence had determined the nature of state propaganda concerning the war. Anything that could potentially question the sense of war as a 'sacred' conflict or a 'blessing' had to be omitted from the state-controlled media. Some realities, however, could not be removed by censorship. One such reality was the refugee crisis as it was not possible to erase or hide the presence of such a large number of war refugees in major Iranian cities. The refugee crisis as a subject was not only discussed in the media including state television and newspapers, but it was also allowed to be addressed in cinema within the governmental guidelines that evolved in the mid-1980s with the rise of the new genre labelled as 'Sacred Defence cinema'. Naser Gholamrezaei's *Harim-e Mehrvarzi* (Kindness Territory), which was released six years after the start of the war in 1986, was one such film about war refugees. The film focuses on the story of a couple housed in a hotel in Tehran as war refugees and on how they meet in the hotel and eventually marry. Using the case of a couple finding love due to their status as refugees, the film's premise was that while the war had uprooted people from their homes and normal lives, it was still a 'blessing' as it brought new forms of blessing to life and was a manifestation of God's will.

Bahram Beyzaie's *Bāshu Gharibeh-ye Kuchak* (Bāshu, the Little Stranger) was another film on the refugee crisis which was made in 1985 and was ready for release in January 1986. It was the story of a young refugee boy named Bāshu who ended up in a village in the north of the country. Despite its simple story, the film was banned for more than three years and was not approved for screening until after the war in 1989 when it was allowed to be screened in a limited number of theatres. The question posed here is why the film was banned. This question is important because the film had been produced by *Kānun-e Parvarash-e Fekri-ye Kudakān va Nojavānān* (Institute for the Intellectual Development of Children and Young Adults), targeted a younger audience, and had not broken any government mandates.[4] The film depicts the story of a refugee boy who is adopted by a woman named Nāei in Gilan Province. Thus, it fulfilled one of Ayatollah Khomeini's decrees on the subject:

> The officials should inform the people that these (refugees) are our brothers. They have become refugees for the sake of Islam and Islamic war. Consider them like your own kins and your own children. If there are orphaned children among them, and someone can adopt them and keep them, they should keep them.[5]

The issue, however, was that despite its simple narrative and its general fulfilment of state requirements, the film departed from the propaganda requirements and policies of the state in its depiction of the refugee status itself. This is evident in the statement below in which Mirsalim quotes Ayatollah Khomeini to clarify the policy of the state: 'in that meeting Imam made a good point'. He said, 'Saddam thought that war refugees would become a problem for us, but they are now forming the army against Saddam himself. You should put yourselves in God's care as well and things will be taken care of.'[6] In another instance, Khomeini had mentioned that war refugees were put to a test by God and the more they persevere and pass this test patiently, the more they would be rewarded by God's benevolence.[7]

Working in response to these statements and similar speeches, the regime attempted to create a generic identity for war refugees as people who should consider their condition as ordained by God and make it their mission to stand against the enemy despite having lost their homes and being subjected to other forms of devastating hardships and traumas. People from the host cities were likewise defined as those who should consider the war a blessing and be willing to open their doors to war refugees due to their religious fervour.

One of the main reasons for the ban on *Bāshu* was the departure of Bāshu's and the villagers' characters from the prescribed identity promoted by the state in a filmic context that depicted the traumatic impacts of the war and the race-obsessed exclusion of a war refugee. This chapter aspires to demonstrate why and how this departure was significant at different levels. Since such an analysis requires analysing the specific qualities of Bāshu's character and situation, the chapter also engages with naming and choosing the epithet for Bāshu as metaphors that determine the specifics of his situation. In dramatic and fictional narratives, names function like windows into the characters' identity. Thus, my analysis of naming also reflects on how Beyzaie creates his counternarrative against state propaganda through his depiction of Bāshu as a stranger. In its denotations, the name 'Bāshu' is gender neutral, means 'stay' and suggests someone who is present, and his presence cannot be denied. Beyzaie, however, makes this more specific by adding the epithet 'the little stranger'. The word 'little', of course, refers to the young boy's age, but the term *stranger*, in addition to its literal meaning, delves into a framework of contexts and meanings which require analysis and elaboration. Apart from Bāshu being a 'little stranger', which will be elaborated further, one can identify other attributes that define Bāshu's identity as an immigrant and an outsider who suffers the traumas of loss and rejection. I also analyse this identity to show how it gradually expands in the film to portray the difference between the 'war refugee' in Beyzaie's vision and the clichéd image of a war refugee in state propaganda. Thus, the chapter, in general, focuses on Bāshu's character to explore the various aspects of this identity and answer the following questions: What was Bāshu's image as a war refugee that the regime did not tolerate during the war? What were the characteristics demonstrated by the villagers who had hosted Bāshu in their village which further contributed to the ban on the film? What are Bāshu's unmentioned names and why did Beyzaie choose the epithet 'stranger' from amongst other names and attributes?

Bāshu, the Little Immigrant

Judging based on what happens in the film, the film could be titled *Bāshu, the Little Immigrant* as Bāshu's condition is best defined by his status as an immigrant. According to *Merriam-Webster Dictionary*, 'immigration' means 'the movement from one country, place or locality to another'. Thus, an immigrant is a person who moves from one cultural and geographical milieu to another. In the film, Bāshu migrates from a war-torn village near the Persian Gulf to a tranquil village near the Caspian Sea. If examined with attention to Everett S. Lee's points about the causes of migration, Bāshu has both a reason to leave his home region and a reason to stay in an unfamiliar place. In his case, the 'push factors', the 'things that are unfavourable about the area one lives in', are loss of family, home and school and an ongoing war. His 'pull factors' the 'things that attract one to another area' also include finding a new family, a place of work and a home in a peaceful location far from the place in which he suffered.[8]

The film begins with a detailed exposition of these push factors. The first fourteen shots depict a series of explosions and their casualties. Village houses are destroyed in explosions, a woman wearing traditional Arabic clothing from southern Iran is engulfed in flames and a man wearing traditional southern clothing falls in a hole caused by an explosion. War is the most readily understandable reason for migration, and the film provides ample visual evidence for why this is the case. When a truck stops and Bāshu secretly jumps onto its back, the audience understands the reason behind his flight in a pure cinematic style without any single dialogue.

The sequence, thus, reveals the first aspect of Bāshu's identity as an emigrant: a person who must flee a land of fire and blood in order to survive. Before realizing his status as a stranger, Bāshu finds that he is an emigrant who must secretly escape by hiding on the back of a truck. In a short scene, the truck driver tells another person who wishes to travel with him that he will never take any passengers. This scene is overlooked in the narrative, but the driver's attitude reveals another aspect of Bāshu's condition as his status suggests that of an illegal migrant: a person who was otherwise fated to stay and probably die in the land of fire and blood, just like what happened to his family. If the driver had known that someone was taking a ride on his truck, he would most probably have refused to take him. Bāshu's push factor is the war and his pull factor is safety. Safety is the foremost criterion for a migrant but another more complicated necessity arises when the migrant's life is no longer in immediate danger: the problem of identity. As specified by many scholars, 'religion, political administration, and economic and other forms of shared experiences provide individuals with a sense of cultural identity'.[9] Thus, moving from one geographical area to another can have major impacts on cultural identity.

This framework is relayed in *Bāshu* as once Bāshu's life is not in danger anymore, the issue of identity crisis becomes central to the plot. As an immigrant Bāshu is torn between his former identity and the new identity that is to be defined in a new place. Among the many factors that define identity the film first focuses on language. Language is regarded as one of the most important factors in shaping a person's individual or group identity. As John Joseph states, 'Language and identity are ultimately inseparable.'[10] Language is one of the first alienating elements that Bāshu has to grapple with as an immigrant. Having migrated from a region in the southwest of Iran to a north-western region of Iran, he belongs to the same nationality as the people of the village, but they speak completely different languages, and this is one of the main reasons why the villagers do not consider him Iranian. Thus, both his individual identity and his group identity are threatened by his new status as an immigrant. As Edwards states, '[e]veryone is used to accent, dialect and language variations that reveal speakers' membership in particular speech communities, social classes, ethnic and national groups'.[11]

At this point in the film a significant dramatic arc develops: Nāei and Bāshu face a challenge as the newcomer refugee needs to communicate with the village residents via language. In fact, one of the most important scenes of the film depicts this attempt to form a language connection. The first words that Nāei and Bāshu teach to each other from their respective local languages are sickle (a tool for harvesting), a well bucket (a tool for drawing water), rice (the staple food in northern Iran), tomato (a bounty of the earth), oil barrel (necessary for keeping the oven fire), egg (a symbol of birth) and doll (a transformed depiction of a mythical goddess). All these words reflect the matriarchal aspects of the culture of Gilan province, an agricultural culture that is intimately intertwined with water, earth, harvest and fertility. The doll can also be understood as a feminine symbol of this culture and a symbol associated with rain rituals.[12]

There is a mystery in the arrangement of these words. Nāei has an instinctive understanding of the hidden aspects of language and the connection between vocabulary and culture. It is, thus, as if by teaching him the new words, Nāei teaches Bāshu about the new culture as well. Bāshu's vocabulary is full of fire, fear and death, but Nāei introduces him to a new culture via new words. At the end of the scene, Bāshu and Nāei tell their names to each other and reveal the first aspect of their identity. Thus, under the overarching influence of names, all the words previously used are defined within the context of identity.

In a later scene, when Bāshu gets into a fight with children of his age group, instead of throwing the stone held ready in his hand, he picks up a Persian textbook and reads the text aloud in eloquent formal Persian. The idea of a book replacing a stone conveys a profound sense in the context of language and identity, particularly because Bāshu has fled a war-stricken land. Immediately after the reading scene, to show others what has happened to his school, he throws a stone at a makeshift toy house. The stone is a symbol of an identity that is rooted in war, rage and a desire for destruction. The phenomenon can be viewed as a tendency towards violence in immigrants, but Bāshu puts the stone aside and picks up the book. He reads: 'Iran is our homeland. We are of one soil and water. We are the children of Iran.' Thus, by replacing the stone with the book, the film regards the immigrant's tendency towards violence to be a result of the immigrant's unfamiliarity with the language and the culture of the host and his inability to defend himself with words when ridiculed or cornered by others. Expressing himself with the Persian textbook is the first stage in Bāshu's attempt to find an individual as well as group identity as the boys realize with admiration and wonder that Bāshu is literate.[13]

At another level, Bāshu's reading from the Persian textbook, which is his first step in forming a relationship with the other children, is also a reflection of nationalist sentiments. In the first decade after the Islamic Revolution the ruling regime insisted on defining the bond between Iran's various ethnic groups as something beyond belonging to the same country and nation and promoted an Islamic religious sense of unity. One of the most frequently repeated slogans after the revolution was 'Not Eastern, not Western, Islamic Republic', an exact reflection of the rhetoric of Islamic unity which was to replace patriotic nationalist unity.

Immigrants' individual and group identities are defined by their encounters with the host region's identity. Nāei is the first person to whom Bāshu looks for protection. As a host, Nāei is the ideal human figure. She even transcends the national bond and nationalist sentiment. She does not care what language Bāshu speaks. Although she is the first person who tries to teach Gilaki to Bāshu, his inability to understand Gilaki does not change her attitude towards him. Bāshu's identity is specifically defined by his status as an 'immigrant' or the 'little one' for her. For the young helpless refugee, Nāei is an epitome of the archetypal goddess, Anahita, the goddess of water and fertility in Iranian mythology. This is also reflected in the fact that Nāei's name is an altered Gilaki version of Nahid which is in turn the new Persian term for Anahita, which is ultimately derived from the Avestan language.[14] This feature is also important as it highlights an archetypal aspect of the matriarchal culture into which Bāshu has entered.

It can be assumed that the features of the host region and its people are also important in the divide between the film and the government's policies regarding the subject of war refugees. Neither Nāei nor the other villagers reflect the regime's preferred image of a community of believers competing to provide support for the refugees. Nāei does not accept Bāshu into her home because the state has advised it or because she hopes for a divine reward. Her identity is rooted in the cultural practices that reflect ancient Iranian and Mesopotamian mother goddess figures and her motivations are ultimately humane.[15] The other residents of the village, on the other hand, are even farther from the state's ideal image of a refugee-accepting community.

After attempting to teach him the language and realizing his ability to communicate in Persian, Nāei encourages Bāshu to expand his group identity, and in an important scene, takes Bāshu to a village market. In the framework of the economic, social and cultural relationships between farming villages, the market is not only an economic centre but also a place for socialization and cultural exchange. While selling her products, Nāei gives Bāshu some money to buy something for himself. Bāshu mingles in the crowd and browses the products. This is his first experience as an immigrant who wants to enter the village's social life. But his experience is distorted by two symbolic signs. The first is a horseman riding fast which signifies aggression; the second is a poster of a film entitled *Attack* depicting a soldier on the wall behind Bāshu. As a person trying to find his place in a new social setting, once more he experiences fear and doubt and runs to the imaginary figure of his mother. Here, as in some other scenes, including when Bāshu hears a roadwork explosion and runs away screaming or when he thinks they are being bombarded due to the noise from the oven, Beyzaie highlights an important point about an immigrant's identity: a neurotic fear of aggression rooted in traumatic experiences of loss. This focus on fear and trauma made *Bāshu, the Little Stranger* one of the first films in Iranian cinema that addresses post-traumatic stress disorder, a subject that could potentially be in direct opposition to the view of war as a 'divine blessing'. Indeed, the state rhetoric refused to recognize this aspect of the identity of war refugees or war veterans until 1989 when Mohsen Makhmalbaf, who was at the time still religious and backed by the state, addressed the impacts of war trauma in *Arusi-ye Khubān* (The Marriage of the Blessed).

Bāshu's absence after the market scene is a dilemma in the film as the audience is not informed about what he has done off-screen. It is also not clear whether this absence was intentional or due to the deletion of a scene by the censor. Nevertheless, when Bāshu returns from wherever he has been off-screen he distances himself further from his former identity as an immigrant. In the next scene after his return Bāshu is wearing a new shirt that Nāei has bought for him in the marketplace. The orange T-shirt which he has been wearing since the beginning of the film has signified his identity as a refugee who has fled through fire from a hot sunny land. Wearing the new purple shirt is, thus, like Bāshu's farewell to his former refugee self. In the scene, Bāshu is seen standing in the middle of the farm with his purple shirt on and acting like a person who considers himself the owner of the land. He plays a rhythm on a bucket and performs a ritual dance for the farm's fertility while singing. Thus, the film displays how Nāei's attempts to initiate him into his new farming culture have been successful. Another important detail depicted in this scene occurs when Bāshu and the other children have a ritual fight before he is accepted among them. The other children accompany him in this ritual. Bāshu plays the role of the land's guardian, and the other children play as invaders. They all share a culture now. Bāshu the immigrant has found a new identity within the new culture. This identity, however, is not that of the zealous protector of Islamic values promoted by the state but one that, as Talajooy states, marks Bāshu as an agent of art, fertility and prosperity.[16]

Bāshu, the Little Outsider

Another apt title for the film could be *Bāshu, the Little Outsider*. The reason for this is that Bāshu is marked by visible features that mark him as different from the villagers. As Linda Alcoff argues, 'skin tone, hair texture, shape of facial features', which are the 'physical features conventionally used to differentiate the races are almost laughably insignificant', but she also admits that 'the visible is a sign [...] and thus invites interpretation to discern what is behind it, beyond it, or what it signifies'.[17] In Bāshu's case, one of these insignificant physical differences, his skin tone, functions as a decisive factor in the villagers' refusal to accept Bāshu. Bāshu's skin colour is a sign that differentiates him from others and suggests a racial difference. Even before speaking he is immediately distinguished from others by his darker skin tone. In his first encounter with Nāei, she remarks about his skin colour: 'He is so black.' Later when Bāshu appears before other villagers beside Nāei and her children it is his skin tone that draws their attention. No one asks where the boy has come from or what he is doing in the village. This difference also means that from the start the villagers define his identity as an outsider and not an immigrant. It is at this point that Nāei and the villagers embark upon different paths regarding their relationship with Bāshu. For Nāei, Bāshu is an immigrant in need of shelter but for them he is an outsider. She declares that she is 'safekeeping' Bāshu for his parents who are likely to come looking for him. What makes Nāei the main character in contrast to others is her attempt to subvert the idea that Bāshu is an unwelcome outsider. Nāei's natural wisdom and maternal instincts enable her to understand that to transform Bāshu from an 'outsider' to a 'local' she needs to teach him her language and culture. She knows that Bāshu must learn the language and the culture of his new society to transcend the label of an outsider so that their relationship is not based on a power struggle. Nāei does not want to use her power as a 'local' to suppress Bāshu as an 'outsider'. The best example to verify this statement is, once more, the language teaching sequence. Being able to identify with and understand Bāshu's feelings as an outsider, Nāei seeks to demonstrate their equal status in this relationship. Her ability to understand Bāshu and step down to establish a relationship based on equality may arise from her status in the village as a lonely and somehow independent and rebellious woman. She, the unbending woman, and Bāshu, the stranger boy, have something in common, which as Nasrin Rahimieh argues, has to do with the fact of their status as contrary to or 'peripheral to existing linguistic, social, and cultural system of signification, which isolate and vilify difference'.[18]

Nāei tries to overcome the impact of Bāshu's physical appearance as a marker of being an outsider by washing him to make him white and teaching him her language and culture. That is why she buys a bar of soap in one of the early scenes. However, before she finds the opportunity to wash Bāshu, the film depicts her walking in the rice paddy, ringing a bell and telling Bāshu 'the seeds will grow better with this sound' in a tone that suggests she is introducing the immigrant to an important aspect of the agricultural culture she belongs to. The scene is followed by the one in which while trying to teach him her language, she learns his name: 'Bāshu', a person who is here to stay and whose presence cannot be denied. After this scene, the villagers come to Nāei's house to see the stranger, and Nāei confidently introduces Bāshu and talks about his ability to speak. Perhaps she thinks that merely by confirming that he can speak and can learn their language, she has prepared the path for his acceptance and the villagers may now forget about his identity as an 'outsider' and accept him as one of them. Soon, however, she realizes her mistake. During the villagers' visit, an old man stands before Bāshu and calls him a 'wonder'; another stands before him and calls him 'the soot covered boy'. At this point Nāei realizes that Bāshu's status as an 'outsider' has as much to do with his skin colour as it does with his unfamiliarity with the culture and the language.

Bāshu is an immigrant to Nāei and an unwelcome outsider to the villagers. The difference is that an immigrant possesses an unfamiliar language and culture, but an 'outsider' is not recognized by his language, culture and humanity. The scene in which Nāei washes Bāshu and is shocked to realize that his darkness cannot be washed away may seem simplistic, but it has a metaphorical significance. Several scholars have analysed the scene as a comment on racist attitudes. Hamid Dabashi, for instance, states: 'In their first encounter, Na'i makes a nasty reference to his dark complexion [...]. The leitmotif of racism persists in *Bāshu*, resulting in one of the most definitive scenes, in which Na'i ritually gives birth to Bāshu, but not before buying a new bar of soap to wash his dark skin in an attempt to make him white.'[19]

I would, however, argue that Nāei's reaction to the colour of Bāshu's complexion seems to be more because of her ignorance. She has never seen somebody in this colour, so she tries to make him white. Such a reaction has nothing to do with racism. Nāei is aware that for the villagers Bāshu's identity is intertwined with his colour. Thus, she tries and fails to liberate him from what has made him an outsider to the villagers. This realization enables Nāei to accept Bāshu as he is.[20] After washing Bāshu, Nāei gives him her husband's clothes to wear. Clothing is doubtlessly an important part of human culture and identity. Wearing the father's clothing has a meaning beyond simple dressing as it means that he has been accepted in the small family. It also suggests that Nāei has accepted Bāshu's skin tone as part of his identity. By dressing an unfamiliar body in familiar clothes, she takes another step to make others forget that Bāshu is an 'outsider'. At a psychological level, however, wearing the father's clothes can also suggest an oedipal overtone as it means that in the father's absence it is Bāshu who fills his role.

The father's refusal to endorse keeping Bāshu as expressed in his letter and later in a verbal argument with Nāei after his return is a vague reflection of this oedipal overtone. Dabashi also mentions this issue by referring to father's return 'with his right hand, an obvious phallic symbol, cut off'.[21] However Dabashi does not mention that Bāshu in some parts stands between being a son and a husband for Nāei. He analyses Nāei and Bāshu's relationship just as a mother and son, while it seems that Bāshu may also function as the image of the ideal father/male figure, who, in contrast with the father who carries the markers of an oppressive outsider in his first scene with Nāei, is always gentle and helpful. Bāshu himself is an oppressed outsider and even wearing the father's clothes does not turn him into a dominant, oppressing male figure. This is also suggested in that towards the end, Bāshu puts the father's clothes on a scarecrow. The father of the family had objected to Bāshu's presence, and Bāshu has, in turn, consciously or unconsciously, reduced his agency to that of a scarecrow which has no power to move and has no serious role in the family. In the scene depicting the father's return the camera angle puts him right in front of the scarecrow and makes them appear as one. The semiotic meaning of the scarecrow reflects Bāshu's perspective in which the father's body is a scarecrow that does not fulfil any roles in the family. The image, however, once more confirms the oedipal overtones of the relationship between Bāshu and the father of the family.

This implied conflict puts the narrative in yet another level of contrast with the state's war propaganda. The films that were dependent on the official rhetoric had a different take on the father figure serving at the front. This man was supposed to be a role model for his wife, children and relatives even in his absence, a man whose demands and views were to be regarded as especially important. In *Bāshu*, however, that image is distorted in a way that contradicts the ideas of the leader of the revolution. Furthermore, the villagers do not speak of the absent man, who is serving at the front, as a sacred figure. In his absence, Nāei can manage her life with ease without being dependent on his return. Moreover, the man who returns from the war has nothing in common with the veterans in other films from the same decade.[22]

Wearing the father's clothes invokes yet another symbolic meaning. Putting aside children's clothing and wearing the costume of the man of the house can also indicate Bāshu's maturity.

In fact, Bāshu's experience in the new geographical location can be understood as a rite of initiation: 'Adolescent initiation ceremonies move individuals from the social stage of childhood to the social stage of adolescence.'[23] One of these stages is bidding farewell to a child's body by changing a children's clothing to an adult's clothing. In Zoroastrianism, one of the requirements for the rite of initiation (Navjote) is to wear the sacred garment and girdle called Sudreh and Kusti, respectively. One can speculate that Beyzaie intended an allusion to such rites of passage in general and Zoroastrian Sudreh and Kusti in particular.[24] Other stages of such rites of initiation include a symbolic return to the mother's womb in the shape of staying alone in a dark room, a ritual fight to demonstrate strength, and self-harm which, once more, signifies putting aside the body of childhood to be able to greet the body of adulthood.

During the film, Bāshu undergoes all these stages: replacing his orange T-shirt with the father's clothes and then a new shirt, fighting with other teenagers of the village, being confined to a dark room and sickness. This exposure to darkness is, of course, significant as it means subjecting the initiate to pain and fear in controlled settings.[25] All these stages indicate Bāshu's entry into adolescence and adulthood, which, in turn, prepare him for the final scene in which he accompanies Nāei and Qesmat Shanbesarāei (her husband) in protecting the farm.

Yehudi A. Cohen, in his study of boys' initiation ceremonies, proposed that the boys, who are 'traumatized and denied the comfort of their families, are forced to identify emotionally with their initiators. This redirects their identification from the family to the male cohort'.[26] In a cliché plot, Qesmat (the father figure) would be the initiator and the head of the male cohort, but Beyzaie makes Nāei the main initiator in Bāshu's initiation journey. Traumatized and far from the comfort of his family, Bāshu identifies with Nāei instead of Qesmat. Replacement of a male initiator with a female one is beyond the normal clichés of father figures and defamiliarizes the stereotypes, but it also allows Bāshu to gradually recreates his own visible identity while defining a new social identity for himself as the protector of the farm.

Earlier in this chapter, I mentioned that Bāshu is an immigrant to Nāei and an outsider to the villagers. In fact, for the villagers, his unknown body is a source of anxiety. In the village gathering, the villagers warn Nāei of the potential dangers of this new unknown entity. The small community wishes to reduce this black outsider to an 'abject' that must be discarded without further concern: 'The rejection', therefore, 'is played out through an abjection'. Such a situation is inevitable because, abjection, as Kate Cregan states, is both 'a semiotic' and 'an embodied' phenomenon. 'It is the rejection of and revulsion at what both is and is not the body.' Thus, the term 'abject' is used for the phenomena which are not either subject or object, and society has a tendency to repel them: 'Abjected matter is a remnant of the uncontrollably chaotic *chora*, which threatens to "irrupt" into (disrupt) the Symbolic order.'[27]

Although the term is not used for human beings, by expanding its definition, one can perceive that in close communities with strict borders between 'us' and 'them' the outsiders are turned into social abject, potential threats that must be oppressed, rejected and removed so that order and safety can return to society.[28] The villagers call Bāshu 'the monster'. They do not recognize his sickness and attempt to prohibit Nāei from keeping him. Bāshu's presence with his unknown face and body is a cause of disorder. The most significant instance of such a disorder occurs when Nāei as a member of this small community chooses a different path and throws the villagers out as abject. This is a key moment that, if considered from another perspective, suggests that she is an animist reviver, someone who can even elevate objects to the status of a subject. She talks to dogs and birds and plays a bell for the plants to grow.

After the gathering in Nāei's house which takes place thirty minutes into the film, Bāshu becomes ill, suggesting that the villagers' attitudes have made Bāshu realize that they intend to reject and ultimately banish him. Bāshu's illness takes him to the point of death. Nāei runs wailing to the other villagers to seek help, but until later when the apothecary shows some humanity, they all turn their backs to her as if Bāshu's illness is a solution for getting rid of the offending abject. Later, the film creates a parallel to this scene when Nāei becomes ill, and Bāshu runs to the villagers to bring help. The villagers react the same way to Nāei's illness as if Nāei herself has become a troublesome object that must be rejected. Bāshu saves Nāei on his own by performing a southern healing ritual. Thus, the culture of the immigrant who was assigned the role of the unwanted 'outsider' enables him to save Nāei when her own ethnocentric people have rejected her.

When Nāei rises from her sickbed, the narrative moves towards its end. Nāei and Bāshu have both been saved from banishment and death. Both have survived and now, untied together, they can repel any invaders from their farm. Once more, one can compare Bāshu's image as an outsider with the official image of a refugee in the official rhetoric during the war. The fact that the villagers do not consider Bāshu as one of them contradicts the premises of the idea of religious unity promoted by the state. The villagers are oblivious to the 'blessings of the war' and are far from the refugee accepting Muslims of the state's propaganda. They even go so far as rejecting one of their own people when she opens her door to the unwelcome 'outsider'.

Bāshu, the Littler Stranger

As argued before, based on Bāshu's different identities, one could give the film different titles, but from among all those potential titles, Beyzaie chose *Bāshu, the Little Stranger*. This shows that for Beyzaie, Bāshu's position and identity as a stranger are central to the plot, which, in turn, raises the questions of who this stranger is and what the term stranger means in Beyzaie's oeuvre. Both 'outsider' and 'immigrant' are terms used in sociology and philosophy. *Stranger*, however, has no place in academic terms. It is an informal word with many connotations, but a review of Beyzaie's oeuvre suggests a straightforward and frequently appearing meaning for the term. In one of his lectures at Stanford University, Beyzaie argues that 'awareness is the beginning of change', that 'a saviour will not come unless we turn into our own saviours by self-awareness', that 'as long as we wallow in self-deception, there can be no salvation', and that 'breaking free from self-deception is only possible by awareness'.[29] For Beyzaie, therefore, achieving and giving awareness enable human beings to avoid self-deception which, in turn, leads to salvation. His frequent use of the figure of a stranger who fulfils a collective duty and overcomes self-deception to oppose ignorance also suggests that his own identity as a creative thinker has evolved from the same image.

In Beyzaie's cinematic and theatrical works, strangers are those who, due to their high level of 'awareness', cannot conform to society and attain a coherent and acceptable group identity to join the people around them. The stranger is someone who remains solitary, and the majority fail to accept him as one of their own. Beyzaie's oeuvre contains a long line of strangers. In one of his first plays titled *Ārash* which draws upon ancient Iranian mythology, the eponymous hero is a stranger both among his compatriots and the enemies of his country. He carries the awareness of a national burden and shoots a single arrow that determines the borders of Iran. In his first feature film *Ragbār* (Downpour, 1972), a teacher who epitomizes knowledge redefines his identity as a person dedicated to raising awareness in a district populated by people who do not welcome change. In another film *Gharibeh va Meh* (Stranger and the Fog, 1974), Beyzaie went so far as including the term *stranger* in the title. Āyat, the stranger of the film, seems to have returned from the realm of the dead. He is, thus, like Bāshu in that both have come from a world of death with the difference that Bāshu's world of death is tangible as he has come from the frontlines of a contemporary war. In *Cherikeh-ye Tārā* (Ballad of Tārā, 1978–80), another stranger who possesses historical awareness emerges from the water. Beyzaie continued to use the figure of the stranger after *Bāshu* with the grandmother in *Mosāferān* (Travellers, 1990) being a special case as her conception of life and death which is radically different from the people around her enables her to understand and insist on the continuity of her daughter and her family who have died in a road accident.[30]

It seems that the 'awareness' that Bāshu and others lack is his profound historical awareness which he acquired through personal experience. He has witnessed the war, and his dark skin, overall appearance and orange shirt represent the same historical and geographical awareness of war that he brings to a community which has had no awareness of it. The villagers represent all the people who have ignored the war and are living obliviously. Bāshu's mere presence, skin tone and language have, thus, brought them the news of a distant war, an awareness of a historical incidence, an awareness of the history itself and the necessity to change. Bāshu's mythical counterpart in Ferdowsi's *Shāhnāmeh* could be Zāl, the boy who is abandoned in the wilderness at birth by his father because of his white hair (Zāl literally means albino) and is raised by the mythical gigantic bird Simurgh. Zāl, who is also associated with the sun, returns to human society by descending from the top of the mountain to the low plains at an age similar to Bāshu's. Like Bāshu, Zāl has been raised in a different geographical location, and like Bāshu, he was a child who has become old before going through adulthood and middle age. Zāl's white hair, like Bāshu's black skin, sets him apart from others. But both the white-haired stranger and the black-faced stranger embody awareness. In the *Shāhnāmeh*, Zāl (as an old child) is associated with wisdom and knowledge. This is a quality that is also clearly reflected in Bāshu's gradual rise in the film.[31] As Taqi Pournamdariyan states, in Shahboddin Sohrewardi's interpretation of the legend (*ca.* 1185) 'Zāl is a great sign who is manifested by his light. His high honour is hidden from the ignorant ones'.[32] Zāl has attained awareness due to being associated with the sun and the mythical/mystical bird Simurgh. Bāshu, however, attains awareness due to being exposed to the fire of the war and being displaced. The awareness that Bāshu possesses is informed by his nightmares and memories of the war. The structure of the narrative does not allow the spectator to forget how Bāshu frequently remembers the flames that consumed his home, his parents and his sister, but his recollections are neither framed as flashbacks nor pushed to the edges of the main narrative. Instead, they are made palpable as if they are happening in the present. They impose themselves on Bāshu in such intense ways that they disrupt his connection with his current environment. In several scenes the past becomes so prominent that it completely clouds the present. One particularly important scene in this regard is the one in which Nāei needs help to move a ladder, but Bāshu initially does not help her. The camera reflects his vision of being in the dry terrains of southern Iran walking along his parents and sister in a direction opposite to where Nāei is walking with the ladder. In this significant scene, Bāshu's mental conception of his geographical domain is so strong that it has overcome the reality of his physical surroundings.

Bāshu's confusion about his geographical location and identification with his dead kinsmen who share his original identity is the result of his trauma. At a more metaphorical level, however, the film also highlights other forms of self-deception and ignorance in society. The idyllic village in the film represents a society which wallows in self-deception and continues the peaceful flow of life by being wilfully oblivious to reality. Any stranger that compromises their peace and quiet is, therefore, doomed to being shunned and banished. This reality can be a war or any other significant incident. Bāshu's awareness also has another layer. While he is being beaten by the other boys, he picks up the Persian textbook and reads a passage aloud. Although the scene contradicts the otherwise minimalistic narrative of the film which avoids a direct message, it reflects the essence of Bāshu's awareness which he also attempts to communicate to the people around him – the awareness that all of them 'belong to one soil and water' and are 'Iranian'. This is what the villagers are oblivious to. Their lack of awareness is, thus, both historical and geographical. Burdened by superstitions, the older people even think that Bāshu is a 'monster' and have no awareness of the possibility that he may be a dislocated citizen of their country. Thus, Bāshu brings geographical and historical awareness to the secluded village and shatters some of their superstitious beliefs. Together Bāshu and Nāei present a stance which is neither reflective of the villagers' racism nor of the Iranian pre-revolutionary royalist nationalism or the state's revolutionary religious nationalism. As Rahimieh puts it, 'the film exposes the manner in which the construction of Iranian national identity has insisted upon the erasure and elision of gender, language and ethnicity'.[33] However, as Talajooy argues, 'while transcending nationalism, the film introduces a new form of togetherness which transcends the exclusionist obsessions of nationalist or religious discourses and is more concerned with inclusion and mutual support for guaranteeing fertility and prosperity'.[34]

This reading of the film also reveals a subtle critique of the state's rhetoric and propaganda during the war. First and foremost, the focus on Bāshu as a living example of the calamity of the war and the number of orphaned children that remain stranded due to military conflicts contradicts the glorification of the war as a blessing in the state media. Furthermore, whereas the media constantly depicted a sacred image of the war and claimed that the people had a united national will to continue the conflict against foreign forces, the villagers do not seem to know anything about or care about the war and are oblivious to what is happening to their country. Of course, as Talajooy argues, it can be assumed that it is the initial stage of the war, and thus, either the news has not yet reached this remote corner of the country or the villagers do not associate Bāshu's arrival with the recent news of the war.[35] After all, Beyzaie's original idea occurred to him when he thought about 'what would be the situation of the first southerner who had fled the war and migrated to the north'.[36] Nevertheless, it is still important that they do not care about what is going on outside their community and the state's slogans and propaganda have had no impacts on the small community of the villagers.

Another important element to consider when it comes to Bāshu's role in the community is that, like some of the other strangers in Beyzaie's works, at one level, he seems to act like a saviour. Examples of such strangers include the ostracized Ārash in *Ārash*, who restores Iran's borders by shooting an arrow, or the grandmother in *Travellers*, who brings the dead back to life. Bāshu reveals similar qualities. He can be compared to mythical figures of saviour children such as Moses (Hebrew culture), Joseph (Canaanite culture), Gilgamesh (Sumerian culture) and Oedipus Rex (Hellenic culture). All these mythical figures are exposed to death during childhood, escape death by different means, arrive in a new land (usually with the aid of a woman) and continue their lives until they emerge as saviour figures. Bāshu's story is narrated exactly with the same mythical pattern.[37] From a semiotic perspective, the purple shirt that Bāshu wears in the second half of the film can be viewed as a mythological/religious allusion to the violet robe of Christ as the saviour figure. Considering such an interpretation, the ending scene where Bāshu rises to protect the farm from wild animals can have an apocalyptic significance with Bāshu as the saviour. Beyzaie does not usually discuss such interpretations in the public, but one can assume that the officials in charge of censoring films may have suspected these semiotic suggestions and they may have played a role in banning the film.

An important factor which drives the narrative towards its conclusion is when Bāshu, who is a stranger himself, calls Qesmat a stranger. Calling the father of the family a stranger is the first step towards their mutual understanding as it is where the first bond for the potential connection occurs. Bāshu knows that being a stranger may mean possessing a higher level of awareness or having an unknown experience. Thus, he knows that there is a similarity between the man and himself. Qesmat also witnesses that when he acts like an invader by shouting at Nāei, Bāshu arrives holding a stick to protect the woman. This functions like the last stage of Bāshu's role as a provider of awareness. He teaches the father that there is a difference between him and the invaders that he has 'probably' seen in the war. He teaches the father that not every 'stranger' is necessarily untrustworthy. Now the father believes that he can trust this 'stranger' and perhaps he can be like the hand that he has lost. He, thus, accepts Bāshu.

Nevertheless, even when it comes to a stranger's potential to raise awareness in a distant community about a historical event, the discourse promoted by Beyzaie's film is completely different from the one desired by the state. The discourse of acceptance is humanistic, cultural and in service of fertility rather than religious, and the discourse on war as highlighted by Bāshu and Qesmat is devastation and loss of potential for prosperity and fertility. In other words, Beyzaie's film offers a constructive universal discourse on human relationships with themselves and their primary role as protectors of life and nature. The official discourse, however, was obsessed with propaganda for a violent Islamic discourse that celebrated the war as a blessing and was already taking its toll on people's lives.

Conclusion

On the surface *Bāshu, the Little Stranger* is a simple film with a child protagonist. It neither explicitly says anything against the regime or its policies nor opposes the war that was labelled 'the Sacred Defence' by the official rhetoric.

Nevertheless, the film was banned for three years because, as argued above, it did not fulfil the demands of the regime in any of the assumed identities that this chapter suggested for Bāshu. Bāshu's threefold identities are all given to him by different sources. Nāei considers him an immigrant, the villagers consider him an outsider and reduce him to an abject, and Bāshu considers himself a stranger who must find a way to belong and become familiar. These three identities form the various layers of his characterization, and it appears that the totality of the three identities given to Bāshu resulted in the three-year ban that was imposed on the film.

In all the assumed identities that Beyzaie gives to Bāshu, he refuses to conform to the official policies regarding the war or offer direct criticism against them. Bāshu's position contradicts the image of host communities being open to immigrants. Instead, it uses the semiotic motifs of the outsider and the abject to demonstrate a realistic and unidealistic image of the immigrant-accepting communities and the humanitarian crisis of war. Bāshu's position also poses a criticism towards the state media by depicting his identity as a stranger. The essence of this analysis can also be understood if one compares Bāshu with Hussein Fahmideh (1967–80). Fahmideh, who was slightly older than Bāshu, was a thirteen-year-old boy, who tied hand grenades to himself and jumped under an enemy tank to destroy it. He was, for years, the ideal heroic image that the regime presented to other Iranian boys. A Bāshu, who could have been acceptable to the regime, would have been neither an immigrant, nor an outsider, nor a stranger; but one that did not flee the war, faced the enemy and asserted his identity as a martyr.

Of course, apart from these hidden aspects, there were also some obvious reasons for the three-year ban on *Bāshu*. For example, the close-ups of an actress's face did not follow the modesty codes that had been imposed on Iranian cinema after the revolution. Furthermore, the director's personal history had defined him as one who was outside the circle of state-approved directors. In any case, however, when *Bāshu, the Little Stranger was* screened, the war had already ended. Perhaps the censor assumed that with the end of the war, the film no longer had an impact on the public and would be regarded past its expiration date, but the thirty-six years that have passed since the making of the film have proved that it is one of the best films of Iranian Cinema, and one of the most important films about the war between Iraq and Iran.

Notes

1   Garshasbi, 'Gharibeh-hāye Āshnā', 16.
2   Rabi'i, 'Bonyād-e Omur-e'.
3   Mirsalim, 'Revāyat-e Mirsalim'.
4   The Institute was founded in January 1966 with the purpose of producing books and films and organizing cultural activities for younger audiences. The Institute continued its activities after the 1979 revolution, but it became much more aligned with official discourses. 'Film-hā-ye Kānun' (Institute's Films), as they were popularly known,

focused on subjects related to children and were mostly apolitical, which made them easier to pass censors.
5   Khomeini, *Isār va Shahādat*, 205.
6   Mirsalim, 'Revāyat-e Mirsalim'.
7   Khomeini, *Isār va Shahādat*, 205.
8   Lee, 'Theory of Migration', 47–57.
9   Kamrava, *Modern Middle*, 13.
10 Joseph, *Language and Identity*, 13. Quoted in Edwards, *Language and Identity*, 20.
11 Edwards, *Language and Identity*, 21.
12 The doll used in the scene is a traditional doll from Gilan province called 'Chamcheh Khatun' (Lady Ladle) which is one of the key objects in a rain ritual in northern Iran.
13 See also Rahimieh, 'Marking Gender', who examines the use of Persian as a book language in *Bashu*.
14 For an analysis of Nāei as Anahita, see also Talajooy, 'Jābejāei-ye Marzhā', 48–51.
15 Humanization of mythical figures is a recurring element in Beyzaie's oeuvre. This is even reflected in his first play, *Ārash* (1959), in which Beyzaie depicts a mythical hero as a normal human being conflicted by doubts.
16 Talajooy, 'Jābejāei-ye Marzhā', 50–1.
17 Alcoff, *Visible Identities*, 7 and 199.
18 Rahimieh, *Marking Gender*, 241.
19 Dabashi, *Close-Up*, 101.
20 See Talajooy, 'Jābejāei-ye Marzhā-ye', 49–50.
21 Dabashi, *Close-Up*, 106.
22 See, for instance, Ebrahim Sultanifar's *Toei Keh Nemishenākhtamat* (You, Whom I Did Not Know, 1990).
23 Schlegel and Berry III, *Pain, Fear*. 435.
24 Chiniwalla, *Sequel to Essentials*. 6–11.
25 Schlegel and Berry III, *Pain, Fear*. 440.
26 Quoted in Ibid., 442.
27 Cregan, *Sociology*, 96.
28 The refugee camps can likewise be considered a place for such abject humans – a place where immigrants are forced to remain in the fringes of society far from the centre.
29 Beyzaie, 'Bahram Beyzaie Discusses', 58'.30"–62'.20".
30 The evidence can be seen easily in all of Beyzaie's films, but for more on the subject of outsiders and strangers in his films, see the introduction to this book and Talajooy, *Iranian Culture*; 'Bahram Beyzaie', 34–47, 'Downpour', 'Stranger and the Fog', 'The Crow', 'Maybe Some Other Time', 'Ballad of Tārā', 'Bashu, the Little Stranger', 'Uncle Moustaches', 'The Journey', 119–21, 133–5, 139–41, 148–50, 210–13, 234–6, 236–8.
31 For more on the similarities of Zāl and Bashu from another angle, see also Talajooy, 'Jābejāei-ye Marzhā' in which he also compares Nāei with Simurgh.
32 Pournamdarian, 'Ramz va Dāstān-hā-ye', 200–8.
33 Rahimieh, 'Marking Gender', 238.
34 For Beyzaie's take on nationalism in *Bashu*, see Talajooy, *Mythologizing*, 238–82 and 'Shifting the Borders'.
35 Talajooy, *Mythologizing*, 270.
36 Beyzaie in 'Mosāhebeh', 44.
37 See Talajooy, 'Jābejāei-ye Marzhā', 48, who examines this aspect of Bashu's character from another angle.

Bibliography

Alcoff, Linda. *Visible Identities: Race, Gender and the Self*. Oxford: Oxford University Press, 2006.

Beyzaie, Bahram. 'Mosāhebeh bā Bahram Beyzaie: Gharibeh-ei dar Pe-ye Tafāhom'. *Māhnāmeh-ye Sinemāei-ye Film* (Film Journal). Vol. 8. No. 87 (March 1990). Pp. 44–51.

Beyzaie, Bahram. 'Bahram Beyzaie Discusses Crossroads'. Video Recording. *Stanford University: Bahram Beyzaie*. Online: https://beyzaie.sites.stanford.edu/lectures-conferences-and-discussions (Dated 23 April 2018) (Accessed 24 June 2022).

Cregan Kate. *The Sociology of the Body, Mapping the Abstraction of the Embodiment*. London: Sage, 2006.

Dabashi Hamid. *Close up: Iranian cinema, Past, Present and Future*. London: Verso, 2001.

Edwards, John. *Language and Identity: An Introduction*. Cambridge: Cambridge University Press, 2009.

Chiniwalla, Framroze. *A Sequel to Essentials of Zoroastrianism*. Online: www.dnzt.org: https://tinyurl.com/2w4uv72j. (Accessed 5 June 2022).

Garshasbi, Mohamad. '*Gharibeh-hā-ye Āshnā*'. *Iran* (Daily Newspaper). No. 7479 (31 October 2020). P. 16.

Joseph, John. *Language and Identity: National, Ethnic, Religious*. Basingstoke: Palgrave Macmillan, 2004.

Kamrava, Mehran. *The Modern Middle East, a Political History since the First World War*. Barkley: University of California, 2005.

Khomeini, Ruallah. *Isār va Shahādat dar Maktab-e Emām Khomeini*. Tehran: Moʻasseseh-ye Nashr-e Asār-e Imām Khomeini, 2011.

Lee, Everett S. 'A Theory of Migration'. *Demography*. Vol. 3. No. 1 (March 1966). Pp. 47–57.

Mirsalim, Mostafa. 'Revāyat-e Mirsalim az Sāmāndehi-ye Yek Million O Sad Hezār Āvāreh-ye Jangi dar Tul-e Defāʻ-e Moqaddas'. Interview. *ISNA: Iranian Students' News Agency*. 13 Mehr 1399 (4 October 2020). Online: https://www.isna.ir/news/99071309348/%D8%B1 (Accessed 21 June 2022).

Mohammadi, Sara. *Osarā-ye Zan va Zanān-e Farāmush Shodeh dar Jang-e Iran va Iraq*. *BBC Persian*. Online: https://www.bbc.com/persian/blog-viewpoints-49381116. (Dated 17 August 2019) (Accessed 21 May 2022).

Pournamdarian, Taqi. *Ramz va Dāstān-hā-ye Ramzi dar Adab-e Fārsi*. Tehran: Elmi va Farhangi, 1996.

Rabiʻi, Manizheh. 'Bonyād-e Omur-e Mohājerin-e Jangi'. In *Dāneshnāmeh-ye Jahān-e Eslām*. Vol. 1 (Encyclopaedia of Islamic World). Tehran: Bonyād-e Daeratolmaʻāref-e Eslāmi, 2011. Vol. 1. P. 1946. Online: https://lib.eshia.ir/23019/1/1946. (Accessed 21 June 2022).

Rahimieh, Nasrin. 'Making Gender and Difference in the Myth of the Nation: The Post-Revolutionary Iranian Films'. In *The New Iranian Cinema: Politics, Representation And Identity*. Ed. Richard Tapper. London and New York: I. B. Tauris, 2002. Pp. 238–53.

Reed-Sandoval, Amy. *Socially Undocumented: Identity and Immigration Justice*. Oxford: Oxford University Press, 2020.

Schlegel, Alica and Herbert Berry III. 'Pain, Fear, and Circumcision in Boys' Adolescent Initiation Ceremonies'. *Cross Cultural Research*. Vol. 5. No. 5 (January 2017). Pp. 435–63.

Talajooy, Saeed. *Mythologizing the Transition: A Comparative Study of Bahram Beyzaee and Wole Soyinka*. PhD thesis. University of Leeds. Jan. 2008. Online through *Whiterose eTheses* https://etheses.whiterose.ac.uk/406/. (Accessed 5 June 2022).

Talajooy, Saeed. 'Bahram Beyzaie'. In *Directory of World Cinema: Iran 2*. Ed. Parviz Jahed. Bristol: Intellect, 2017. Pp. 34–47.

Talajooy, Saeed '"Downpour", "Stranger and the Fog", "The Crow", "Maybe Some Other Time", "Ballad of Tārā", "Bāshu, Little Stranger," "Uncle Moustaches", "Journey"'. In *Directory of World Cinema: Iran 1*. Ed. Parviz Jahed. Bristol and Chicago: Intellect, 2012. Pp. 119–21, 133–5, 139–41, 148–50, 210–13, 234–6, 236–8.

Talajooy, Saeed. 'Shifting the Borders of Belonging in the Myth of the Nation: (A Ritual of Exorcism)'. Video Presentation for the Conference, *Celebrating Bahram Beyzaie's 10 Year Anniversary at Stanford University*. (May 2021). Online at YouTube https://www.youtube.com/watch?v=UzaayPZPR9w (Accessed 27 June 2022).

Talajooy, Saeed. 'Jābejāei-ye Marzhā-ye Taʿlloq: Qomiyat, Zabān va Hovyat Melli dar Bāshu, Gharibeh-ye Kuchak'. *Film-e Emruz* (Today's Film). Vol. 1. No. 8 (January 2022). Pp. 48–51.

Section C

BEYZAIE THE FILMMAKER – GENRES AND TECHNIQUES

Chapter 7

THE CINEMATIC TRANSLATION OF *TA'ZIYEH* IN BEYZAIE'S *TRAVELLERS*

Farshad Zahedi

Introduction

Mosāferān (Travellers, 1991) is the fourth film that Beyzaie made after the 1979 Revolution. He made the film during a short period of time in the late eighties when by the emergence of more liberal policies for Iranian cinema, he found the opportunity to return to filmmaking. With Mohamad Khatami as minister of culture and Islamic guidance (1982–92) the state launched new organizations to implement more supportive cinematic policies while maintaining its main aim of promoting Islamic ideological values. The creation of these organizations originated in the idea of supervising the film industry and educating a new generation of filmmakers. Nevertheless, the plan also involved giving new opportunities to veteran filmmakers to allow them to adapt to the new coordinates.[1] The new cultural politics of the Islamic Republic, thus, gradually introduced new opportunities for filmmakers. Consequently, in the period between 1985 and 1991, Beyzaie produced three films: *Bāshu Gharibeh-ye Kuchak* (Bāshu, the Little Stranger, 1985), *Shāyad Vaqti Digar* (Maybe Some Other Time, 1988) and *Travellers*. The films, however, became uneasy cases for new cinematic authorities. Beyzaie's films hardly adapted to the ideological rules set by the state. Instead, they subtly displayed critical positions. As a result, the screening of each film was possible only after fierce negotiations with the censors. The case of *Bāshu* is remarkable: it took three years for the film to gain screening permission because of the filmmaker's 'refusal to make some eighty changes demanded by the official censors. This may have had as much to do with the anti-war message [...] as with the bold transgression of the codes of modesty, the direct relay of diegetic gazes, and spectator positioning'.[2] Ironically, the film was a victim of censorship because of its peaceful narrative as the anti-war story of *Bāshu* was marked as a message that must not be conveyed to the audience. Presenting a counternarrative to the official policies on depicting 'the sacred defense' as just and heroic, this was enough to make the film unwelcomed in official views at least during wartime. Similar situations occurred with his two other films made during this period. The release of *Bāshu* and the production of

Travellers coincided with a remarkable historical period in Iran: the end of Iraq-Iran war in 1988 and the death of Ayatollah Khomeini a year later. *Travellers* also suffered objections from the censors. The filmmaker had to eliminate 'some joyful marriage scenes [...] this partly alludes to the fact that during the long war with Iraq, the display of joy and happiness was officially frowned on, unless it was to congratulate the families of the martyrs on their deaths'.[3] Beyzaie again persistently resisted bending to censor's requirements, and the film finally received the permission for screening after nine months. *Travellers*, however, became his only film of the 1990s. Due to a combination of different elements, particularly the imposition of more conservative cultural policies between 1993 and 1997, Beyzaie could not make any films until 1999 when he began making *Killing Mad Dogs* (*Sagkoshi*, 2001) during Khatami's presidency.

This historical background suggests that *Travellers* concluded Beyzaie's first period of creative involvement with post-revolutionary conditions and that a retrospective examination of the film is likely to produce interesting discoveries about the film and the period in which it was made. As the author himself states, the film is an intentional celebration of life produced in reaction to those Iranian films that praised death.[4] However, one can read the film as an outstanding defiance of the state's ideological use of Shi'i martyrdom culture for mass mobilizations during the wartime. Beyzaie's film subtly stages a deconstructed narrative of martyrdom while using the technical elements borrowed from the Iranian traditional theatre *ta'ziyeh*. My attempt in this chapter is to explore the film to examine these elements. I will demonstrate how *ta'ziyeh* techniques become cinematic and how Beyzaie interpretations of traditional *ta'ziyeh* and classical filmmaking style shape the film's aesthetics.

Ta'ziyeh is a ritual theatre genre that primarily stages the tragic martyrdom of Hossein, the grandson of the prophet of Islam and the third Imam of Shi'i Muslims.[5] Saeed Talajooy's summaries of the features and history of the form and its function as a tradition of passion plays, quoted below, highlight the significance of the form in Iran and its potential for modern reformulations, which I will be discussing in relation to Beyzaie's *Travellers*:

> *Ta'ziyeh* [... is] associated with Ashura ceremonies, the annual mourning rituals commemorating the martyrdom of [...] Hussein and the male members of his family. With the establishment of Imami Shiism as Iran's official religion in the sixteenth century, these annual rituals became a locus for the reinforcement of an imagined national identity based on religious cohesion. During the seventeenth and eighteenth centuries, due to royal patronage, the semi dramatic aspects of these rituals transformed into dramatic forms, creating passion plays about sacrificial figures in Shiite and Islamic historiography, including plays on Abel, John the Baptist, etc. *Ta'ziyeh* reached its highest status in the nineteenth century when it gave birth to about 2,000 plays on more than 270 subjects, including secular and comic ones. *Ta'ziyeh* is a treasure house of dramatic techniques from expressionist and minimalist depictions to grand scale re-enactments. The audience knows the events and the outcomes of the plays, which are written and

recited in verse. The unities are not observed: the characters might go from one city to another by circling the stage and the time is usually announced in the dialogue. Costume and makeup are essential, but the scenery is usually minimal: a basin of water may stand for the Euphrates, a palm branch in a vase for a grove of palms, a black handkerchief for mourning. Yet during the nineteenth century it was also possible to see *ta'ziyeh*(s) of epic grandeur with hundreds of people performing.[6]

Ta'ziyeh was performed by amateur or professional actors, called *shabih* in circular stages, where the relationship between the audience and the actors was close. Since actors played sacred figures or violently hated villains, many participatory conventions evolved in which actors or directors explained that actors were just actors, commented on a situation, cursed the villains, asked for blessing, or invited the audience to comment and weep for the martyrs, which, in turn, necessitated conscious acting and carrying of the role rather than impersonating the saints and the villains. Thus, like other indigenous forms, *ta'ziyeh* involved various participatory and innovative techniques.[7]

Fascinated by these techniques and the potential of the form as a source of innovative techniques for modern drama and cinema, early in his career, Beyzaie conducted in-depth research on the form and wrote the history of the formation and evolution of *ta'ziyeh* in a chapter of his research book on Iranian theatre.[8] According to Talajooy, Beyzaie's first contacts with *ta'ziyeh* was in the mid-fifties when he joined other theatre practitioners of National Arts Group (1956–73). The idea of the group was to promote the creation of 'an Iranian theatrical tradition by refashioning indigenous dramatic forms'.[9] Later, between 1961 and 1965, he accomplished his research on Iranian theatre which was published in the book mentioned above. In his interview with Zaven Qukasian, he points to the discovery of *ta'ziyeh* as an important event for him in this period, especially when he accidentally found out that his ancestors were among the most important *ta'ziyeh* directors (*ta'ziyeh gardān*) of his native town.[10] This contact with indigenous theatrical forms and narratives and the intensive research on the subject which followed it drove him to bring ancient forms to the present. He adamantly followed his ideal of framing *ta'ziyeh* and other Iranian artistic forms in modern theatrical and filmic works. From the early 1960s, therefore, he brought his knowledge of Iranian forms to the practice arena and 'began to combine these with eastern and western forms to create the most expansive collections of experimental works in Iranian theatre and cinema'.[11] This tendency of the author evolved with time and culminated arguably in *Travellers*: a film in which, one can find a modern and subversive reading of *ta'ziyeh* and some other Iranian theatrical techniques such as dramatic storytelling forms of *naqqāli* and *pardeh khāni*.[12]

Talajooy points to Beyzaie's subversive use of *ta'ziyeh* as a counterculture and as a response to the dominant ideology of post-revolutionary Iran:

> The government's use of Ashura rituals and Shiite historiography for mythologizing its political discourse encouraged Beyzaie to expand his

counternarrative on heroism to create a deconstructive tragic paradigm, in which creative intellectuals and artists, historically victimized by radical elements in Iran's religious and political establishments, were depicted as sacrificial heroes.[13]

Drawing upon this view, I will argue that in *Travellers* this counternarrative becomes cinematic. My approach to the film is to examine its formal use of global filmic and *ta'ziyeh* techniques. I will, particularly, focus on the combination of *ta'ziyeh* theatrical conventions with cinematic ones such as objective/subjective shots to construct the film narrative. I will also discuss how this combination of *ta'ziyeh* and film engages the audience in a collective ritual. In this regard, I follow Hamid Dabashi's opinion about *Travellers* when he considers the film a brilliant example of what he calls Beyzaie's 'mythical realism'.[14] For Dabashi, Beyzaie's works 'portray a communal ritual, but they transform the act of spectatorship itself into a communal ritual'.[15] I will demonstrate how the participation of the viewers in the ritual becomes possible by engrafting *ta'ziyeh* rules into the grammar of classical film. The relations between the shots, the framing and editing techniques and finally the thorough play of the author with objective and subjective shots give consistency to the ritual. This, the use of *ta'ziyeh* and other Iranian theatrical techniques such as *naqqāli* makes the film *materially* Iranian.

The opening scene: The wreckage

Many Iranian scholars detect powerful traces of *ta'ziyeh* narrative techniques in *Travellers*' opening sequence.[16] Outside a house near the Caspian Sea, Mahtāb and his family are preparing for a trip to Tehran to participate in the wedding ceremony of her sister Māhrokh. Her husband Heshmat and a driver named Safar are setting their luggage in the vehicle that will take them along with their twin young boys, Keyvān and Keyhān, to the city. Special attention is paid to a mirror, which must be taken to the destination for the marriage to take place. Later, the audience is given more information about this mirror: it is part of their family heritage, and traditionally it must remain with the person who has married last. It is, therefore, supposed to be brought to weddings as a token of continuity and good omen. When Mahtāb is ready to get in the car, she unexpectedly looks directly at the camera and explains, in an impassive tone, that they never reach their destination. They will have an accident, and they will all die (Figure 7.1). In the car, while driving through a meandering mountain road to Tehran, all car occupants also look straight into the camera and introduce themselves. The audience know their names, ages and professions. Because the spectator knows that they are going to die, their joyful introduction becomes more ritualistic and impressive. First Mahtāb's family talk to the camera. These include the two children, Keyvān and Keyhān, and then their father, Heshmat, whom the spectator learns is a headteacher in the town they live. The next persons are Safar, the driver, and Zarrinkolāh, a farming woman who is requesting a ride to the city to visit doctors for curing her infertility. Finally, Mahtāb herself says she is a housewife and a teacher. For Negar Mottahedeh, this

Figure 7.1 Mahtāb directly addressing the camera.

introduction is given as if 'registering the necessary details for the imminent police report on the accident'.[17] *Travellers* energetic and happy introduction, nevertheless, promises something less official than a serious introduction before the law and order's agents. Talajooy's interpretation points to the narrative structure of this moment. He considers this sequence as a *taʿziyeh* pre-recital, or *pish-khāni*, in which actors introduce their characters prior to starting their performance.[18] By introducing themselves while addressing the camera directly, the characters transmit the information to the audience as *taʿziyeh* actors do when they talk about their roles, intentions, or destinations. The point is why they directly address the camera to introduce themselves, or rather, why the film makes the audience aware of the existence of the camera. I will argue that this is an efficient strategy as it highlights the role of the camera and gives it a role like the role of the mirror in the plot.

An accordion-based cheerful music accompanies this introductory scene. This is cut to a truck image that comes up the same road. The image and the sound of the truck introduce an atonal ominous music in the soundtrack. Once more, one can find similarities with *taʿziyeh* in which the actors of saints and martyrs (*moālef khān* or *mazlum khān*) sing their lines harmoniously, while those performing the roles of evil antagonists (*mokhālef khān or ashghiā*) just recite their dialogues with a loud, harsh and authoritarian voice.[19] The sequence, then, reaches the scene of the wreckage, which opens with a voice-over that introduces himself as a police officer and then gives details of a fatal accident. A set of plans identify the car and the truck that the spectators have seen before, and the voice of the police officer confirms what Mahtāb said a moment earlier: they have all died.

In his book on Iranian theatre, Beyzaie enumerates some important characteristics of *ta'ziyeh*. He asserts that at the beginning of each *ta'ziyeh* performance, sometimes the actors introduce themselves and briefly explain the role they are about to perform. Since the plays involve religious figures, the actors are to remind the audience that they are not the saintly figures or the villains that they represent. At times, the actors read and sing their lines from scraps of paper that they have in their hands. The director is always close to the scenes and conducts all actions. He could even stop the play to directly address the audience 'to pay attention to some important detail, or begging their compassion, or even reminding the audience of some important moral lesson'.[20] These distancing techniques must be considered structural since *ta'ziyeh* is a regularly performed ritual for an audience who knows the narratives by heart. Furthermore, *ta'ziyeh*, like many other medieval forms, maintains an iconic relationship to a mystified reality. Hence, distancing here contains what was for Walter Benjamin a sense of sacred aura of premodern artwork.[21] In other words, the audience and the cast of a *ta'ziyeh* performance are, indeed, participants of a passion play in which they are all regularly reminded of their distance from the sublime, original reality on which the play is based. Nevertheless, although the audience know what is before them is just a representation, they never lose the imaginary significance. The result is the active engagement of the public with the cathartic play. That means this information does not turn into an obstacle to their enjoyment of the plot, or better say, to their participation in the ritual. After all, *ta'ziyeh* has been shaped through the time as a ritual staging of significant religious myths.

In *Travellers* something similar to *ta'ziyeh* happens as 'the spectators know the story's outcome before the performance begins'.[22] This pre-given information, however, does not block their engagement with the cathartic scenario of the final mourning-wedding ceremony.[23] On account of this structural character, one can find ritualistic qualities in *Travellers*. By using a *ta'ziyeh* technique in the opening scene, the film transfers a certain authority to the audience to participate in the ritual/narrative and ultimately to accept the final returning of the mirror holders from the realm of death.

The ritual structure of the film also engages the audience with the allegorical representation of a collective traumatic memory. This allegorical dimension is underscored in the opening sequence when a series of autonomous objective shots show images of the car and the mountain road: the cover of the mirror which is on the roof rack is blown away by the wind. The 'naked' mirror reflects the sky. This is cut to the car's wheels, and then some road landscapes are framed from outside the car. These shots do not reflect the characters' perspectives as the camera captures these images from a position that cannot be occupied by a human subject in real day-to-day life. They have been filmed from the exterior of the moving car or from the inside of the car in a position that just a camera can occupy. The result of the juxtaposition of these shots by the film editing opens a way for conceiving the scene as if some phantom who has the knowledge of this historical destiny is watching the car and its occupants.[24] In other words, the allegory arises as a possibility to interpret the images when the car occupants and the audience share the same knowledge about what is going to happen. If in Hitchcock's cinema, in some critical sequences, the audience have more knowledge than the characters, here the audience and characters have equally the same information. The result is the deconstruction of the cinematic grammar of classical style by the traditional *ta'ziyeh* techniques, which leads to the emergence of a ritual narrative that invites the audience to consider the narrative allegorically. The key to this allegory, the mirror, is also of central importance in this opening sequence and the whole film. The very first shots of the film show the mirror on the ground. Someone – probably Safar the driver – lifts it up and turns it around to reflect the sea and the sky and finally the car. These images are combined with the film credits. Negar Mottahedeh's reading of this scene sheds a thorough light on the allegorical dimension of the mirror: 'as the film melds the camera's look with mirror's gaze, it brings the two frames together to configure a single point of view'.[25] It is as if both the film and the mirror become effective tools for illusory access to reality. The mirror, like cinema itself, works as a framing tool that generates self-awareness and offers what Talajooy calls Beyzaie's 'paradigms of being and belonging'.[26]

The question that arises is how the mirror, the camera and the ideas borrowed from *ta'ziyeh* merge together for constructing an allegorical narrative. To begin with, the camera gaze, to which the characters in the film's opening scene talk and introduce themselves, must be analysed. The film combines the pre-recital or *pish-khāni* convention of *ta'ziyeh* in which actors explain their role, situation, and fate, with the classical filmic tools that subjectify the objective shots. Thus, when Mahtāb and other characters address the camera, in cinematic terms they return an objective gaze which belongs to nobody in the diegetic space. Classical filmmaking requires that such objective shots are subjectified to avoid confusing the spectator. This is basically to guide the audience to understand the narrative through the viewpoints of the characters. In cinema, an autonomous objective shot is a source of fear. It is particularly used in horror films when e.g. a monster's no-human wandering gaze is directed towards a haunted house. The audience comes into radical otherness of this autonomous shot precisely because no recognizable subject occupies the position of this gaze.[27] In a similar way in *Travellers* the objective shots which portray the car occupant's introduction are never subjectified to reflect any given perspective in the film. They look at the camera directly as if it was a mirror. While it is true that the audience will ultimately be behind this *mirror*, the process gives a complex position to the camera. It reflects a certain self-knowledge of the characters and at the same time it mediates between the audience and this knowledge. The emphatic staging of the mirror, thus, has an important role in the plot and takes the camera and the mirror on the same grounds. Thus, the relationship between the mirror and the audience in the film is embodied by the autonomous objective shots. Whereas these autonomous gazes belong to nobody, they have the potential to embody the multiple autonomous images reflected by the film's smashed mirror.

These ominous objective shots are also combined with other *ta'ziyeh* convections to construct the accident scene. A voice-over delivers some information about the mortal accident. This autonomous voice accompanies images of the wrecked truck and the car.[28] The bloody broken front windscreen and the crumpled family photo that Safar had in the car visor make the audience identify the car. Then Lieutenant Fallāhi is framed. The autonomous voice is now subjectified. He also starts his formal report by introducing himself. Then he delivers the information that Mahtāb provided at the beginning of the film. The difference between the two is to whom they are addressed: while Mahtāb's message is to inform the audience, Lieutenant Fallāhi's message is intended to inform his superior officer. Mahtāb performs her *ta'ziyeh*-based role as a cultural act; the police officer, however, does the same to fulfil a bureaucratic duty.

As mentioned above, as the police officer describes the accident scene in detail, the spectators observe traces of the wreckage on the screen. Following a basic rule of *ta'ziyeh*, while the police officer describes the accident, no image of the bodies appears on the screen. The viewer, nevertheless, finds identifiable objects that confirm the tragic event. As Beyzaie points out, one of the oldest conventions of *ta'ziyeh* is not to show the violent circumstances of a martyr's death. Normally what happens is that a wounded actor riding a horse goes outside the scene, villains follow him and a few seconds later the horse comes back to the scene covered in blood with several arrows in its body and without its rider.[29] Rather than showing the scene of martyrdom realistically, the use of 'jump cuts' allows the viewer to imagine it. Apart from this, one can find evidence of *naqqāli* and *pardeh khāni* in the wreckage scene of *Travellers*. In these traditional theatrical forms, the storyteller draws the audience's attention to details of a figurative painting while narrating the heroic scenes with different voice tones.[30] Something similar happens in *Travellers* when Lieutenant Fallāhi's off-screen descriptions confirm the information that the audience has received earlier.

The objective shots in the wreckage scene are, nonetheless, subjectified: a camera in motion shows the driver Allāhqoli and his assistant Mochul. As if responding in reaction to the camera of a reporter, they reject being filmed and turn their back to the camera as a sign of protest. The next shot shows a journalist cameraman with a video camera recording the scene, confirming the situation. The combination of Fallāhi's narration and the journalist's presence stands in deep contrast with the tragic images of the accident. With the presence of journalist photographers and TV reporters, a new set of cameras come into the stage to emphasize the link between the camera and the mirror as devices which reflect reality. In Beyzaie's films, mirror and camera become 'equal partner in the narration of film story'.[31] The tragic accident is framed by different cameras: the film camera through which the travellers addressed the audience directly, and the reporter's camera that explores the accident scene with the logic of journalistic storytelling. Mottahedeh interprets these camera-mirror interactions in terms of national allegories as depictions of the different levels of access to reality:

> In the scenes that bear witness to the accident, these questions of constitutive address and framing are further elaborated to probe the link between the image of actuality and the imaginal. They are widened to embrace the specificity of the nation's collective relation to the real, especially when the trope of the newspaper

arrives to function as the textual counterpart of the documentary lens used by the film and actualized within its narrative in the scene of the wreckage. The film halts to ask itself, reflexively: 'How may post-Revolutionary Iranian cinema define and frame the nation's real?'[32]

Mottahedeh's reading of 'nation's real' could be expanded to the historical grounds. The family house as a locus of historical events gives more clues to the audience to take the mirror not just as a sheer lost object but in what it signifies symbolically for the family's identity as an important object for their communal memory. By having this in mind, the allegorical aspects of the wreckage scene could be read in its historical background. The crisis that is produced by the accident transcends the totality of the relationship of its parts with reality. In addition to its tragic impact on the members of the family, the wreckage produces a traumatic encounter with the void that is behind the images of the real: as if in the absence of the historical mirror, a collective access to the historical background of the reality would also vanish. The mirror, after all, is a significant object for the collective memory of the members of the family. The predicament now is how to make a new image of the self, a solid national imaginary, in the absence of historical coordinates provided by the collective memory.

In addition to this, the wreckage scene is significant in relation to its suggestions about figures of authority. As mentioned before, at the beginning of the sequence, the spectator sees the accident scene while hearing Lieutenant Fallāhi's voice-over. This is cut to a medium shot of Fallāhi delivering his report and watching the scene from a distance, as if what the audience was seeing, in fact, was the officer's point of view. Fallāhi's viewpoints are defied in the following sequences by the grandmother, but it is also questioned in this very sequence by a long shot from over the mountains that covers the accident scene. Apart from being a standard establishing shot, this autonomous view functions as if it was the same autonomous gaze to which the car occupants introduced themselves earlier. It observes the complete crash scene from above. This holistic vision stands in contrast to the officer's focus on details. In the next sequence, this liberated gaze is transported to the grandmother's house in Tehran. It is combined with feminine subjective shots to construct a cinematic space that, once more, has allegorical qualities.

Grandmother's house: Wedding preparations

At the beginning of the next sequence, which is set in the grandmother's house in Tehran, the spectator finds that they know more about the stats of the travellers than the characters in Tehran and that they are preparing for a wedding. The house is painted in white, and the people are in motion: the bride Māhrokh, her grandmother Khānum Bozorg, painters, servants, and in-laws are all working together to prepare for the wedding. Simultaneously, however, they are waiting for the travellers and know nothing of the mortal accident. Māhrokh is Mahtāb's sister and Khānum Bozorg is the grandmother of both. They have a brother, Māhu, who is a university professor. Later the audience is informed that their parents also died in a car accident years ago. The grandmother, who is supervising the activities, is concerned about preparing Mahtāb's room. As mentioned earlier, at this stage, the audience has the privilege of having more knowledge than the characters, but soon the phone rings to give the bad news. Now that the characters and the spectator are both aware of the accident, Beyzaie focuses on the reactions of the characters. The grandmother is the only one who refuses to accept the travellers' death. The rest and the audience prepare themselves for the funeral, which in Beyzaie's hands become a cathartic ceremony.

When the news reaches the house, the film enters again on the *ta'ziyeh* arena. Mottahedeh finds similarities between *ta'ziyeh* of Qasem and this part of *Travellers*. Qasem was Imam Hossein's nephew, and the *ta'ziyeh* narrates his wedding and his heroic martyrdom before consummating the marriage.[33] Mottahedeh also compares the preparation of the funeral space with that of a *takiyeh* which has been traditionally used for *ta'ziyeh* performances:

> In mother's home, the characters are in constant motion. [...] The film edits and bridges shots by linking its transitions from shot to shot, from space to space, to the movement of the bodies and to sounds. Significantly, the house appears, by way of this movement, as the circular space of the *takiyeh*.[34]

It is important to highlight that the circularity of the *takiyeh* is because of its ritualistic character. *Takiyehs* were spaces in Iranian cities for holding mourning ceremonies during the month of Muharram. As a multifunctional space dedicated temporally for Muharram's ceremonies, *takiyehs* were traditionally 'fluid social spaces, rather than fixed architectural sites'.[35] The circularity of the *takiyeh* stages should be understood with attention to this architectonical logic as a circular stage is a natural space for ritual performances held in temporal sites. In *takiyehs*, the circular stage is located centrally and around which people gather to see and interact with characters of the play. In *Travellers*, after receiving the news, the house is redecorated. It is reshaped to be prepared as a *takiyeh*: the white-painted walls become black. The decorative and ceremonial objects associated with weddings are quickly replaced with those of a funeral, and the space is recreated to receive mourners. All these preparatory actions also contribute to the creation of a natural circular stage in the middle of the main hall.

What I would like to add to Mottahedeh's points about the cinematic recreation of space in the grandmother's house is an analysis of the special role of the bride's point-of-view shots. The bride is worried about the delayed arrival of her sister and the mirror and at the same time maintains the happy face required for her upcoming wedding. Throughout the film, Māhrokh never leaves the house, and her subjective shots make the spectators identify with her. These shots include among others the shots in which she looks at the street, passers-by, garden and messenger; the shots in which she talks to the groom Rahi, the family members, servants and guests, and even the shot in which the film registers her gaze at the objects such as the telephone, the invitation letters and garden's trees. Finally, her point-of-view shots are crucial to observe the magical final return of the travellers. The ominous objective shots, however, again dominate the sequence when the family receives the accident news. First, Hekmat, Heshmat's brother, is covered by a tracking autonomous shot while talking to Lieutenant Fallāhi over the phone. Subsequently, Hekmat leaves the house clearly shocked. Then the second call is staged: the black telephone is framed in the centre of the image, having the reaction of Māhrokh, Mastān (her sister-in-law and Māhu's wife) and Khānum Bozorg in the background (Figure 7.2).

The following sequence in the furniture rental shop also begins with an autonomous objective shot. Māhu, in a furniture rental shop, is ordering the additional housewares that they need for the wedding. The camera pans from the shop owner and his assistant when they are loudly checking a repertoire of traditional objects to Māhu reading a book in a dark corner of the place. An off-screen sound effect of a door opening informs the viewers and the characters alike that someone has entered. Then, in a chain of shots/reverse shots Hekmat informs Māhu of the disastrous situation. Again, an objective shot pans to the owner of the rental shop and his assistant, checking the traditional objects that Māhu has already ordered for decorating the house for the wedding. The objects' names reveal Māhu's concern with cultural authenticity: the glassware stamped with congratulatory *mobārak bād*; the illustrated screens (*pardeh*) with images of mythical lovers Khosrow/Shirin and Bahram/Golandam and the sequin handmade panels (*pulaki*) illustrated with flowers, birds, water, fish, moon, stars and the sun.

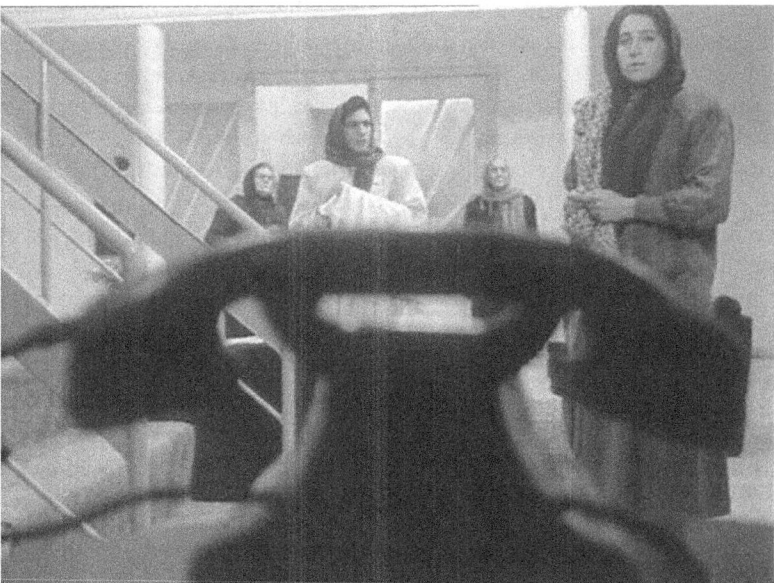

Figure 7.2 The black telephone at the centre of the frame.

The next shot shows Māhu affected by the news. The list of objects must now be modified as the wedding celebration is to be transformed into a funeral ceremony. The owner and his assistance suggest new objects for the mourning ceremony: an illustrated screen *pardeh* of archangel Raphael blowing the last trumpet *Soor-e Erāfil*; the dark *termeh* tablecloths, and the metallic hand *panjeh* with the image of the sun. Māhu accepts the offer. The objective autonomous shot functions as if an external *historical* force makes Māhu admit the *objective* reality. Considering the relationship between the mirror and the camera, one can find a second interpretation for this scene: as if the smashed mirror becomes detached and autonomous cinematic images which observe the reactions of the members of the family when receiving the tragic news.

The relationships between the shots also create possible meanings for the film's spaces. If the grandmother's house is a place of familiar remembrance, here the furniture rental shop is a place of objects linked to the communal memory. In Beyzaie's previous film *Maybe Some Other Time* the main characters seek traces of their lost identity in an antique store. Both the antique store and the furniture rental shop are spaces in which memories are materialized in objects. Beyzaie's nostalgic view of the repertoire of traditional objects reveals his critical vision towards the amnesiac present. In this regard, one can interpret such an emphasis on mirrors in the film. As a reflective device, beyond its traditional meanings and uses, a mirror generates an image of immediate reality. This image could refresh imaginaries of the self that, in the symbolic framework of the film, could be read as an *authentic* modern identity. Tradition here must be understood as the layers of memory with which the very particular mirror of the film has been framed. These palimpsestic layers of memory have shaped a shifting significance for the film's mirror through the time, and what the film ultimately suggests is that the character's access to their modern identity only becomes possible through the ritual/ceremonial practices of remembrance and belonging – hence the importance of mirror in the film's ceremonies. It is, therefore, not out of character to see a mirror among the furniture in the rental shop. At the beginning of the sequence, while listening to the assistant's voice naming the objects on the wedding list, Māhu finds a mirror covered with a layer of dust deep inside a dark part of the shop. He passes his finger on the mirror surface, which results in a shining reflection of his image in the cleaned line. In the second part of the sequence, when he goes to the dark corner of the rental house again to reflect on the news that he has just received from Hekmat, once more he finds his image in the mirror. He looks at himself, comes to a conclusion about the traveller's death and decides to cancel the order. However, instead of cancelling the order, he accepts the offer to rent a set of different objects: the wedding objects, thus, join the missing family mirror, and together they comprise the film's absent objects. The funeral objects now come to form the *present* stage.

These objects become political signs if the film is examined in its historical context. Discussing the historical context that led the author to create *Travellers*, Beyzaie states that the film was the result of 'my psychological need [to respond] to the ruins I stood on'.[36] Hence the grandmother's (Khānum Bozorg's) refusal to accept such a destiny could be read as a sign of cultural defiance against the dominant ideology of the time.

Grandmother's resistance

As Talajooy puts it: 'Beyzaie's oeuvre has generated techniques and templates that delineate the aesthetics of indigenous-style modern Iranian theatre, yet it has also wrought a counterhegemonic space in which marginalized ideas, people and forms appear to resist dominant socio-political discourses.'[37] In this context, one can find meanings for Khānum Bozorg's apparently irrational reaction when she receives the news of the accident, particularly because the process of this reaction is staged in her house. To begin with, there are enough signs to suggest that the house presents a national allegory. The most important signs for this allegorical suggestion are presented in the final scene which brings together in the house people from all walks of life from the members of the family to many other people who are indirectly involved with the accident: the truck driver and his assistant, their families, their co-workers and the police officer. The argument for this becomes more solid if one notes that Beyzaie's film comes in a long list of films and novels using houses as allegorical representations of Iran. As examples, one can refer to the houses in Sadeq Hedyat's *Blind Owl* (*Buf-e Kur*, 1936) or Houshang Golshiri's *Shazdeh Ehtejāb* (Prince Ehtejab, 1968), and Iraj Pezeshkzad's *Dāei Jān Nāpeleon* (My Uncle Napoleon, 1973). In Iranian cinema, the best examples of such depictions can also be found at the oeuvre of directors of Beyzaie's generation, including Forough Farrokhzad's *Khāneh Siāh Ast* (The House Is Black, 1962), Dariush Mehrjui's *Ejāreh Neshin-hā* (The Tenants, 1986) and Ali Hatami's *Mādar* (Mother, 1990). In *Travellers*, the house is proved to be a necessary space to stage the author's concerns with the collective identity. A more important point, however, is to highlight how this allegory is expressed and to what end it is formulated. To this end, Khānum Bozorg's resistance and her deep belief in the arrival of the travellers and the mirror are of primary importance. Just before he receives the news of the accident, Hekmat provokes a short discussion with Mastān when he states that the house can be a source of good business if they accept to demolish it, build a high-rise building and sell its apartments at a good price. He is criticized for his speculations about the economic advantages of demolishing the house. Khānum Bozorg ends the discussion by rejecting any idea that may involve demolishing the house and, instead, recounts the story of the mirror:

[The mirror] is a family heritage. Munis [the servant] remembers. It has been present in the wedding of all of us for many generations. After every wedding, the new bride had the responsibility to keep it safe until the following wedding. Last time, it got lost by accident. It had been sent, by mistake, to the furniture rental shop. Mahtāb searched for it everywhere and finally found it. Then we decided that she will keep it herself.[38]

About the mirror's possible meanings, Beyzaie states that its sense has been produced through time by its role in weddings. Through time it has found a ritual significance as a sign of a good omen: 'Thus, the mirror is what they must bring along. It means – and this is not my invention – bonding, fertility and luck, and the breaking of a mirror for people signifies bad omen and the breaking of a bond.'[39] I argue that what is important here is not just the mirror as a reflective object; it is how to keep believing in and maintaining the rituals that give meanings to the mirror. That is exactly what Beyzaie's film through refashioning traditional storytelling techniques does: making the viewer participate in a ritual ceremony as a re-signifying process for the mirror and in so doing *bringing the smashed mirror back to life*, at least on the screen. The grandmother tries to convince others of the importance of this ceremony. She knows that if they give up and accept what seems to be *historically* determined, the mirror will never come back. The objective knowledge of the official history, that of Lieutenant Fallāhi's narrative, does not have to make them believe in the culture of death. If they resist the official death-centred versions of the idea of martyrdom and continue to celebrate life, the reappearance of the mirror will just be a matter of time. For the author the cultural roots beneath objects such as the mirror are important. This means that if a community keeps their ancestors' rituals alive and does not reject them as backwards and old-fashioned, the rituals evolve with time, lose their superstitious aspects and become modern cultural rituals. The celebration of this cyclic ritual makes people construct the future based on their own memories. Only a study of the historical past and a thorough examination of the traditions will provide the people of a community with the possibility of finding their authentic modern identities.

One can find this reaction of Beyzaie among other authors of non-Western cultures in the era of postcolonial awakening. Fredric Jameson made a Hegelian reading of such reactions among the authors of the countries which were then called 'the third world':

> One important distinction would seem to impose itself at the outset, namely that none of these cultures can be conceived as anthropologically independent or autonomous, rather, they are all in various distinct ways locked in a life-and death struggle with the first-world cultural imperialism – a cultural struggle that is itself a reflexion [sic] of the economic situation of such areas in their penetration by various stages of capital, or as it is sometimes euphemistically termed, of modernization.[40]

Jameson demonstrates that these reactions are necessarily expressed as national allegories when it is expressed in modern Western conventions such as realism. For Jameson, in the Western modernist and realist works, one encounters the split of the poetic and the political, between the private domain of sexuality and the public space of social struggles. In the peripheral realist works, the poetic and the political are interrelated and 'necessarily project a political dimension in the form of national allegory: the story of the private individual destiny is always an allegory of the embattled situation of the public third-world culture and society'.[41]

In this regard, Khānum Bozorg's – and by extension the author's – resistance could be read against the political and cultural forces that give distorted meanings to national identity. As Nacim Pak-Shiraz argues, Beyzaie maintains a critical view of the politics of mass modernization in his urban films before the revolution.[42] It seems to me that Beyzaie's works after the revolution show his position towards the ideological readings of religion as a negative aspect of the same forms of modernization. Both versions of these officially promoted national identities have left untouched the cultural degeneration whose crucial sign is destroying invaluable heritages of the past and historical memories. This position does not turn the author necessarily into a traditionalist but rather a modern thinker who reads and refashions national traditions in his intellectual struggle against the alienating forces of global cultural hegemonies.

The last challenge of Māhu and others in *Travellers* is how to convince Khānum Bozorg to accept the deaths of Mahtāb and her family. Lieutenant Fallāhi is invited to tell her the official version: to testify in person and present the empirical evidence that certifies the reality of the mortal accident (Figure 7.3). Khānum Bozorg's response is a question to the police officer: 'Did you find a mirror?' Fallāhi replies that no mirrors were found in the scene of the accident. Khānum Bozorg asserts: 'Your evidence is not enough. Mahtāb is coming with the mirror. She gave me her word.' Then she encloses herself in her room. Māhrokh, Mastān and others see Khānom Bozorg's reaction as an acceptance of the accident. As a result, they break the house's mirrors, tear or hang the paintings of flowers backwards and smash colourful glassware. Munis and other servants throw the dry leaves of the garden

Figure 7.3 Lieutenant Fallāhi presenting the official version of the accident.

into the air in a style similar to the reaction of *ta'ziyeh* actors to the news of Imam Hossein's martyrdom.⁴³

The final catharsis

The final sequence also follows *ta'ziyeh* conventions for staging the mourning ceremony. As in *ta'ziyeh* in which seats that belong to the main martyred characters are left empty, some chairs are left unoccupied. The house is decorated in black, with the emblems of mourning similar to those decorating a *takiyeh* hanging on the walls. The chairs are arranged in a way that in the centre a natural stage is made. While the ceremony goes on, Khānum Bozorg introduces a key concept for understanding her belief in the travellers' return: 'They died, but never ended.' For Talajooy the fact that the film is based on *ta'ziyeh* rules is confirmed in this very belief: the travellers, as well as the *ta'ziyeh*'s martyrs 'can never be dead because they are being performed'.⁴⁴ In light of this interpretation, one can read the final return of the travellers to the scenario. The film deconstructs the realist rules of classical cinema and reconstructs them on *ta'ziyeh* grounds. This means, in the final sequence, *Travellers* abandons the realist storytelling methods of classical cinema. It rather tells the story that reminds the audience of the existence of a possible mythical reality in the same way that *ta'ziyeh* does. Considering this, the final appearance of the dead travellers is linked directly with the self-introductions of the opening sequence of the film. As specified above, they are not actors in the Western realist sense of the term; they are modernized *ta'ziyeh shabihs*, who are to remind the audience of the possibility of the continuity of a cultural and spiritual form of reality. At the allegorical level, they bring the mirror to celebrate life and fertility. The futile ideologies that are obsessed with death, therefore, are to be replaced with a prospering form of knowledge that is capable of recreating traditions as authentic modern practices and ideas.

The final sequence turns into a cathartic stage in which social conflicts are also staged. Different people come onto the stage to narrate their version of the story that links them to the Travellers: Safar's workmates and family, Zarrinkolāh's husband Sha'bān, Lieutenant Fallāhi and finally the truck driver Allāhqoli, his assistant Mochul and their wives and children. Lieutenant Fallāhi again speaks to the public about his version of the accident and his sense of duty. Khānum Bozorg again defies him. When he affirms that nothing remains unseen in the eye of the law, she replies: 'yes, but you never found the mirror'. Then, she tells Māhrokh to put on the wedding dress. 'They are coming,' she says, 'and it's not good if they find you dressed in black'. A series of reaction shots show the funeral guests whispering about Khānum Bozorg's madness. Māhrokh reacts angrily to the whispers. She goes upstairs to her room and puts on her wedding dress. Meanwhile, the last visitors, Allāhqoli and Mochul, come into the house. They have requested temporary leave from the prison to express their condolences and respect to the traveller's family. Once more, a *ta'ziyeh* technique is used to stage their arrival: Safar's sons and Zarrinkolāh's husband attack them out of anger. They do not really fight but show how the fight might be. Mochul's wife, Effat, raises her baby up as she begs for compassion. This action reminds the audience of a typical scene in *ta'ziyeh*, in which Imam Hossein's baby son, Ali Asghar, is represented. The fight finally comes to an end. Allāhqoli and Mochul tell the story of the accident to the public and finally beg for collective forgiveness. They painfully explain that they could not do anything. Lieutenant Fallāhi's report also corroborates their claim, given the circumstances caused by an oil spill from an oil tanker; the accident was inevitable. Thus, Beyzaie's film uses *ta'ziyeh*'s techniques to deconstruct the Manichean duality that is central to *ta'ziyeh*: there is no evil in this collective tragedy. The accident has occurred because of a combination of situations which involved negligence but not guilt. Now the collective reaction is important.

Māhrokh surprises everyone by appearing in her wedding dress. Outstanding reaction shots register the guests' confusion. Some applaud this gesture and some reject it. Finally, Mahtāb and the other travellers arrive with the mirror. The mirror brings light to the darkened house and reflects the main characters one by one. An outstanding point-of-view shot, shaped by the form of the mirror's frame, displays Mahtāb greeting everyone. That is the most important shot of the film as Mahtāb's gaze corresponds with that of the camera and the mirror. The scene suggests that Māhrokh's reaction and her appearance in her wedding dress was the move required for the appearance of the mirror. Rahi, the groom, also prepares himself to accompany Māhrokh. Thus, at the last minute, another transformation changes the funeral into the wedding ceremony. Gradually, all the guests join in to express their happiness as if in the light of the mirror, and due to the metaphorical return of the travellers, all sorrows and social conflicts end momentarily. Mahtāb brings the mirror forward until it finally frames Māhrokh. The film reaches its denouement with Khānum Bozorg's greetings (Figure 7.4).

Figure 7.4 Mahtāb and her family enter with the mirror.

In addition to what was mentioned before, one can interpret this emphasis on the mirror as Beyzaie's consideration of mirrors as devices of self-reflexivity and self-consciousness. The above-mentioned relation between objective shots and the mirrors also suggests that the cinema itself is a device whose social function could be like mirrors: a source of self-knowledge. This use of mirrors as the medium for reflecting light into houses proceeds from two – apparently contradictory – sources. On the one hand, it certainly has deep roots in Persian traditions, and on the other hand, it is undoubtedly a powerful legacy of modernism. As to the meaning of the mirror in Persian traditions, it suffices to consider its communal meaning as a sign of good omen. I also argue for a possible modern significance for mirrors in *Travellers* as mirrors are also presented as sources of knowledge due to their illuminating quality. As Michel Foucault puts it, following the enlightenment preoccupations with illumination, the modernist culture was obsessed with illuminating objects and elucidating concepts because of 'the fear of darkened spaces, of the pall of gloom, which prevents the full visibility of things, men and truths'.[45] In Beyzaie's film these two concepts merge together to show the author's responses to his historical context. The mirror here is a desired lost object that becomes a meaningful device by the virtue of its symbolic role. It could reflect an honest image of the self that would be a source of knowledge and identity. This knowledge will bring back fertility and life force to the allegorical communal house. That is to say, the mirror materializes the author's ideal and praxis regarding the urgent necessity of having new readings of history for refashioning traditions and constructing *authentic* modern identities.

Conclusions

Travellers is, on the one hand, a response to the government restrictions in the 1980s, and on the other hand, it is a *ta'ziyeh* translated for the screen. These two aspects of the film are interrelated. Beyzaie in *Travellers* defies the official culture of martyrdom in a creative and experimental treatment of theatrical forms of a passion ritual play. The martyrs of *Travellers* are not saints but educated secular individuals who are concerned with their own identity. This predicament in the film is never articulated verbally, but it is expressed in the relationship of characters with emblematic objects such as mirrors. The film stages this relation with subjective shots that show characters – particularly Māhrokh and Khānum Bozorg's viewpoints. However, the objective autonomous shots show an uncanny view, which by the virtue of some framing and editing techniques are related to the reflected images of the mirror itself. This narrative strategy, specially at the beginning when the Mahtāb announces their death looking directly at the camera as if it was a mirror, makes the audience participate in the ritual. *Ta'ziyeh* conventions then come into the stage to make the ritual Iranian. The mirror must reach the house to augment the allegorical dimensions of the narrative. Then the house which hosts a collective ceremony of death becomes the space for a ceremony of life and fertility with the arrival of the mirror. *Travellers*, therefore, is a national allegory in which the author's concerns with the identity of Iranian people and his effective way to resist dominant ideologies come together to make a communal ritual of life which celebrates the fertility of new ideas in an Iranian version of modernity.

Notes

1. For the historical context of these circumstances see Naficy, *Social History*, Vol. 2, 127–30. Regarding the cinematic politics of Khatami's era as minister of culture and Islamic guidance see Omid, *Tārikh-e Sinamā*, 218–31. See also the statements of the first director of *Bonyād-e Sināmei-ye Fārābi* (Farabi Film Foundation), Mohammad Beheshti; and the first Minister Deputy of General Department of Cinematic and Audiovisual Affairs *Sāzman-e Omure Sinemāi va Sam'i Basari*, Fakhroddin Anwar, in Farzollahi, *Sinemā-ye Novin-e*.
2. Naficy, *Social History*, Vol. 4, 38.
3. Ibid.
4. See Beyzaie in Amiri, *Jedāl*, 95.
5. Chelkowski, '*Ta'ziyeh*: Indigenous'.
6. Talajooy, 'Indigenous Performing'. See also Chelkowski, *Ta'ziyeh: Ritual*; and Malekpour, *Islamic Drama*.
7. Talajooy, 'Iranian Indigenous'. See also Talajooy, *Mythologizing*, 15–20 and 101–6; and Chelkowski, '*Ta'ziyeh*: Indigenous'.
8. Beyzaie's *Namāyesh dar Irān*. (1965) is a key publication in Persian on the history of theatre in Iran.
9. Talajooy, 'Indigenous Performing', 498.
10. Qukasiyan, *Goftogu*, 7.
11. Talajooy, 'Beyzaie's Formation', 692.
12. See Talajooy's chapter on Beyzaie's *Ārash* and *naqqāli* and in this volume.
13. Talajooy, 'Indigenous Performing', 501. See also Talajooy, 'Intellectuals as Sacrificial'.
14. Dabashi, *Masters*, 255.
15. Ibid.
16. See, for example, Nurai, 'Barkhāstan az gur'; Dabashi, *Masters*, 266; and Mottahedeh, *Displaced*, 69–88.
17. Mottahedeh, *Displaced*, 19.
18. Talajooy, *Mythologizing*, 102.
19. This mentioned musical techniques of the *ta'ziyeh* must be nuanced: each *moālef khān* sings his line in a certain traditional musical mode or *Dastgāh-e Musiqi*, such as *Chahrgāh*, *Navā* or *Shur*; the *mokhālef khāns*, however, recite their lines loudly and sometimes out of tune. See Beyzaie, *Namāyesh*, 137–8.
20. Beyzaie, *Namāyesh*, 140.
21. See Benjamin, *Work of Art*.
22. Naficy, *Social History*, Vol. 4, 195.
23. Ibid., 195.
24. See Gunning, 'Landscape and the Fantasy'. I borrow 'phantom' from the study of Gunning that explores the depictions of landscape in early cinema by a ghostly image that was provided by positing the camera in front of moving trains. The films that

contained these panoramic views were catalogued as 'Phantom rides' to underscore their uncanny effect on the viewer.
25 Mottahedeh, *Displaced*, 72.
26 The expression is the subtitle of Talajooy's *Iranian Culture in Bahram Beyzaie's Cinema and Theatre: Paradigms of Being and Belonging.*
27 See, e.g., Žižek, *Fright*, 31–54. In my reading of subjective/objective shots of the film, I had in mind the Hegelian/Lacanian approach of Žižek to these cinematic standard techniques. For him, the film provides a space to project our subjective position from which we engage with objective reality using our cultural/ideological perspectives.
28 See Chion, *Voice in Cinema*. I follow the psychoanalytic readings of Chion of the autonomous voices in film diegetic space that he calls the *acousmêtre*.
29 Beyzaie, *Namāyesh*, 120.
30 See Talajooy's chapter on Beyzaie's *Ārash* and *naqqāli* in this volume.
31 Mottahedeh, *Displaced*, 76.
32 Ibid., 76–7.
33 Ibid., 70–1.
34 Ibid., 77.
35 Rezvani-Naraghi, 'From Architectural', 141.
36 Amiri, *Jedāl*, 95.
37 Talajooy, 'Reformulation', 695.
38 My translation. *Travellers*. Dir. Bahram Beyzaie. 1991.
39 Amiri, *Jedāl*, 93.
40 Jameson, 'Third-World Literature', 68.
41 Ibid., 69 (italicized in the original).
42 Pak-Shiraz, 'Exploring the City', 811–28.
43 In *Ta'ziyeh* when Imam is martyred, other *shabihs* throw straws into the air. See Beyzaie, *Namāyesh*, 138.
44 Talajooy, *Mythologizing*, 102.
45 Quoted in Strathausen, 'Uncanny Spaces', 15.

Bibliography

Amiri, Nushabeh. *Bahram Beyzaie, Jedāl bā Jahl: Goftogu*. Tehran: Sales, 2009.
Benjamin, Walter. *The Work of Art in the Age of Mechanical Reproduction*. Trans. J. A. Underwood. London: Penguin, 2008.
Beyzaie, Bahram. *Namāyesh dar Irān*. Tehran: Roshangarān va Motāleāt-e Zanān, 2001.
Chelkowski, Peter. 'Ta'ziyeh: Indigenous Avant-Garde Theatre of Iran'. *Performing Arts Journal*. Vol. 2. No. 1 (Spring 1977). Pp. 31–40.
Chelkowski, Peter. Ed. *Ta'ziyeh: Ritual and Drama in Iran*. New York: New York University Press, 1979.
Chion, Michel. *The Voice in Cinema*. Trans. Claudia Gorbman. New York: Columbia University Press, 1999.
Dabashi, Hamid. *Masters and Masterpieces of Iranian Cinema*. New York: Mage books, 2007.
Farzollahi, Amir. *Sinemā-ye Novin-e Irān*. Tehran: Afrāz, 2014.
Gunning, Tom. 'Landscape and the Fantasy of Moving Pictures: Early Cinema's Phantom Ride'. In *Cinema and Landscape*. Ed. Graham Harper and Jonathan Rayner. Bristol: Intellect, 2010. Pp. 31–70.

Jameson, Fredric. 'Third-world Literature in the Era of Multinational Capitalism'. *Social Text*. No. 15 (Autumn, 1986). Pp. 65–88.
Malekpour, Jamshid. *The Islamic Drama*. London: Frank Cass, 2004.
Mottahedeh, Negar. *Displaced Allegories: Post-Revolutionary Iranian Cinema*. Durham: Duke University Press, 2008.
Naficy, Hamid. *A Social History of Iranian Cinema*. Vol. 2 and Vol. 4. Durham: Duke University Press, 2012.
Nurai, Jahanbakhsh. 'Barkhāstan az Gur'. In *Majmu'eh-ye Maghālāt dar Naghd va Mo'arrefi-ye Āsār-e Bahram Beyzaie*. Ed. Zaven Qukasian. Tehran: Agah, 1999. Pp. 554–68.
Omid, Jamal. *Tarikh-e Sinemā-ye Irān (1358–1369)*. Tehran: Rozaneh, 1991.
Pak-Shiraz, Nacim. 'Exploring the City in the Cinema of Bahram Beyzaie'. *Iranian Studies*. Vol. 46. No. 5 (2013). Pp. 811–28.
Qukasian, Zaven. *Goftogu bā Bahram Beyzaie*. Tehran: Agah, 1992.
Rezvani-Naraghi, Ashkan. 'From Architectural Entities to Social Spaces: Redefining the Notions of Takiyeh and Takiyeh Dowlat'. *International Journal of Islamic Architecture*. Vol. 8. No. 1 (2019). Pp. 141–65.
Strathausen, Carsten. 'Uncanny Spaces: The City in Ruttman and Vertov'. In *Screening the City*. Ed. Mark Shiel and Tony Fitzmaurice. London: Verso, 2003. Pp. 15–40.
Talajooy, Saeed. *Mythologizing the Transition: A Comparative Study of Bahram Beyzaee and Wole Soyinka*. PhD thesis. University of Leeds, January 2008.
Talajooy, Saeed. 'Indigenous Performing Traditions in Post-revolutionary Iranian Theatre'. *Iranian Studies*. Vol. 44. No. 4 (2011). Pp. 497–519.
Talajooy, Saeed. 'Beyzaie's Formation, Forms and Themes'. *Iranian Studies*. Vol. 46. No. 5 (2013). Pp. 689–93.
Talajooy, Saeed. 'Reformulation of *Shahnameh* Legends in Bahram Beyzaie's Plays'. *Iranian Studies*. Vol. 46. No. 5 (2013). Pp. 695–719.
Talajooy, Saeed. 'Iranian Indigenous Forms'. In *Modernity and Iranian Theatre* (forthcoming).
Žižek, Slavoj. *The Fright of Real Tears: Krzysztof Kieslowski between Theory and Post-Theory*. London: BFI Publishing, 2001.

Chapter 8

CRIME THRILLER ELEMENTS IN BAHRAM BEYZAIE'S FILMS

Parviz Jahed

Introduction

The crime thriller is a cinematic genre that offers a suspenseful account of a crime presented in a way that evokes in the audience intensive feelings of suspense, excitement, surprise, anticipation and anxiety. According to the *Oxford Dictionary of Film Studies*, a crime film is 'an extremely wide-ranging group of fiction films that have crime as a central element of their plots'.[1] Susan Heyward's definition of the term confirms this by specifying that crime thrillers are films of suspense that rely on the intricacy of plot and relations to instil terror in the audience.[2]

Whereas the crime film as a genre is a feature of almost all national cinemas, with distinct versions in European, American and Far East cinemas such as Korean and Japanese cinema, in Iranian cinema, the genre remained marginal and exceptionally rare in the pre-revolutionary period. Nevertheless, it left its impact on Iranian films in different films. Examining the progression of these impacts reveals aspects of Iranian cinema which have remained understudied. This is mainly because though film noir qualities began to appear in the late 1950s with imitations of Hollywood noir films by Samuel Khachikian, these qualities were soon adopted by a few New Wave directors such as Masoud Kimiaei, Amir Naderi, Kamran Shirdel and Bahram Beyzaie who created new forms in dialogue with this genre. Among these directors, Bahram Beyzaie imprinted his films with a unique beat akin to that of the masterpieces of the crime thriller genre, particularly Alfred Hitchcock's films, and used the major technical elements of the genre to create suspense and a dark ambiance while remaining true to national colours and narratives both before and after the 1979 revolution.

Much has been said and written about the mythical, metaphorical, ritual, philosophical, existential and feminist aspects of Beyzaie's films. His representation of the world of criminals and his use of the main thematic and stylistic elements and methods of the crime thriller genre, however, have rained understudied. In this chapter, I engage with this gap by analysing his approach to creating suspense, tension and mystery, his inclusion of plot events that involve kidnapping, missing people, murders, rape, revenge, investigations, unexpected twists, death traps, nightmares, identity crisis, paranoia, false accusations, and his use of low-key lighting, revealing camera movement, and noirish atmosphere and iconography. To reveal these elements, I will focus on Beyzaie's *Kalāgh* (The Crow,1977), *Shāyad Vaghti Digar* (Maybe Some Other Time, 1988) and *Sag Koshi* (Killing Mad Dog, 2001) and analyse how Beyzaie conveys his ideas about social, mythical and philosophical issues through the framing devices of the crime thriller plot and narrative structure. Pointing out and analysing the discreet yet highly conscious and pervasive influence of the genre, I argue that in all these three films Beyzaie has crafted a noir-like plot that moves swiftly and unexpectedly towards unpredictable denouement. Nevertheless, I also argue that, as a filmmaker whose films cannot be pigeonholed in a specific genre, Beyzaie transcends the genre because, while using its elements, he subverts the boundaries of its generic conventions and stereotypes to create a special filmic experience.

The key points that I find examples for in Beyzaie's films while linking them to film noir as a genre include narrative structure, detective figures and heroism, suspense and tension, living under surveillance, subjective point-of-view shots, the power of the dark city, plot twists, crime thriller iconography, and phobia and traumatic memories. This arrangement may make the chapter look fragmented and like a catalogue of features, but it is the best way to offer a clear picture of how his filmic style is in dialogue with film noir as a genre. Given the fact that the main source of Beyzaie's dialogue with the crime thriller genre is Alfred Hitchcock's cinema and Beyzaie has even written a monograph on his cinema, I also briefly compare the general features of Hitchcock's and Beyzaie's visions towards the end of the chapter.

Film Noir narrative structure in Beyzaie's cinema

The narrative structure of film noirs is often formed around a crime but not always. A crime thriller narrative is mainly based on a conflict between good and evil in a context that has both physical and psychological aspects. Thus, a constant conflict between the protagonist and the outside or inside forces become the driving engine of the plot. It is usually a villain-driven plot, whereby the villain presents obstacles that the protagonist must overcome.[3] Similarly, Beyzaie uses narrative structures that tease the audience by presenting puzzles or riddles to be solved by the end of the films. The puzzles which are introduced in an increasingly darker and more threatening situation create mystery, tension and suspense and lead to a prevalent sense of paranoia in the main character. Beyzaie intensifies these by shocking situations and menacing atmospheres where loyalty, honesty and safety have no place, and everybody feels threatened.

In *The Crow*, the narrative device which initiates and develops the plot and drives the characters is the TV advert about a missing girl. Although no crime is committed in the film, the narrative points which gradually unfold take the shape of those observed in a crime thriller. The film, therefore, captivates its audience in the style of films that focus on murder, kidnapping or inexplicable disappearance. In *Maybe Some Other Time*, Kian, the female protagonist, who seems unstable and is overwhelmed by confusing memories of loss, struggles to discover her true identity. In *Killing Mad Dogs*, which is the closest to a contemporary film noir, a highly intricate mystery narrative revolves around a female protagonist encountering the tough and, in several cases, illegal world of Iranian business life. The film contains all the narrative elements of the genre including murder, chases, shootouts, and double crossings. Golrokh Kamāli (played by Mozhdeh Shamsaie) struggles in the crime-ridden world of business in Tehran to buy back the checks that his husband's creditors have used to put him in prison.

While the conflict in *Killing Mad Dogs* is between Golrokh and the criminally minded businessmen, in *Maybe Some Other Time*, the conflict has a psychological nature and is rooted in Kian's subconscious misgivings and memories. The threat here is more emotional and mental than physical. Indeed, as in some film noir films, the plot includes an extended dream sequence and a flashback which display the subconscious turmoil in the mind of the female character, Kian. Highlighting the traumatic memories of her childhood when her poverty-ridden mother abandoned her in the corner of a street or when she was frightened by darkness or a street dog, the film uses surrealistic sequences to reflect the nightmarish world of her paranoia. In *The Crow* both forms of conflict exist: the psychological between the old lady and her memories and the physical and psychological between Āsiyeh and her kidnapper in a superbly depicted scene of kidnapping, fighting back and chasing.

As to the pace of the plot, which is often fast in recent crime thrillers, while both *The Crow* and *Maybe Some Other Time* are average in their pace due to their focus on their protagonists' emotions and a mystery that requires attention to details, *Killing Mad Dogs* has a fast-paced plot with a high level of tension as it is directly concerned with a crime. This fast-paced plot enhances the relentless sense of paranoia, suspense, anxiety, tension and the ever-increasing risk of death for the protagonist and turns *Killing Mad Dog* into Beyzaie's most noir-like film.

Film noir detective figures in Beyzaie's cinema

When analysing the characters of Beyzaie's thriller films, one may find elements that go against the conventions of the genre, and the character types may not always conform exactly to the genre's rules. Unlike American thrillers, in Beyzaie's films, the protagonists are frequently ordinary citizens unaccustomed to danger. Although there are no detectives or private eyes in Beyzaie's thriller films, as Saeed Talajooy also argues, the protagonists gradually evolve to act as detective figures. Thus, following the pattern of a mystery detective story, their principal function in the narrative becomes investigating a case to uncover a hidden truth.[4] As Susan Hayward states, 'generally speaking, in the film noir the woman is central to the intrigue and it is therefore she who becomes the object of the male's investigation'.[5] However, in Beyzaie's films, the gender of the detective is sometimes used to subvert this aspect of the genre. Thus, while protagonists of thrillers have traditionally been men, in Beyzaie's films, the detective figure can be male or female but is often a strong-willed woman who becomes the leading character as she gets involved in unshrouding a mystery at great risk to herself. These women are often the victims of a male-dominated patriarchal society where they have been persecuted or suppressed by their husbands, people, or authorities.

In *The Crow*, though Esālat is ostensibly the film's protagonist, in fact, it is the vulnerable but brave Āsiyeh who discovers the truth at the end. Thus, as Talajooy argues, it is Āsiyeh who assumes the role of the detective and delves into the case of the missing girl advertised in the newspaper by an unknown person.[6] In *Maybe Some Other Time*, which was made under the male-oriented censorship codes of the 1980s, Modabber (Kian's husband), a documentary filmmaker, serves as the detective who embarks on a mission to find out if his wife has been unfaithful to him. This mission ultimately resolves the mystery when he finds that Kian has a twin sister from whom she was separated in childhood. The detective in *Maybe Some Other Time* is, therefore, a man, but the focus is primarily on the identity of a woman. In *Killing Mad Dogs*, however, once more, the detective is a female protagonist who becomes embroiled in the violent world of Iranian business.

The latter two films are particularly in dialogue with Hitchcock's films which has in itself produced a major trend in making thrillers. Like Hitchcock, Beyzaie places an innocent woman in a strange, life-threatening and terrorizing situation. According to Gilles Deleuze, in Hitchcock's films, 'the criminal has always done his crime for another', for an innocent person, 'who, whether we like it or not, is innocent no longer'. That is why 'one does not commit a crime in Hitchcock, one delivers it up, one gives it, or one exchanges it'.[7] In *Killing Mad Dogs*, Golrokh must fight and make sacrifices for the sake of her husband to restore the equilibrium that she thinks has been disrupted by her husband's work partner. Everything turns against her assumptions by the end as the whole process has been her husband's plot. Thus, in the end there is no equilibrium, or as Gilles Deleuze says of Hitchcock's plots, a 'terrible equilibrium' is attained.[8] In the course of the film, Golrokh must deal with villainous businessmen to whom her husband owes money, and Beyzaie successfully relies on Golrokh's vulnerability and desperation to create tension and suspense in the narrative.

In a particularly memorable scene in *Killing Mad Dogs*, Golrokh meets an Iranian version of a yuppie businessman who is working in a fancy office, wearing nice clothes and, most notably, inserting an inordinate number of English words into every sentence he speaks. He is a caricature of the typical Westernized Iranian crook, a greedy, unfeeling capitalist out to get whatever he wants at the expense of others. When he forces Golrokh to meet him for dinner, she appears coy, distraught and helpless, but then when he lures her into his flat, Beyzaie subverts expectations by showing that Golrokh is not only wise to yuppie's scheme, but is ready and willing to confront him with a gun to get what she wants.[9] Immediately after this sequence, however, the spectator comes to realize that although she found a way to empower herself and take control in a difficult situation, she has entered a domain that is far beyond what she can imagine. In this sequence, Golrokh, who has meticulously planned to avoid danger, goes to confront another set of villains on the upper floor of a house, but she is trapped and raped by the villains. The suggested rape scene is a turning point in the narrative as after this encounter Golrokh is no longer the naïve and sentimental woman she has been before. By the end of the film, after she has discovered that her husband has used her to con his debtors, the spectator has gone through the same process of transformation that she has. Being tortured, raped and humiliated, she is now on a quest to bend these crooks to her will, not for the sake of her husband but for herself.[10]

The film offers one of the good examples of how Beyzaie deconstructs the stereotypes of heroism and female characters in Iranian cinema. Unlike most Iranian films, women are not passive elements in Beyzaie's films but play active roles in their society and family. They are either farmers, like Nāei in *Bāshu, the Little Stranger*, or teachers, like Āsiyeh in *The Crow*, and being employed gives them the power to survive in a patriarchal society. As Talajooy argues, he even depicts women as savours and sacrificial figures, who, even when victimized, confront and overcome the agents of their corrupt power-obsessed patriarchal societies.[11] Thus, in Beyzaie's thriller or mystery films, though the representation of women is in dialogue with Hitchcock's films, he often transcends the varied spectrum of Hitchcock's 1940s psychological thrillers such as *Rebecca* (1940) and *Suspicion* (1941), or George Cukor's *Gaslight* (1944).

Thriller-like suspense and tension in Beyzaie's films

One of the key features of crime thrillers is suspense. Filmmakers use suspense to create tension and excitement in viewers as the film approaches its climax. Tension is built through situations that are menacing or where escape seems impossible. Suspense in thrillers is often created with the interplay of hope and anxiety, which are aroused in anticipation of the conclusion – the hope that things will turn out all right for the protagonists and the fear that they may not.[12] In cinema, suspense occurs when the viewer knows that the protagonist is in danger, but the protagonist does not, or when neither the viewer nor the character knows what comes next.[13] In the thriller tradition, Hitchcock is often regarded as one of the greatest masters of suspense. Philp Kemp's analysis of how this is achieved in *Psycho* and how it is done in a way that pushes the spectator out of their normal way of looking at things provides a great example: 'There is a parallel trick in his *Psycho* when Norman Bates, the antagonist tries to sink Marion Crane (the protagonist)'s car, with her body in the boot, in a swamp and it stops, half-submerged, involuntarily we sigh with relief when it starts sinking again.'[14]

In Beyzaie's city films, suspense plays an important role, but Beyzaie's approach to suspense is less intense. In his films the suspense is timed by long takes, camera movement or cross-cutting to steadily increase engaging the viewer's concern. In *The Crow* and *Killing Mad Dogs*, the anticipation of violence creates a high level of excitement and suspense which is further boosted by the fear of being trapped in a world where nothing is safe. There are also conscious Hitchcockian touches and references in the narrative as the protagonist faces dangerous situations. The most overt example in *The Crow* is the sequence in which Āsiyeh, the female protagonist, gets into a kidnapper's car by accident but manages to make a dramatic escape.[15] From the onset of the scene, as the kidnaper's car passes through the streets of modern Tehran and the reflections of the buildings are seen on the windscreen and juxtaposed with Āsiyeh's horrified face, the viewer hears an orchestral piece of music composed by Babak Bayat in style similar to those written by Bernard Herman for Hitchcock. Āsiyeh is further terrified when the driver brandishes a knife in a haunting and dramatic shot. Then when she seizes an opportunity to get away, the film makes a range of Hitchcockian references in which everything that she runs past becomes a point of tension inducing. The sequence even includes an homage to the filmography of the master of suspense with a gigantic billboard of an upbeat female face selling 7UP and a shot of a passer-by who appears to take a voyeuristic enjoyment in her peril. She then goes into a clock store and breathes a sigh of relief. The tense music stops and after a moment of silence, the intense deafening tick-tucks of the clocks from all around her become overwhelming and the feeling of anxiety returns. As the clocks chime, the music starts again.[16]

Up to this point in *The Crow*, Beyzaie has used a series of shots to refer to Hitchcock's *The Birds, Psycho, Spellbound* and *Vertigo*. Āsiyeh, then, passes a Shia relic of an upright hand symbolizing protection from evil but also appearing very much like a call to stop. This is followed by a mirror and then she runs past a canon pointing at her and a terrifying window displaying dozens of mannequin heads. A high-angle shot then captures the image of her running into and disrupting a huge flock of birds which is a direct reference to Melanie's situation in *The Birds*. During her flight, she is also surrounded by scaffoldings and other forms of menacing urban imagery – a motif that occurs in several of Beyzaie's films including *Killing Mad Dogs* which was made three decades later. She runs down a long set of steps which in the shot make a reference to Hitchcock's *The 39 Steps* (1935). Finally, when she believes that she is safely home, the film reflects the most threatening view so far by showing her from behind as she gets into the shower to relieve her stress.[17] The spectators are, thus, left in a continued state of suspense even here because if they are familiar with the famous shower scene in Hitchcock's *Psycho*, they know that the shot reflects the view of Norman Bates in *Psycho*.[18]

Thriller-type surveillance in Beyzaie's cinema

Surveillance is one of the major concerns of the modern era and is addressed by many filmmakers particularly Hitchcock in *The Rear Window* (1954). Surveillance and being observed closely are also one of Beyzaie's main thematic preoccupations. One of Beyzaie's iconic motifs in his films is the shot of a large pair of glasses. The shot functions as a metaphor for the ever-present, watchful eyes of a source of social and political control as the camera monitors people in public spaces and shows that they live under the constant gaze of others.[19]

In *The Crow* the camera captures Āsiyeh from above through a big decorative pair of glasses from an optical shop as she runs away from her kidnapper.[20] Similarly, in *Maybe Some Other Time*, a high-angle long shot of the pavement on which Kian is walking captures her under a similar pair of glasses.[21] In the latter film, surveillance becomes an overwhelming element of the plot as Kian feels that she is being observed all the time whether she is in bed or in the street. In a very surrealistic scene, reminiscent of Scottie's nightmare in *Vertigo* and also Rosemarie's feverish nightmare scene in Polanski's *Rosemarie's Baby*, Kian is shown sleeping on her bed in a long corridor feeling disturbed by being under the gaze of a surgical team. The film, then, marks her words to her psychologist: 'I'm under surveillance from every side. Escape is impossible'.[22] The zooming camera to the ceiling, the shadowed lighting and the ominous, atmospheric music, all create a very impressive nightmarish scene. Beyzaie uses multiple camera angles during Kian's nightmare scene including the low-angle and high-angle shots. These shots and those of a rocking bed join the interplay of the lights and shadows that surround Kian and the music to reflect Kian's fears and her subconscious memories of her traumatic childhood. All these elements work together to reflect at social and psychological levels the impact of surveillance on creating an imbalance in human identity formation.

Surveillance is also essential in *Killing Mad Dogs*. Golrokh is watched and bugged by the receptionist of the hotel and several people outside the hotel. In a scene at the beginning of the film, Nasser Moaser is driving a car at night as his partner Javad Moghadam is hiding in the back seat. As Nasser drives on the street, Basiji paramilitary groups and revolutionary guards are shown approaching the car and peering through the window.[23] Such scenes increase the tension, but they also suggest the overwhelming presence of surveillance in Iranian society.

Noir-like, subjective POV shot in Beyzaie's cinema

POV or first-person shots are frequently used in thrillers. This kind of subjective shot reflects the viewpoint of a character looking at someone or something or shows the character's reaction. Such shots put the spectator in the shoes of the protagonists or antagonists and allow them to see everything they see and feel what they feel. As Joseph V. Mascelli states,

> A point-of-view shot is as close as an objective shot can approach a subjective shot – and still remain objective. The camera is positioned at the side of a subjective player – whose viewpoint is being depicted – so that the audience is given the impression they are standing cheek-to-cheek with the off-screen player. The viewer does not see the event through the player's eyes, as in a subjective shot in which the camera trades places with the screen player. He sees the event from the player's *viewpoint*, as if standing alongside him.[24]

Beyzaie uses POV shots to put the viewer in the position of the protagonist facing a threat or entering a dangerous place. In *Maybe Some Other Time,* Beyzaie uses the POV shot to blur the boundaries between reality and imagination. In a significant scene a medium shot of Kian shows her sitting at a table and listening to her husband who talks to her from outside the frame. Then Beyzaie cuts to Kian's POV shot to show an empty chair signifying that it was all in Kian's imagination.[25] In *Killing Mad Dogs*, he intensifies the complexity of his narrative by a sophisticated orchestration of points of view and filmic time. For instance, early in the film, a POV shot of Golrokh shows her looking out through the window of a car at the chaos of the city which looks like a war zone: ominous tower-like constructions, trenches, slogans written on the walls in support of the war and the paramilitary Basij marching in the streets.

Beyzaie's aesthetic approach to constructing his thriller-like vision, including his camera movement and tracking shots and mise en scène are consistent in his entire filmography but are most present and iconic in *The Crow*. In a very dramatic scene, when Āsiyeh goes into a shed-like room full of old items in search of clues about the fate of the missing girl, the use of low-key lighting, the continuous cawing of the crows, the sharp lines of the structural beams, a rat and a close up of her horrified face, all serve to create an effectively dreadful and expressionistic atmosphere.[26] In the pivotal reveal sequence in *The Crow*, Āsiyeh goes into the room which is full of her mother-in-law's (Ālam's) belongings. The opening offers a very Hitchcockian turning of a doorknob shot. This continues with Āsiyeh looking around the room as the camera proceeds to adopt her POV to examine the items around the room. She checks Ālam's preserved possessions and finally finds the photo that had been used for the missing person advert. She, thus, realizes that the photo features Ālam's youth and concludes the investigation that she and her husband had embarked upon by establishing that the old lady was behind the whole affair in a desperate attempt to remind the people around her of her existence and her past. The world around the old woman has changed to an extent that it is no longer recognizable. As Talajooy argues, the process can, therefore, be read to comment on how unbridled modernization cancels the possibility of preserving the positive elements of cultural traditions and learning from the past, which has been one of the ongoing issues in Iran since the early 1900s.[27]

Beyzaie, thus, illustrates the interaction between the present and the past, between the habitual memory and the virtual memory as Bergson outlines it. In Deleuze's terms, 'Bergson's major theses on time are as follows: the past coexists with the present that it has been; the past is preserved in itself, as past in general (non-chronological); at each moment time splits itself into present and past, present that passes and past which is preserved'. What Deleuze calls 'The crystal-image' is 'the point of indiscernibility of the two distinct images, the actual and the virtual, while what we see in the crystal is time itself'.[28] Thus, according to Deleuze, the 'past does not follow the present that it is no longer, it coexists with the present it was. The present is the actual image, and *its* contemporaneous past is the virtual image, the image in a mirror'.[29] This is exactly the anachronistic aspect of Beyzaie's films, a kind of crystal image similar to what is suggested by Deleuze, a representation of the splitting of time, the movement of past and present reflected through the images, the simultaneous existence of the past and present where the pure-virtual image interacts fleetingly with present.

The pure crystal image, where the actual meets its virtual image, occurs in *Maybe Some Other Time* in the scene in which Kian is facing a portrait of a woman similar to herself among the historical objects of an antique shop. It is a painting of her twin sister, which could be the virtual image of herself and her mother as well. In fact, by choosing Susan Taslimi to play the roles of both sisters and their mother, Beyzaie shows that the actual and the virtual cannot be separated as, at that specific moment, there can no longer be a distinction between the present and the past for Kian. The virtual image becomes actual. Once more, these technical elements are juxtaposed with noir and crime cinema elements to reflect on the psychological impacts of separation, hesitation, the feeling of having no control and being under surveillance by people whom one does not know or cannot react to or control.

The dark city of noir films in Beyzaie's cinema

Although the films in the crime thriller genre may be set, wholly or partly, in exotic settings such as remote areas and deserts, they are generally more likely to have urban or ordinary suburban settings. Thus, a city that is initially shown to be a relatively safe place becomes a place for evil forces engaged in criminal activities. Beyzaie's cinema, especially *The Crow* and *Maybe Some Other Time*, do not have crimes at the centres of their plots but they use the major elements of crime thriller genre in the urban spaces of modern Tehran. All three films convey a sense of fear and living in a dangerous and threatening place. The façade of the city in *The Crow* and *Killing Mad Dogs* is noxious and menacing. The city is a place in which people can get lost, be kidnapped, raped, tortured and murdered. In *Killing Mad Dogs*, like American classic noirs, the big city symbolizes the corruption and darkness that threaten the lives of the characters, and the chaos of the capital foreshadows what awaits Golrokh in the brutal male-dominant culture of Iranian business life.

Thus, Beyzaie's city films, especially the ones that I have been analysing in this chapter make major use of the idea of the dark city. Nevertheless, among noir elements, the use of the dark city or town and plot twists, which I will examine in the following section, also exist in most of Beyzaie's historical and mythical films including *Marg-e Yazdgerd* (Death of Yazdgerd, 1981) and *Gharibeh va Meh* (Stranger and the Fog, 1974). Indeed, although *Death of Yazdgerd* has a historical setting, as Talajooy also argues, it is structurally a detective mystery using and subverting the tropes and trademarks of the genre.[30] The film is set in a dark world of fear and war, opens with a shot of a corps and is framed in the manner of a murder mystery that needs to be investigated. Beyzaie challenges the givens of history by employing a *Rashomon* style multi-layered non-linear narrative in which the Miller, his wife and their daughter while trying to exculpate themselves, offer their own versions of how the murder occurred and the identity of the corpse. By using a complex narrative structure and by concealing the real identity of the slain person and the motives behind his murder, Beyzaie invites his viewers into a mysterious and suspenseful world in which war, crime, greed and oppression have distorted human life.

Noir-like plot twists in Beyzaie's films

The plot twist is a common narrative device in crime thrillers. This occurs with a radical change in the expected direction or outcome of the plot of a film which usually comes as a surprising yet perfectly justifiable revelation near the end of the film. In *The Crow*, the twist happens when it is revealed that it was Ālam, who sent the photo of her youth for the advert of the missing girl, not the girl's parents, murderer, or kidnapper. The plot twist of *Maybe Some Other Time* occurs also in the final sequence when the twin sisters meet in Vida's home, and Modabber realizes that the woman in the unfamiliar car with another man was not his wife but her twin sister Vida, who had remained with their mother when Kian was left for adoption. *Killing Mad Dogs* is also characterized by a sudden reversal of the narrative when it is revealed that Golrokh's husband was not wronged by his business partner, Javad Moqaddam, and that he had concocted the whole plot to frighten Moqaddam and use Golrokh to retrieve his checks so that he can get away with the money and marry his secretary Fereshteh who also functions like a film noir femme fatal. In a skilfully arranged sequence, the camera captures a medium shot of Golrokh and then tracks back to reveal in the corner of the frame Javad Moqaddam and his gang menacingly walking towards Nasser and Fereshteh who are shown in the background running away in the plain. The last long-take shot is an ambitiously choreographed crane shot in the style of Miklós Jancsó, a balletic act of violence that shows Nasser Moasser getting shot like a mad dog. Then after a gunshot is heard from out of the frame, Golrokh, who is sitting in her car, murmurs to herself, 'So this is the end of killing mad dogs.'

Crime thriller iconography in Beyzaie's cinema

Iconography is what spectators visually associate with a genre. The usual icons of crime thrillers and noir films include dark streets, car chases, guns and other types of weaponry, bars, cigarettes, alcohol, raincoats and fedoras, police sirens, low-key lighting, shadows, and a few other visual motifs regularly used in these films. The iconic motifs of crime genre are recognizable in all three films. In *The Crow* there is a scene in which Āsiyeh and her husband, Esālat, are heading by car to the scene of a crime after they are informed that a girl has been murdered. This scene features an array of film noir icons. Heavy rainfall, dark streets, neon city lights reflected upon the wet asphalt, police sirens, flash photography, and shadowed figures carrying umbrellas moving under the rain, are all used to set a noir filmic mood. As Talajooy states, the film even reflects its noir iconography in well-orchestrated meta-cinematic scenes of danger and mystery in the underworld of the city. The best example of such scenes is the ominous-looking sequence in which, following a phone call from someone who claims to know the whereabouts of the missing girl, Esālat goes to a junkyard to meet him.[31]

Similar forms of presentation can also be seen in *Maybe Some Other Time*, which is more like a psychological thriller in that everything bares the mark of suspicion and doubt which is a driving force for many crime thriller protagonists. The low-key lighting, stylized cinematography, and the arrangement of the shots accompanied by a film score similar to Bernard Hermann's compositions all help to create a nightmarish world. This is also the case in *Killing Mad Dog*, where anything may pose a threat. From constantly ringing telephones to the turning of a door handle or the construction workers who watch Golrokh through her window from the street, all serve as devices that make the viewer as uneasy as the protagonist. The film also includes scenes with weapons and blood on display which fully qualify for suggesting the film as a crime thriller. The perturbing opening sequence begins with a pan on an image of dead dogs in the street with air raid sirens heard from out of the frame and faded into a full shot of a window in a dark room. As the film proceeds, the viewer sees how Golrokh comes into contact with people unknown to her and the audience. A man in a taxi arrives to collect her from the airport purporting to have been sent by her husband. He takes her to a five-star hotel again reserved supposedly by her husband where she receives deliveries which contain a bouquet of flowers and then a pistol.[32] All of these impregnate the ambiance of the film with doubt and anxiety about the nature of what is going to happen to her. The viewer knows that something nefarious has been set up but cannot tell by whom. The film also makes use of telephone sets in a style similar to thrillers in that it is not only a means of creating panic and anxiety in the main character but also a hearing device for the criminals to control and follow Golrokh by listening to her conversations.

Thriller-like phobia and traumatic memories in Beyzaie's films

In psychological thrillers the characters often suffer from phobia or paranoia. As in Hitchcock's *Marnie*, they may have had a traumatic childhood or later experience that constantly affects their lives and generates inexplicable phobias. Beyzaie's use of female protagonists having nightmares in the three films analysed in this chapter highlights the fears that these women struggle with in their respective situations. They all need to go through a psychological journey of revelation and confrontation to overcome their phobias and anxieties. In *The Crow*, Āsiyeh's anxiety is rooted in the fear of being kidnapped and murdered. Although she manages to escape from the kidnapper who intended to sexually assault her, the experience has had a traumatic effect on her so that the sequence becomes a turning point in the narrative of the film. Before this sequence and this traumatic experience, Āsiyeh does follow the news of the missing girl, which her husband is interested in, but after the assault, she becomes obsessed about it and decides to follow the case herself.

In *Maybe Some Other Time*, these traumatic memories have led to Kian's identity crisis, which is one of Beyzaie's main thematic interests. Kian's character is like Hitchcock's Marnie. They both suffer from a traumatic experience. She has had a traumatic childhood. She knows that she was adopted when she was very young, but now she has become obsessed with discovering her real identity, why she has no picture of her childhood and why she was left for adoption. Kian's fear is a childhood trauma which has also triggered an aversion to darkness and dogs. Her anxiety, therefore, is ingrained and explains her nightmares and her confusion about her identity. In the final sequence of the film, when she meets her twin sister, they start to recall their blurred memories, and through a long and well-structured flashback, Beyzaie takes the viewer to their traumatic past. The camera, thus, moves through the walls of Vida's house, whose paintings along with the items of the antique shop metaphorically represent the corridor of history and time, and enters the streets of old Tehran where the twin's mother had to leave one of them for adoption because of poverty. By weaving in flashbacks and meta-cinematic footage, the narrative takes the viewer back and forth in time towards the family suffering that lies at the film's core.[33] While it could be argued that the film is partly a psychological thriller, there are also crime elements spread all over the film and the mystery that is to be resolved is as important as the psychology of the characters.

Hitchcockian elements in Beyzaie's cinema and concluding remarks

As suggested above, though Beyzaie's films are in dialogue with noir films and thrillers in general, the most important source of inspiration and subversion for Beyzaie's vision seems to be Hitchcock. This argument can also be supported if one notes that the most technically significant book on Hitchcock's cinema is a monograph written by Beyzaie. It, therefore, seems appropriate to close this chapter with a brief discussion of the link between the two.

Deleuze argues that Hitchcock has a sound understanding of human relations and that in his films 'actions, affections, perceptions, all is interpretation, from the beginning to end'.[34]

> There are many excellent commentators on Hitchcock (for no film director has been the object of so many commentaries) and there is no need to decide between those who see him as a profound thinker and those who see him merely as a great entertainer. There is, however, no need to make Hitchcock a Platonic and Catholic metaphysician, as do Rohmer and Chabrol, or a psychologist of the depths, as does Douchet. Hitchcock has a very sound conception of theoretical and practical relations.[35]

I argue that one can attribute the same to Beyzaie and his works and that Beyzaie's thriller-like films display an intentional similarity to Hitchcock's. As Beyzaie himself states in his book on Hitchcock, Hitchcock never goes into the details of an espionage incident or ideological issue. He rather forms new relationships between and focuses on those who, knowingly or unknowingly, are stuck in the middle of the incident.[36] Beyzaie refers to *Topaz* (1969) and *The Torn Curtain* (1963), as two examples of Hitchcock's spy films that do not praise an idea (such as the anti-communist discourses of the 1950s) but focus on the insecurity of human conditions under the shadow of such invisible wars.[37] He also adds that Hitchcock reflects his perception of the world without judging or turning it into an intellectual theory.[38]

Like Hitchcock, Beyzaie has found something in Iranian society that is highly congenial to the crime thriller genre and has used the genre to cast a spotlight on the nature of life in modern-day Iran. Beyzaie uses almost all crime thriller elements without strictly adhering to the dogma of the noir and crime thriller genre. In these three films, therefore, the prominent aspects remain concerned with an examination of different types of criminality in Iran. The films also reveal Beyzaie's intellectual and artistic interests in the mythical and ritualistic realms. Thus, in the same way that Hitchcock's films reflect his catholic ideology, Beyzaie constructs his themes, narratives and atmosphere around the ritual, mythical and historical aspects of Iranian culture. Hitchcock once said his intention was 'to give the public good healthy mental shake-ups'. Beyzaie is also out to make his audience think about his characters and their reactions to the psychological and social problems they observe in his films.

As explained earlier, Beyzaie's films are also depictions of women's struggles in a repressive, male-dominated culture. But unlike Hitchcock's women, Beyzaie's women are not weak or naive, or if they originally are, they rise to become strong survivors. They may act emotionally, but they are clever, intellectually gifted, determined and brave. They are also willing to sacrifice their interests for love. This is one of the several ways in which Beyzaie's cinema goes beyond the expected Hitchcockian dramatic turns and suspenseful tropes and expectations that the audience might have of the classic crime thriller. The others include incorporating social and cultural issues that characters must face and showing how their struggles are like those faced by the ordinary people of Iran or people of similar backgrounds.

Like most great suspense thrillers, Beyzaie's thrillers are structured to raise questions in the minds of their spectators, and their ability to make these questions inevitable is essential to their success in engaging their spectators with their narratives and characters. Beyzaie does this well not only at personal and existential levels, as Hitchcock does, but also at cultural and socio-political levels to the extent that he makes this questioning one of the hallmarks of his work and establishes an interactive and participatory relationship with his viewers. Thus, though the plot and structures of his thrillers echo some of the principles and rules of crime thrillers, the themes that he grapples with are multifaceted and include commentary on various socio-political and existential relations and situations.

In the chapter above, I tried to trace some of these qualities and reflect on how Beyzaie used the technical features of crime thrillers and film noir genre and how he conveys his social and philosophical themes through this curious lens. Due to the limited space, I could not go in depth and cover all aspects of crime elements in Beyzaie's filmography and could not explore his unmade film scripts such as *Haqāyeqi Darbāreh Leila Dokhtar-e Edris* (Truths about Laila, the Daughter of Edris, 1975) and *Eshghāl* (Occupation, 1980).[39] Nevertheless, the technical and thematic elements of the films that I examined and Beyzaie's monograph on Hitchcock clearly suggest Beyzaie's preoccupation with the genre and his ability to transcend the limitations of the genre to create some of the most important films of the Iranian New Wave Cinema.

Notes

1. Kuhn, *Oxford Dictionary*, 101–2.
2. Hayward, *Cinema Studies*, 128.
3. Luhr, Film Noir, 50–72.
4. Talajooy, 'Khāneh, Khānevādeh', 153.
5. Hayward, *Cinema Studies*, 131.
6. Talajooy, 'Khāneh, Khānevādeh', 153–4.
7. Deleuze, *Cinema 1*, 201.
8. Ibid., 203.
9. Beyzaie, *Killing Mad Dogs*, 85–90.
10. Ibid.,102–6.
11. Talajooy, 'Intellectuals as Sacrificial'.
12. Ortony, Clore, and Collins, *Cognitive Structure*, 132.
13. Kemp, 'Master of Suspense', 14.
14. Ibid., 14.
15. Beyzaie, *The Crow*, 30'–36'.
16. Ibid., 32'.47".
17. Ibid., 32'–34'.
18. See also Talajooy, *Iranian Culture*, 211–14, which examines this sequence from several angles.
19. See also Talajooy, 'Khāneh, Khānevādeh', 143 and 146.
20. Beyzaie, *The Crow*, 31'.55".
21. Beyzaie, *Maybe Some*, 32'.54".
22. Beyzaie, *Maybe Some*, 105'–106'.
23. Beyzaie, *Killing Mad*, 6'.40"–7'.04".
24. Mascelli, *Five Cs.*, 22.
25. Beyzaie, *Maybe Some*, 21'.44".
26. Beyzaie, *The Crow*, 95'–97'.
27. See also Talajooy, 'Khāneh, Khānevādeh', 142–61; and *Iranian Culture*, 193–236.
28. Deleuze, Cinema 2, 82.
29. Ibid., 79.
30. Talajooy, 'History and Iranian', 196.
31. Talajooy, *Iranian Culture*, 217–19.
32. Beyzaie, *Killing Mad Dogs*, 11'–20'.
33. For a more detailed analysis of the film and Kian's identity crisis, See Talajooy, 'Khāneh, Khānevādeh'.

34 Deleuze, *Cinema 1*, 200.
35 Ibid., 202.
36 Beyzaie, *Hitchcock dar Qāb*, 33.
37 Ibid., 35.
38 Ibid., 62.
39 For an analysis of *Occupation* which also touches upon the script's thriller elements, see Talajooy, 'Bahram Beyzaie', 128–50.

Bibliography

Deleuze, Gilles. *Cinema 1: The Movement-Image*. Minneapolis: Minnesota University Press, 1986.
Deleuze, Gilles. *Cinema 2: The Time-Image*, London: Continuum Books, 1989.
Hayward, Susan, *Cinema Studies: The Key Concepts*. London and New York: Routledge, 2013.
Kemp, Philip. 'The Master of Suspense'. *39 Steps to the Genius of Hitchcock*. Ed. James Bell. London: BFI, 2012. Pp. 14–15.
Kuhn, Annette and Guy Westwell. *Oxford Dictionary of Film Studies*. Oxford: Oxford University Press, 2012.
Luhr, William. *Film Noir (New Approaches to Film Genre)*. Oxford: Wiley and Blackwell, 2012.
Mascelli, Joseph V. *The Five C's of Cinematography: Motion Picture Filming Techniques Simplified*. Hollywood, Calif.: Cine/Graphic Publications. 1965.
Ortony, Andrew, Gerald Clore and Allan Collins. *The Cognitive Structure of Emotions*. Cambridge: Cambridge University Press, 2015.
Talajooy, Saeed. 'Khāneh, Khānevādeh va Shahr: Revayāt Tajaddod dar Kalāgh va Shāyad Vaqti Digar'. *Iran Nameh*. Vol. 27. No. 1 (2012). Pp. 142–61.
Talajooy, Saeed. 'Bahram Beyzaie va Jang-e Jahāni-ye Dovvom: Revāyat-e Eshghāl va Degardisi-e Mafhum-e Mellat'. *Iran Nameh*. Vol. 28. No. 1 (2013). Pp. 128–50.
Talajooy, Saeed. 'History and Iranian Drama: The Case of Bahram Beyzaie'. In *Perceptions of Iran; History, Myths and Nationalism from Medieval Persia to the Islamic Republic*. Ed. Ali M. Ansari. London and New York: I.B. Tauris, 2014. Pp. 183–210.
Talajooy, Saeed. 'Intellectuals as Sacrificial Heroes: A Comparative Study of Bahram Beyzaie and Wole Soyinka'. *Comparative Literature Studies*. Vol. 52. No. 2 (July 2015). Pp. 379–408.
Talajooy, Saeed. *Iranian Culture in Bahram Beyzaie's Cinema and Theatre: Paradigms of Being and Belonging (1959–1979)*. London and New York: I.B. Tauris, 2023.

Section D

BEYZAIE'S FILMS IN THEIR COMPARATIVE CONTEXTS

Chapter 9

MULTILINGUALITY IN IRANIAN CINEMA:
A COMPARATIVE ANALYSIS

Saeed Zeydabadi-Nejad

Introduction

'Persian is sugar', a story by Mohammad Ali Jamalzadeh published in the first collection of modern Persian short stories in 1921, tells the story of a young man who spends a night in jail struggling to understand the way two of his cellmates speak. One of the two, a western educated Iranian, mixes his Persian with a strong dose of French and the other, a mullah, with Arabic. The young man, who has never faced such a situation before, assumes they are genies rather than humans but the narrator, who is also sharing the same cell, assures him that the two are in fact Persian speakers and, therefore, Iranians. As the four inmates are freed as arbitrarily as they were imprisoned, they pass another man who has just been arrested. The latter speaks in another equally difficult way for the young man to understand. The narrator contemplates reassuring the young man that the new prisoner is also a Persian speaker and Iranian, but he does not do so as he thinks that the young man may assume that he is teasing him.[1]

In February 2003, when I attended Fajr Festival in Tehran, it was the first time that I had the chance to watch a large range of Iranian films within a few days, from art-house ones such as Asghar Farhadi's first feature *Raqs dar Ghobār* (Dance in the Dust, 2003) to the B-rated state-sponsored ones like Abolghasem Talebi's *Naghmeh* (2003). To my surprise, a common feature of a large number of films, including *Dance in the Dust* and *Naghmeh*, was that they had one or more scenes in a regional language or strong dialect with no subtitles. To me this was an interesting development which broke the hold of ethnocentric Persian monolinguality on film. As reflected in Table 9.1, a review of this change in Iranian cinema shows that more recently, from 2006 to the present, films with large parts in languages other than Persian, which include some with subtitles, have exponentially increased in number.

In this chapter, I explore the phenomenon of increasing multilinguality in Iranian cinema and its relationship to ethno-linguistic otherness. I seek to find out whether the relatively new phenomenon of heterogeneity of languages in Iranian films contests the hierarchy between the Persian centre core and the speakers of peripheral languages in Iran.[2] I will examine whether the inclusion of those languages signals *otherness*, or it problematizes the power relationship between the Persian nation core and the various other ethnicities in Iran. To answer the question, I focus on three films, *Che* (Hatamikia, 2014), *The Night Bus* (Pourahmad, 2007) and *Bāshu, the Little Stranger* (Beyzaie, 1985). The reason for choosing these films is that they are all set in the context of conflict between the Islamic Republic of Iran and a linguistically 'other' enemy. In *Bāshu, the Little Stranger*, the young boy at the centre of the narrative is an Arabic speaker in a story set at the time when Iran was at war with its Arab neighbour Iraq. *The Night Bus*, which is also set at the time of Iran-Iraq war, has large sections in Arabic. In *Che*, the narrative features the Iranian regime's war with the Kurds fighting for autonomy in the early 1980s and includes conversations in the Kurdish language. The chapter will explore whether the films constitute what Chris Wahl refers to as 'polyglot' films in which linguistic inclusiveness signals universal humanism that excludes no one as the *other*.[3]

Table 9.1 Films with languages other than Persian between 2006 and 2017

Film	Languages
Sargijeh (Vertigo). Dir. Mohamad Zarrindast (2006)	Persian, English
Otobus-e Shab (The Night Bus). Dir. Kiumars Pourahmad (2007)	Persian, Arabic
Farzand-e Khāk (Child of the Soil). Dir. Mohammad Ali. Bashe Ahangar (2007)	Kurdish, Persian
Zād o Bum (Motherland). Dir. Abolhassan Davoodi (2008)	Persian, German
Ketāb-e Qanun (The Book of Law). Dir. Miri (2008)	Persian English, Arabic
Haft-o-Panj Daqiqeh (7:05). Dir. Mohamad Mehdi Asgarpour (2009)	Persian, French
Siy-o-seh Ruz (33 Days). Dir. Jamal Shurjeh (2010)	Arabic, English
Zabān-e Madari (Mother Tongue). Dir. Ghorban Mohammadpour (2010)	Persian, Spanish
Esterdād (Give Back). Dir. Ali Ghaffari (2012)	Persian, Russian
Berlin Manfi-ye Haft (Berlin −7°). Dir. Ramtin Lavafipour (2013)	Persian, German
Tanhā-ye Tanhā-ye Tanhā (All Alone). Dir. Ehsan Abdipour (2013)	Persian, Russian
Fereshtegān-e Qassāb (Butcher Angels). Dir. Soheil Salimi (2012)	Persian, English
The Past (Produced in France). Dir. Asghar Farhadi (2013)	French, Persian
Farsh-e Qermez/Red Carpet (Red Carpet). Dir. Reza AtTārān (2013)	English, Persian, French
Che (Mostafa Chamran's epithet, which compares him with Ernesto Che Guevara). Dir. Ebrahim Hatamikia (2014)	Persian, Kurdish
Abu Zeynab. Dir. Ali Ghafari (2015)	Persian, English, Arabic
Kārgar Sādeh Niāzmandim (Simple Worker Needed). Dir. Manouchehr Hadi (2017)	Persian, Azari Turkish
Ābba Jān (Abba Jaan). Dir. Hatef Alimardani (2017)	Persian, Azari Turkish

Multilinguality and film

At the most basic level, a multilingual film is one in which two or more languages are spoken. Wahl, however, distinguishes between genuine 'polyglot' films and others that either include a few short sentences in a foreign language or use the inclusion of a foreign language as a marker of otherness.[4] Accordingly, in a society where various languages are spoken their inclusive representation in a polyglot film subverts the mask of homogeneity which a single language on film would portray. Discussing *Midnight Express* (1978), a Hollywood film set in Turkey, he dismisses it as not qualifying as 'polyglot' in his definition because

> foreign language is, in places, relegated to noise and is solely used to symbolise otherness, and secondly because the interaction between speakers of different languages is only integrated for the sake of plot narration, and not as a conscious statement on the difficulties or the miracles of communication.[5]

By extension, I argue that including another language in a film can be more than an acknowledgement of diversity in a society as it has the potential to question the power dynamics between the dominant and dominated ethnicities. If the act of communication itself becomes a focus of representation, the characters trying to communicate *can* be portrayed as equals as they attempt to overcome the barrier of language difference. In nation states like Iran consisting of a dominant nation core and a variety of subjugated ethnolinguistic groups, the foregrounding of linguistic differences can question the power dynamics between the nation core and the peripheral ethnicities.

Power relationships are inherent in any reflection of linguistic differences in films, Iranian or otherwise. In the context of Hollywood films, as Ella Shochat and Robert Stam state,

> Inscribed within the play of power, languages are caught up in artificial hierarchies rooted in cultural hegemonies and political oppression. English, for example, as a function of its colonising status, became the linguistic vehicle for the projection of Anglo-American power, technology and finance. Hollywood, especially, came to incarnate a linguistic hubris bred of empire. Presuming to speak for others in its native idiom, Hollywood proposed to tell the story of other nations not only to Americans, but also for the other nations themselves, and always in English.[6]

While the power imbalance is more evidently inscribed in the hegemonic dominance of American English language in Hollywood cinema, internal linguistic diversity within a nation, be it in Iran, China or the UK, is less so. In the UK, otherness is inscribed in accents spoken in film. As Shochat and Stam put it,

> Even monolingual societies are characterised by heteroglossia; they englobe multiple 'languages' or 'dialects' which both reveal and produce social position, each existing in a distinct relation to the hegemonic language. [...] In many

British New Wave films, upper-class English is worn like a coat of arms, an instrument of exclusion, while working-class speech is carried like a stigmata.[7]

Finally, the inclusion of subtitles, Wahl contends, turns the sounds of the other language into a comprehensible dialogue, and hence the use of subtitles is a step in the direction of polyglossia in film. Naficy, however, points out that to include subtitles or not, or even how to include them is a complex decision that some filmmakers make according to their auteurial style and/or the sense which they seek to convey.[8] Hence, whether and how the three Iranian films have used subtitles is important to consider in relation to the three films analysed here.

Iranian cinema and multilinguality

Prior to *Bāshu, the Little Stranger*, regional languages other than Persian hardly ever featured in Iranian cinema or more generally in the Iranian mass media. This is while a third of Iranians are estimated to be native speakers of other languages such as Azari Turkish, Kurdish, Arabic, etc.[9] Persian is the official language of the country and that of education. Therefore, with Iran's relatively high level of literacy 86.8 per cent,[10] one can conclude that bilingualism is the norm for over 25 per cent of Iranians. However, this sociolinguistic reality has been subjected to the political hegemonies of the two recent regimes in Iran, the Pahlavis (1925–79) and the Islamic Republic (1979 to present). Before the 1979 revolution, state-controlled media tried to portray a modern image of Iran, centred on the Iranian capital with its high-rise buildings and other putative emblems of urban modernity. Film and television were major vehicles of such propaganda in which standard Persian, generally with a Tehrani accent, featured almost exclusively. In mainstream cinema, theatre and television speaking in a regional variety of Persian was primarily used for derision and people with accents other than the one spoken in the putative modern capital were generally dismissed as fools or simpletons.[11] To speak Persian with a Tehrani accent was thus constructed as a marker of being modern, following the tradition of early twentieth-century Persian prose written by Jamalzadeh and Sadeq Hedayat.[12] This attitude towards regional varieties of Persian still continues and is exemplified in state-sponsored TV programmes (e.g. Mehran Modiri's popular series *Pāvarchin* [On Tiptoes] or *Shabhā-ye Barareh* [Barareh Nights]), popular Iranian jokes and the Iranian exiled community television channels. The power relationship constituted a centre-periphery model that values the Persian-speaking nation core at the expense of peripheral ethnic groups who speak either regional varieties of Persian or other languages.

While the 1979 revolution shook Iran in many ways, the Persian language and its speakers remained central to the new regime. The post-revolutionary ideological Islamization went against the modernization drive before the revolution. However, when it came to regional people and their languages, there was hardly any change after the revolution, partly because almost all leading religious clerics came from the Persian-speaking provinces.[13] In the early post-revolution period, some peripheral nations within Iran, such as the Kurds and the Turkmen, attempted to gain self-determination through armed struggle. However, their short-lived struggles were abandoned in the face of the military might of the central government. When it came to cinema, the regime acknowledged the derisory treatment of provincial peoples in films made before the revolution. Formulated in 1982, the Islamic Republic's censorship code banned 'derision of provincial dialects' on film.[14] However, the stipulation in the filmmaking code does not have any practical implications for the filmmakers such as Mehran Modiri's TV series named above which does not abide by the codes.

Bāshu, the Little Stranger (Beyzaie 1985)

Bāshu, the Little Stanger (see Figure 9.1) is written and directed by Bahram Beyzaie, a veteran filmmaker of the 1970's *Sinemā-ye Motefāvet* (Alternative Cinema). Many of his films are about strangers who enter a society as the others against whom societal norms are questioned. His films often feature strong female

Figure 9.1 *Bāshu, the Little Stranger* (film poster).

characters who take a central role in the narrative.[15] *Bāshu* is by far his most highly acclaimed film among critics in Iran.[16] In order to situate my analysis, I will briefly outline the plot below.

The story centres on Bāshu, an eleven-year-old Arab boy living in the war zone, who loses his family to war early in the film. He hides in the back of a truck which heads across the country, ending up in the lush green environment of Gilan province in the north of Iran, by the Caspian Sea. A young woman named Nāei and her two children discover Bāshu, hiding in the corner of their rice field. Naei's husband is away, and she looks after her children on her own. Nāei attempts to communicate with the Arab boy without much success. She speaks Gilaki, a regional variety of Persian spoken in Gilan, which is difficult to comprehend for people from other parts of Iran. She is startled by the boy's very dark complexion that contrasts with the fair complexion of people of Gilan. Nāei shelters him and gradually begins a cross-lingual exchange of very basic words, captured in an improvised scene in the film (Figure 9.2).

When the other villagers find out about this stranger's presence, they approach Nāei to warn her about all the possible problematic consequences of sheltering the 'black stranger'. However, by refusing to do so, Nāei antagonizes the whole village. The village children intimidate the little stranger who cannot converse with them. In the end, Nāei's husband returns with an amputated arm, which he has lost while working in the war zone.

Early in the film, the spectators witness Bāshu losing his family to the war. Towards the end, Naei's husband comes back, and the film implicitly suggests that he has been to the war and lost his arm as a result. However, unlike nationalism would dictate, he is not treated as a war hero and instead Nāei reprimands him for having lost an arm. Beyzaie refuses to give in to the logic of othering on the basis of the war. The war and its manifestations in the use of violence are central to the inclusion of Bāshu, the Arab boy in the family of the nation, when Iran was at war with an Arab neighbour.

War and its logic of violence are rejected in multiple ways in *Bāshu, the Little Stranger*. Beyzaie asserts that 'war is the ultimate logic of the patriarchal world'.[17] The film recounts the horrors of the war that affected all Iranians regardless of

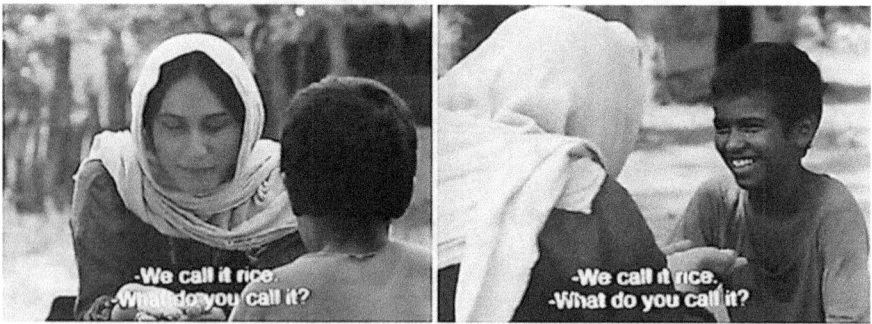

Figure 9.2 Nāei and Bāshu communicating across languages.

their geographical distance from the war zone. Like Bāshu, many Iranians became displaced as refugees in other parts of Iran. Throughout the film, Bāshu's traumatic recollections of the devastating effects of the war appear as his visions. During the period, the state propaganda machine was ceaselessly glorifying the war, Beyzaie's vision clearly constitutes a critique of the official discourse of the time. Just as importantly, despite its nationalistic overtone, the film did not fall into the trap of nationalistically demonizing the Iraqi people as 'the enemy of the nation'. Although as an Iranian nationalist Beyzaie highlights the centrality of the Persian language to the nation, his stranger, Bāshu is a speaker of Arabic, the language spoken in Iraq.

In the film, there is no direct mention of where Naei's husband is working. However, attention to mise en scène of one of the shots in the film provides the clue as to where he is. In the shot, Nāei is dictating a letter to Bāshu for her husband. In a 360-degree shot, the camera follows Naei, as she dictates the letter while hanging the clothes on the line. Behind Naei, in the background, the camera displays the route that the letter must pass through to reach her husband in the form of a series of 'backdrops'. This includes a letter box, road signs, soldiers around army vehicles and sandbag shelters. To the Iranian viewer this indicates that the letter is going to the war zone, but for a reason that later becomes clear Beyzaie refers to where the husband is only indirectly.

In the end, when the husband arrives home, with one arm amputated, Nāei asks him why he had to take such a job, to which he answers there was no other job available. When Bāshu is confronted with him and finds out that he is Naei's husband, he asks where he has been. The husband answers, 'I have been looking for you'. This hints to the Iranian viewer that the husband has been to the war zone, where Bāshu is from. To have directly mentioned that the war has caused the amputation that Nāei so laments and criticizes the husband for would have been unacceptable to the censors because such criticism of the 'holy defence' would not have been allowed.

The use of the Gilaki and Arabic languages, which are almost incomprehensible for the majority of Iranians, is an important feature of the film which is at one level about Iranian national identity. In Iran, the film was not subtitled. Apart from the small percentage of Iranians who speak Gilaki, other viewers are left to feel like Bāshu, strangers in their own country. Therefore, watching the film challenges the ethnocentric expectation of the Iranians from the privileged Persian nation core and unsettles them. Non-Iranians who follow the film through subtitles miss out on the intricacies of the relationship that is built gradually between Naei, Bāshu and the Iranian viewers. The subtitles fail to differentiate between Gilaki, Standard Persian, and Arabic as spoken on different occasions in the film.

The use of Gilaki in the film was an unprecedented move in Iranian cinema. Before *Bāshu, the Little Stranger*, films were almost always in Standard Persian, generally with a Tehrani accent. The nation-making efforts of the state promoted Standard Persian through the education system and the state-controlled mass media in contrast to the regional varieties of Persian that are derided and/or ridiculed. This attitude towards regional varieties of Persian still continues and is exemplified in Iranian jokes and also in the Iranian exiled community television channels. The disdain for people with a difference constituted a centre-periphery model that values the Persian-speaking nation core at the expense of peripheral ethnic groups who speak a language other than Persian or regional varieties of Persian. Beyzaie, by locating his nationalist story in a regional area and using a regional variety of the language, constituted a critique of this centre-periphery model that has continued after the revolution.

Until almost halfway through the film, the Iranian viewer is challenged to follow the story by catching words and phrases here and there, but more importantly, by the feelings evoked by pictures and the body language of the actors. Nevertheless, the masterly visual style of Beyzaie more than compensates for the lack of an easily comprehensible language. As the two main characters, Bāshu and Nāei begin to understand each other through an emotional connection, a similar bond is forged between the viewer and the two characters. Thus, within the confines of the film the use of Gilaki is normalized.

In an interview, Beyzaie states that he wanted to focus attention on Gilaki because, in his opinion, it is very close to the 'purer' origin of Standard Persian, i.e. the pre-Islamic Pahlavi language.[18] He laments the fact that no official institution exists to research varieties of Persian to extract the ancient Persian forms of the language. He adds, '[H]ow can anyone mock Gilaki, with its many pure words and combinations?'[19] Therefore, in the use of Gilaki, Beyzaie not only attempts to destabilize the ethnocentric views of the mainstream Iranian viewer but also reveals his nationalistic sentiments in search of purity of language and hence Iranian culture.

This search for purity is a response to the Western 'impurities' reinforced by the Shah's modernization ideology and the present regime's agenda. The nationalists have been advocating a return to an 'Iranian identity' rooted in the long Iranian pre-Islamic history. The phenomenon of searching for purity and authenticity is not unique to Iran and applies to all modern societies. Dean MacCannell asserts, 'modern man [sic] has been condemned to look elsewhere, everywhere, for his authenticity, to see if he can catch a glimpse of it in the simplicity, poverty, chastity or purity of others'.[20] While modernity may appear 'alienating, wasteful, violent, superficial, unstable and inauthentic', 'the authentic' has been imbued with the opposite of those adjectives.[21]

Erik Cohen argues that anthropologists in their search for 'the ethnographic present' 'seek to recapture the society and culture of the people who they study as these had been before the "contaminating" contact with the Western world'.[22] His criticism of anthropologists is not accurate within current practices of the discipline since a commitment to scrupulousness demands that 'the existing situation, as experienced by the ethnographer and subjects be fully explored for the reader'.[23] Although Beyzaie does not claim to have made a documentary or to have engaged in ethnographic representation, he explicitly declares that he means to analyse cultural norms.[24] However, there are no traces of 'modern life', such as a vehicle, a radio, or electricity in the village. This 'unrealistic' depiction of village life has been criticized by Iranian film critics.[25] While this could be due to romanticization, it could also be due to the filmmaker's desire to heighten the sense of isolation of the village which is necessary for the narrative to work.

In *Bāshu, the Little Stranger*, the exclusive use of Gilaki continues until the point when, after a fight with the local children, Bāshu picks up a book off the ground and begins to read out in Standard Persian, with some degree of difficulty. The famous passage from a grade school text reads 'Iran is our homeland. We are from the same water and soil. We are the children of Iran'. The fighting stops and the children begin to talk to him in Standard Persian for the first time. The children who would generally speak Gilaki, like Bāshu, speak Standard Persian almost as a second language. Bāshu's revelation that he can speak Persian and is also an Iranian paves the way for his acceptance among the children. Here, Beyzaie pragmatically begins to use Standard Persian, the official language used all over Iran, as a shared basis for a national identity. Apart from language, being from the same 'water and soil' or 'homeland' is a basis for Beyzaie's vision for the nation. Clearly, Beyzaie's ingredients of nationhood, i.e. shared homeland, language and history, constitute a contestation of the Islamic Republic's nation-building efforts with Islam as the basis for forming a nation.

Beyzaie pushes multilinguality and polyglossia, in Wahl's sense of the term, to a mythical level in his film. Nāei refers to Bāshu as 'a child of the sun and the Earth' for whom Nāei is the mother. According to Beyzaie, Nāei personifies the mythical goddess Nahid or Anahita.[26] Anahita is an Iranian pre-Islamic mythological goddess who is the protector of women and children on Earth. In the film, Nāei talks to the animals and understands them. Therefore, Nāei, the central character of the film, is the mother to the nation, to humanity and to all creatures, and recognizes no otherness.

This ethno-linguistic nuance is flattened in the exported version of the film which includes subtitles for all characters. However, when I saw *Bāshu, the Little Stranger* at Cinema Azadi in Tehran in 1989, it was screened without subtitles. The absence of subtitles for Persian viewers was a deliberate ploy by Beyzaie to defamiliarize Iran to his ethno-centric Persian viewers by forcing them off the centre of his narrative about the nation.

Beyzaie's representations of multilinguality have not been beyond criticism. Rahimieh critiques *Bāshu, the Little Stranger* for its penultimate scene depicting the return of Naei's husband.[27] In an argument that takes place between the husband and Bāshu in standard Persian, Nāei stands silently in the background. Rahimieh considers this argument and its ensuing formation of the new family, which now includes Bāshu, as re-establishing patriarchy. To Rahimieh the reinstallation of Naei's husband as the head of the family signals Naei's 'final submission to patriarchy' because she is excluded from the negotiations of power between the two male characters in standard Persian, the language of power. To Rahmieh, the nation is thus masculinized. I question Rahimieh's position by drawing attention to the ultimate scene of the film rather than the penultimate one. At the very end, when the farm is attacked by invading hogs and birds, it is Nāei and not either of the male characters who leads the charge to frighten them away. Her now-handicapped husband and Bāshu follow behind. Nāei is at the centre of the final shot of the film (Figure 9.3).

Figure 9.3 The ending of *Bāshu, the Little Stranger*.

Beyzaie's representation of Iran ironically validates the power relations between the Persian nation core and the peripheral nations within Iran. In the film, the Arab boy is protected by a Persian mother. He is the adopted child who is sheltered by the Persians, although he does not belong in the community. He finds acceptability partly through the use of Standard Persian. Beyzaie's own ethnocentricity is further exemplified in his choice of a *Persian* name for the *Arab* boy. Beyzaie states that the name Bāshu is a pseudo-derivative which he made up from the Persian root verb *Bāshidan* (to stay; referring to the ending of the story when Bāshu is accepted in the family and stays on).[28] Furthermore, Beyzaie claims that 'to Bāshu, Persian is not a foreign language'.[29] However, he contradicts himself later saying Bāshu's problem in reading the aforementioned Persian passage is like Persian children reading 'foreign' [generally English] school texts, which they can read with difficulty.[30] Beyzaie also states that his focus on Gilaki was because, in his opinion, it is very close to the 'purer' origin of Standard Persian, i.e. the pre-Islamic Pahlavi language.[31]

The Night Bus (Pourahmad 2007)

Kiumars Pourahmad, the director of *The Night Bus* (see Figure 9.4), trained in filmmaking before the revolution but found fame as a mainstream filmmaker making family dramas and comedies after the revolution. *The Night Bus* stands apart from any other film that he has made as it addresses the controversial topic of Iraqi prisoners of war, it features black and white cinematography, and its script was written by Pourahmad in collaboration with Asghar Farhadi, who became one of the most renowned Iranian filmmakers subsequently.

Set at the time of the Iran-Iraq war, the film is about the journey of two *Basijis*,[32] Issa and Emmad, who are transporting Iraqi POWs on a bus traveling away from the war zone. The two and the bus driver, Rahim, are the only Iranian characters in the film. The story takes place over 24 hours and has a simple plotline about the captors managing the unfolding situation on the bus while the driver drives the bus through unmarked routes to its destination. A sense of suspense and drama

Figure 9.4 *The Night Bus* (film poster).

in the film emanates from the aerial bombardment of the bus route, the driver losing the way, mine fields along the route and the captives' temporary success in taking control of the bus and their captors at one stage during the journey. Towards the end of the film, Emad, the older of the two captors dies off camera in a mine explosion, when he is forced to walk blindfolded into an area with mines, during the POWs' temporary takeover of the bus. The film ends with close-ups of Emad's widow as the driver and Issa struggle to tell her about his death.

Arabic is spoken by the POWs and in a broken manner by the Iranian captors in many parts of the film. The film is unique in how the Iraqi enemy is humanized in a rare instance of an Iranian film about the war. They are shown to be suffering in conditions that cannot be considered humane. They are blindfolded, their hands are tied behind their backs and their young captor, Issa, does not even allow them to talk to each other because their conversation frightens the captors, who are concerned about them plotting against the captors. The blindfold of one of the captives, Sirvan, is removed only when he reveals he has medical training to help a POW who on a few occasions has seizures.

As they advance in the journey, the two sides find more commonalities. Emad recognizes one of the POWs as Sirvan, an old Kurdish Iraqi friend, whom he met years ago on a trip to Turkey. The two then begin a conversation in English and Persian. The driver, Rahim, who witnesses the conversation between the two old friends, comments to Issa: 'Each one of these [POWs] is as close to us as these two [are to each other]. ... People have no enmity toward each other. ... However, those with [political] party leanings are different from us.' Praising the film, Vatanabadi asserts,

> In sharp contrast to the battle over boundary acted outside the bus, the interior of the bus becomes a space of heteroglossia, where the sharp dichotomies of the two nations at war are brought into question. The bus becomes a metaphoric microcosm of ethno-linguistic diversities and hybrids. The bus and the interaction among its passengers become a contrasting zone revealing cultural overlaps, dialogism, and interconnections among the 'enemies.'[33]

I would argue that the film is more complex than Vatanabadi suggests and that despite its attempt at universal humanism, it does not go far enough to question the rootedness of 'national' identities. The most revealing part of the film in this regard is when at some stage during the night journey, the Iraqis free themselves and disarm the Iranians. The tables are turned and the Iraqi leader of the group, who looks remarkably like Saddam Hussein (Figure 9.5), beats up both Iranians and surprisingly even Sirvan, the Iraqi Kurd POW for suggesting that the Iranians are

Figure 9.5 Saddam Hussein's lookalike leader in *The Night Bus*.

also humans. The rebellion is brought to an end by another Iraqi POW, Farouk, who sides with the Iranians and disarms the Iraqi ringleader. The reason which he gives for his switching sides is very telling. In answer to the Saddam lookalike leader who enquires, 'Aren't you our compatriot?' Farouk answers, 'My mother was from their country, my father from ours. Where is my country?' Thus, the logic of nationalist feelings based on one's biologic/ethnic roots is hardly challenged in this film. The divided loyalty of Farouk and Sirvan can be explained by the sense of socio-political belonging into which they were born. Sirvan is a Kurd whose ambiguity towards the Iraqi regime is what causes him to side with the Iranians. Similarly, Farouk's mixed parentage determines his leaning towards the Iranian captors.

The Night Bus at times lapses into the Iranian regime's so-called sacred defence cinema which are propagandist films about the internal and external armed conflicts of the Islamic Republic.[34] Distinct from war cinema elsewhere in the world, the 'sacred defence' films focus on the sacrifices of the Iranian volunteer soldiers, rather than any other aspect of the regime's armed conflicts. As Varzi states,

> After the inauguration of the War Films Bureau for the Sacred Defence, there was a clear move toward films that sought to represent the war as spiritual rather than military in character. This move [...] is marked by the presence of Islam, which serves to promote the war as Sacred Defence rather than a matter of cold-blooded strategy. [...] Films made after the Sacred Defence film programme was put into effect mark a clear departure from the earlier 'action' films by providing the space for the 'sacred' in defence. These films emphasize the role of martyrdom and belief in the action scenarios of the films.[35]

In those ideologically charged narratives about the so-called sacred defence, the fact that Iran was also the aggressor for parts of the eight-year war is thus disregarded. A major element of most 'sacred defence' films is the focus on the martyrs whose sacrifice for the 'Islamic' cause is foregrounded. Shots of the dog tag of a missing or martyred Basiji are common visual motifs of these films. *The Night Bus* uses one of the clichéd motifs of 'sacred defence' cinema, which is the close-up of the dog tag of Emad (Figure 9.6) who dies off camera because of a mine explosion. By glorifying the loss of life on one side of the war, *The Night Bus* cannot escape the logic of othering inherent in the state-sponsored cinema of war.

Nevertheless, what redeems the film is the foregrounding of the humanized Arabic-speaking captives and their suffering. In particular, their Arabic dialogue is made intelligible to Iranian audiences through the use of subtitles and in key moments of the film the captors are reminded of the suffering of the human fragility of the POWs when one of them has seizures. Thus, in various moments, captors and captives are shown to be linked in their common humanity.

Figure 9.6 Dog tag close-up.

Che (Hatamikia 2014)

Che (Figure 9.7) is the eighteenth feature film produced by Ibrahim Hatamikia (1961–), a prolific post-revolutionary Iranian filmmaker. Hatamikia began his career with documentaries in support of the war efforts of the Islamic Republic during the Iran-Iraq conflict in the 1980s. With increasing familiarity with filmmaking techniques and access to state funds available to those committed to the Islamic regime, Hatamikia was able to progress into making feature films. From his earliest films, he was a 'sacred defence' filmmaker, and gradually honed his filmmaking technique to become one of the most commercially successful directors, critically and commercially, inside Iran.

Che tells the story of an episode in the life of Mostafa Chamran (1932–81), a US-educated Iranian physicist turned revolutionary commander, in which he takes part in an internal conflict against the Kurdish rebels in the early 1980s. At the time, the mainly socialist Kurdish rebels were fighting for self-determination against the central Iranian regime. The biographical film denotes that Chamran has sacrificed his comfortable life in the United States and abandoned his wife and family in the 1970s to fulfil revolutionary causes in Iran and elsewhere. The bulk of the narrative, however, is concerned with the conflict in Paveh, a town in Iranian Kurdistan which is taken over by the rebels. Chamran, who has been assigned by Ayatollah Khomeini to the task of 'liberating' Paveh, arrives in the area and attempts to rally some Kurdish locals against the rebels. The film has a simple

Figure 9.7 *Che* (film poster).

narrative: Chamran arrives in Paveh, attempts unsuccessfully to negotiate with rebel leaders, and tries to lead the armed resistance against the rebels who control the town, and when his side appears to be on the verge of defeat, they miraculously succeed in gaining control of the town. The narrative timing is interrupted on a few occasions when Chamran has flashbacks about his family and particularly his children.

Kurdish is spoken in a few scenes in the film. In the first, the viewer sees Chamran speaking in a hospital to Sirvan, a local man who has been injured in the conflict apparently while fighting on the side of the central government. Chamran encourages the man to fight on his side. As he is leaving the room, he places a flower that he was holding in his hand on Sirvan's gun placed on Sirvan's hospital bed. When Chamran leaves the room, Sirvan's wife, Hana, who is holding her infant in her arms, picks up the flower and throws it away. Hana, then hands her husband the baby, kneels in front of him and starts to address him in Kurdish in the first instance of the use of the language in a dialogue in the film. The camera captures Hana's tearful face in close-up from Sirvan's point of view (Figure 9.8) as

Figure 9.8 Hana pleading with Sirvan.

she pleads with him to think of their baby and not to risk his life, to no avail. Non-diegetic sentimental tune is played in the background, and the scene is subtitled. While this conversation and many other short sections in Kurdish are subtitled, there is hardly any need for it as the visual language, the soundtrack and the tone of speech convey the meaning.

The two Kurdish characters, Sirvan and Hana, feature again in the film where they need the protection of Chamran and his fellow Persian speakers. In one scene, when the Basiji commander is running out of options, he hands guns to women including Hana. Looking at the gun, Hana hands it back to the Basiji commander saying she does not wish to use it. In another related scene, her husband, Sirvan, appears once again injured near the end of the film as he is about to be airlifted out of the area. Through the three scenes Sirvan and Hana, and, by extension, the Kurds, are contrasted with the able-bodied and masculine fighters on the Iranian regime's side. They are shown to be unable to fight on the 'righteous' side of the conflict from the filmmaker's perspective.

The representation of the phallic symbol of the machine gun separates the two sides from each other very early in the film. As the opening titles appear, the camera captures a bird's-eye view of a large city square with street markets and political gatherings in the town of Paveh which is under Kurdish rebels' control. Guns appear everywhere with many Kurds appearing to be examining them as goods in the market. On three occasions, the rebels shoot the guns in the air, two of which are for no apparent reasons while the third is fired as two men appear to be in a scuffle over it, while others in Kurdish garb appear to be wrestling with each other (Figure 9.9). The town and its people appear out of control with no authority in charge. Thus, the guns appear as dangerous and threatening in the hands of the Kurds in contrast to the Persian Basijis in whose hands the guns are suggested to belong.

Figure 9.9 Kurds scuffling over a gun as it is fired in the air (top right-hand corner).

The second time Kurdish is spoken in the film in a sequence when Chamran is going to a pre-arranged meeting to negotiate with the rebels. He is being led there by Latifi, a Kurd who has arranged the meeting. As Chamran and his companions pass through a narrow valley, they are shouted at in Kurdish, one or two words each time, from above by the rebels who fire warning shots at them intermittently. Chamran's companions blame Latifi for having deceived them, but when they drop their guns, the shooting ends and Chamran is led to meet a rebel leader. The negotiation between the two is unsuccessful.

The film ends with Chamran 'freeing' the town of Paveh from the rebels rather miraculously as they are outnumbered and outgunned. In the final shots in Paveh, Chamran emerges from a building; he and his *basiji* companions embrace each other as they shed tears of joy. Hana is hugging her child as she is surrounded by other Kurdish women and wounded men. The film establishes Kurdish speakers and Kurds, by extension, as feminized, emasculated and in need of protection (Hana and Sirvan) or out of control, dangerous and threatening (the rebels). Here, gender is added to ethnicity and language to build the Kurd as the 'Other'. Guns are also used in the film as phallic symbols representing the able-bodied masculine agency of Chamran and his companions protecting the feminized/emasculated disabled Kurds from themselves. The Persian centre is thus portrayed as the saviour of the peripheral peoples in Iran.

Conclusion

I raised a question early in this chapter about whether the recent phenomenon of multilinguality in Iranian cinema can be interpreted as a trend away from othering of speakers of regional languages or dialects in cinema. In the films that I saw at the Fajr Festival in 2003, to which I referred in the introduction of this chapter, multilinguality is not integral to the storylines as one could remove the short segments in the regional languages or dialects with no disruption to the narratives. In the two recent films that I analysed, multilinguality does not seem to disrupt the deep-rooted 'othering' of speakers of regional languages in Iran. In this sense, *Bāshu, the Little Stranger* remains seminal in its ethno-linguistically significant representation of Iran.

Let us now return to Jamalzadeh's 'Fārsi Shekar Ast' (Persian Is Sugar, 1921), which I recounted at the start of the chapter. The narrator's recognition of the characters in the story as Iranians in this allegorical short story is based on his acknowledgement of them speaking Persian, a language which Jamalzadeh considers sweet as sugar, as the title of the story denotes. Hence, in a similar way to Beyzaie, for Jamalzadeh, Persian language is central to Iranian identity. In a broader perspective, as testified by Meskub as well as Fischer and Abedi,[36] to Iranian intellectuals in general the centrality of the Persian language as the basis for an Iranian identity is unquestionable. Non-Persians are included by the Persians in the allegories of the nation not as equals but out of 'compassion': a little Arab war refugee to be adopted or the wounded/helpless Kurds to be rescued by the Persian nation core. While *Bāshu, the Little Stranger* is certainly progressive in its inclusiveness, there is still some way to go in Iranian cinema for it to problematize Persian speakers' ethnocentricity at a fundamental level.

Notes

1. Jamalzadeh, *Yeki Bud*.
2. This chapter excludes a discussion of films that include European languages and focuses only on languages spoken within Iran.
3. Wahl. 'Discovering a Genre', 336.
4. Ibid., 336–8.
5. Ibid., 338.
6. Shochat and Stam, 'Cinema after', 36.
7. Ibid., 53.
8. Naficy, *Accented Cinema* 51–2.
9. Amani, 'Karbord-e Zabanha-ye', 44.
10. CIA Factbook (2017).
11. Notable exceptions include films that featured the actors Arham Sadr or Nosratollah Vahdat, who spoke with Isfahani dialect and were protagonists in the film.
12. Honarmand, *Impact of*, 285.
13. Abrahamian, *Iran Between*, 475.
14. Golmakani, 'New Times', 21.
15. Examples include *Stranger and the Fog, The Crow, Ballad of Tara, Killing Mad Dogs*.
16. Golmakani, 'New Times', 22.
17. Qukasiyan, *Goftogu*, 228.
18. Qukasiyan, *Goftogu*, 226–7.
19. Ibid., 224.
20. MacCannell, *Tourist: A New*, 41.

21 Ibid., 2.
22 Cohen, 'Authenticity and Commoditisation', 375.
23 Marcus and Fischer, *Anthropology as Cultural*, 116.
24 Jafarinejad, 'Goftogu ba Bahram', 48.
25 Kavousi, 'Bashu Gharibeh', 71; Eshqi, 'Beyzaie va Hāfezeh-ye', 450.
26 Qukasiyan, *Goftogu*, 263.
27 Rahimieh, 'Marking Gender'.
28 Jafarinejad, 'Goftogu ba Bahram,' 50.
29 Qukasian, *Goftogu,* 242.
30 Ibid., 242.
31 Ibid., 226–7.
32 A member of the ideologically committed paramilitary force called *Basij* which was founded by Ayatollah Khomeini in 1979.
33 Vatanabadi, 'Narratives of Border', 27.
34 Zeydabadi-Nejad, *Politics of Iranian*, Chapters 2 and 3.
35 Varzi, 'Ghost in the Machine', 157.
36 See Meskub, 'Iranian Nationality' and Fischer and Abedi, *Debating Muslims*.

Bibliography

Abrahamian, E. *Iran: Between Two Revolutions*. Princeton: PUP, 1982.
Ale Ahmad, J. *Gharbzadegi*. Tehran: Jam'e Daran, 1962.
Amani, M. 'Kārbord-e Zabānhā-ye Mahalli dar Iran'. *Nāmeh Olum-e Ejtemāei*. Vol. 12. No. 12 (Autumn 1998). Pp. 43–50.
CIA Factbook (2017). *Iran*. Online: https://www.cia.gov/the-world-factbook/countries/iran/. (Accessed 5 December 2017).
Cohen, Erik. 'Authenticity and Commoditisation in Tourism'. *AOTR*. Vol. 15 (1988). Pp. 371–86.
Eshqi, Behzad. 'Beyzaie Va Hāfeze-ye Tārikhi'. In *Majmu'eh Maqālāt dar Naqd va Mo'arrefi Āsār-e Bahram Beyzaie*. Ed. Zaven Qukasiyan. Tehran: Āgah, 1989.
Fischer, M. and M. Abedi. *Debating Muslims: Cultural Dialogues in Postmodernity and Tradition*. Madison: University of Wisconsin Press, 1990.
Gomakani, Houshang. 'New times, Same Problems'. *Index on Censorship*. Vol. 21. No. 3 (1992). Pp. 19–22.
Honarmand, Saeed. *The Impact of the Modernity Discourse on Persian Fiction*. Ohio: OUP, 2011.
Jafarinejad, Sharam. 'Goftogu ba Bahram Beyzaie: Gharibeh-ei dar pe-ye Tafāhom'. *Film*. Vol. 7. No. 87 (March 1990). Pp. 44–51.
Jamalzadeh, M., *Yeki Bud, Yeki Nabud*. Tehran: Nashr-e Electronik-e Bahman, 2000.
Kavousi, H. 'Bāshu, Gharibeh-ye kuchak va Nāei Histerik-e Bozorg'. *Film*. Vol. 9. No. 115 (November 1991). Pp. 71–2.
MacCannell, Dean. *The Tourist: A New Theory of Leisure Class*. New York: Shocken Books, 1976.
Marcus, G. and M. Fischer. *Anthropology as Cultural Critique: An Experimental Moment in the Human Sciences*. Second Edition. Chicago: University of Chicago Press, 1999.
Meskub, S. 'Iranian Nationality Vis-à-vis Language and History'. In *Iranian Nationality and the Persian Language*. Ed. J. R. Perry. Washington, DC: Mage Publishers, 1992.

Naficy, H. *An Accented Cinema: Eexilic and Diasporic Filmmaking*. Princeton: Princeton University Press, 2001.
Qukasiyan, Z. *Goftogu ba Bahram Beyzaie*. Tehran: Āgah, 1993.
Rahimieh, N. 'Marking Gender and Difference in the Myth of the Nation: "Bāshu", a Post-Revolutionary Iranian Film'. In *The New Iranian Cinema: Politics, Representation and Identity*. Ed. Richard Tapper. London: IB Tauris, 2002. Pp. 238–53.
Shochat, Ella and Robert Stam. 'The Cinema after Babel: Language, Difference, Power'. *Screen*. Vol. 26. No. 3–4 (May–August 1985). Pp. 35–58.
Varzi, R. 'A Ghost in the Machine: The Cinema of the Iranian Sacred Defence'. In *The New Iranian Cinema: Politics, Representation and Identity*. Ed. Richard Tapper. London: I.B. Tauris, 2002.
Vatanabadi, S. 'Narratives of Border and beyond'. In *Moments of Silence: Authenticity in the Cultural Expressions of the Iran-Iraq War, 1980–1988*. Ed. Arta Khakpour, Mohammad Mehdi Khorrami and Shouleh Vatanabadi. New York: New York University Press, 2016.
Wahl, Chris. 'Discovering a Genre: The Polyglot Film'. In *Shifting Landscapes: Film and Media in European Context*. Ed. Miyase Christensen and Nezih Erdogan. Cambridge: Cambridge Scholars Publishing, 2009.
Zeydabadi-Nejad, Saeed. *The Politics of Iranian Cinema*. London and New York: Routledge, 2010.

Chapter 10

LITTLE STRANGERS: REPRESENTATIONS OF
DISPLACED YOUTH IN IRANIAN NEW WAVE CINEMA

Nina Khamsy

Introduction

Like the masterpiece *Bāshu, the Little Stranger* (1985), many Iranian films have depicted Iran's cultural and linguistic diversity through the vantage point of 'little strangers'. Set during the Iran-Iraq war, the film emblematically tells the story of an Arab Iranian boy from the south of Iran fleeing to the north of the country, where he is eventually adopted by a new family. I rely on this film to analyse the positions of other young, displaced characters in Iranian cinema. In Jafar Panahi's *The White Balloon* (1996), a young balloon-selling Afghan boy is the character who ultimately helps the protagonist, the little girl, to retrieve the banknote she has dropped, and no one else has managed to retrieve it. The lives of young Kurds have also been featured in Samira Makhmalbaf's *Blackboards* (2000) that depicts a group of Kurdish teachers walking near the Iraqi border with blackboards strapped to their backs, looking for students. Kurdish-Iranian filmmaker Bahman Ghobadi has also made numerous films to depict the struggles of Kurds from the perspectives of displaced youth. Arab Iranians have also been depicted in multiple films, such as *Iron Island* (2005) by Mohamad Rasoulof, which features a group of Iranians and Arab Iranians living on a mothballed oil tanker in the Persian Gulf. More recently, Iranian Afghan filmmaker Navid Mahmoudi's *A Few Cubic Meters of Love* (2014) is the story of the forbidden love between an Iranian boy and an Afghan girl working in a factory in a shantytown on the outskirts of Tehran. It portrays the discriminations and exclusions of Afghans in Iran which negatively impacts Iranians as well, and the struggle of the new generations to overcome them. In Majid Majidi's *Sun Children* (2020), the young Iranian protagonist from an impoverished family shares a genuine friendship with another street child of Afghan origins and his older sister who sell items in Tehran subway to support their family.

It is widely recognized that child actors and children-related themes were among the main components of the New Wave in Iranian filmmaking and thus form a thematic category.[1] A common, if unsatisfactory, explanation of this significant presence has been to link it with the imposition of authorities' regulations following the 1979 Revolution. The prohibition to depict intimate relationships between non-married couples is said to be the reason which led filmmakers to resort to pre-gendered characters to tell their stories. Yet Iranian cinema scholars have linked this presence not merely to the directors' socio-political considerations and regulatory obligations but also to their stylistic choices ingrained in a long-term Persian tradition and inspired by their individual sensitivities.[2] Such an approach avoids the trap of categorizing filmmakers' actions as only being directed against state's power.

Questions of the representation of displaced youth are brought to the forefront at a time when domestic and transnational migration is increasing and when meaningful new Iranian films featuring displaced children are released. While economic hardship and declining living conditions in rural areas force people to migrate to cities where socio-economic gaps are further widening,[3] second-generation refugees – particularly Afghans – form an ever-expanding part of Iran's socio-economic landscape due to continuous cycles of political conflicts and natural disasters in the region.[4] These social, economic and political issues have led to the production of many recent films by established and young filmmakers who examine different aspects of the lives of displaced youths. Being conscious of the significance of these films, this chapter engages with some of these films by comparing the representation of displaced children and young adolescent heroes in Iranian post-revolutionary New Wave films.

The purpose at one level is to answer the following questions: How do these latest productions relate to Beyzaie's way of dealing with children and dislocation since the 1970s? How do filmmakers map diversity onto the bodies of little strangers? And, in turn, what does the representation of little strangers tell us about the evolution of the Iranian New Wave in the last four decades? However, while attempting to answer these questions, I will also explore how cinematic language is used in these films to represent children, displacement, and the nation. These three concepts are problematic and ambiguous. I argue for the need to overcome the trap of political under- and over-interpretation of child figures.[5] Children are not used only to represent a biological age-bound category or to bypass the Islamic Republic's restrictions on gender relations on screen. Recognizing the polysemy of the figure of the child opens the field of enquiry to wider horizons and problematizes nationalistic understandings of displacement.

The national 'Self' is commonly held as symbolic figure of domestic genealogies to indicate its stable and continuous nature (foreigners 'adopting' countries that are not these foreigners' native home).[6] Usual metaphors of the nation draw on a *natural* jargon between the nation and its children. Botanical terminologies referring to 'roots' and 'uprootedness' are anchored in the 'national order of things' described by Malkki,[7] whereby the borders of nation states constitute a natural order and crossing them is pathological. In representing displaced children, filmmakers produce discourses on what should or should not constitute the nation, which, in turn, challenge or reproduce exclusion. They can complicate our understanding of what is deemed 'natural' and 'national', and what is considered the 'Self' and what 'Other'.

The Persian traditions of poetry and images, which are themselves constantly reinvented, are key for an interpretation that moves beyond the political over-interpretation and provide an alternative – Persian – repertoire that transcends nationalistic discourses. As they have already been present in Iranian cinema before the Revolution, children's presence is more of a sign of continuity rather than rupture in Iranian cultural productions. Yet, at the core of the interpretation of children's representation, there is a fruitful ambiguity, which makes it oscillate between an allegory and a social reality. In engaging with this ambiguity, filmmakers can draw on the form and content of Iranian poetic tradition. At one level, they play with the open nature of their narrative to avoid closed and obvious messages. At another, they depict displacement, belonging and longing, both within and outside Iran, which are notions that are strongly situated within Persian poetic tradition.

The study of 'little strangers' opens a path for decentring Persian ethnocentrism and engaging with critical studies on youth culture in Iran. In Saeed Zeydabadi-Nejad, 'Linguistic minorities in Iran are neither "strangers" nor "little". But in the culture in which we Persian speakers have grown up, they are considered so.'[8] In her study on second-generation Afghans in Iran, Zuzanna Olszewska notes that English-language literature on youth culture in Iran excessively focuses on urban, middle-class, mostly secular youth and on the 'social phenomena that are interpreted as acts of resistance to and rebellion against the political establishment and the moral order it espouses'.[9] Wellman also notes that 'the people in Iran we best understand are the urban, secular, middle – or upper-middle-class youth who take to the streets in protest of the state or who pursue creative self-expression despite its strictures'.[10] A similar trend in the literature tends to reduce the music produced in Iran to a narrow discourse of 'resistance' and 'freedom'.[11] Little strangers invite us to question the 'center' and the 'margins'. As shown by Till Mostowlansky, the ways we look at borderlands and the people who inhabit them can challenge 'assumptions about which places are central and which are marginal within these spaces and how they are connected to or detached from the world beyond'.[12] For instance, in defining his objects of study of Karimabad in northern Pakistan and Khorog in eastern Tajikistan – borderlands in both countries – as 'marginal hubs', Mostowlanski indicates 'that their status is ambivalent and relational'.[13] What counts is 'who renders them both central and marginal from different vantage points and at different points in time'.[14] Displaced children in Iranian New Wave cinema can highlight such changes in time.

To illustrate my argument, I begin by analysing the constitutive role afforded to children and displacement in New Wave Iranian cinema over the last four decades. I then move on to analyse *Bāshu* (completed in December 1985, released in 1989) by Bahram Beyzaie, *Baran* (2001) by Majid Majidi (1959–) and *Sonita* (2016) Rokhsareh Ghaemmaghami (1976–). The two latter films also represent the figure of the displaced child but relate to *Bāshu* in different ways. They focus on the links between Afghans, Iranians and the idea of the nation. *Baran* (2001), features the love of Lateef, an Azari teenager working on a construction site on the outskirts of Tehran,[15] for an Afghan worker. *Sonita* (2016) is the story of a Tehran-based teenage Afghan refugee, who attempts to fulfil her full potential as a singer and flee from a forced marriage with the help of the film director. These three films put in sharper focus the important socio-economic place these young characters occupy in Iranian society.

Children of the multi-ethnic nation

Iranian films representing cultural diversity in Iran give insights into the elements that led some to be perceived as 'insiders' and others as 'outsiders'. This dichotomy can be understood against the grid of the 'national order of things' which is held as the natural, self-evident configuration. While 'real' nations are supposed to be static and delimited by fixed borders,[16] Iran is a multi-ethnic and multilinguistic country with rich transnational ties stemming from the Persian civilization at large.[17] Iran shares economic, religious, cultural, linguistic and historical links with today's Azerbaijan, Iraq, Turkey, Afghanistan and Pakistan. As a result of historical regional mobility, and conflicts and natural disasters since the 1970s, refugees and migrants, mainly from Iraq and Afghanistan, form an important portion of Iran's population. Iraqi immigration intensified with Kurdish inflows after Saddam Hussein and Shah's agreement in 1975, Iran-Iraq war (1980–8), the first Golf war in 1991 and the American invasion in 2003.[18]

Afghan immigration to Iran also intensified since the late 1970s,[19] particularly with Shi'i and Hazara population targeted by the widespread violence during the civil conflict (1992–6), the Taliban rule (1996–2001) and the ongoing violence during the NATO American-led intervention (2001–21). Iran's policies towards Afghan refugees have frequently shifted, from a period of 'open doors', to that of restrictions, keeping Afghan labour at a minimum cost 'in an atmosphere of both official and popular xenophobia'.[20]

In depicting social issues of their time, some New Wave directors have played an important role in bringing attention to the ongoing issue of the lack of a proper socio-legal framework to integrate those who have been excluded from citizenship. This is, for instance, significant for people of Afghan origin as many Afghans are still considered non-Iranian although they were born on Iranian soil. These films, therefore, deal with real situations and often subvert the institutional exclusion and othering of some groups of people by displaying the ability of people to forge ties and join in practices across boundaries, leading individuals to imagine themselves across racial, ethnic or civilizational divisions.[21] In their attempts to go beyond the 'insiders'/'outsiders' dichotomy, Iranian New Wave filmmakers have also featured displaced children and adolescents in a number of films that deserve examination.

In the Iranian context, the nationalistic discourse selects the main historical sources of identity to determine who is considered the 'insider'. Examined in its most basic form, this category is mainly built against what ought not to be

Iranian: not Arab but Persian, not Islamic Sunnite but Shiʻi. The 'Indo-Europeanist' linguistic discourse began to take shape in Europe towards the end of the eighteenth century and began to be adopted in Iran over time, being instrumental to the construction of the idea of Iran as a nation state.[22] Iranian nationalism of the early twentieth century coincided with the construction and hierarchization of its ethnicities. Displaced children and adolescents are, thus, meaningful tropes to build a discourse on the relationship between the Iranian nation and its children. Even more so as the national 'Self' conveys domestic genealogies to indicate its stable and continuous nature.[23] With the Iranian nationalism of the 1920s and 1930s, the production of Persian poems as well as patriotic discourses of *vatan* (the Iranian 'patry') increased, in which Iran was conceptualized either as a beloved or a mother.[24] The figure of the child is then used to complicate discourses based on biological and botanical metaphors to determine who is part of the nation and who is not.

Displacement has a particular place in Persian literature. Classical Persian poetry is centred around the key tension of the lover's separation from and longing for the beloved. Sufi (mystic) poetry, especially, is like a great cultural capital based on which Iranians can portray and express their feelings of belonging and exile. Perhaps most famously, thirteenth-century Sufi poet Jalāl ad-Dīn Muhammad Rūmī's *Nei-nāmeh* (Reed's Account) is an example of a poem expressing the pain of separation and longing for reunification. In the poem of Rūmī, who was himself born in Balkh, present-day Afghanistan, the reed laments its separation from the reedbed. According to Hamid Naficy, the poem 'provides the paradigmatic worldview and language of exile, embodying a variety of journeys, returns, and unifications'.[25]

The role of media is central in narrating the idea of the nation and building the national identity. For Benedict Anderson, 'nation-ness is the most universally legitimate value in the political life of our time'.[26] Members of modern nations cannot possibly know all their fellow members, yet they maintain an image of their communion.[27] In his study, Anderson analyses how printed media underlies the concept of a nation, as the imagined community emerges with a common language and discourse that is generated from the use of the printing press. Michael Billig draws on Anderson and argues that the tendency to understand nationalism within a political framework that highlights separatism or ethnic division ignores the 'banal' side of nationalism, embedded in nationalist practices of ritual and everyday life.[28] Films showing everyday interactions between individuals who are portrayed as being of different ethnicities can thus subvert or preserve a desired or imagined idea of a nation. To link nation and cinema conceptually, I acknowledge the synergy existing between the socio-political organization and culture. This approach follows the example of the film scholar Susan Hayward who writes:

> [F]ilm functions as a cultural articulation of a nation (even if it subverts it, it still addresses/reflects it, albeit negatively or oppositionally) [...]. In this way, cinema – a 'national' cinema – is ineluctably 'reduced' to a series of enunciations that reverberate around two fundamental concepts: identity and difference.[29]

While the space in this paper does not allow for the in-depth analysis that theories of nationalism and the case of Iranian nationalism deserve, what is of importance is that cinema participates in maintaining an image of the nation's imagined communion. In the words of Fariba Adelkhah, the study of travel, margins and borders questions the imperturbable representations that society draws of itself as Iranian, Shiite and authentic (*asil*). To paraphrase her, this is because the historical and social contexts that have been used to create difference have done so in a paradoxical way that enable us to imagine Iranian history differently.[30] Displaced children and adolescents represent allegories of a multi-ethnic nation, tell stories about their everyday struggles for integration and reflect on the hierarchization of who is the 'Self' and who is the 'Other'.

Interpreting children's cinema

With Bahram Beyzaie and other prominent directors, themes revolving around children and actors became prevalent in the Iranian New Wave filmmaking that had begun in the 1960s. While cultural and cinematic movements from abroad, including French New Wave and Italian neorealism inspired and influenced the new cinema,[31] award-winning pre-revolutionary films with children include Beyzaie's *Journey* (1972), Kiarostami's *The Traveller* (1974) and Amir Naderi's *Harmonica* (1974). New films, distinct in their sophistication in filmmaking style and their socially conscious tone, were formulating a subtle critique of the difficulties Iran was facing under the Pahlavi regime and illustrated the complexities of their social and political contexts.[32] This style, marked by the fragmentation of boundaries between the fictional and the every day, 'between temporal and spatial boundaries', has become an emblem of art house Iranian cinema.[33] The presence of non-professional actors who often perform their own role in life has also led to what Naficy refers to as the 'dense intertextuality and self-referentiality of Iranian art movies: one film spawns another'.[34] Filmmakers used children and amateur actors as central characters to expose social reality. Both types of actors share something unique and precious: they are not film stars but ordinary people and can, therefore, disseminate the narrative's values more authentically and persuasively,[35] exposing the audience to a unique performance owing to the ephemeral nature of these characters. However, whereas amateur actors lose their amateurism and ordinariness once they have appeared on screen, the meanings attached to a child in films' narrative remain manifold, particularly because the films can be designed to address children and adults and can, thus, be viewed from several angles.

There are many ways children can appear on screen. Naficy cites two Iranian critics who divide children's films into four categories.[36] It includes films *for* children, films *about* children, films in which children are *substitutes* for adults or a *pretext* for dealing with adult issues, and films with children acting in them. This typology is a useful starting point as most films with children protagonists relate to one or some of these categories. Films in which children are *substitutes* for adults or a *pretext* for dealing with adult issues (third category) have most often been associated with the post-revolutionary period due to the new set of regulations on cinema that restrict the representation of non-married men and women's intimate contacts.[37] However, one should be aware that as significant conceptual figures, they may and are often used to reflect on discourses of nationhood, belonging and heroism or represent a dialogue with a literary tradition rather than just be there to bypass regulations.

A child is defined as someone between the stages of birth and puberty. Cinematically, however, the definition is more open, offering many grounds for interpreting children's filmic representations. Children can be approached as (passive) objects of socialization and cultural transmission by focusing on mechanisms through which culture passes between generations or as (active) members of society with a determinant role in socializing processes.[38] Media scholars have warned against seeing kids primarily as passive victims and 'focus[ing] on a single element of media culture [...] presumed to affect all children in the same way'.[39] For Karen Lurz, 'the child and childhood, and indeed children themselves, occupy a situation in which they are "other": other to the supposedly rational, civilized, "grown up" human animal that is the adult'.[40] An accurate reading of children in cinematic representations and the 'otherness' they represent needs to remain attentive to cross-cultural distinctions and historical and social contexts since children experience diverse kinds of childhood in different societies. What is particularly relevant is that the figure of displaced children who geographically or socially move from one context to another may reveal embodied social norms of the (ancestral) original place and trigger questions about the status quo of the new place they inhabit.

Bahram Beyzaie is one of the first Iranian directors to have children in leading roles prior to the 1979 revolution, and he is a major reference for the popularization of this type of film. His *Uncle Moustache* (1970) is one of the first films featuring children in cinema and conveying serious cultural intentions through these characters.[41] While, as specified above, films can be *for* or *about* children, questions remain as to whether children are represented as social agents.[42] The following analysis of *Uncle Moustache* (1970) is illustrative of the active role that Beyzaie gives to his young characters. Moreover, it shows the ambiguity in qualifying a film as being *about* children or a *pretext* for dealing with adult issues, already before the Islamic Revolution.

Bahram Beyzaie's twenty-nine-minute film *Uncle Moustache* deals with the confrontation between a retired middle-aged man and a group of young boys who disturb his peace. The film takes a comic tone, tapping into the genre of melodrama. The man wishes to stay in his house, alone, far from the city but is disrupted by the noise of a large group of enthusiastic young boys who organize a football contest next to his house. This is followed by a period of confrontation between the man and the children who call him 'Uncle Moustache' (*Amu Sibilu*) to mock him for his large handlebar moustache, which, as Talajooy states, can be interpreted as a marque of masculinity and attachment to society's old-fashioned values.[43] Indeed, he seems to cherish his individual self and has a flourishing ego.

Gradually, the man gets more and more frustrated by the children whom he considers as a source of annoyance, but the children persist in gathering and playing football and finally break one of his windows. He explodes with rage and chases them until one of the boys falls and gets injured. When the children leave, Uncle Moustache feels guilty to have caused them harm. He buys a ball and goes to the hospital to reconcile with the children. The film exemplifies the way children are used to disrupt conformism and can push society forward, for example by imposing interactions leading to better mutual understanding. The middle-aged man can represent the ideals of an individualistic society, where neighbours wish to live isolated and pursue their own desires selfishly. Their persistent presence puts him on the defensive side, and he wants to chase them to protect his own identity and way of living. The harmonious end is suggestive of hope: after the confrontation, Uncle Moustache is the one questioning his exclusionary behaviours, showing that this step is needed to leave together in conviviality.

As in Persian poetry, what is seen by the eyes is not the primary focal point. In this sense, within the category of films *about* children in post-revolutionary period, the films in which children do not appear on screen but are meaningfully evoked, 'hors-champs', can also be included. In Kiarostami's *A Taste of Cherry* (1997), the protagonist Mr Badi'i who is planning to commit suicide, is looking for someone to bury him correctly after his suicide. This means he wants to abide by the religious rituals according to which the burial should be done on the day of death. The Persian-speaking Mr Badi'i drives through a mountainous region on the outskirts of the city where construction sites abound. He approaches a series of men who all seem to be from poor social backgrounds and are involved in menial work. On the way, he encounters different Iranian ethnic groups and a few end up in the car – a young Iranian Kurd (army conscript), a young Afghan (seminary student) and a middle-aged Iranian Turk. His generous financial offers are all rejected by the individuals he accosts on religious and legal grounds. Finally, the insistence pays off and the Iranian Turk accepts. However, the Iranian Turk tries to dissuade Mr Badi'i and shares the story of his own suicide attempt that was hampered by the revelation of the taste of a cherry, the sunshine and the landscape brought to him, notably, by a kid. He had planned to hang himself from a cherry tree, but when about to commit the act, the children and his wife asked him to help them pick cherries. Children, therefore, play an implicit role in shaking Mr Badi'i's determination to end his life.

Children in Iranian New Wave cinema

The number of films with child protagonists increased after the 1979 revolution. To cite just a few, Naderi's *The Runner* (1984) featured a determined orphan child who struggled to win a race. Abbas Kiarostami's *Where Is the Friend's House?* which was made in 1986–7 and released in 1988, also has a child protagonist who takes a long journey to return his classmate's notebook to him to save him from being expelled from school. Made in 1985 and released in 1989, Beyzaie's

Bāshu, the Little Stranger was also the result of a similar approach with variations that were specific to Beyzaie. Similarly at international level, the 1980s and 1990s marked a period when many child-centred films came to the screen.[44] Scholars have examined these films and the reasons for their proliferation in the 1980s and 1990s from different angles but displaced children as a recurring thematic cycle have not been scrutinized so far.

Under the previous regime, many thinkers, both religious and secular, were against what they considered to be an immoral cinema that facilitated what they perceived to be an obsession with Westernization. With the establishment of the Islamic Republic in 1979, the Iranian film industry came to a halt, but from 1982, the newly established Farabi Cinema Foundation and the film office of the Ministry of Culture and Islamic Guidance took numerous measures to revitalize the film industry and shape its regulations according to their standards. The new officials emphasized the role of the director as the creative force behind a film, which benefitted the art cinema and festival films.[45] For Hamid Sadr, child-centred films allow 'the projection of ideas about what people should ideally be like'.[46] The author links children's presence to the emerging desire to 'renegotiate an image of Iranian society' after the Iran-Iraq war (1980–8) that is to give a more positive image of this society through children.[47] Another related aspect, according to him, is the urgency of the subject due to censorship. While criticism about the social realities in Iran both before and after the Islamic Revolution was never tolerated, the censorship rules became stricter after the revolution. The state issued laws that imposed an Islamic dress code on women and men in films and prohibited them from demonstrating any signs of sensual or sexual acts.[48] Sadr's conception of children in these films is thus akin to the one arguing that they are mainly *substitutes* for adults or a *pretext* for dealing with adult issues.

Zeydabadi-Nejad's complementary explanation for the presence of children in films is that 'rather than a conscious decision on the part of filmmakers or the MCIG', this presence was 'necessitated by factors such as funding and stylistic considerations',.[49] He explains that since the beginning of the New Wave in the 1960s, *Kānun-e Parvaresh-e Fekri-e Kudakān va Nojavānān* (the Institute for the Intellectual Development of Children and Young Adults) was one of the major funders of child-centred films. Since the Institute was not under strict control of the government, this financial support was important for secular filmmakers missing access to other governmental sources.[50] The revolution did not bring major changes to the Institute's responsibilities and funding activities as most of its creative personnel and its mission statement remained unchanged, but its main target was now Islamization.[51] The Institute produced three of the most important child-centred films of the 1980s: *The Runner*, *Bāshu, the Little Stranger*, and *Where Is the Friend's Home?*. In addition to the Institute and other institutions such as the Farabi Cinema Foundation, which was established in 1983, the Iranian state TV has also been a key source of influence before and after the revolution with some successful examples of children's series and films, both for pre-school and school ages as well as young adults.[52] During the presidency of reformist Mohammad Khatami (1997–2005), his moderate views on the regulation of art and culture allowed space for more children cinema and Majid Majidi's *Children of Heaven* (2000) became the first ever Oscar nominated film from Iran. However, according to Hosseini-Shakib, who draws on Sadr's substitution theory, the metaphorical levels decrease due to the relative freedom felt by the artists.[53] She explains that with the easing of many monitory processes in the 2000s, 'more direct ways of dealing with social issues emerged that put an end to the symbolism and poetic realism of 1990s children cinema'. She further argues that 'Khatami's pro-women and young people campaign provided new spaces to breathe for the two neglected and denied categories'.[54] It is worth nuancing this statement. As noted in this chapter, women and children had already occupied a central position in Bahram Beyzaie's works for two decades. There is, therefore, no clear-cut relationship between films representing children and women and the socio-political contexts of their release.

In the last decade, Iranian films with child characters and child protagonists have grown, testifying to the vitality of this figure which is not only a pretext for dealing with other issues.[55] These films produce a subtle discourse on social issues of their time in the same tradition as major films of the pre-revolutionary New Wave films, especially by including non-professional actors. However, in this new trend, children are more likely to personify themselves rather than represent adults or ideas with allegorical significance. Many recent youth films deal with tensions around generational differences and how children are often the ones who are most affected by the adults' misdeeds. For example, Gholamreza Sagharchiyan's *Houra* (2015) is set in the desert and features a teenager whose family is affected by water shortage issues. The family's garden is drying up due to the destruction of the precious waterway surrounding them. Sagharchiyan, thus, focuses on how children are impacted by the environmental challenges linked to the mismanagement of water resources that the country is facing.

To sum up, what might be broadly called the 'Iranian children cinema' is not only born out of a combination of directors' material and stylistic motives but also mostly out of the poetic layers and open-ended stories that this trope offers. While at the beginning of the New Wave cinema, children carried an allegorical tone, often acting as substitutes for adult characters, more recent child-centred productions have shifted towards more explicit discourse on social issues affecting children. However, though the allegorical use of children has remained a major component in recent production, many seemingly allegorical films about children bring up concerns with children's rights and their position in the multi-ethnic Iranian society. In what follows, the rich texture of the figure of the child will be illustrated through the prism of displacement in three post-revolutionary films. The displaced child is a powerful figure to produce both an allegorical evocation and a social commentary. It can debunk the natural metaphors that unproblematically link the monolithic nation with its homogenous children.

Three little strangers

The first film, *Bāshu, the Little Stranger*, which was made in 1985 and released in 1989, features the interaction between two characters pertaining to different ethnolinguistic minorities in Iran during the Iran-Iraq war (1980–88). Bāshu, a young boy from southern Iran, flees the war that has ravaged his hometown and killed his family. Having jumped on the back of a truck in a moment of fear, he wakes up the next day to find himself in the Gilan province in northern Iran. There, as an Arab Iranian, he stands out by his different ethnic and linguistic backgrounds. He is adopted by Nāei, a Gilaki speaker, whose absent husband is later revealed to have been employed as a seasonal worker near the front. Nāei, the mother of two young children, accepts Bāshu into her family, defying the authority of her relatives and village elders.

The second film, Majid Majidi's *Baran* (2001) features the love of Lateef, an Azari adolescent, for an Afghan labourer who works in the same construction site as him on the outskirts of Tehran. Inspectors' constant tracking of illegal labourers obliges illegal Afghan refugee labourers to constantly hide themselves. Lateef meets Baran when she arrives as a new Afghan worker dressed up as a boy. This mysterious character never speaks a word. When Lateef discovers that she is a girl, he deeply falls in love with her, but Baran is forced to escape due to an inspection. Lateef embarks on a long journey across the city and finally finds her in the community where Afghan refugees live. He decides to help her and gives all his valuable belongings to Baran's family anonymously so that she can return to Afghanistan.

The third film, Rokhsareh Ghaemmaghami's *Sonita* (2016), is a documentary featuring a talented young female Afghan who lives as a refugee in a social centre in Tehran. Sonita dreams of becoming a famous rapper. When her family from Afghanistan tries to sell her off into an arranged marriage, the director, Ghaemmaghami decides to move to the other side of the camera and become an active character in the story. She supports Sonita by paying the amount needed by her family (2,000 dollars) to cancel her forced marriage temporarily and helps Sonita realize her potential as a rap singer. They record Sonita's rap song and release it on social media to win an Arts Academy scholarship in the United States of America.

All three Iranian filmmakers tackle the social and economic predicaments of their time in relation to internally displaced or cross-border migrants and the varying degrees of acceptance in society. Each hero experiences some form of exclusion. Bāshu faces the rejection of the villagers who call him 'coal' due to his dark complexion, Baran faces Lateef's animosity, when, believing that she has stolen his job, he calls her 'Afghani' in an insulting tone, and Sonita, whose family is selling her into an arranged marriage, is perceived as someone with no future in Iran and a mere bargaining chip to pay for her brother's bride.

The locations where these child-centred stories are filmed highlight the often-neglected social issues that often occur in the margins of society but are shaped by and shape broader national and transnational processes. The viewer, thus, enters a northern rural village unimpacted by the war, a construction site on the outskirts of Tehran where mainly Afghan immigrants work, and a small social centre in Tehran where mostly second-generation refugees stay. These films invite the spectator to question the space allocated to minority groups, in particular children. They reflect on the places that have been allocated to them in the nation and suggest that the margins they inhabit are ambiguous and relational rather than absolute.

The encounters of those who are considered Iranian 'insiders', ethnic Iranians and migrant 'outsiders' formulate discourses about the nation. While displacement is the chore of these child protagonists, other kinds of movements are portrayed albeit metaphorically. Characters embarking on journeys to help the 'others' of their society is illustrative of the move towards their 'recognition'. Spatial features are explored similarly in *Baran* and *Sonita* as both Iranian characters travel to Afghanistan (or an Afghan neighbourhood) to help their counterparts. The directors, thus, show border spaces to highlight the everyday encounters between nationals and non-nationals. In these encounters, representations reflect the cultural politics of the time. To reflect on the way this is done in the films and discuss what these features reveal about Iranian cinema, in the following section I will offer in-depth analysis of these three films' main themes with a particular focus on the representations of the figures of displaced youth.

Bāshu: Setting the tone for a renewed vision of the Iranian nation

Bomb explosions open the first scene of the film. As reflected in the palm trees, the setting is Khuzestan, where the conflict with Iraq was the most intense during the war that began in 1980. A few minutes later, Bāshu, appears out of a corn field and jumps on a truck to flee the war-torn area. The background Khuzestani music starts as the truck takes Bāshu to a destination unknown to him. When Bāshu gets out of the vehicle, he finds himself in the forest and fields of Gilan, a province in the north of Iran. Differences are so stark that he thinks that he may be in another country. The camera that has followed the truck from the south of the country to the north has already informed the spectator of the geographical distance between the conflict zone and the Gilan province. In Gilan, Bāshu stands out by his different language and appearance as an Arab Iranian. A set of other contrasts illustrate the distance and the divide. The green province of Gilan is the opposite of the rather dry areas of the south.

When Nāei discovers Bāshu in the field, she assumes he is not from Iran. The first scene where Nāei stares through the camera, looking for Bāshu, has become a classic scene as she gazes at the camera and breaks the camera's gaze and the fourth wall that implies what we see on screen is authentic and real. Throughout the film, Beyzaie draws our attention to the relationship between the little stranger and his new mother. Nāei's husband has left the village in search of work. When she welcomes Bāshu in her family despite the objections of other villagers, she is ostracized because despite the advice and the beliefs of her community, she welcomes and protects an outsider and tends to his fever when even the doctor refuses to help him. In another scene, she saves Bāshu from drowning with a fishing net when he falls into the river. As Beyzaie explains in an interview, Nāei is, at one level, a projection of the ancient goddess of fertility, Anahita. Therefore, her illness can also be read metaphorically which also signifies why she is brought back to life ritualistically, when Bāshu beats the drums.[56] Referring to Bāshu, Nāei calls him 'a child of the Sun and the Earth'. Nāei feeds children and animals and talks to birds, which highlights her mythical level. As Bāshu is from an Arab ethnic group and thus shares his language and origins with the Iraqi enemy, the union between him and Nāei demonstrates conviviality and rejects the logic of animosity pervading at times of war.

Bāshu's arrival triggers many reactions in this northern village. Villagers do not know where Bāshu has come from because they cannot conceive that he belongs to the same nation as them. His very existence questions many of the elements that constitute the imagined community as homogeneous. The protagonist child becomes a catalyst for the community to rethink concepts of national identity. As an outsider, the child is like a metaphor for the 'pre-socialized' or 'pre-gendered' character, providing a neutral outlook on the closed environment where he enters.

In several cases, Beyzaie reflects Bāshu's perspective with a circular movement of the camera which depicts how he observes the attitudes of the villagers. This is one of the signatures of Beyzaie's cinema and a tribute to the round arena of ta'ziyeh.[57] A revealing sequence occurs early in the film, when Nāei, hosts her neighbours for a tea reception. From the beginning of the scene even as they are being welcomed by Nāei, the crowd criticizes her decision to keep Bāshu.[58] A few minutes in, when everyone is enjoying their tea, Bāshu, who is visibly frightened and is sitting in a corner receives villagers' suspicious glances. As part of the many comments made by villagers to discourage Nāei from hosting Bāshu, a woman asks in a provocative way which country Bāshu comes from and a young girl touches Bāshu's face to verify if his black complexion is due to some oil or dirt. A few seconds later, seeing that Bāshu is physically suffering from this atmosphere, an exasperated Nāei suddenly decides to push all the guests out. The villagers, not agreeing with her stance, ostracize her. In a later scene, Bāshu enters a fight with local boys.[59] Nāei intervenes by dripping a bucket of cold water on the boys. Bāshu, trying to defend himself, chooses to pick up the nearby schoolbook instead of a stone and reads, 'Iran is our country. We are all Iran's children'. The children and Nāei are surprised as now they all realize that Bāshu is in fact from Iran.

The location of the small village, as a relatively closed environment enables the little stranger to function as a powerful character disrupting social norms. In this microcosm, the protagonists' (the 'other') geographical displacement leads to a readjustment in the host space (the 'self'). Beyzaie is also concerned with telling a story about Nāei as a woman who can stand for Iran as a modern nation, as she welcomes Bāshu by going beyond the backward prejudices of the villagers. The film's release was delayed for its tacit critique of the war and the depiction of Nāei, who, in the famous first scene, gazes directly at the camera, challenging modesty laws.[60] As part of the regulations of the Ministry of Culture and Islamic Guidance which issues permits for national film productions, directors are required to give a positive image of the war between Iran and Iraq. For this reason, Bāshu, which was produced in 1985, was banned until 1989 because the war was presented in a 'negative' image and, at the same time, not of any concern to Gilan province.[61] According to Devictor, the instructions insisted on the necessity of showing solidarity on the front, camaraderie among soldiers, the faith of warriors and their individual will to sacrifice their lives for their country and their religion but Beyzaie refused to implement any of the eighty-five changes that the censors had commanded.[62] In the film, the signs of the war are only seen in the first scenes in the south of Iran, before Bāshu escapes. Throughout the film, several signs of the war keep the conflict in mind: the sounds of military air crafts, visions from Bāshu's imagination of his lost family, Nāei's husband's letters and finally, the return of the injured father with a missing hand. Shot during the Iran-Iraq war, the film represents an alternative way to consider how the social-historical context of the war is felt. Instead of shooting the war frontline, spectators see how it is felt and impacts the lives of people in less visible places.

Iranian filmmakers have been particularly prolific in producing war fiction films, in a genre that has been called 'sacred defence films' (in Persian: *Sinemā-yi Defā'-e Moqaddas*).[63] Though occasionally critical of the war, these films were mostly concerned with fostering national cohesion and an acceptance of the conflict and its massive mobilization.[64] In *Bāshu*'s case, however, the film's vision fosters an anti-war stance and offers an idea of the nation which contradicts the dominant discourses of the nation. The notion of the nation as a motherland becomes even more conceptually related to the protection of women. In this framework, the country is represented as a female body that needs male protection against alien intrusion,[65] which is extrapolated during interstate conflicts that put the nation at risk of invasion or destruction. As a leading playwright and scholar of Iranian performing arts, Beyzaie's vision of the nation provides an interesting alternative approach to that of the ethnocentric Vatan. Indeed, as Saeed Talajooy argues, like the other subjects or artistic forms that he has dealt with, his vision of the nation has been particularly concerned with the marginalized and the unacknowledged aspects of Iran's culture, history and mythology.[66] Indeed, according to Talajooy this attention to the marginalized has always been at the centre of his work:

> Thus, when he began his theatre activities in the late 1950s, his main concerns were to reclaim the marginalized cultural and artistic practices and to reread historical and mythical accounts in plays that undermined the reductive narratives of nationhood, leadership, modernity, development, modernization, war, heroism, sacrifice, intellectuality, womanhood, myth, history and culture.[67]

His handling of the idea of nationhood, therefore, offers a much more progressive view of the nation than the dominant discourses of nationhood in Iran.[68]

In Beyzaie's cinema, as seen in Uncle Moustache, dislocation and crises of identity are constantly featured in contexts that use archetypal suggestions to present a social critique against conformism. Similarly, in his other films, historical events are highlighted to show how they shape and reshape the modern Iranian subject. In *Journey* (1972), the expedition of two orphan boys is depicted in a context in which Beyzaie's protagonists are two boys who want to change their world. The film uses realistic and symbolic representation to make these children transcend their individual figures and represent life in a large city. Similarly, in *The Crow* (1976) and *Maybe Some other time* (1988), profound ideas evolve with the film's focus on the individuals' experience of living as orphans or being dislocated.[69]

Thus, Beyzaie's films display contemporary or historical narratives with echoes of mythical figures to suggest the continuity of certain practices or undermine the regressive beliefs that have created present oppressive discourses.[70] His works have, thus, continually challenged 'the diktats of official pedagogies of nationhood and development by depicting the realities of people in the streets and by going back to historical and mythical origins to produce alternative narratives and highlight details that deconstruct grandiose political constructs'.[71] In his plays and films, one of his signatures is a tribute to the round arena of *ta'ziyeh* which is also the basis for his filmic movement between the real and the mythical, the past, present and future.[72]

The discursive function of the displaced child in this film is built against the backdrop of the context of the Iran-Iraq war. The nationalist conception of Iran, particularly during the Iran-Iraq war, shaped the way the nation was imagined as a female geo-body that needed to be protected and defended against the invader other, which in this case was the Arab other. In *Bāshu*, the representation of the little stranger challenges the homogenous discourse of national identity and critiques the myth of a linguistically, racially and culturally homogenous Iran. The displaced child in this context can be understood as a pre-socialized human being and a powerful mirror for the society into which he walks.

Nevertheless, from my perspective, the film's representation of ethnic diversity in Iran is ambiguous. In Zeydabadi-Nejad's terms, by using Gilaki, 'while Beyzaie unsettles the Persian speakers' ethnocentricity, he does not do so in any fundamental manner' because 'at its depth, the film endorses ethnic inequality between Persians and the rest'. 'Non-Persians are included by the Persians in the allegories of the nation not as equals but out of "compassion"'. Thus, 'a little Arab war refugee' is 'adopted by the Persian nation core' to reflect the positive aspects of Iranian culture. As a result, one may argue that while '*Bāshu, the Little Stranger* is certainly progressive in its inclusiveness, there is still some way to go in Iranian cinema for it to problematize Persian speakers' ethnocentricity at a fundamental level'.[73]

Baran: Romantic encounter with the silent neighbour

The film starts with a contextualization of Afghan refugees' presence in Iran – '1.5 million hosted in Iran'. The explanation ends with 'Most members of the younger generation were born in Iran and have never been home'. The first scene opens with a close-up shot of bakers' hands preparing *nān lavāsh*, an Iranian traditional bread, at a local bakery in Tehran, where Lateef is buying some bread. The camera then follows him walking past a park, noticing an Iranian couple and smiling at them. When looking at himself in the mirrored door of a rather luxury apartment building, he receives a condescending look from a well-dressed man exiting the building. Later, while walking back towards his workplace, he kneels to discreetly pick up a coin. At a local shop, the owner takes note of the amount of credit based on which Lateef is buying food for his co-workers at a construction site and leaves the note in Lateef's birth certificate which he puts in his drawer. The official birth certificate clearly shows that he is an Iranian from Zanjan. The camera then follows Lateef to the construction site where he works – the space he belongs to. Lateef is an Azari Iranian boy working as a handyman, serving tea and shopping for the workers of construction site. Owing to his impoverished background illustrated from the outset, he is detached from the bourgeois Iranian urban society. This marginalization is illustrated both narratively and visually throughout the film.

Meʿmār (the Architect), a good-hearted if often bad-tempered Iranian man, who is responsible for the site, employs many Afghans for menial work. Lateef proves to be a hot-blooded young boy. After an Afghan worker is injured, a family friend, Soltān, presents the man's son called Rahmat. Meʿmār gives him Lateef's job which infuriates Lateef. As he slaps Rahmat on the chin, he calls him 'Afghani', a common yet derogatory term to address Afghans in Iran. However, Lateef's anger is turned into compassion when he later realizes that Rahmat is, indeed, a girl dressed as a boy. Lateef starts acting as her protector on the site and even lands in jail after defending her when she is to be arrested by two government inspectors. When Baran disappears after escaping an inspection on the site, Lateef struggles to track her down. When he finally finds her in her new employment, as she struggles to haul rocks into the river, he is moved to tears. In his desperate attempt to help her, Lateef hands over his entire year's wages to her family anonymously and sells his national birth certificate for her.

Lateef's physical and emotional journey to find his beloved Baran contains allegorical motifs that can be traced back to Sufi tradition, a recurrent theme in Majidi's filmography. Lateef's acts of love also allude to long-established tropes in Persian poetry. As Dominic Parviz Brookshaw notes, in pre-modern Persian poetry and prose, the 'perils of passionate love' inspired poets 'to compose some of their most profound and lasting poetry, whether mystical, profane, or a subtle and complex blend of the two'. He further illustrates:

> With love comes yearning [...], both for the Divine beloved, and for His earthly counterparts or representatives, whether the Prophet, one of the imams, the royal patron, the idealized courtly beloved, or the alluring wine-server. Given the variety of possible beloveds, the lover's desire as portrayed in pre-modern Persian literature can range from one of selfless devotion and yearning for (re-)union with God or the earthly beloved [...] to a much baser, lustful desire for sexual gratification [...], often with a social inferior.[74]

Lateef's gesture of giving away everything he owns to help Baran suggests his selflessness. His journey to track back Baran can also represent a metaphor for his attempt to get closer to her. His quest leads him to cross Tehran by bus, walk further away from the city through long and deserted alleys, and get across a river. The ability to overcome one's ego to reach the ideal form of freeing oneself of being (*faqr o fanā*) is at the core of Sufi tradition. This notion, which is sometimes translated as 'spiritual poverty' or 'annihilation', is central in the works of Sufi poet Jalāl ad-Dīn Muhammad Rūmī. In his oeuvre, *Nafs* refers both to ego and to the part of the soul that incites men to do evil.[75] For Rūmī, *faqr o fanā* has the potential to bring one to an awareness of one's dependence on God, which is emphasized as a fundamental requirement for avoiding the belief that one is independent of the divine will.[76]

Lateef's actions seem to show his acceptance of his equal status with Baran and the Afghan refugees. In this sense, he literally exchanges his birth certificate for what he thinks is best for Baran – the money that may enable her to cross the border and go 'home' to be free from heavy menial work in Iran. However, the depiction of the figure of the Afghan in this film is subject to debate. It puts into question whether Majidi's representation of diversity is contesting or confirming social reality which subordinates Afghan refugees in Iran. The implicit benevolent intention of Lateef is compromised by what can be seen as the fascination and exoticization of the 'other'. This sympathetic portrayal of Afghan refugees can be seen as problematic because of Baran's muteness, which reflects the reluctance of Iranians to hear what Afghans have to say and reduces the Afghan girl into a mirror for Lateef's fantasies.[77] Thus, though Baran's father speaks, the mysterious Baran is only a ploy for Lateef's self-realization. The film, therefore, seems to reproduce the silencing of children, women and refugees. It depicts refugees as not only 'helpless' but also 'speechless' and in need of someone who can speak for them. Forms of silencing and speechlessness are particularly evident in visual representation of refugees, especially in photography and documentary film.[78]

Yet Baran's muteness can also represent structural obstacles that physically and metaphorically suppress the Afghan other. As mentioned above, Majidi's plot is a vehicle for a mystical allegory in which his representation of love is inspired by the Sufi figure of the silent beloved awaiting the lover to reach her. Silence is one of the main themes in Rumi's poetry. It is the last stage of a mystic's attempt to speak to God. Rumi argues for this silence by emphasizing the limited capacity of language to express the truth, the inexpressibility of God and the need to be liberated and remain liberated from the material world and human language.[79] Majidi critiques and contests the unequal status of Iranians and Afghans who work side by side and formulates a possibility for conviviality based on the mystic tradition where the distance between the two entities, Lateef and Baran, can be bridged through divine intervention. Yet Majidi's representation of Afghans also perpetuates unequal schemes of exclusion.

Children and displacement are recurrent figures in Majidi's filmography. Majidi's films are highly allegorical. As in *Baran*, his *Children of Heaven* (1997) has Sufi motifs. It tells the story of a brother and a sister whose determination to continue their normal life and education despite having to share a pair of shoes leads to a spiritual quest of self-sacrifice and transcendence. Majidi's films also depict the socio-economic hardship felt by children. In *Baduk* (1992), for instance, he depicts child slavery in a film that shows how a brother and his sister are separated and how the boy has to become a 'Baduk', a person hired to smuggle merchandises across the Pakistani border. In *Sun Children* (2020), Majidi goes one step further towards a more engaging depiction of the people of Afghan origin. The twelve-year-old hero Ali is an Iranian street boy whose companion in petty crimes, Abolfazl is of Afghan origin. Ali is in love with Abolfazl's sister Shamila who sells items in Tehran subway to support her family. When Ali leads Abolfazl to take part in risky actions, Shamila furiously criticizes him. Her genuine audible voice contrasts with Baran's silence. While the protagonist is still Iranian in his ethnolinguistic features, Majidi gives central stage to his Afghan characters and the acts of conviviality and disobedience that Iranian characters take on to denounce the exclusion of Afghans.

Sonita: *An Afghan Iranian rapping for change*

The film starts with the eighteen-year-old Sonita speaking about what she wants to become as a grown-up. The camera stands above her shoulder, allowing us to see from her perspective, that she is cutting a magazine picture illustrating a concert to paste it in her notebook. On the next page, there is a note with a prayer or poem written in Persian. By pasting her head onto an artist's picture, this photo montage shows how she would like to see herself as a grown up. She is a student at the 'Tehran-Society for Protection of Working and Street Children' where she also works as a helper. It is a centre with caring Iranian staff welcoming mostly Afghan youth. A few moments later in the centre, the camera captures Sonita as a thriving artist, singing a rap song at an animated crowd of about twenty young schoolgirls who sing along, repeating her lyrics. This is the highlight of Sonita's day. Her home is in a relatively poor neighbourhood of Tehran where she lives with her sister and niece. She tells the camera that about half of her seven siblings are in Afghanistan and half of them are in Iran. She uses family pictures and phone calls as links to connect with her relatives in Afghanistan.

The film then introduces Sonita's past when she takes part in a group exercise based on 'the theatre of the oppressed' at the social centre. The technique of rehearsing a scene with actions that the protagonist would like to try out in real life creates a new reality. Sonita is, thus, asked to recreate the narrative of how she and her family crossed the border to Iran. She is first asked to depict it as it happened and then the way she would have liked it to happen. This is a performance within the performance. Sonita, who, in the first version, only acts as a passive viewer who rewinds her sad memories, becomes active in the second version to shape the story at her convenience. This scene foreshadows the later moment in the film when the film director Ghaemmaghami gets involved to help Sonita change her life story. Ghaemmaghami allows the young artist to achieve her dreams and become the persona she has constructed in her photo montages. The contrast between the Sonita's aspiration and her reality, between her daily life and her possible futures is an ongoing theme of the film.

At the social centre, Sonita talks with her female school comrades who express their despair regarding the issue of selling brides. They confess their future engagement with husbands who may be their age or much older. Young girls do not have any choice as their consent is hardly considered. Due to economic hardships emanating from decades of conflict and foreign presence, Afghan families often find themselves forced to sell their lands, limbs and even daughters. Sonita finds herself in this very situation: her family wants her to go to Afghanistan to get married because her brother wants to use Sonita's bride price to pay for his own bride. In this transaction, Sonita is worth 9,000 dollars. Trying to get support and help from her mother, she calls her, but she soon finds out that her mother wants her back in Afghanistan or her brother will come to take her back.

Even though this film is categorized as a documentary, the director is voluntarily blurring the line between the documentary and the fiction to invite the audience to be more critical of what can be considered a representation of reality. Owing to its similarity with themes of Iranian New Wave cinema, it is a relevant film to analyse in this light. A symptomatic scene happens after the mother says she needs 2,000 dollars, or she will take Sonita back. The school's official in charge of Sonita explains to the director that the school can neither interfere nor pay this amount. As Ghaemmaghami sits in the office of the school's official and helplessly discusses what can be done to help Sonita, the sound engineer holding the microphone joins the conversation. The camera turns to film him as he declares that Sonita's mother wants to sell her has as she has no mercy for her child. He addresses himself to Ghaemmaghami and states: 'She expects you to do something [for Sonita], but we are total strangers to her!'[80] As the debate continues, and Ghaemmaghami is hesitant on whether she should pay the amount, the cameraman also shares his opinion by stating: 'You are a filmmaker, you shouldn't intervene.' At that moment, the viewer empathizes with Ghaemmaghami who needs to take a stance – either let the young girl leave for Afghanistan with her family or interfere and help her film's protagonist whom she has followed for three years. The next scene in which Sonita disappears is pivotal. Fearing that Sonita may be forced to return to Afghanistan for the arranged marriage, Ghaemmaghami drives around Tehran with her film crew to find her. On the second day of search, anxious, she addresses the camera: 'so does it mean that if we don't find her, we'll have to finish the film right here?'.[81] Fortunately for her and for the film, she eventually finds Sonita. Here, once more, the film reflects the fragmentation of the boundaries between the mise en scène and the documentary emblematic of Iranian cinema.[82]

Ghaemmaghami eventually supports Sonita by paying the 2,000 dollars her family needs to temporarily avoid her forced marriage. Furthermore, she helps Sonita to record her first song, uses social media to gain online attention for her, and helps her win a scholarship to attend the Wasatch Academy in Utah. They release *Dokhtar forushi*, which can be translated as Daughter Selling or Daughters for Sale, a video in which Sonita raps against child marriage. The circulation of a video made during the filming of the documentary on social media, and later seen by other characters also extends the narration's space and time and intertextuality as one film spawns another.[83] The ripple effect expands as Sonita's younger cousins in Afghanistan learn her song and sing it. Sonita's clip, therefore, is widely circulated and has an impact on the younger generation in Afghanistan. When Sonita learns that she has been selected, she realizes that she needs to go to Herat in Afghanistan to get her birth certificate. The stakes are high because if her papers are not produced, she might lose this opportunity and not even be able to return to Iran. Both in Iran and Afghanistan, Sonita's feeling of in-betweenness and powerlessness is palpable. While she cannot record a rap song in Iran because women are prohibited from singing solo, she has also lost the trust of her family and fears that they may detain and force her into the marriage from which she has been escaping. Sonita wants to be an active agent of change. As a rapper, she voluntarily becomes the rebel who questions conservative gender norms in Iran (prohibition of women's solo singing) and Afghanistan (child marriage). Sonita's mother was herself forced into child marriage, but Sonita refuses this fate. In doing so, one can imagine that she also prevents another girl from being bought for Sonita's brother marriage. Yet the solution presented for her to live up to her ambitions is to leave.

The film demonstrates the ambiguity of discourse production on Afghan refugee girls. Sonita does speak, but what remains ambiguous is that at one level even this speech may reproduce the idea of 'helpless' and 'speechless' refugees in need protection.[84] The film denounces the treatment of girls who are forcibly married at very young ages and echoes their voices speaking about how they are sold off to grown-up husbands who may even beat them. Sonita uses rap music with engaging lyrics and rhythm to provoke outrage about this issue that she experiences herself. Yet she provides little context to denounce such forms of gender violence against girls or reflect on how the broader socio-economic context leads to such traditions. As a result, the film *Sonita* both counters and reproduces a common representation of Afghan women as victims of patriarchy in need of rescue. This is particularly the case with the clip, which, to win the scholarship, is clearly directed towards an American audience and thus fits media discourses on Afghanistan. In the study of Afghan societies, gender has taken a central stage and has been politically used to justify wars with humanitarian poses. The American military intervention in Afghanistan (2001–21) was partly justified by the rhetoric of 'liberating' oppressed Afghan women.[85] In this discourse, Afghan women are represented as helpless human beings who need to be 'saved' from their own culture, thereby reproducing the pattern of 'white men saving brown women from brown men'.[86] As reflected in Hollywood films produced after the 9/11, it also focuses on oppressed women in burkas or on refugees in need of assistance, portraying the nation as one ridden by fundamentalist Islam, misogyny, and inter-ethnic battles, downplaying external forces leading to conflicts.[87] Yet what is neglected in a process that leads to further distortions is the contexts and the daily conflicts that Afghan men and women face and how further conflicts postpone the possibility of grassroots change.

The three films contrast in their representation of exclusion and conviviality. Ghaemmaghami accompanies Sonita to Afghanistan in order for her to receive her identity papers and continue her journey to the United States. Likewise, in *Baran* Lateef goes to find his beloved to give the money to his family so she, the 'other', can return to its 'natural' place Afghanistan. Nāei, however, being the product of 'Beyzaie's concern with expanding the borders of belonging', refers to Bāshu as 'a child of the Sun and the Earth' and manages to adopt him.[88]

Conclusions

The subject of little strangers in Iranian cinema highlights them as an analytical category to explore how both the 'child' and the 'outsider' are portrayed at different historical periods and what these portrayals reveal about the nation. Exploring the position of displaced children in Iranian cinema leads to new ways of understanding the nation and the construction of the 'other' grounded on people's relationships rather than on grandiose nationalist narratives. Bāshu, Baran and Sonita are not archetypal, but they illustrate the variations in representing little others, and new stakes, in the ever-changing idea of Iranian nation. Displacement is portrayed according to the socio-historical context: in 1980, the theme of the Iran-Iraq war is portrayed, while in the 1990s, the phase of post-war reconstruction is highlighted, and in 2015, the conditions of migrants and their dire economic status are accentuated. In each period, the 'other' is constructed based on different hierarchies, which tells us more about the cultural politics of the time they were produced than about the content under consideration.

While children are a main theme in the Iranian New Wave cinema, child 'strangers' comprise a heuristic category that enables the researcher to observe shifts in their representation. The depiction of displaced children on screen can be attributed to the New Wave cinema's poetic roots as well as the filmmaker's own sensitivities to pressing socio-political transformations. Sadr argues that at the end of the 1990s, 'the focus shifted away from the heroic past to the prosaic present', and thus, the co-optation of the narrative into the socialized adult gaze changed to an attention to the point of view of young people themselves.'[89] Though this is correct, at another level, the portrayal of displacement in many cases remains highly polysemic and in dialogue with Persian poetic tradition. Furthermore, the figure of the displaced child enables Iranian New Wave filmmakers to feature social issues in tandem with the ability of people to forge ties across boundaries.

In this context, *Bāshu, the Little Stranger* maintains its contemporary significance as it highlights the construction of the imagined Iranian nation made of different ethnicities and languages and is a call to forge convivial bonds. This is mainly because Beyzaie's way of seeing children as active contributors to social processes and not as mere reproducers attributes an important role to the youth for the future of the nation. In turn, it has also had an impact on the rise of the other films like the ones I examined in this chapter as they also seem to celebrate multi-ethnicity by acknowledging the presence of minorities, migrants and refugees and showing how they play significant roles in society and are integral to the socio-economic landscape in today's Iran. In general, therefore, the presence of displaced child characters in films questions what is held as the 'national order of things',[90] and challenges the domestic genealogies used to indicate the stable and continuous nature of the nation.[91]

Notes

1. Sadr, *Iranian Cinema*, 152, Zeydabadi-Nejad, 'Iranian Intellectuals', 383. Naficy, *Social History 4*, 209.
2. Ibid.
3. Adelkhah, *Les mille*.
4. Adelkhah, and Zuzanna, 'Iranian Afghans', 145–7.
5. Veyne, 'L'interprétation et l'interprète', 241–72.
6. McClintock, *Imperial Leather*, 375.
7. Malkki, 'Refugees and Exile' 495–523.
8. Zeydabadi-Nejad, 'Farsi shekar ast'.
9. Olszewska *Pearl of Dari*, 842.
10. Wellman, 'Sacralizing Kinship', 506.
11. Nooshin, 'Whose Liberation?', 164.
12. Mostowlanski, 'Faraway Siblings'.
13. Ibid.
14. Ibid.
15. Azaris are an Iranian minority from the northeast of the country.
16. Malkki 1992: 26.
17. According to the UNHCR, Iran is home to nearly 3 million Afghan migrants and refugees, 204,000 Iraqis and about 8 million Kurds. See also Michelle, 'Cultural Diversity', 261.
18. Jadali. 'L'Iran, Pays d'accueil', 13–20.
19. Turton, and Marsden, 'Taking Refugees'; Monsutti, *War and Migration*.
20. Adelkha and Olszewska, 'Iranian Afghans', 145.
21. Gilroy. *Postcolonial Melancholia*, 65; Marsden. *Trading Worlds*, 290.
22. Asgharzadeh, *Iran and the Challenge*, 2.
23. McClintock, *Imperial Leather*, 375.
24. Brookshaw, 'Women Poets'. 272; Najmabadi. 'The Erotic Vatan', 445–6, Tavakoli-Targhi. *Refashioning Iran*, 113. According to Tavakoli-Targhi, 'motherland' prevails (*madar-i/mam-i vatan*).
25. Naficy. 'Poetics and Practice', 286.
26. Anderson. *Imagined Communities*, 3.
27. There are many kinds of imagined communities, and Anderson provides the following definition of the nation: 'it is an imagined political community – and imagined as both inherently limited and sovereign', Ibid., 5–6.
28. Billig. *Banal Nationalism*, 6.
29. Hayward, *French National*, ix–x. That is, in a neo-Marxist approach, the material production finds reflection in the aesthetic (superstructure) in a two-directional relationship.

30 Adelkhah, 'Les mille', 9.
31 Mirbakhtyar, *Iranian Cinema*, 38.
32 Zeydabadi-Nejad, 'Iranian Intellectuals', 394, Sadr, *Iranian Cinema*, 152.
33 Mottahedeh, 'Displaced Allegories', 15.
34 Naficy, *Social History*, 235.
35 Sadr, *Iranian Cinema*, 232.
36 Jahangirian, *Farhang-e filmha-ye*; Mehrabi, *Farhang-e Filmhā-ye*, cited in Naficy, *Social History*, 209.
37 E.g. Sadr, *Iranian Cinema*, 152.
38 Christensen and Allison's *Research with Children* specifies that children's active contribution to society can occur through, for example, their membership in families and their participation in leisure, labour and schooling.
39 Kinder, *Kids' Media*, 3.
40 Lury, 'Child in Film', 2.
41 Talajooy. 'Uncle Moustache', 234.
42 Naficy notes that in the first decade following the revolution 'only the best of the films involving children dealt with children as makers of meaning and culture' but the dismissive attitude that looks at children as being shaped by adults has been steadily replaced by other forms of looking at children's agency. Naficy, *Social History*, 209.
43 Talajooy. 'Uncle Moustache', 234–5.
44 For example, *Pixote, Survival of the Weakest* (Hector Babenco, 1981), *Salaam Bombay!* (Mira Nair, 1988), *Pelle the Conqueror* (Bille August, 1988), *Toto the Hero* (Jaco van Dormael, 1991), *Ponette* (Jacques Doillon, 1997), *Tito and Me* (Goran Markovic, 1992) and *Silences of the Palace* (Moufida Tlatli, 1994) were internationally successful (Sadr, 2002: 229).
45 Zeydabadi-Nejad, 'Iranian Intellectuals', 379.
46 Sadr, *Iranian Cinema*, 232.
47 Ibid.
48 Ibid., 228.
49 Zeydabadi-Nejad, 'Iranian Intellectuals', 383.
50 Ibid., 384.
51 Ghorbankarimi, *Colourful Presence*, 11.
52 Hosseini-Shakib, 'Image of Children', 228.
53 Ibid.
54 Ibid., 232.
55 For example, in *A Separation* (2011) by Asghar Farhadi, *Under the Shadow* (2016) by Babak Anvari. Recent Iranian child-focus films include *The Promise* (2014) by Mohammad Ali Talebi, *Ava* (2014) by Siamak Kashef Azar, *The Other's Father* (2015) by Yadollah Samadi, and *House on 41st Street* (2016) by Hamid Reza Ghorbani.
56 Donmez-Colin. *Cinemas of the Other*, 30.
57 In the traditional staging of the *ta'ziyeh* performance, the audience sits on the ground around a circular platform in a large courtyard, and the play is performed both on- and offstage. Mottahedeh, *Displaced Allegories*, 17.
58 Beyzaie, *Bashu*, 31'.28".
59 Ibid., 57'.37".
60 Naficy, *Social History*, 140.
61 Devictor, *Politique Du Cinéma*, 45.
62 Ibid., 45.
63 See Abecassis, 'Iranian War', 387–94, and Khosronejad, *Iranian Sacred*.

64 Ibid.
65 Tavakoli-Targhi, *Refashioning Iran*, 113.
66 Talajooy, 'Beyzaie's Formation', 691, and *Mythologizing*, 238–82.
67 Ibid., 689.
68 For analysis of the idea of the nation in Beyzaie's oeuvre and *Bashu*, see Talajooy, *Mythologizing*, 238–82.
69 For more on these films, see Talajooy, 'Journey', 'Crow', and 'Maybe Some'. See also 'Khāneh, Khānevadeh' which analyses *The Crow*, and *Maybe Some Other Time*.
70 See Amjad, 'From the Land', and Talajooy, *Mythologizing*, for analysis of this quality in Beyzaie's oeuvre.
71 Talajooy, 'Beyzaie's Formation', 690.
72 Khalili Mahani. 'Bahram Baizai'. *Ta'ziyeh* is the annual Shiite mourning rituals representing the struggle that marked the defeat of the family of the Prophet Muhammad against the caliph in Karbala in 680. Beyzaie's oeuvre is popularly considered by Iranians to be genuinely and traditionally Persian in its scope and in dialogue with the form. See Talajooy, *Mythologizing*, 15–20 and 101–7 and Mottahedeh, *Displaced Allegories*, 17.
73 Zeydabadi-Nejad, 'Farsi Shekar'.
74 Brookshaw, 'Love and Desire', 673.
75 Zarrabi-Zadeh, 'Jalal al-Din Rumi's', 48.
76 Ibid., 50.
77 Olszewka, *Pearl of Dari*, 51.
78 Malkki, 'Speechless Emissaries', 388.
79 Kakayee and Behrani, 'Karkardehā-ye Elahyiati', 129–50.
80 Ghaemmaghami, *Sonita*, 33'.20".
81 Ibid., 36'.00".
82 Mottahedeh, 'Displaced Allegories', 15.
83 Naficy, *Social History*, 235.
84 Malkki, 'Speechless Emissaries', 388.
85 Billaud, *Kabul Carnival*; Hirschkind, and Mahmood. 'Feminism, the Taliban', 339–54.
86 Spivak, 'Can the Subaltern Speak?'.
87 Rastegar, 'Global Frames'; Graham, *Afghanistan in the Cinema*.
88 Talajooy, 'Shifting the Borders'.
89 Sadr, *Iranian Cinema*, 249.
90 Malkki, 'Refugees and Exile', 495–523.
91 McClintock, *Imperial Leather*, 375.

Bibliography

Abbasi-Shavazi, Mohammad Jalal, Rasoul Sadeghi, Hossein Mahmoudian and Gholamreza Jamshidiha. 'Marriage and Family Formation of the Second-Generation Afghans in Iran: Insights from a Qualitative Study'. *International Migration Review*. Vol. 46. No. 4 (Winter 2012). Pp. 828–60.

Abecassis, Michaël. 'Iranian War Cinema: Between Reality and Fiction'. *Iranian Studies*. Vol. 44. No. 3 (May 2011). Pp. 387–94.

Adelkhah, Fariba, *Les mille et une frontières de l'Iran, Quand les voyages forment la nation*. Paris: Karthala, 2012.

Adelkhah, Fariba and Zuzanna Olszewska. 'The Iranian Afghans'. *Iranian Studies*. Vol. 40. No. 2 (Spring 2007). Pp. 137–65.
Anderson, Benedict. *Imagined Communities: Reflections on the Origin and Spread of Nationalism*. London: Verso, 2006.
Amjad, Hamid. 'From the Land of the Pure, in Search of the Lost Origin: An Interview with Bahram Beyzaie on Siyavush-Khani (Siyavush Recitation) and Its Mythological and Literary Roots'. *Iranian Studies*. Vol. 46. No. 5 (May 2013). Pp. 721–36.
Billaud, Julie. *Kabul Carnival: Gender Politics in Postwar Afghanistan*. Philadelphia: University of Pennsylvania Press, 2015.
Billig, Michael. *Banal Nationalism*. London: Sage, 1995.
Brookshaw, Dominic Parviz. 'Love and Desire in Pre-modern Persian Poetry and Prose'. *Iranian Studies*. Vol. 42. No. 5 (December 2009). Pp. 673–5.
Brookshaw, Dominic Parviz. 'Women Poets'. In *A History of Persian Literature: Literature of the Early Twentieth Century*. Ed. Ali-Asghar Seyed-Gohrab and Ehsan Yarshater. London: I.B. Tauris, 2015. Pp. 240–310.
Christensen, Pia and Allison James. Eds. *Research with Children: Perspectives and Practices*. 2nd Edition. New York and London: Routledge, 2008.
Devictor, Agnès. *Politique Du Cinéma Iranien: De L'Ayatollâ Khomeyni Au Président Khâtami*. Nouvelle Edition. Paris: CNRS Editions, 2004.
Dönmez-Colin, Gönül. *Cinemas of the Other: A Personal Journey with Film-Makers from the Middle East and Central Asia*. Bristol and Portland: Intellect, 2006.
Ghorbankarimi, Maryam. *A Colourful Presence: The Evolution of Women's Representation in Iranian Cinema*. Newcastle upon Tyne: Cambridge Scholars, 2015.
Gilroy, Paul. *Postcolonial Melancholia*. New York: Columbia University Press, 2005.
Graham, Mark. *Afghanistan in the Cinema*. Urbana: University of Illinois Press, 2010.
Hayward, Susan. *French National Cinema*. 2nd Edition. London and New York: Routledge, 2005.
Hirschkind, Charles and Saba Mahmood. 'Feminism, the Taliban, and Politics of Counter-Insurgency'. *Anthropological Quarterly*. Vol. 75. No. 2 (Spring 2002). Pp. 339–54.
Hosseini-Shakib, Fatemeh. 'The Image of Children'. In *Directory of World Cinema: Iran*. Ed. Parviz Jahed. Bristol and Chicago: Intellect, 2012. Pp. 226–33.
Jadali, Safinaz. 'L'Iran, Pays d'accueil, un Point de Vue Juridique sur les Migrants et les Réfugiés'. *Hommes et Migrations*. 1312 (December 2015). Pp. 13–20.
Kakayee, Ghasem and Eshkan Behrani. 'Kārkardhā-ye Elāhyiāti Sokut dar Āsār Mowlānā'. *Fasslnāmeh-ye Falsafe va Kalām Eslāmi*. Vol. 42. No. 1 (Autumn & Winter 2009). Pp. 129–50.
Khosronejad, Pedram. Ed. *Iranian Sacred Defence Cinema: Religion, Martyrdom and National Identity*. Canon Pyon: Sean Kingston Publishing, 2012.
Kinder, Marsha. Ed. *Kids' Media Culture*. Durham and London: Duke University Press, 1999.
Langford, Michelle. 'Cultural Diversity in Iranian Cinema'. In *Directory of World Cinema: Iran*. Ed. Parviz Jahed. Bristol and Chicago: Intellect, 2012. Pp. 258–82.
Lury, Karen. *The Child in Film: Tears, Fears, and Fairy Tales*. London and New York: I.B. Tauris, 2010.
McClintock, Anne. *Imperial Leather: Race, Gender, and Sexuality in the Colonial Contest*. London: Routledge, 1995.
Magnus, Marsden. *Trading Worlds: Afghan Merchants across Modern Frontiers*. Oxford: OUP, 2016.

Mahani, Najmeh Khalili. 'Bahram Baizai, An Unknown Master of Iranian Cinema Pre and Post-Revolution'. *Offscreen*. Vol. 7. No. 1 (January 2003). Online: http://offscreen.com/view/bahram_baizai (Accessed 3 December 2021).

Malkki, Liisa. 'Refugees and Exile: From "Refugee Studies" to the National Order of Things'. *Annual Review of Anthropology*. Vol. 24 (1995). Pp. 495–523.

Malkki, Liisa. 'Speechless Emissaries: Refugees, Humanitarianism, and Dehistoricization'. *Cultural Anthropology*. Vol. 11. No. 3 (August 1996). Pp. 377–401.

Mirbakhtyar, Shahla. *Iranian Cinema and the Islamic Revolution*. Jefferson and London: McFarland, 2006.

Monsutti, Alessandro. *War and Migration: Social Networks and Economic Strategies of the Hazaras of Afghanistan. Middle East Studies: History, Politics, and Law*. New York and London: Routledge, 2005.

Mostowlanski, Till. 'Faraway Siblings, So Close: Ephemeral Conviviality across the Wakhan Divide'. *Modern Asian Studies*. Vol. 53. No. 3 (2019). Pp. 943–77.

Mottahedeh, Negar. *Displaced Allegories, Post-Revolutionary Iranian Cinema*. Durham: Duke University Press, 2008.

Naficy, Hamid. 'The Poetics and Practice of Iranian Nostalgia in Exile'. *Diaspora: A Journal of Transnational Studies*. Vol. 1. No. 3 (Winter 1991). Pp. 285–302.

Naficy, Hamid. *A Social History of Iranian Cinema, Volume 4: The Globalizing Era, 1984-2010*. Durham: Duke University Press, 2012.

Najmabadi, Afsaneh. 'The Erotic Vatan [Homeland] as Beloved and Mother: To Love, to Possess, and to Protect, Society for Comparative'. *Society for Comparative Study of Society and History*. Vol. 39. No. 3 (January 1997). Pp. 442–67.

Nooshin, Laudan. 'Whose Liberation? Iranian Popular Music and the Fetishization of Resistance'. *Popular Communication*. Vol. 15. No. 3 (Summer 2017). Pp. 163–91.

Olszewska, Zuzanna. *The Pearl of Dari: Poetry and Personhood among Young Afghans in Iran*. Bloomington and Indianapolis: Indiana University Press, 2015.

Rastegar, Kamran. 'Global Frames on Afghanistan'. In *Globalizing Afghanistan*. Durham, London: Duke University Press, 2011.

Sadr, Hamid Reza. 'Children in Contemporary Iranian Cinema: When We Were Children'. In *The New Iranian Cinema: Politics, Representation and Identity*. Ed. Richard Tapper. London: I. B. Tauris, 2002. Pp. 227–37.

Sadr, Hamid Reza. *Iranian Cinema: A Political History*, London: I. B. Tauris, 2006.

Spivak, Gayatri Chakravorty. *Can the Subaltern Speak?* Basingstoke: Macmillan, 1988.

Talajooy, Saeed. *Mythologizing the Transition: A Comparative Study of Bahram Beyzaee and Wole Soyinka*. PhD thesis. University of Leeds. January 2008. Online through Whiterose eTheses <https://etheses.whiterose.ac.uk/406/>. (Accessed 5 January 2021).

Talajooy, Saeed. '"Uncle Moustache", "The Journey", "The Crow", and "Maybe Some Other Time"'. In *Directory of World Cinema: Iran*. Ed. Parviz Jahed. Bristol: Intellect, 2012. Pp. 139–41, 148–50 and 234–8.

Talajooy, Saeed. 'Khāneh, Khānevādeh va Shahr: Revayāt-e Tajaddod dar *Kalāgh* va *Shāyad Vaqti Digar*'. *Iran Nameh*. Vol. 27. No. 1 (2012). Pp. 142–61.

Talajooy, Saeed. 'Beyzaie's Formation, Forms and Themes'. *Iranian Studies*. Vol. 46. No. 5 (May 2013). Pp. 689–93.

Talajooy, Saeed. 'Shifting the Borders of Belonging in the Myth of the Nation: (A Ritual of Exorcism)'. Video Presentation for the Conference, *Celebrating Bahram Beyzaie's 10 Year Anniversary at Stanford University*. (May 2021). Online at YouTube: https://www.youtube.com/watch?v=UzaayPZPR9w (Accessed 27 October 2022).

Tavakoli-Targhi, Mohamad. *Refashioning Iran: Orientalism, Occidentalism and Historiography*. New York: Palgrave Macmillan, 2001.
Turton, David and Peter Marsden. 'Taking Refugees for a Ride? The Politics of Refugee Return to Afghanistan'. *Issues Paper Series*. Islamabad: The Afghanistan Research and Evaluation Unit (AREU), 2002.
Veyne, Paul. 'L'interprétation et l'interprète. A propos des choses de la religion'. *Enquête 3* (November 1996). Pp. 241–72.
Wellman, Rose. 'Sacralizing Kinship, Naturalizing the Nation: Blood and Food in Postrevolutionary Iran'. *American Ethnologist*. Vol. 44. No. 3 (Summer 2017). Pp. 503–15.
Zarrabi-Zadeh, Saeed. 'Jalal al-Din Rumi's Mysticism of Love-based Annihilation'. *Mawlana Rumi Review*. Vol. 5. No. 1 (January 2014). Pp. 26–72.
Zeydabadi-Nejad, Saeed. 'Iranian Intellectuals and Contact with the West: The Case of Iranian Cinema'. *British Journal of Middle Eastern Studies*. Vol. 34. No. 3 (December 2007). Pp. 375–98.
Zeydabadi-Nejad, Saeed. 'Farsi Shekar Ast'. Conference Paper. A revised version of this paper has been included in this volume under the title of 'Multilinguality in Iranian Cinema'.

Films:

Bāshu, the Little Stranger. Directed by Bahram Beyzaie, IIDCYA, 1990.
Baran. Directed by Majid Majidi, produced by Majid Majidi and Fouad Nahas, 2001.
Sonita. Directed by Rokhsareh Ghaemmaghami, Tag/Traum GmbH Filmproduktion, Intermezzo Films, RTS Radio Télévision Suisse, SRG SSR, Rokhsareh Ghaemmaghami, 2016. https://www.swissfilms.ch/en/film_search/filmdetails/-/id_film/48CAFED2CCFF47379F4CBBC886DABF1A

INDEX

Adonis (Greek god) 26
Aphrodite (Greek goddess) 26
Aesthetics/aesthetic 2, 6, 7, 8, 11, 13, 14, 47, 75, 100, 102, 186, 238
Afhami, Sirus 88
 Pahlevānān (*Pahlevāns*) 88
Afghan/Afghanistan (including Afghan refugees, migrants, labourers, women, children) ix, 17, 217, 220, 224, 227–28, 231–36, 238, 241
Afrāsiyāb/Afrasiab (Shahnameh/Avesta) 34–39, 51, 55
Ahmadi, Ahmadreza 107
Ahura Mazda 34, 35, 36, 51, 54
Akutagawa, Ryūnosuke 50
 In A Grove 50
 Rashomon 50. *See* Kurosawa
Al-e Ahmad, Jalal 11, 18, 19, 49, 77, 74, 90, 101
Amateur acting/actor 49, 159, 222
Amateur gaze/vision (thinking outside the box) 2–3, 17
Amjad, Hamid xii, 18, 19, 89, 91, 112, 240
Anahita 46, 64, 73, 140, 151, 205, 229
Anti-war 109, 157, 230
Apush/Aposh 36, 51
Arab/Arabic 32, 49, 54, 129, 198, 202, 206, 214, 217, 221, 227–31
Ashoori, Dariush 7, 17, 18, 19
Ashura/Karbala 62, 158–59, 240
Aslani, Mohammad Reza 101
 Badbade (*The Quail*) 101
Authentic/authenticity (identity, cultural) 3, 7, 11, 24, 83, 84, 86, 167, 168, 170, 172, 174, 204, 215, 216, 222, 228
Authoritarian 3, 4, 24, 161
Avesta 14, 35–6, 50, 51, 53, 54, 140
Ayyār, Ayyāri 5, 9, 10, 14, 18, 40, 57–59, 61, 70, 75, 77, 88, 90, 93. *See* Javānmardi and Pahlevān

Background 2, 3, 13, 17, 25, 98, 103, 105, 106, 158, 165, 167, 188, 191, 203, 205, 212, 224, 227, 228, 232
Bahaism/Bahai 3, 47–48
Bahram Chubin (Shahnameh) 34–37, 51, 54
Bahram (pre-Islamic Iranian deity) 43
Behrangi, Samad 98
 Māhi-ye Siāh-e Kuchulu (The Little Black Fish) 98
Belonging v, 2, 14, 25, 44, 46, 54, 57–93, 104, 113, 133, 140, 153, 163, 168, 176, 193, 209, 219, 221, 223, 237, 242. *See* Recognition
Benjamin, Walter 33, 44, 51, 52, 53, 162, 175, 176
Bergson, Henri 186
Beyzaie's Works
 Account of Bondār, the Premier (*Kārnāmeh-ye Bondār-e Bidaksh*) 6, 9, 24, 25, 28, 30, 32, 33
 Afrā, or the Day Is Passing 10, 18, 39, 50, 52, 54
 Ārash v, 5, 9, 13, 14, 16, 23–55, 57, 59, 60, 75, 76, 146, 148, 151, 175, 176
 Ardāvirāf's Report 5
 Azhdāhāk 24, 25, 28–30, 33, 48, 57
 Ballad of Tārā (*Cherikeh-ye Tārā*) v, vii, 5, 9, 15, 43, 88, 108, 115–17, 118–20, 124–27, 129–31
 Bāshu, the Little Stranger v, vi, viii, 10, 14, 15, 16, 17, 43, 89, 97, 102, 106, 107–13, 115–20, 127–34, 135–53, 157, 183, 198, 200, 201–6, 214–15, 216, 217, 219, 225, 227, 228–31, 237, 239, 240, 243
 Crow 5, 9, 16, 90, 106, 151, 153, 179–93, 214, 231, 240, 242
 Death of Yazdgerd 6, 10, 18, 107, 108, 187
 Downpour (*Ragbār*) 9, 12, 18, 89, 90, 105, 146, 151, 153

Feast (*Ziyāfat*) 11, 102
Film in Film 110
Four Boxes 11, 18, 71
Journey (*Safar*) v, 9, 14, 16, 39, 89, 97, 102, 104–07, 109, 111, 112, 113, 151, 153, 222, 231, 240, 241, 242
Kallāt Claimed (*Fathnāmeh-ye Kallāt*) 6, 10, 20
Killing Mad Dogs (*Sagkoshi*) 16, 106, 158, 179–93, 214
The Landscape (*Cheshm Andāz*) 110
Lonely Warrior (*Ayyār-e Tanhā*) 9
Mahi 12, 18, 19
Maybe Some other Time 5, 11, 16, 68, 106, 151, 153, 157, 168, 179–93, 231, 242
Memoirs of the Actor in a Supporting Role 10, 18
Mirās (Heritage) 102
Mourning Wail (*Nodbeh*) 9
New Preface to the Shahnameh 5, 10
Occupation (*Eshghāl*) 192, 193
The One Thousand and First Night 10, 12, 18
Parchment of Master Sharzin (*Tumār-e Sheikh-e Sharzin*) 5, 6, 10, 39
Puppet Trilogy (*Marionettes/puppets, Sunset in a Strange Land, Tale of the Hidden Moon*) 9, 11, 18, 20
Reed Panel (*Pardeh-ye Ne-ei*) 10
Siyāvush Recitation (*Siyāvushkhāni*) 10, 91, 241
Snake King (*Soltān Mar*) 5, 9, 11
So Dies Pahlevān Akbar (*Pahlevān Akbar Mimirad*) vii, 5, 9, 13, 14, 19, 57–93
Stranger and the Fog (*Gharibeh va Meh*) 9, 11, 15, 39, 43, 89, 90, 106, 115, 118, 120–24, 130, 134, 146, 151, 153, 187, 214
Travellers (*Mosāferān*) vi, 15, 146, 149, 157–77
Truths about Leila the Daughter of Edris 9, 192
Uncle Moustache (*Amu Sibilu*) 9, 14, 16, 97, 102–4, 108, 110, 111, 112, 113, 151, 153, 223–24, 231, 239, 242
When We Are All Sleeping 106

Biruni, Mohamamd Abu Reihān 35, 51, 53
Bonyād-e Omur-e Mohājerin-e Jang-e Tahmili (Foundation for the Affairs of the Immigrants of the Imposed War) 135, 152
Bourdieu, Pierre 2, 3, 17, 19
Boyce, Mary 26, 50, 51, 53
Brecht, Bertolt 2, 8, 45
  The Decision 45
Burke, Edmund 67–8, 89, 91

Camera 7, 103, 104, 143, 147, 160–64, 167, 168, 173, 174, 175, 180, 183, 185, 186, 188, 190, 203, 207, 209, 211–12, 227, 228–30, 232, 234, 235
Capitalist/capitalism 12, 177
Carnival 5, 6, 9, 10, 18, 240, 241
Catharsis 6, 28, 106, 162, 166, 172
Chamran, Mostafa 210–13
Children 8, 9, 11, 14, 16–17, 75, 88–93, 97–113, 116–18, 126–31, 134, 135–153, 160, 172, 202, 205, 206, 211, 217–43
Chronological 13, 186
Chubak, Sadeq 73
  Tangsir (*Tight Corner*) 73
Cine Club (*Kānun-e Film*) 7, 18, 19
Cinematography 189, 193, 206
Citizenship/citizen 5, 11, 14, 25, 31, 39, 43, 46, 49, 72, 81, 148, 181, 220
Classical Cinematic Techniques 16, 158, 160, 163, 172, 157–77
Closeup 17, 127, 150, 151, 207, 209, 210, 211, 232
Collective 39, 45, 62, 108, 146, 160, 162, 164–65, 169, 173–74
Collective memory 62, 165
Comedy/comic 5, 6, 7, 10, 18, 61, 63, 71, 81–82, 97, 105, 158, 206, 223
Comic Relief 71, 81, 82
Constitutionalists/constitutionalism 4, 47, 76. *See also* Mosaddeq
Corbin, Henry 51, 53, 62, 89, 91
Cosmopolitanism/cosmopolitan 4, 7, 17, 76, 77
Creativity 8, 13, 16, 17, 23, 25, 32, 121
Crime thriller/Noir film elements vi, 16, 179–93
Cukor George 183
  Gaslight 183

Index

Culture 1–5, 7, 8, 11, 13, 25, 27, 41, 47, 49, 50, 54, 57–58, 72, 76–77, 84, 86–87, 89, 93, 99–100, 108, 111, 112, 117, 136, 139, 141–43, 145, 149, 157, 158, 170, 174, 175, 187, 191, 204, 219, 221, 223, 225, 230, 231, 236, 239

Cultural Production 2, 7, 8, 11, 13, 111

Death/dying 9, 15, 18, 28, 45, 57–93, 116, 122, 124–27, 129, 139, 145–46, 149, 157–77, 180, 181, 187, 207, 224

Deleuze, Giles/ crystal image 182, 186, 190, 192, 193

Detective. *See* Crime thriller elements

Diba (Pahlavi), Farah 97, 98, 112
  The Little Mermaid (*Dokhtarak-e Daryā* [Translation]) 98

Double/hamzād 6, 14, 42–3, 52, 59, 66–9, 72, 76, 78, 79, 126, 181

Dominant Discourses x, 4–8, 11, 12, 13, 15, 23, 24, 27, 30, 39–40, 60, 76, 77, 86, 97, 100, 101, 102, 117, 131, 148, 150, 169, 191, 218, 219, 221, 223, 228, 230, 231, 236

Ebrahimi, Nader 38
  Arash in the Realm of Doubts 38

Ecocritical 15, 115–17, 133

Ecological 132, 133

Emasculated/feminized 213

Emancipatory/emancipation/emancipate 5, 7, 8, 9, 10, 11, 12, 25, 28, 32, 40, 44, 48, 49, 81

Environment 15, 108, 115–33, 147, 202, 226, 229

Epic/Anti-epic 9, 14, 24, 26, 27, 34, 37–39, 47, 57, 63, 69, 70, 87, 105, 107, 159

Epistemic/epistemic privilege/epistemic authority 1, 2, 8, 18, 19, 33

Esfandārmaz/Spandārmaz 35–37, 46, 51

Esfandiyār (Shahnameh) 75, 77, 78–81

Ethnocentric 15, 108, 145, 197, 203, 204, 206, 214, 230, 231

Exclusionism/exclusionist 4, 7, 11, 12, 14, 15, 23–25, 28, 29, 32, 45, 46, 59, 60, 61, 72, 86, 148, 203, 224

Expressionism/Expressionistic 30, 40–42, 45, 46, 52, 64, 68, 106, 158, 186

Fantastic (The) 14, 68–9, 89, 93

Farhadi, Asghar 198, 206, 239

Farrokhzad, Forough 169
  The House Is Black 169

Fathi, Hasan 88
  Pahlevānān Nemimirand (*Pahlevāns Do Not Die*) 88

Feminist/Feminism/Ecofeminism 15, 58, 116, 115–34, 117–18, 121, 132, 133, 139, 165, 179, 213, 240, 241

Ferdowsi, Abulqasem 34, 36, 51, 53, 80, 88, 89, 90, 92, 147. *See Shahnameh*

Fereydun (*Shahnameh*) 40, 70, 89

Fertility agents/rituals 9, 10, 11, 15, 34–37, 43, 63–64, 73, 109, 131, 139–41, 148, 149, 170, 172–75, 229

Filmfarsi ix, 100, 105–6, 111, 113. *See* Tough Guy films/culture

Folk (culture, art forms, drama, lore, tales) 3–7, 9, 12, 14, 18, 24–27, 32, 34, 37, 41, 57, 60, 63, 66, 69–70, 79, 86

Forsi, Bahman 24, 60, 61
  Chub-e Zir-e Baghal (Crutches) 72

Fotovvat 70, 88, 92. *See* Javānmardi

Foucault, Michel/Foucauldian 1–2, 8, 17, 20, 33, 51, 53, 118, 174

Frame/framing/reframing vii, 7, 15, 16, 65, 75, 103, 104, 132, 159–60, 163–65, 167, 173, 174, 180, 186, 188, 189

Freud, Sigmund 2, 67, 79, 89, 90, 92, 188

Gender/gender relation 13, 91, 115, 117, 133, 137, 148, 151–52, 182, 213, 215, 216, 218, 229, 236, 241

Genre 5, 65, 93, 105, 107, 136, 155, 158, 179–82, 187, 188, 191, 192, 193, 214, 216, 223, 230

Ghaemmaghami, Rokhsareh
  Sonita 16, 219–20, 227, 234–37, 240, 243

Ghaffary, Farrokh ix, 7, 18, 50, 53, 61. *See* Cine Club
  South of the City (*Jonub-e Shahr*) 61

Gharibpour, Behruz 107, 111, 112, 113

Gholamrezaei, Naser 136

Golshiri Houshang ix, 169
  Shazdeh Ehtejāb (*Prince Ehtejab*) 169

Gorgani, Fakhreddin Asʻad/ *Veis o Rāmin* 37, 52, 53
Gosān 25, 53. *See* Naqqāli
Goshtasp (Shahnameh) 26, 51
Greek/Greek plays 24, 37, 49

Harim-e Mehrvarzi (*Kindness Territory*) 136
Hatami, Ali 88, 90, 169
   Bābā Shamal 88, 89
   Mādar (*Mother*) 169
   Qalandar 88
   Toqi (*Wood Pigeon*) 88
Hatamikia, Ebrahim 16, 198, 210–13
   Che vii, 16, 210–13
Hedayat, Sadeq 19, 25, 60–1, 69, 200
   Arusak-e Posht-e Pardeh (*The Doll behind the Curtain*) 69
   Buf-e Kur (*The Blind Owl*) 69
   Dash Akol 25
   Mohallel (*Divorce Resolver*) 25
   Mordeh Khorhā. (*Burial and Inheritance Opportunists*) 25
   Seh Qatreh Khun (*Three Drops of Blood, 1932*) and
   Shabhā-ye Varāmin (*Varāmin's Nights*) 69
Hegel, Georg Wilhelm Friedrich 84, 90, 92, 170, 176
Hercules/Heracles 38, 79
Heteroglossia 25, 199, 208
Hitchcock, Alfred 82, 163, 179, 180, 182–84, 189, 190–92, 193
   The Birds 184
   Marnie 189
   Psycho 183, 184
   The Rear Window 184
   Rebecca 183
   Spellbound 184
   Suspicion 183
   Topaz 191
   The Torn Curtain 191
   The 39 Steps 184, 193
   Vertigo 184, 185
Hossein (Imam) 124, 158–60
Host culture, region, community, etc. (for immigrants) 15, 16, 108, 137, 139, 140, 150, 229
Hystaspes 26

Ibsen, Henrik 2, 8, 41
   Brand 41
   Peer Gynt 41
Identity vi, 2, 6, 7, 8, 13, 16, 25, 60, 63, 65, 66, 68, 70, 72, 78, 82, 106, 108, 116, 12, 123, 133, 135–53, 158, 165, 168, 169, 171, 174, 175, 180, 181, 182, 185, 188, 190, 192, 203–5, 214, 216, 220, 221, 224, 229, 231, 237, 241, 242
Imaginal (The) 28, 53, 57, 61–62, 81, 89, 91, 164. *See* Nā-Kojā-Ābād
Immigrant. *See* Migrant
India/Indian 36, 75, 78
Indigenous forms, rituals, drama x, 2, 7, 8, 9, 10, 14, 16, 18, 20, 24–28, 48, 50, 92, 158–60, 169, 175, 176, 177
Initiation 58, 103, 118, 144, 152
Institute/ The Institute for the Intellectual Development of Children and Young Adults. *See* Kānun-e Parvaresh-e Fekri …
Intellectual/intellectuality v, 3, 4, 5, 6, 8, 9, 10, 11, 12, 14, 15, 17, 18, 19, 20, 31, 37, 38, 39, 41, 59, 62, 68, 70, 75, 76, 77, 88, 89, 90, 91, 97–103, 105, 113, 118, 134, 136, 153, 160, 171, 175, 176, 191, 193, 214, 225, 230, 238, 239, 241, 243
Iraj (*Shahnameh*) 70, 89, 169. *See* Sacrificial Heroes
Iran-Iraq war 117, 130, 198, 206, 210, 216, 217, 220, 225, 227, 230, 231, 237
Islam/Islamic/Islamist 2, 4, 5, 11, 15, 17, 18, 23, 26, 32, 34, 35, 55, 57, 58, 62, 64, 70, 76, 77, 111, 124, 133, 135, 136, 140, 141, 149, 152, 157, 158, 175, 177, 193, 198, 200, 201, 204, 205, 206, 209, 210, 218, 221, 223, 225, 230, 236, 242, 243

Jamalzadeh, Mohamad-Ali 197, 200, 214, 215
   Persian Is Sugar (*Farsi Shekar Ast*) 197, 214
Japan/Japanese theatre/cinema x, 7, 50, 179
Javanmard, Abbas 50, 54, 57, 86–87, 90, 92
Javānmard/Javānmardi 3, 14, 57–61, 68, 70, 84, 86, 87, 88, 92. *See* Ayyāri and Pahlevān)

Kafka, Frantz/Kafkaesque 2, 64
Kānun-e Parvarash-e Fekri-ye Kudakān va Nojavānān (Institute for the Intellectual Development of Children and Young Adults) 12, 14, 97–113, 134, 136, 150, 225
Kānun-e Nevisandegān (Writers' Association) 12
Kasraei, Siyavush 38, 52, 54, 59
  Ārash Kamāngir (Ārash the Archer) 38, 52, 54, 59
Kaveh (Shahnameh) 40, 43, 89
Kaykhsorow (*Shahnameh*) 31, 89
Khanqah/Khanaqah/Kanaqah 58, 88, 91
Khatami, Mohammad 157, 158, 175, 225, 226, 241
Kheimeh-Shab-Bāzi (Puppet Plays) 7, 9. *See* Puppet
Khomeini, Ruhollah 136, 137, 151, 152, 158, 210, 215
Khosrow Parviz (Shahnameh) 34, 51
Kiarostami, Abbas x, 107, 110, 222, 224
  A Taste of Cherry (*Ta'm-e Gilās*) 224
  The Traveller (*Mosāfer*) 222
  Where Is the Friend's House? (*Khāneh-ye Dust Kojāst?*) 110, 224
Kimiaei, Masoud 89, 100, 179
  Qeysar 89
  Dāsh Ākol 89
  Reza Motori (*Reza Motorcyclist*) 89
Kurds/Kurdish/Kurdistan (region, rebels, language) viii, 16, 40, 50, 198, 201, 208–14, 217, 220, 224, 238
Kurosawa, Akira 50, 187
  Rashomon 50, 187. See Akutagawa
Kushan, Esmāeil 89
  Kolāh Makhmali 89

Lacan, Jacques/Lacanian 103, 176
Language v, viii, 5–7, 11, 16, 17, 18, 32, 36, 39, 46, 49, 51, 61, 62, 67, 77, 80, 84–6, 88, 90, 115, 120, 129–31, 132, 136, 139–40, 142–43, 147, 148, 151, 152, 197–216, 218, 219, 221, 228–29, 233, 237
Leadership/leader 10, 14, 25, 31, 32, 36, 38, 49, 57, 58, 72, 75, 81, 82, 84, 99, 144, 208, 209, 211, 213, 230

Left/leftist 4, 11, 23, 29, 37, 38, 77, 98–99, 101, 102, 103
Lighting 16, 180, 181, 185–89
Love/beloved/lover 7, 11, 14, 18, 28, 43–45, 61, 63, 67, 71–73, 76, 79, 82, 84–86, 100, 109, 115, 116, 122–27, 130–31, 136, 191, 217, 220, 227, 232–34, 237, 240, 242, 243
Lout/Lāt 61. *See* Tough Guy films & Luti
Luti (chivalrous man) 61. *See* Tough Guy films

Mahmoudi, Navid 217
  A Few Cubic Meters of Love 217
Majidi, Majid 16, 217, 219, 226, 227, 232–34, 243
  Bachcheh-hā-ye Āsemān (*Children of Heaven*) 226, 233
  Baduk 234
  Baran 16, 219, 227–28, 231–33, 237, 243
  Khorshid (*Sun Children*) 217, 234
Makhmalbaf, Mohsen 14, 141
  Arusi-ye Khubān (*The Marriage of the Blessed*) 141
Makhmalbaf, Samira 217
  Takhteh Siāh (*Blackboards*) 217
Maleki, Khalil 4, 19
Manuchehr (Shahnameh) 34–37
Marcuse, Herbert 44, 52, 54
Marginalized/marginalized perspectives/marginalization v, 1–2, 5, 8, 10, 11, 12, 13, 14, 15, 16, 23–55, 57–93, 24, 25, 29, 30, 37, 43, 44, 46, 48, 49, 57, 59, 61–64, 70–71, 75, 76, 80–83, 87, 105–7, 111, 169, 230, 232
Martyr/martyred/martyrdom 62, 89, 124, 150, 158–59, 161, 164, 166, 170, 172, 174, 176, 209, 241
Marxist 11, 102, 238
Masculinity (hegemonic, toxic or ideal) 9, 10, 57–58, 88, 91, 92, 105, 223, 225
Medieval 5, 6, 14, 27, 41, 57, 58, 69, 88, 92, 162, 193
Mehrjui, Dariush 169
  Ejāreh Neshin-hā (*The Tenants*) 169
Metaphor/metaphorical 15, 46, 63, 84, 86, 103, 115, 118, 123, 137, 143, 147, 173, 179, 184, 190, 208, 218, 221, 226, 228, 229, 233

Meta-cinematic. *See* Self-reflexive
Migrant/Immigrant/Emigrant 15, 108, 135, 137–43, 145, 146, 150, 151, 220, 227–28, 237–38, 241
Migration/immigration/emigration 86, 108, 135, 138, 151, 152, 218, 220, 238, 240, 241, 242
Mise en scene 7, 24, 31, 103, 105, 106, 108, 109, 110, 186, 203
Mithra/Mithraism 4, 34, 35, 46, 58–59, 64, 73, 88, 89, 93
Minority perspective/minority 1–4, 8, 9, 11, 70, 71, 80, 105, 219, 227–28, 238
Mirror 30, 61, 66–67, 72, 103, 122, 124, 160–75, 184, 186, 231, 232, 233
Modernist/modernism 14, 38, 85, 86, 99, 170, 174
Modern/modernity 2, 3, 4, 5, 7, 8, 14, 15, 17, 18, 19, 24, 25, 32, 37, 38, 39, 40, 41, 48, 49, 50, 53, 57, 60, 66, 69, 70, 71, 72, 78, 79, 83, 86, 90, 93, 106, 151, 152, 158, 159, 168–72, 174, 184, 187, 191, 197, 200, 204, 221, 229, 231, 241, 242
Modernization/modernizing/modernized 3, 4, 5, 8, 32, 61, 70, 71, 86, 105, 170–72, 186, 200, 204, 230
Mohseni, Majid 61
  Lāt-e Javānmard (*Chivalrous Lout*) 61
Momayez Morteza 101
  Siā Parandeh (*Black Bird*) 101
Monologue/monological 23–5, 29–31, 39, 40, 50, 68, 78, 80–82
Mosaddeq, Mohamad 47, 105
Mourning Rituals/Rites 55, 158, 240
Multilingual/polyglot 197–203, 205, 207, 209, 211, 213–16, 220, 243
Music/musician/film music x, 26, 28, 63, 64, 80, 104, 161, 175, 184, 185, 219, 228, 236, 242
Mythologize/demythologize 32, 43, 50, 54, 64, 75, 151, 159, 175, 176, 177, 240, 242

Naderi, Amir 89, 100, 101, 107, 179, 222, 224
  Davandeh (*The Runner*) 107, 110, 224
  Sāzdahani (*Harmonica*) 101, 222
  Tangsir (*Tight Corner*) 89

Nā-Kojā-Ābād/Eqlim-e Hashtom/ 28, 51, 62, 89. *See* The Imaginal
Na'lbandiyan, Abbas 50
Naqqāli/ Naqqāl 7, 9, 10, 14, 16, 23–31, 33, 38–41, 48, 50, 52, 54, 55, 62, 159, 160, 164, 175, 176
Nassirian, Ali 25, 40, 50, 53, 60, 86, 90, 92
  Af'ei-ye Talāei (*Golden Viper*) 25, 60
  Bolbol-e Sargashteh (*Wandering Nightingale*) 25, 60
  Siāh (Blackface Prankster) 25
Nativism/nativist 4, 17, 19, 37, 76–77, 91
Nation/national/nation-building 4, 5, 33, 140, 152, 153, 198–206, 214, 216, 218–31, 237, 238, 240, 242, 243
Nationalism/nationalist/nationalistic 4, 5, 27, 32, 37, 41, 51, 140, 148, 151, 193, 201–6, 209, 218, 219–22, 231, 37, 238, 214
New Wave/Alternative Cinema vi, ix, 100, 106, 110–11, 179, 192, 200, 201, 217–20, 222, 224–26, 235, 237
Nightmare/nightmarish 17, 41, 52, 67–69, 106, 125, 147, 180–81, 185, 189–90, 191
Noir Films. *See* Crime Thriller

Objective/subjective shots 15, 160, 162–66, 174, 176, 185
Odatis 26. *See* Zariadres
Oedipal/Oedipus 90, 103, 143, 144, 149
One Thousand and One Nights x, 10
O'Neill, Eugene 41, 52, 71–2
  All God's Chillun Got Wings 52
  The Emperor Jones 41
  Long Day's Journey into Night 71–2
Outsider 67, 137, 141–46, 150–51, 220, 228, 229, 237. *See* Stranger

Pahlavi, Farah. *See* Farah Diba
Pahlavi era 3, 32, 76, 77, 84, 87, 91, 98, 100, 107, 200, 222
Pahlavi (pre–Islamic script/language) 34, 204, 206
Pahlbod, Mehrdad 77
Paranoia 180, 181, 189
Panahi, Jafar 217
  The White Ballon (Bādkonak-e Sefid) 217

Passion plays 18, 51, 158, 162. *See* Ta'ziyeh
Past/time/concept 1, 7, 8, 9, 16, 19, 23–25, 28, 32, 33–5, 38, 44, 48–9, 57, 60, 62, 70, 72, 88, 104, 147, 150, 152, 170-71, 184, 186–87, 190, 198, 231, 232, 234, 237
Patriarchy/patriarch/patriarchal 5, 59, 103-04, 109, 116–18, 123, 127, 131, 132, 182-3, 202, 205, 236
Persian (language, literature, culture) vii, ix, x, 3, 5–7, 10, 12, 16, 17, 18, 26–8, 31–2, 36–7, 42, 49, 51, 52, 53, 54, 57, 62, 69, 79, 85–6, 92, 93, 131, 138–40, 148, 151, 152, 174, 175, 197–216, 217–21, 224, 230–32, 234, 237, 240, 241. *See* Language
Pezeshkzad, Iraj
   Dāei Jān Nāpeleon (*My Uncle Napoleon*). 169
Phobia 180, 189, 220
Point-of-view/POV shots 166–67, 173, 175–76, 180, 185–86
Polanski, Roman 185
   Rosemarie Baby 185
Post-revolutionary 20, 32, 92, 101, 152, 158, 159, 165, 177, 200, 210, 216, 218, 223, 224, 226, 242
Pourahmad, Kiumars 16, 198, 206–10
   Otobus-e Shab (*The Night Bus*) viii, 16, 198, 206–10
Pre-Islamic 5, 17, 55, 57, 64, 204, 205, 206
Pre-modern 70, 232, 241
Pre-Revolutionary 99, 148, 179, 222, 226
Propaganda/propagandist 15, 84, 102, 136–37, 144, 146, 148–49, 200, 203, 209
Purification/purgation/cleansing 35, 44, 58
Puppet plays/puppets 7, 9, 11, 18, 23–4, 57, 60, 63–65, 68, 81, 86. *See* Kheimeh-Shab-Bāzi
Puriyā-ye Vali 60, 64, 66, 70, 78, 85, 86

Qezel Qal'eh Zendān/Red Castle Prison 80

Radi, Akbar 24
Rap/rapper 227, 234, 236

Rasoulof, Mohamad 217
   Jazireh Āhani (*Iron Island*) 217
Rebel/rebellion/rebellious 2, 6, 10, 25, 29, 34, 39, 41, 44–45, 61, 142, 209–13, 219, 236
Rebirth/reborn 104, 38
Recitation Plays v, 14, 23–55, 23–30, 32–3, 38, 48, 50–1, 57, 91, 241. *See* Naqqāli
Recognition (psychological and social) 2, 14, 44, 57–93, 82, 214, 228. *See* Belonging
Reformulation/reformulate (artistic forms, culture, rituals) 3, 7, 8, 12, 14, 15, 16, 18, 20, 33, 34, 47, 48, 51, 52, 54, 60, 62, 65, 70, 76, 84, 89, 92, 158, 176, 177
Refugee 17, 104, 107, 117, 119, 135–37, 139–41, 145, 146, 151, 203, 214, 218, 220, 227, 228, 231, 236, 238, 240, 241, 242, 243
Regime (patriarchy, Pahlavi and Islamic Republic) 99, 118, 137, 140, 149, 150, 198, 200, 201, 204, 209, 210, 212, 222, 225
Resistance x, 6, 20, 47, 70, 77, 81, 98, 99, 102, 105, 158, 169, 170, 171, 175, 211, 219, 242
Return-to-the-roots Discourses 4, 77. *See* Nativism
Revolution/revolutionary (1979 R) x, 6, 11, 13, 14, 15, 19, 20, 32, 44, 46, 49, 53, 92, 97, 98, 99, 100, 101, 102, 107, 109, 110, 111, 135, 140, 144, 148, 150, 152, 157, 158, 159, 165, 171, 171, 177, 179, 185, 200, 201, 204, 206, 206, 210, 215, 216, 218, 219, 222, 223, 224, 225, 226, 239, 241, 242, 243
Ritual/ritualization/ritualize 4, 6, 8, 9, 10, 15, 18, 19, 32, 35, 44, 50, 53, 55, 57–59, 62, 68–71, 75, 80, 87, 89, 133, 139, 141, 143–45, 151, 153, 158–60, 162–63, 166, 168, 170, 172, 174–76, 179, 191, 209, 221, 224, 229, 233, 240, 242
Romance (Genre) 18, 27, 34, 70, 88
Romantic 41, 60, 119, 126, 204, 231

Rostam 28, 38, 57, 60, 69, 70, 75, 77–78, 80–81, 88, 89
Rumi (Mulana Mohammad Balkhi) 70, 71, 84, 221, 233, 240, 243

Sacred 53, 91, 122, 133, 136, 144, 148, 149, 157, 159, 162
Sacred Defence 107, 136, 149, 209, 210, 216, 230, 239, 241
Sacrificial hero/sacrifice 6, 10, 13, 14, 20, 30, 31, 33–36, 38, 40, 45, 48–49, 58, 63, 65, 68, 70, 73, 73, 79, 84, 87, 98, 111, 117, 122, 158, 160, 175, 182, 183, 191–93, 209–10, 230, 234. *See* Zarir, Iraj, Siyāvush
Saddam Hussein viii, 137, 208, 209, 220
Sagharchiyan, Gholamreza 226
  Houra 226
Said, Edward 2, 7, 18, 20
Samak-e Ayyār 40, 88, 90
Sāzemān Cherikhā-ye Fadāei Khalq (Organization of Iranian People's Sacrificial Guerrilla) 98
SAVAK 98–99
Self-reflexive/self-reflexivity/reflexivity 8, 28, 155, 174, 189, 190
Sepehri, Sohrab 17, 77
Sex/sexual/sexuality 81, 91, 92, 170, 189, 222, 225, 232
Shadow (psychology) 40–42, 52, 63, 65, 67–68, 82. *See* Double
Shadows (lighting) 89, 185, 188
Shah (Mohammad Reza Pahlavi) 5, 47, 48, 87, 105. *See* Pahlavi Era
Shahnameh (Ferdowsi) vii, 5, 10, 20, 26–28, 34, 36, 36, 40, 45, 51, 53, 54, 62, 87, 88, 89, 90, 92, 147, 177
Shakespeare, William 2, 6, 49, 71, 72, 81, 82. *See* Comic Relief
  Hamlet 72, 82
Shamlou, Ahmad 77, 90
Shelly, Percy Bisshe 52
Shi'i/Shiite 3, 17, 18, 26, 51, 62, 89, 90, 91, 98, 99, 100, 102, 111, 124, 158, 159, 184, 220, 221, 222, 240
Shirvanlu, Firuz 98–100, 102, 111
Silence/silent (nature, woman) 34, 41, 79, 123, 205, 231, 233
Simurgh/Simorgh 80, 147, 151

Siyāvush (*Shahnameh*) 10, 70, 89, 91, 241. *See* Sacrificial Heroes
Sohravardi Shahabuddin 62. *See* Nā-Kojā-Ābād & Imaginal
  Aql-e Sorkh (*Crimsoned Archangel/ Red Reason*) 62
  Sedā-ye Āvāz-e Par-e Jebreil (*Rustlings of Gabriel's Wings*) 62
Soltanpur, Saeed 11, 18, 19, 102, 112, 232
Sophocles 84
  Antigone 84
Stranger (concept) v, vi, viii, 9, 10, 11, 13, 14, 15, 16, 17, 26, 39, 43, 62–63, 70, 80, 83, 89, 90, 97, 102, 106, 107–12, 115–34, 135–38, 141, 142, 146–51, 153, 157, 183, 187, 198, 200–3, 205, 206, 214, 217–43
Strindberg, August 41
  The Road to Damascus 41
Stylized 28, 50, 189
Sublime 14, 59, 66–68, 162
Surreal/Surrealistic 46, 132, 181, 185
Surveillance 66, 73, 87, 100, 122, 127, 180, 184–85, 187
Suspense/suspenseful 16, 179–84, 188, 191, 192, 193, 206

Taghvai, Nasser 89, 100, 101
  Rahāei (*Salvation*) 101
  Sadeq Kurdeh 89
Takhti, Gholamreza 83, 90, 91
Takiyeh 166, 172, 177. *See* Ta'ziyeh
Taliban 220, 241
Taqlid/Tamāshā (Improvisatory comedy) 5, 7, 9, 10, 11, 18
Ta'ziyeh vi, ix, 3, 9, 10, 15, 18, 28, 30, 31, 51, 52, 53, 55, 61, 62, 157–77, 229, 231, 239, 240. *See* Passion Plays
Tension 179–85, 221
Thriller. *See* Crime Thriller
Thugs 12, 47–48, 52, 61, 80, 83, 87, 105
Tough Guy films/culture 14, 45, 47, 59, 61, 68, 69, 77, 84, 88, 90, 100, 105, 181. *See* Filmfarsi
Tishtar/ TIŠTRYA 33, 36, 51
Todorov, Tzvetan 68–69, 89, 93. *See* The Fantastic and The Uncanny

Tradition/traditional 4, 5, 7, 8, 10, 13, 17, 20, 24, 24, 25, 32, 40, 48, 51, 53, 58, 59, 63, 69, 78, 81, 88, 90, 92, 100, 106, 117, 119, 124, 131, 138, 151, 158–59, 160, 163, 164, 166–68, 170–72, 174–75, 177, 182, 183, 200, 215, 218, 219, 223, 226, 232, 233, 236, 237, 239, 240

Tragedy/tragic 28, 30, 38, 41, 46, 60–62, 66, 72, 75, 81–82, 84, 90, 92, 158, 160, 164–65, 168, 173, 236

Trauma/traumatic 2, 3, 46, 49, 65, 82, 108, 129, 135, 137, 141, 144, 147, 162, 165, 180, 181, 185, 189–90, 203. *See* Marginalization

Turān/Turāniān/Tur 13, 34, 38, 39, 40, 43, 49, 57, 89

Turk, Turkmen, Turkish, Turkic/Azeri Turk 36, 37, 49, 70, 87, 104, 198, 200, 201, 220, 224, 227, 232, 238

Turkey 199, 208

Uncanny (The) 41, 60, 66–69, 89, 92, 174, 176, 177. *See* The Fantastic

Utopian/dystopian 29, 44, 62, 105

Violence/violent 2, 3, 4, 7, 12, 17, 30, 39, 48, 58, 66, 71, 75, 80, 87, 89, 98, 103, 109, 123, 139, 149, 159, 164, 182, 183, 188, 202, 204, 220, 236

Voice/noise 23–25, 27, 28, 29, 32, 33, 39, 81, 84, 99, 100, 102, 107, 109, 116, 118, 125, 130, 132, 141, 161, 163, 164, 168, 176, 199, 223, 234, 236

Voyeurism/voyeuristic 184

War 15, 38, 82, 107–9, 116, 117, 119, 129–31, 135–41, 144–50, 152, 157, 158, 186–88, 198, 202–3, 206–10, 214, 216, 217, 220, 225, 227–31, 237, 238, 239, 240

Western/Westernized/Westernization 4, 5, 17, 24, 25, 32, 49, 71, 77, 89, 93, 139, 140, 159, 170, 172, 182, 197, 204, 225

Westoxicated/West-obsessed 5, 71, 77

Yarshater, Ehsan 37, 51, 52, 55, 86, 90, 93, 241

Yasemi, Siamak 89
   Ganj-e Qaroun (Qaroun's Treasure) 89

Zahedi, Fazlollah 59–60

Zahedi, Homa 98

Zahhāk 12, 29, 29, 33, 40, 54, 89

Zāl (*Shahnameh*) 70, 80, 89, 147, 151

Zarir (*Shahnameh*) 36, 38, 70. *See* Sacrificial Heroes

Zariadres 26, 53

Zoroastrian 33, 34, 70, 80, 81, 144, 152

Zurkhāneh/ZUR-ḴĀNA 4, 9, 47, 53, 58–60, 78, 87, 88, 91, 57–93

www.ingramcontent.com/pod-product-compliance
Lightning Source LLC
Chambersburg PA
CBHW071819300426
44116CB00009B/1365